Contents

Introduction

The markets for derivative securities have developed enormously during the past two decades. Where only futures contracts on agricultural commodities have traded on futures exchanges since the mid-1800s, today futures, option, and futures option contracts are traded not only on physical commodities but also on stocks and stock indexes, bonds and bond indexes, and currencies.[1] The first financial futures contracts were the foreign currency futures contracts introduced by the Chicago Mercantile Exchange (CME) in May 1972. Interest rate futures contracts followed suit shortly thereafter. The Chicago Board of Trade (CBOT), in collaboration with members of the mortgage industry, launched futures contracts on Government National Mortgage Association (GNMA) mortgage-backed securities in October 1975. The first exchange-traded options were stock options. In April 1973, the Chicago Board Options Exchange (CBOE)—formed by the CBOT as the first exchange to trade stock options—began trading in call options on 16 New York Stock Exchange (NYSE) stocks. Today, calls and puts on nearly 500 common stocks trade on five U.S. exchanges. Options on a variety of other financial instruments are also traded. Among the most active contracts currently are the CBOT's Treasury bond futures option contract and the CME's Eurodollar futures option contract (launched in October 1982), and the CBOE's S&P 100 index option contract (March 1983).[2]

Concurrent with the rapid development of new financial instrument markets have been rapid advances in the theory that describes the interrelations between the prices of the derivative instruments traded in these markets and the prices of the underlying commodities. The landmark contributions of Black and Scholes [1973], Merton [1973], Black [1976], and Cox, Ingersoll, and Ross [1982] have provided a solid theoretical base upon which the standards of the valuation of futures and option contracts are based. In particular, the Black and Scholes (option)

---

[1]For a more complete treatment of the history of commodity futures and option contract markets, see Chicago Board of Trade [1989, Ch. 1].

[2]Stoll and Whaley [1985] provide a detailed listing of the noncommon stock option markets that have been developed in the eighties.

and Black (futures option) pricing models underlie many facets of the futures and option industries, ranging from their use by portfolio managers in tailoring return/risk characteristics of asset positions to their use by exchanges and clearinghouses in setting margins and computing risk exposures.

The purpose of this volume is to bring together some of the important research contributions in the futures and option literature. These articles are intended to provide the origins of the theoretical pricing relations that link futures, option, and futures option markets to the prices of the underlying commodity.[3] Where previous volumes in this series have dealt primarily with futures/commodity markets, this volume deals primarily with option and futures option markets. The focus is primarily on valuation.

Section 1 begins with a historical recount of the key contributions that underlie option and futures option valuation. Black [1989] provides a historical perspective on how modern-day option pricing theory evolved. This introductory article is then followed by three seminal contributions to option pricing theory: Black and Scholes [1973], Merton [1973], and Cox and Ross [1976]. The framework used in these articles (which we subsequently refer to as the "Black-Scholes framework") relies on two crucial assumptions. The first is that the underlying asset/futures price follows geometric Brownian motion. Roughly translated, this means that at any point in time in the future, the asset/futures price is lognormally distributed. Although this book contains mostly readings that rely on this assumption, there is considerable literature that examines the pricing implications of competing distributional forms. Periodically, throughout the book, we refer to some of this work. The second crucial assumption is

that a riskless hedge may be formed between the option and the underlying commodity. This notion permits the derivation of certain option pricing results without introducing explicit investor preference functions.

Section 2 deals with some important extensions of the Black-Scholes option pricing framework. Geske [1979], for example, deals with the valuation of compound options. Unlike options on commodities or commodity futures, compound options are options on options. Compound option valuation results are important for three reasons. The first is that certain exchange-traded options can be viewed as compound options. For example, a call option on a stock may be viewed as a call option (the exchange-traded security) on a call option on the value of the firm (the common stock of the firm). The second is that the compound option valuation formula can provide useful insights on the value of the early exercise premium embedded in American-style options, which we will see in Section 4. The third is that compound option markets are beginning to emerge. Calls on calls, calls on puts, puts on calls, and puts on puts actively trade in OTC markets.

Margrabe [1978] extends the Black-Scholes framework in yet another way. He derives a valuation equation for an exchange option, that is, the right to exchange one asset or commodity for another. While, on face appearance, this type of option may seem to have little practical significance, its role in pricing the options embedded in futures contracts is essential. For example, Stulz [1982] and Johnson [1987], based on the work of Margrabe [1978], derive pricing equations for options on the maximum and minimum of two or more risky assets. Conceptually, many of the futures contracts that currently trade are options on the minimum. With the CBOT's Treasury bond futures, for example, the short holds the

---

[3] For those interested in contract-specific valuation results, see Stoll and Whaley [1992].

right to deliver the cheapest of a number of deliverable T-bond issues and, therefore, has an option on the minimum. Such options, called *quality options*, are also embedded in many of the CBOT's grain futures contracts where a number of grades are eligible for delivery. All of these options can be priced accurately and effectively.

Section 3 contains three articles on physical commodity or asset options. The Black-Scholes framework is sufficiently general to permit valuation of any options where it is reasonable to assume that the underlying commodity has a constant, continuous cost-of-carry rate. In general, this is a good working approximation. There are some cases, however, where the framework needs to be modified to account for discrete cash flows—payments or receipts—on the underlying commodity during the option's life. A good example of this type of security is a stock option, where the stock pays a discrete cash dividend during the option's life. Roll [1977] and Whaley [1981] modify the Black-Scholes framework to deal with discrete cash flows on the underlying security.

Another case where the Black-Scholes mechanics may be inappropriate for commodity options is where the underlying commodity is a foreign currency. In foreign currency option valuation, the underlying source of uncertainty is the volatility of the spot exchange rate. Unfortunately, the Merton [1973] model, which is commonly used to price foreign currency options, assumes that the interest rates in both the domestic and foreign markets are constant. But, the same economic factors that cause the exchange rate to be volatile should cause interest rates to be volatile. Grabbe [1983] develops foreign currency option pricing formulas with stochastic interest rates.

Section 4 contains three articles on futures option valuation. The first is Black's [1976]

development of a pricing formula for European-style options on forward contracts. This follows straightforwardly from the Black-Scholes model, when it is recognized that the cost of carrying a forward contract equals zero. (The Black-Scholes model implicitly assumes that the cost-of-carry rate is the riskless rate of interest.) The contribution of the Cox, Ingersoll, and Ross [1982] article to futures option valuation is that it shows the equivalence of forward and futures prices under the Black-Scholes assumptions. This means that the Black model applies to European-style futures options as well as forward options. Finally, since all exchange-traded futures options in the U.S. are American-style, an article by Whaley [1986] that provides an approximation method for pricing American-style futures options is included.

Section 5 contains four articles on American-style option approximation methods. Unlike the European-style option results provided by Black and Scholes, Merton, and Black, many exchange-traded options are American-style. For example, all commodity futures options, the more active foreign currency options traded on the Philadelphia Exchange, and all stock options may be exercised prior to expiration. The four articles in this section show four different approximation methods for pricing American-style options in the order that they appeared in the finance literature. The first two approaches replace the continuous commodity price movement assumption in the Black-Scholes framework with a discrete-jump movement. Both the finite difference method introduced by Brennan and Schwartz [1978] and the binomial method of Cox, Ross, and Rubinstein [1979] create a lattice of possible paths that the commodity price may travel during the option's life, value the option at expiration conditional on the various levels of terminal commodity price, and then bring the option values back to the present accounting for the probabilities of certain commodity price moves and the riskless rate of interest. Of the two, the finite difference method is the most accurate. Unfortunately, it involves considerable computation and is generally not practical for real-time applications. The binomial method is faster, albeit less accurate. Geske and Johnson [1984] use a compound option valuation approach in their attempt at American-style option pricing. While the concept is novel, the computational expense is high when great accuracy is demanded. Finally, Barone-Adesi and Whaley [1987] present a quadratic approximation, which provides fast and accurate pricing of short-term American-style options.

Section 6 contains two articles on the dynamic replication. Underlying the development of the Black-Scholes model is the premise that an option position can be dynamically replicated using an investment in the underlying commodity and some riskless bonds. The two articles contained in this section, Rubinstein and Leland [1981] and Rubinstein [1985], discuss dynamic replication in the context of portfolio insurance, that is, buying a put option against a long position in a portfolio of common stocks.

At the beginning of each of the sections, a brief introduction is provided. This introduction describes the role of the articles included in the section as well as some of the related research. In addition, each introduction provides a bibliography of articles that have either built upon or are related to the articles reprinted here. The bibliographies are by necessity incomplete. The option and futures option literature continues to develop at an extraordinary rate. Omissions of relevant research in each category are purely oversights.

Robert E. Whaley
The Fuqua School of Business
Duke University
Durham, NC

References

Barone-Adesi, G., and R.E. Whaley, 1987, "Efficient Analytic Approximation of American Option Values," *Journal of Finance* 42(June), 301-20.

Black, F., 1976, "The Pricing of Commodity Contracts," *Journal of Financial Economics* 3, 167-79.

———, 1989, "How We Came Up with the Option Formula," *Journal of Portfolio Management* (Winter), 4-8.

———, and M.S. Scholes, 1973, "The Pricing of Options and Corporate Liabilities," *Journal of Political Economy* 81(May/June), 637-59.

Brennan, M.J., and E.S. Schwartz, 1978, "Finite Difference Methods and Jump Processes Arising in the Pricing of Contingent Claims," *Journal of Financial and Quantitative Analysis* 13, 461-74.

Chicago Board of Trade, 1989, *Commodity Trading Manual*, Chicago: Chicago Board of Trade.

Cox, J.C., F.E. Ingersoll, and S.A. Ross, 1982, "The Relation Between Forward and Futures Prices," *Journal of Financial Economics* 9, 321-46.

Cox, J.C., and S.A. Ross, 1976, "The Valuation of Options for Alternative Stochastic Processes," *Journal of Financial Economics* 3(January-March), 145-66.

———, and M. Rubinstein, 1979, "Option Pricing: A Simplified Approach," *Journal of Financial Economics* 7, 229-63.

Geske, R., 1979, "The Valuation of Compound Options," *Journal of Financial Economics* 7(March), 63-81.

———, and H.E. Johnson, 1984, "The American Put Option Valued Analytically, *Journal of Finance* 39(December), 1511-24.

Grabbe, O., 1983, "The Pricing of Call and Put Options on Foreign Exchange," *Journal of International Money and Finance* 2(December), 239-53.

Johnson, H.E., 1987, "Options on the Maximum or the Minimum of Several Assets," *Journal of Financial and Quantitative Analysis* 22(September), 277-83.

Margrabe, W., 1978, "The Value of an Option to Exchange One Asset for Another," *Journal of Finance* (March), 177-86.

Merton, R.C., 1973, "The Theory of Rational Option Pricing," *Bell Journal of Economics and Management Science* 4, 141-83.

Roll, R., 1977, "An Analytic Valuation Formula for Unprotected American Call Options on Stocks with Known Dividends," *Journal of Financial Economics* 5(November), 251-58.

Rubinstein, M., 1985, "Alternative Paths to Portfolio Insurance," *Financial Analysts Journal* (July-August), 42-52.

———, and H.E. Leland, 1981, "Replicating Options with Positions in Stock and Cash," *Financial Analysts Journal* (July-August), 63-72.

Stoll, H.R., and R.E. Whaley, 1985, "The New Options Markets," in *Futures Markets: Their Economic Role*, A. Peck (editor), Washington, DC: American Enterprise Institute.

———, 1992, *Futures and Options*, Cincinnati, OH: Southwestern Publishing Company.

Stulz, R., 1982, "Options on the Minimum or the Maximum of Two Risky Assets: Analysis and Applications," *Journal of Financial Economics* 10(July), 161-85.

Whaley, R.E., 1981, "On the Valuation of American Call Options on Stocks with Known Dividends," *Journal of Financial Economics* 9(June), 207-11.

———, 1986, "Valuation of American Futures Options: Theory and Empirical Tests," *Journal of Finance* 41(March), 127-50.

Section 1
Foundations

The foundation of modern-day option pricing lies in the seminal articles by Black-Scholes [1973] and Merton [1973]. The key distinction of their work from previous research in option pricing theory is that a riskless hedge may be formed between the option and the underlying commodity. If this is the case, and if the option price is a unique function of the underlying commodity price, then options can be valued under an assumption of risk neutrality, and the valuation equation is the same for risk-neutral investors as it is for risk-averse investors.[1]

The basic structural form of the Black-Scholes European-style call option formula had appeared earlier in the literature. Eight years before, Samuelson [1965] published a valuation equation very much similar to Black-Scholes.[2] The essence of his formula is that the current worth of the call equals the present value of the expected terminal price

[1] The risk-neutrality approach to option pricing was first articulated by Cox and Ross [1975].
[2] Boness [1964] also presents a European-style call option formula similar to the Black-Scholes model. Galai [1978] reconciles the difference between the two formulas.

of the call. The present-value computation is performed at the required rate of return for a risky call option. The expected terminal price of the call depends on the terminal commodity price distribution, which, in turn, depends on the expected rate of return on the commodity over the option's life. The problem with implementing the Samuelson formula is that estimates of the expected rates of return of the call and the underlying commodity are required, and these parameters are difficult to estimate precisely. Moreover, the expected rate of return on the call changes constantly as the commodity price moves and as the time to expiration erodes.

Risk neutrality circumvents these problems. Under risk neutrality, the expected rate of return of the call and the expected rate of return on the commodity are both equal to the riskless rate of interest. Substituting the riskless rate of interest for the expected returns of the call and the commodity in the Samuelson formula produces the Black-Scholes model.

This section reprints the seminal works of modern-day option pricing theory—Black

1

and Scholes [1973] and Merton [1973]. To place these articles in a historical perspective, Black [1989] is reprinted first. Following the works of Black-Scholes and Merton, Cox and Ross [1976] appears. Under risk-neutral valuation, Cox and Ross show that many alternative option pricing models can be developed straightforwardly for commodity price processes other than the geometric Brownian motion process used by Black-Scholes.

References and Bibliography

Bierman, H., Jr., 1967, "The Valuation of Stock Options," *Journal of Financial and Quantitative Analysis* 2, 327-44.

Black, F., 1989, "How We Came Up with the Option Formula," *Journal of Portfolio Management* (Winter), 4-8.

———, and M.S. Scholes, 1973, "The Pricing of Options and Corporate Liabilities," *Journal of Political Economy* 81 (May/June), 637-59.

Boness, A.J., 1964, "Elements of a Theory of Stock-Option Value," *Journal of Political Economy* 72, 163-75.

Brennan, M.J., 1979, "The Pricing of Contingent Claims in Discrete Time Models," *Journal of Finance* 34, 53-68.

Chen, A.H.Y., 1970, "A Model of Warrant Pricing in a Dynamic Market," *Journal of Finance* 25, 1041-60.

Cox, J.C., and S.A. Ross, 1975, "The Pricing of Options for Jump Processes," Working paper, The Wharton School, University of Pennsylvania.

———, 1976, "The Valuation of Options for Alternative Stochastic Processes," *Journal of Financial Economics* 3 (January-March), 145-66.

Galai, D., 1978, "On the Boness and Black-Scholes Models for Valuation of Call Options," *Journal of Financial and Quantitative Analysis* 13, 15-27.

Jagannathan, R., 1984, "Call Options and the Risk of Underlying Securities," *Journal of Financial Economics* 425-34.

Jarrow, R.A., and A. Rudd, 1982, "Approximate Option Valuation for Arbitrary Stochastic Processes," *Journal of Financial Economics* 10, 347-69.

Merton, R.C., 1973, "The Theory of Rational Option Pricing," *Bell Journal of Economics and Management Science* 4, 141-83.

Rubinstein, M., 1976, "The Valuation of Uncertain Income Streams and the Pricing of Options," *Bell Journal of Economics* 7, 407-25.

———, 1983, "Displaced Diffusion Option Pricing," *Journal of Finance* 38, 213-17.

Samuelson, P.A., 1965, "Rational Theory of Warrant Pricing," *Industrial Management Review* 6, 13-31.

———, and R.C. Merton, 1969, "A Complete Model of Warrant Pricing that Maximizes Utility," *Industrial Management Review* 10 (Winter), 17-46.

Smith, C.W., Jr., 1976, "Option Pricing: A Review," *Journal of Financial Economics* 3 (January/March), 3-51.

Stapleton, R.C., and M.G. Subrahmanyam, 1984, "The Valuation of Multivariate Contingent Claims in Discrete Time Models," *Journal of Finance*, 207-28.

Stoll, H.R., 1969, "The Relationship Between Put and Call Option Prices," *Journal of Finance* 24, 802-24.

How We Came Up with the Option Formula

Like many great inventions, it started with tinkering and ended with delayed recognition.

Fischer Black

My paper with Myron Scholes giving the derivation of our option formula appeared in the spring of 1973. We had published a paper on the results of some empirical tests of the formula, however, in the spring of 1972. The work that led to the formula started in the spring of 1969, and the background research started in 1965. Here is the story of how the formula and the papers describing it came to be.

The Short Story   Before I describe the events surrounding our discovery of the formula, here is the idea behind the formula.

Suppose there is a formula that tells how the value of a call option depends on the price of the underlying stock, the volatility of the stock, the exercise price and maturity of the option, and the interest rate.

Such a formula will tell us, among other things, how much the option value will change when the stock price changes by a small amount within a short time. Suppose that the option goes up about $.50 when the stock goes up $1.00, and down about $.50 when the stock goes down $1.00. Then you can create a hedged position by going short two option contracts and long one round lot of stock.

Fischer Black is a Partner and Director of The Quantitative Strategies Group at Goldman Sachs in New York (NY 10004). A short version of this article appeared in *Current Contents/Social & Behavioral Sciences*, Vol. 19, No. 33, 1987, published by the Institute for Scientific Information, Inc., Philadelphia, PA 19104.

Such a position will be close to riskless. For small moves in the stock in the short run, your losses on one side will be mostly offset by gains on the other side. If the stock goes up, you will lose on the option but make it up on the stock. If the stock goes down, you will lose on the stock but make it up on the option.

At first, you create a hedged position by going short two options and long one stock. As the stock price changes, and as the option approaches maturity, the ratio of option to stock needed to maintain a close-to-riskless hedge will change. To maintain a neutral hedge, you will have to change your position in the stock, your position in the option, or both.

As the hedged position will be close to riskless, it should return an amount equal to the short-term interest rate on close-to-riskless securities. This one principle gives us the option formula. It turns out that there is only one formula for the value of an option that has the property that the return on a hedged position of option and stock is always equal to the short-term interest rate.

The same argument works for a "reverse hedge," if you assume that you can sell stock short and invest the proceeds of the short sale for your benefit. A short position in the stock combined with a long position in the option (in the right ratio) will be close to riskless. Your equity in that position will be negative, but there is only one formula such that the return on that position is the interest rate—the same formula that we derive from the direct hedging argument.

We can even get the formula by assuming that a neutral spread must earn the interest rate. If you are short one option and long another option on the same stock in the right ratio, you will have a neutral spread. The argument is plausible even for a spread where you take in money, because you are probably in a position to invest the proceeds of a sale of options for your own benefit.

In fact, we can get the formula without assuming any hedging or spreading at all. We just compare a long stock position with a long option position that has the same action as the stock. In our example, the comparable positions would be long one round lot of stock and long two option contracts. These two positions have the same movements for small changes in stock price in the short run, so their returns should differ only by an amount equal to the interest rate times the difference in the total values of the two positions. We can have equilibrium only if investors are indifferent between the two positions. This gives us the same formula as the hedging and spreading arguments.

The Differential Equation   Jack Treynor was at Arthur D. Little, Inc. when I started work there in 1965. He had developed, starting in 1961, a model for the pricing of securities and other assets that is now called the "capital asset pricing model." William

Sharpe, John Lintner, and Jan Mossin developed more or less independent versions of the same model, and their versions began to be published in 1965. Jack's papers were never published, in part because they never quite satisfied the perfectionist in him, and in part (I believe) because he did not have an academic job.

In any case, Jack sparked my interest in finance, and I began to spend more and more time studying the capital asset pricing model and other theories of finance. The notion of equilibrium in the market for risky assets had great beauty for me. It implies that riskier securities must have higher expected returns, or investors will not hold them—except that investors do not count the part of the risk that they can diversify away.

I started trying to apply the capital asset pricing model to assets other than common stock. I looked at bonds, cash flows within a company, and even monetary assets. One of Treynor's papers was on the valuation of cash flows within a company, and he had derived a differential equation to help in figuring this value. His equation had an error because he had omitted some terms involving second derivatives, but we found out how to put in the missing terms and correct the equation.

With this background, I started working on a formula for valuing a warrant. At that time, we thought about warrants more than options, because the over-the-counter options market was such an imperfect market. I'm not sure when I started work on the warrant problem, but it was probably in 1968 or 1969. I have notes containing the differential equation that are dated June 1969.

Back then, most of the best papers about warrants tried to find the value of a warrant by taking the expected value of the warrant at expiration and discounting it to the present. That method has two problems: you have to know the stock's expected return to find the warrant's expected value at expiration, and you have to choose a discount rate for the warrant. No single discount rate will do, however, because the risk of the warrant depends on the stock price and time. Hence, the discount rate depends on the stock price and time too. None of the papers had dealt with this problem.

One key step in solving the problem is to write the warrant value as a formula that depends on the stock price and other factors. As Treynor had used this approach with his "value equation," I tried it too. And about the same time that I was using this approach, Samuelson and Merton were using it in a paper that appeared in 1969 (although they didn't come up with the same formula).

Another thing that made it possible to solve the problem was to assume away all kinds of complications. I assumed that trading costs are zero, that both borrowing and lending can be done at a single short-term interest rate that is constant over time, and that the volatility of a stock is constant, which means that the future price of the stock follows a lognormal distribution. I made a few other simplifying assumptions, some of which turned out to be unnecessary.

The equation I wrote down said simply that the expected return on a warrant should depend on the risk of the warrant in the same way that a common stock's expected return depends on its risk. I applied the capital asset pricing model to every moment in a warrant's life, for every possible stock price and warrant value. To put it another way, I used the capital asset pricing model to write down how the discount rate for a warrant varies with time and the stock price.

This gave me a differential equation. It was an equation for the warrant formula. It has just one solution, if we use the known value of the warrant at expiration and another condition that I didn't know about at the time.

I spent many, many days trying to find the solution to that equation. I have a Ph.D. in applied mathematics, but had never spent much time on differential equations, so I didn't know the standard methods used to solve problems like that. I have an A.B. in physics, but I didn't recognize the equation as a version of the "heat equation," which has well-known solutions.

I did notice that some of the factors in the original equation were not in the final equation. The warrant value did not seem to depend on how the risk of the stock was divided between risk that could be diversified away and risk that could not be diversified away. It depended only on the total risk of the stock (as measured, for example, by the standard deviation of the return on the stock). The warrant value did not depend on the stock's expected return, or on any other asset's expected return. That fascinated me.

But I was still unable to come up with the formula. So I put the problem aside and worked on other things.

In 1969, Myron Scholes was at MIT, and I had my office near Boston, where I did both research and consulting. Myron invited me to join him in some of the research activities at MIT. We started working together on the option problem, and made rapid progress.

The Formula   First, we concentrated on the fact that the option formula was going to depend on the underlying stock's volatility—not on its expected return. That meant that we could solve the problem using any expected return for the stock.

We decided to try assuming that the stock's expected return was equal to the interest rate. (We were assuming a constant interest rate, so short-term and long-term rates were equal.) In other words, we assumed that the stock's beta was zero; all of its risk could be diversified away.

As we also assumed that the stock's volatility was constant (when expressed in percentage terms) it was easy to figure the likelihood of each possible value of an investment in the stock at the time the option expired. We knew that the stock's terminal value (including reinvested dividends) would have to fit a lognormal distribution.

Other writers on options had made the same sort of assumption about the underlying stock, but they had not assumed an expected return equal to the interest rate. They had, however, assumed a constant expected return, which means a lognormal distribution for the terminal value of a stock that pays no dividends.

If you know the distribution for the stock's terminal value, you can cut it off at the option's exercise price and have the distribution for the option's terminal value. The expected value of that cutoff distribution gives you the expected terminal value of the option.

An article by Case Sprenkle presented a formula for the expected terminal value of an option with these same assumptions, except that Sprenkle allowed the stock to have any constant expected return. By putting the interest rate for the expected stock return into his formula, we got the expected terminal value of the option under our assumptions.

But we didn't want the expected terminal value of the option. We wanted the present value of the option: the value at some time before maturity. So we had to find some way to discount the option's expected terminal value to the present.

Rather suddenly, it came to us. We were looking for a formula relating the option value to the stock price. If the stock had an expected return equal to the interest rate, so would the option. After all, if all the stock's risk could be diversified away, so could all the option's risk. If the beta of the stock were zero, the beta of the option would have to be zero too.

If the option always had an expected return equal to the interest rate, then the discount rate that would take us from the option's expected future value to its present value would always be the interest rate. The discount rate would not depend on time or on the stock price, as it would if the stock had an expected return other than the interest rate.

So we discounted the expected terminal value of the option at the constant interest rate to get the present value of the option. Then we took Sprenkle's formula, put in the interest rate for the expected return on the stock, and put in the interest rate again for the discount rate for the option. We had our option formula.

We checked the formula against the differential equation, and sure enough, it fit. We knew it was right. A few changes, and we had a formula for puts, too.

Our first thought was to publish a paper describing the formula. (Later, we thought also about trying to use the formula to make money trading in options and warrants.) As we worked on the paper, we had long discussions with Robert Merton, who was also working on option valuation.

Merton made a number of suggestions that improved our paper. In particular, he pointed out that if you assume continuous trading in the option or the stock, you can maintain a hedged position between them that is literally riskless. In the final version of the paper, we derived the formula that way, because it seemed to be the most general derivation.

Merton started working on a paper on aspects of the option formula. He was able to prove, along with other important points, that if you don't want a constant interest rate in the formula, you should use the interest rate on a discount bond that matures when the option expires.

Scholes and I started thinking about applying the formula to figuring the values of risky corporate bonds and common stock. Merton began thinking about that too, but neither of us told the other. We were both working on papers about the formula, so there was a mixture of rivalry and cooperation. Scholes and I gave an early version of our paper at a conference on capital market theory sponsored by Wells Fargo Bank in the summer of 1970. We talked then about the application to corporate finance. Merton attended the conference, but he overslept on the morning of our talk, so it was only later that all of us discovered we were working on the corporate finance applications.

The first surviving draft of our paper describing the option formula (dated October 1970) was called "A Theoretical Valuation Formula for Options, Warrants, and Other Securities." I sent it to the *Journal of Political Economy* and promptly got back a rejection letter. They said it was too specialized for them, and that it would be better in the *Journal of Finance.* I then sent it to *The Review of Economics and Statistics* and promptly got back another rejection letter. They said they could publish only a few of the papers they received. Neither journal had the paper reviewed.

I suspected that one reason these journals didn't take the paper seriously was my non-academic return address. In any case, we rewrote the paper to emphasize the economics behind the formula's derivation. The next draft (dated January 1971) was called "Capital Market Equilibrium and the Pricing of Corporate Liabilities."

Merton Miller and Eugene Fama at the University of Chicago took an interest in the paper. They gave us extensive comments on this draft, and suggested to the *Journal of Political Economy* (which is published there) that perhaps the paper was worth more serious consideration. In August 1971, the *Journal* accepted the paper, conditional on further revisions suggested by the referees.

The final draft of the paper (dated May 1972) was called "The Pricing of Options and Corporate Liabilities." It appeared in the May/June 1973 issue of the *Journal of Political Economy*. Meanwhile, we had written a paper on the results of some empirical tests of the formula, which appeared in the May 1972 *Journal of Finance*.

Testing the Formula

While we were working on our paper telling about the formula, we began to look for ways to test it on real securities. We started with warrants.

We estimated the volatility of the stock of each of a group of companies with warrants outstanding. We applied the formula in a simple way to these warrants, ignoring some of the ways in which warrants differ from options. We noticed that several warrants looked like very good buys. The best buy of all seemed to be National General new warrants.

Scholes, Merton, and I and others jumped right in and bought a bunch of these warrants. For a while, it looked as if we had done just the right thing. Then a company called American Financial announced a tender offer for National General shares. The original terms of the tender offer had the effect of sharply reducing the value of the warrants.

In other words, the market knew something that our formula didn't know. The market knew that such a tender offer was likely or possible, and that's why the warrants seemed so low in price. Although our trading didn't turn out very well, this event helped validate the formula. The market price was out of line for a very good reason.

It also illustrates a general rule. The formula and the volatility estimates we put into the formula are always based on the information at hand. The market will always have some kinds of information affecting the values of options and warrants that we don't have. Sometimes the values given by the formula will be better than market prices; at other times the market prices will be better than the formula values.

We learned that rule again in our next set of tests. One of Scholes's students managed to get data on the premiums received by a broker's option-writing customers in the over-the-counter options market. The data covered a period of several years.

We used the formula, with some simple volatility estimates, to test trading rules. We wanted to find out how much money we could have made if we had bought the options whose prices seemed lower than our formula's values, and sold the options whose prices seemed higher than our values.

Ignoring transaction costs, our profits seemed to be substantial. As these were over-the-counter options, we assumed the positions were held to maturity. To highlight the profits and losses, we combined each option position with a continuously changing stock position that created a close-to-riskless hedge all the time. The profits were consistent at around fifty cents per day per contract. Nevertheless, transaction costs in the over-the-counter options market could easily wipe out those profits.

We also tried assuming that we bought the underpriced options and sold the overpriced options at the values given by our formula, rather than at the market prices. Then we had losses of around fifty cents per day per contract. In other words, the formula seemed to have some information the market didn't have, but the market had just as much information that the formula didn't have.

Our findings do not mean that you lose if you use the formula for trading. If you trade at market prices, you get the benefit of what the market knows. But it is not a good idea to insist on trading at the values given by the formula. The market may want to trade at prices away from those values for good reasons that the formula cannot consider.

Later, after the CBOE started trading in listed options, Dan Galai wrote a Ph.D. thesis at the University of Chicago in which he tested trading rules based on the formula. Ignoring trading costs, the profits he found in trading listed options were much larger than the profits we found in over-the-counter options, because he assumed that an option position would be changed every time it became underpriced or overpriced.

For example, he tested the profitability of spreads that are kept neutral continuously. A neutral spread is a long position in one option combined with a short position in another option on the same stock. The position is close to riskless. To maintain a neutral spread, you need to change either your long position or your short position (or both) as the stock price and time-to-maturity change.

Galai figures option values using simple volatility estimates, based on past daily data on stock prices. He has only closing prices for options, but he tries to take out some of their distortions. He assumes that you decide what to do by comparing option values and closing option prices one day, but you execute the trades at closing prices the next day. If closing prices are distorted in the same direction two days in a row, they may still overstate your prices. But if it's possible to trade only at a favorable price, and not at just any next-day's price, then this will understate your profits. This method also ignores profits that market makers can make by opening and closing positions within a single day.

The spreads that Galai looked at involve buying one contract of the underpriced option and selling either more or less than one contract of the overpriced option: whatever is needed to create and maintain a neutral spread. Ignoring transaction costs, the average spread gives a consistent profit of $4.00 or $5.00 per day.

That sounds like a fast way to make money. But it does ignore trading costs, which are especially high for people who have to pay retail commissions. And it does assume trading at the next day's closing prices—a conservative assumption, but one that still may cause profits to be overstated. Finally, the period Galai studied was July 1973 to April 1974. Opportunities like this are harder to come by these days.

One reason for the change is that traders now use the formula and its variants extensively. They use it so much that market prices are usually close to formula values even in situations where there should be a large difference: situations, for example, where a cash takeover is likely to end the life of the option or warrant.

2

The Pricing of Options and Corporate Liabilities

Fischer Black and Myron Scholes*

If options are correctly priced in the market, it should not be possible to make sure profits by creating portfolios of long and short positions in options and their underlying stocks. Using this principle, a theoretical valuation formula for options is derived. Since almost all corporate liabilities can be viewed as combinations of options, the formula and the analysis that led to it are also applicable to corporate liabilities such as common stock, corporate bonds, and warrants. In particular, the formula can be used to derive the discount that should be applied to a corporate bond because of the possibility of default.

Introduction

An option is a security giving the right to buy or sell an asset, subject to certain conditions, within a specified period of time. An "American option" is one that can be exercised at any time up to the date the option expires. A "European option" is one that can be exercised only on a specified future date. The price that is paid for the asset when the option is exercised is called the "exercise price" or "striking price." The last day on which the option may be exercised is called the "expiration date" or "maturity date."

*University of Chicago and Massachusetts Institute of Technology, respectively.

Received for publication November 11, 1970. Final version received May 9, 1972.

The inspiration for this work was provided by Jack L. Treynor (1961a, 1961b).

We are grateful for extensive comments on earlier drafts by Eugene F. Fama, Robert C. Merton, and Merton H. Miller. This work was supported in part by the Ford Foundation.

The simplest kind of option is one that gives the right to buy a single share of common stock. Throughout most of the paper, we will be discussing this kind of option, which is often referred to as a "call option."

In general, it seems clear that the higher the price of the stock, the greater the value of the option. When the stock price is much greater than the exercise price, the option is almost sure to be exercised. The current value of the option will thus be approximately equal to the price of the stock minus the price of a pure discount bond that matures on the same date as the option, with a face value equal to the striking price of the option.

On the other hand, if the price of the stock is much less than the exercise price, the option is almost sure to expire without being exercised, so its value will be near zero.

If the expiration date of the option is very far in the future, then the price of a bond that pays the exercise price on the maturity date will be very low, and the value of the option will be approximately equal to the price of the stock.

On the other hand, if the expiration date is very near, the value of the option will be approximately equal to the stock price minus the exercise price, or zero, if the stock price is less than the exercise price. Normally, the value of an option declines as its maturity date approaches, if the value of the stock does not change.

These general properties of the relation between the option value and the stock price are often illustrated in a diagram like figure 1. Line *A* represents the maximum value of the option, since it cannot be worth more than the stock. Line *B* represents the minimum value of the option, since its value

Figure 1. The relation between option value and stock price

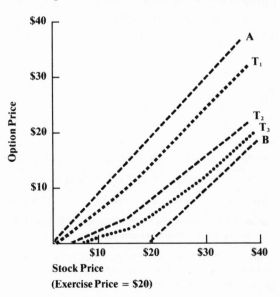

Stock Price
(Exercise Price = $20)

cannot be negative and cannot be less than the stock price minus the exercise price. Lines T_1, T_2, and T_3 represent the value of the option for successively shorter maturities.

Normally, the curve representing the value of an option will be concave upward. Since it also lies below the 45° line, A, we can see that the option will be more volatile than the stock. A given percentage change in the stock price, holding maturity constant, will result in a larger percentage change in the option value. The relative volatility of the option is not constant, however. It depends on both the stock price and maturity.

Most of the previous work on the valuation of options has been expressed in terms of warrants. For example, Sprenkle (1961), Ayres (1963), Boness (1964), Samuelson (1965), Baumol, Malkiel, and Quandt (1966), and Chen (1970) all produced valuation formulas of the same general form. Their formulas, however, were not complete, since they all involved one or more arbitrary parameters.

For example, Sprenkle's formula for the value of an option can be written as follows:

$$kxN(b_1) - k^*cN(b_2)$$

$$b_1 = \frac{\ln kx/c + \frac{1}{2}\,v^2(t^* - t)}{v\sqrt{(t^* - t)}}$$

$$b_2 = \frac{\ln kx/c - \frac{1}{2}\,v^2(t^* - t)}{v\sqrt{(t^* - t)}}$$

In this expression, x is the stock price, c is the exercise price, t^* is the maturity date, t is the current date, v^2 is the variance rate of the return on the stock,[1] ln is the natural logarithm, and $N(b)$ is the cumulative normal density function. But k and k* are unknown parameters. Sprenkle (1961) defines k as the ratio of the expected value of the stock price at the time the warrant matures to the current stock price, and k^* as a discount factor that depends on the risk of the stock. He tries to estimate the values of k and k^* empirically, but finds that he is unable to do so.

---

[1] The variance rate of the return on a security is the limit, as the size of the interval of measurement goes to zero, of the variance of the return over that interval divided by the length of the interval.

More typically, Samuelson (1965) has unknown parameters α and β, where α is the rate of expected return on the stock, and β is the rate of expected return on the warrant or the discount rate to be applied to the warrant.[2] He assumes that the distribution of possible values of the stock when the warrant matures is log-normal and takes the expected value of this distribution, cutting it off at the exercise price. He then discounts this expected value to the present at the rate β. Unfortunately, there seems to be no model of the pricing of securities under conditions of capital market equilibrium that would make this an appropriate procedure for determining the value of a warrant.

In a subsequent paper, Samuelson and Merton (1969) recognize the fact that discounting the expected value of the distribution of possible values of the warrant when it is exercised is not an appropriate procedure. They advance the theory by treating the option price as a function of the stock price. They also recognize that the discount rates are determined in part by the requirement that investors be willing to hold all of the outstanding amounts of both the stock and the option. But they do not make use of the fact that investors must hold other assets as well, so that the risk of an option or stock that affects its discount rate is only that part of the risk that cannot be diversified away. Their final formula depends on the shape of the utility function that they assume for the typical investor.

One of the concepts that we use in developing our model is expressed by Thorp and Kassouf (1967). They obtain an empirical valuation formula for warrants by fitting a curve to actual warrant prices. Then they use this formula to calculate the ratio of shares of stock to options needed to create a hedged position by going long in one security and short in the other. What they fail to pursue is the fact that in equilibrium, the expected return on such a hedged position must be equal to the return on a riskless asset. What we show below is that this equilibrium condition can be used to derive a theoretical valuation formula.

The Valuation Formula

In deriving our formula for the value of an option in terms of the price of the stock, we will assume "ideal conditions" in the market for the stock and for the option:

a) The short-term interest rate is known and is constant through time.
b) The stock price follows a random walk in continuous time with a variance rate proportional to the square of the stock price. Thus the distribution of possible stock prices at the end of any finite interval is log-normal. The variance rate of the return on the stock is constant.
c) The stock pays no dividends or other distributions.
d) The option is "European," that is, it can only be exercised at maturity.

[2]The rate of expected return on a security is the limit, as the size of the interval of measurement goes to zero, of the expected return over that interval divided by the length of the interval.

e) There are no transaction costs in buying or selling the stock or the option.
f) It is possible to borrow any fraction of the price of a security to buy it or to hold it, at the short-term interest rate.
g) There are no penalties to short selling. A seller who does not own a security will simply accept the price of the security from a buyer, and will agree to settle with the buyer on some future date by paying him an amount equal to the price of the security on that date.

Under these assumptions, the value of the option will depend only on the price of the stock and time and on variables that are taken to be known constants. Thus, it is possible to create a hedged position, consisting of a long position in the stock and a short position in the option, whose value will not depend on the price of the stock, but will depend only on time and the values of known constants. Writing $w(x, t)$ for the value of the option as a function of the stock price x and time t, the number of options that must be sold short against one share of stock long is:

$$1/w_1(x, t). \tag{1}$$

In expression (1), the subscript refers to the partial derivative of $w(x, t)$ with respect to its first argument.

To see that the value of such a hedged position does not depend on the price of the stock, note that the ratio of the change in the option value to the change in the stock price, when the change in the stock price is small, is $w_1(x, t)$. To a first approximation, if the stock price changes by an amount Δx, the option price will change by an amount $w_1(x, t)\Delta x$, and the number of options given by expression (1) will change by an amount Δx. Thus, the change in the value of a long position in the stock will be approximately offset by the change in value of a short position in $1/w_1$ options.

As the variables x and t change, the number of options to be sold short to create a hedged position with one share of stock changes. If the hedge is maintained continuously, then the approximations mentioned above become exact, and the return on the hedged position is completely independent of the change in the value of the stock. In fact, the return on the hedged position becomes certain.[3]

To illustrate the formation of the hedged position, let us refer to the solid line (T_2) in figure 1 and assume that the price of the stock starts at $15.00, so that the value of the option starts at $5.00. Assume also that the slope of the line at that point is 1/2. This means that the hedged position is created by buying one share of stock and selling two options short. One share of stock costs $15.00, and the sale of two options brings in $10.00, so the equity in this position is $5.00.

[3]This was pointed out to us by Robert Merton.

If the hedged position is not changed as the price of the stock changes, then there is some uncertainty in the value of the equity at the end of a finite interval. Suppose that two options go from $10.00 to $15.75 when the stock goes from $15.00 to $20.00, and that they go from $10.00 to $5.75 when the stock goes from $15.00 to $10.00. Thus, the equity goes from $5.00 to $4.25 when the stock changes by $5.00 in either direction. This is a $.75 decline in the equity for a $5.00 change in the stock in either direction.[4]

In addition, the curve shifts (say from T_2 to T_3 in fig. 1) as the maturity of the options changes. The resulting decline in value of the options means an increase in the equity in the hedged position and tends to offset the possible losses due to a large change in the stock price.

Note that the decline in the equity value due to a large change in the stock price is small. The ratio of the decline in the equity value to the magnitude of the change in the stock price becomes smaller as the magnitude of the change in the stock price becomes smaller.

Note also that the direction of the change in the equity value is independent of the direction of the change in the stock price. This means that under our assumption that the stock price follows a continuous random walk and that the return has a constant variance rate, the covariance between the return on the equity and the return on the stock will be zero. If the stock price and the value of the "market portfolio" follow a joint continuous random walk with constant covariance rate, it means that the covariance between the return on the equity and the return on the market will be zero.

Thus the risk in the hedged position is zero if the short position in the option is adjusted continuously. If the position is not adjusted continuously, the risk is small, and consists entirely of risk that can be diversified away by forming a portfolio of a large number of such hedged positions.

In general, since the hedged position contains one share of stock long and $1/w_1$ options short, the value of the equity in the position is:

$$x - w/w_1. \tag{2}$$

The change in the value of the equity in a short interval Δt is:

$$\Delta x - \Delta w/w_1. \tag{3}$$

Assuming that the short position is changed continuously, we can use stochastic calculus[5] to expand Δw, which is $w(x + \Delta x, t + \Delta t) - w(x, t)$, as follows:

---

[4]These figures are purely for illustrative purposes. They correspond roughly to the way figure 1 was drawn, but not to an option on any actual security.
[5]For an exposition of stochastic calculus, see McKean (1969).

$$\Delta w = w_1 \Delta x + \frac{1}{2} \; w_{11} v^2 x^2 \Delta t + w_2 \Delta t. \tag{4}$$

In equation (4), the subscripts on w refer to partial derivatives, and v^2 is the variance rate of the return on the stock.[6] Substituting from equation (4) into expression (3), we find that the change in the value of the equity in the hedged position is:

$$- \left(\frac{1}{2} \; w_{11} v^2 x^2 + w_2 \right) \Delta t / w_1. \tag{5}$$

Since the return on the equity in the hedged position is certain, the return must be equal to $r \Delta t$. Even if the hedged position is not changed continuously, its risk is small and is entirely risk that can be diversified away, so the expected return on the hedged position must be at the short term interest rate.[7] If this were not true, speculators would try to profit by borrowing large amounts of money to create such hedged positions, and would in the process force the returns down to the short term interest rate.

Thus the change in the equity (5) must equal the value of the equity (2) times $r \Delta t$.

$$- \left(\frac{1}{2} \; w_{11} v^2 x^2 + w_2 \right) \Delta t / w_1 = (x - w/w_1) r \Delta t. \tag{6}$$

Dropping the Δt from both sides, and rearranging, we have a differential equation for the value of the option.

$$w_2 = rw - rxw_1 - \frac{1}{2} \; v^2 x^2 w_{11}. \tag{7}$$

---

[6]See footnote 1.

[7]For a thorough discussion of the relation between risk and expected return, see Fama and Miller (1972) or Sharpe (1970). To see that the risk in the hedged position can be diversified away, note that if we don't adjust the hedge continuously, expression (5) becomes:

$$- \left(\frac{1}{2} \; w_{11} \Delta x^2 + w_2 \Delta t \right) \Big/ w_1. \tag{5'}$$

Writing Δm for the change in the value of the market portfolio between t and $t + \Delta t$, the "market risk" in the hedged position is proportional to the covariance between the change in the value of the hedged portfolio, as given by expression (5'), and Δm: $- \frac{1}{2} \; w_{11} \text{cov} (\Delta x^2, \Delta m)$. But if Δx and Δm follow a joint normal distribution for small intervals Δt, this covariance will be zero. Since there is no market risk in the hedged position, all of the risk due to the fact that the hedge is not continuously adjusted must be risk that can be diversified away.

Writing t^* for the maturity date of the option, and c for the exercise price, we know that:

$$w(x, t^*) = x - c, \qquad x \geq c$$
$$= 0, \qquad x < c. \tag{8}$$

There is only one formula $w(x, t)$ that satisfies the differential equation (7) subject to the boundary condition (8). This formula must be the option valuation formula.

To solve this differential equation, we make the following substitution:

$$w(x, t) = e^{r(t - t^*)} y \left[(2/v^2) \left(r - \frac{1}{2} v^2 \right) \right.$$

$$\left[\ln x/c - \left(r - \frac{1}{2} v^2 \right) (t - t^*) \right],$$

$$\left. - (2/v^2) \left(r - \frac{1}{2} v^2 \right)^2 (t - t^*) \right]. \tag{9}$$

With this substitution, the differential equation becomes:

$$y_2 = y_{11}, \tag{10}$$

and the boundary condition becomes:

$$y(u, 0) = 0, \qquad\qquad\qquad u < 0$$
$$= c \left[e^{u \left(\frac{1}{2} v^2 \right) \big/ \left(r - \frac{1}{2} v^2 \right)} - 1 \right], \quad u \geq 0. \tag{11}$$

The differential equation (10) is the heat-transfer equation of physics, and its solution is given by Churchill (1963, p. 155). In our notation, the solution is:

$$y(u, s) = 1/\sqrt{2\pi} \int_{-u/\sqrt{2s}}^{\infty}$$

$$c \left[e^{(u + q\sqrt{2s}) \left(\frac{1}{2} v^2 \right) \big/ \left(r - \frac{1}{2} v^2 \right)} - 1 \right] e^{-q^2/2} dq. \tag{12}$$

Substituting from equation (12) into equation (9), and simplifying, we find:

$$w(x, t) = xN(d_1) - ce^{r(t - t^*)} N(d_2)$$

$$d_1 = \frac{\ln x/c + (r + \frac{1}{2} v^2)(t^* - t)}{v\sqrt{t^* - t}}$$ (13)

$$d_2 = \frac{\ln x/c + (r - \frac{1}{2} v^2)(t^* - t)}{v\sqrt{t^* - t}}$$

In equation (13), $N(d)$ is the cumulative normal density function.

Note that the expected return on the stock does not appear in equation (13). The option value as a function of the stock price is independent of the expected return on the stock. The expected return on the option, however, will depend on the expected return on the stock. The faster the stock price rises, the faster the option price will rise through the functional relationship (13).

Note that the maturity $(t^* - t)$ appears in the formula only multiplied by the interest rate r or the variance rate v^2. Thus, an increase in maturity has the same effect on the value of the option as an equal percentage increase in both r and v^2.

Merton (1973) has shown that the option value as given by equation (13) increases continuously as any one of t^*, r, or v^2 increases. In each case, it approaches a maximum value equal to the stock price.

The partial derivative w_1 of the valuation formula is of interest, because it determines the ratio of shares of stock to options in the hedged position as in expression (1). Taking the partial derivative of equation (13), and simplifying, we find that:

$$w_1(x, t) = N(d_1).$$ (14)

In equation (14), d_1 is as defined in equation (13).

From equations (13) and (14), it is clear that xw_1 / w is always greater than one. This shows that the option is always more volatile than the stock.

An Alternative Derivation

It is also possible to derive the differential equation (7) using the "capital asset pricing model." This derivation is given because it gives more understanding of the way in which one can discount the value of an option to the present, using a discount rate that depends on both time and the price of the stock.

The capital-asset pricing model describes the relation between risk and expected return for a capital asset under conditions of market equilibrium.[8] The expected return on an asset gives the discount that must be applied to the end-of-period value of the asset to give its present value. Thus, the capital-asset pricing model gives a general method for discounting under uncertainty.

The capital-asset pricing model says that the expected return on an asset is a linear function of its β, which is defined as the covariance of the return on the asset with the return on the market, divided by the variance of the return on the market. From equation (4) we see that the covariance of the return on the option $\Delta w/w$ with the return on the market is equal to xw_1/w times the covariance of the return on the stock $\Delta x/x$ with the return on the market. Thus, we have the following relation between the option's β and the stock's β:

$$\beta_w = (xw_1 / w)\beta_x. \tag{15}$$

The expression xw_1/w may also be interpreted as the "elasticity" of the option price with respect to the stock price. It is the ratio of the percentage change in the option price to the percentage change in the stock price, for small percentage changes, holding maturity constant.

To apply the capital-asset pricing model to an option and the underlying stock, let us first define a as the rate of expected return on the market minus the interest rate.[9] Then the expected return on the option and the stock are:

$$E(\Delta x/x) = r\Delta t + a\beta_x\Delta t, \tag{16}$$

$$E(\Delta w/w) = r\Delta t + a\beta_w\Delta t. \tag{17}$$

Multiplying equation (17) by w, and substituting for β_w from equation (15), we find:

$$E(\Delta w) = rw\Delta t + axw_1\beta_x\Delta t. \tag{18}$$

[8]The model was developed by Treynor (1961b), Sharpe (1964), Lintner (1965), and Mossin (1966). It is summarized by Sharpe (1970), and Fama and Miller (1972). The model was originally stated as a single-period model. Extending it to a multiperiod model is, in general, difficult. Fama (1970), however, has shown that if we make an assumption that implies that the short-term interest rate is constant through time, then the model must apply to each successive period in time. His proof also goes through under somewhat more general assumptions.
[9]See footnote 2.

Using stochastic calculus,[10] we can expand Δw, which is $w(x + \Delta x, t + \Delta t) - w(x, t)$, as follows:

$$\Delta w = w_1 \Delta x + \frac{1}{2} w_{11} v^2 x^2 \Delta t + w_2 \Delta t. \tag{19}$$

Taking the expected value of equation (19), and substituting for $E(\Delta x)$ from equation (16), we have:

$$E(\Delta w) = rxw_1 \Delta t + axw_1 \beta_x \Delta t + \frac{1}{2} v^2 x^2 w_{11} \Delta t + w_2 \Delta t. \tag{20}$$

Combining equations (18) and (20), we find that the terms involving a and β_x cancel, giving:

$$w_2 = rw - rxw_1 - \frac{1}{2} v^2 x^2 w_{11}. \tag{21}$$

Equation (21) is the same as equation (7).

More Complicated Options

The valuation formula (13) was derived under the assumption that the option can only be exercised at time t^*. Merton (1973) has shown, however, that the value of the option is always greater than the value it would have if it were exercised immediately $(x - c)$. Thus, a rational investor will not exercise a call option before maturity, and the value of an American call option is the same as the value of a European call option.

There is a simple modification of the formula that will make it applicable to European put options (options to sell) as well as call options (options to buy). Writing $u(x, t)$ for the value of a put option, we see that the differential equation remains unchanged.

$$u_2 = ru - rxu_1 - \frac{1}{2} v^2 x^2 u_{11}. \tag{22}$$

The boundary condition, however, becomes:

$$\begin{aligned} u(x, t^*) &= 0, \qquad x \geq c \\ &= c - x, \quad x < c. \end{aligned} \tag{23}$$

To get the solution to this equation with the new boundary condition, we can simply note that the difference between the value of a call and the value of a put on the same stock, if both can be exercised only at maturity, must obey the same differential equation, but with the following boundary condition:

$$w(x, t^*) - u(x, t^*) = x - c. \tag{24}$$

[10]For an exposition of stochastic calculus, see McKean (1969).

23

The solution to the differential equation with this boundary condition is:

$$w(x, t) - u(x, t) = x - ce^{r(t - t^*)}. \tag{25}$$

Thus the value of the European put option is:

$$u(x, t) = w(x, t) - x + ce^{r(t - t^*)}. \tag{26}$$

Putting in the value of $w(x, t)$ from (13), and noting that $1 - N(d)$ is equal to $N(-d)$, we have:

$$u(x, t) = -xN(-d_1) + ce^{-rt^*}N(-d_2). \tag{27}$$

In equation (27), d_1 and d_2 are defined as in equation (13).

Equation (25) also gives us a relation between the value of a European call and the value of a European put.[11] We see that if an investor were to buy a call and sell a put, his returns would be exactly the same as if he bought the stock on margin, borrowing $ce^{r(t - t^*)}$ toward the price of the stock.

Merton (1973) has also shown that the value of an American put option will be greater than the value of a European put option. This is true because it is sometimes advantageous to exercise a put option before maturity, if it is possible to do so. For example, suppose the stock price falls almost to zero and that the probability that the price will exceed the exercise price before the option expires is negligible. Then it will pay to exercise the option immediately, so that the exercise price will be received sooner rather than later. The investor thus gains the interest on the exercise price for the period up to the time he would otherwise have exercised it. So far, no one has been able to obtain a formula for the value of an American put option.

If we relax the assumption that the stock pays no dividend, we begin to get into some complicated problems. First of all, under certain conditions it will pay to exercise an American call option before maturity. Merton (1973) has shown that this can be true only just before the stock's ex-dividend date. Also, it is not clear what adjustment might be made in the terms of the option to protect the option holder against a loss due to a large dividend on the stock and to ensure that the value of the option will be the same as if the stock paid no dividend. Currently, the exercise price of a call option is generally reduced by the amount of any dividend paid on the stock. We can

[11]The relation between the value of a call option and the value of a put option was first noted by Stoll (1969). He does not realize, however, that his analysis applies only to European options.

see that this is not adequate protection by imagining that the stock is that of a holding company and that it pays out all of its assets in the form of a dividend to its shareholders. This will reduce the price of the stock and the value of the option to zero, no matter what adjustment is made in the exercise price of the option. In fact, this example shows that there may not be any adjustment in the terms of the option that will give adequate protection against a large dividend. In this case, the option value is going to be zero after the distribution, no matter what its terms are. Merton (1973) was the first to point out that the current adjustment for dividends is not adequate.

Warrant Valuation

A warrant is an option that is a liability of a corporation. The holder of a warrant has the right to buy the corporation's stock (or other assets) on specified terms. The analysis of warrants is often much more complicated than the analysis of simple options, because:

a) The life of a warrant is typically measured in years, rather than months. Over a period of years, the variance rate of the return on the stock may be expected to change substantially.
b) The exercise price of the warrant is usually not adjusted at all for dividends. The possibility that dividends will be paid requires a modification of the valuation formula.
c) The exercise price of a warrant sometimes changes on specified dates. It may pay to exercise a warrant just before its exercise price changes. This too requires a modification of the valuation formula.
d) If the company is involved in a merger, the adjustment that is made in the terms of the warrant may change its value.
e) Sometimes the exercise price can be paid using bonds of the corporation at face value, even though they may at the time be selling at a discount. This complicates the analysis and means that early exercise may sometimes be desirable.
f) The exercise of a large number of warrants may sometimes result in a significant increase in the number of common shares outstanding.

In some cases, these complications can be treated as insignificant, and equation (13) can be used as an approximation to give an estimate of the warrant value. In other cases, some simple modifications of equation (13) will improve the approximation. Suppose, for example, that there are warrants outstanding, which, if exercised, would double the number of shares of the company's common stock. Let us define the "equity" of the company as the sum of the value of all of its warrants and the value of all of its common stock. If the warrants are exercised at maturity, the equity of the company will increase by the aggregate amount of money paid in by the warrant holders when they exercise. The warrant holders will then own half of the new equity of the company, which is equal to the old equity plus the exercise money.

25

Thus, at maturity, the warrant holders will either receive nothing, or half of the new equity, minus the exercise money. Thus, they will receive nothing or half of the difference between the old equity and half the exercise money. We can look at the warrants as options to buy shares in the equity rather than shares of common stock, at half the stated exercise price rather than at the full exercise price. The value of a share in the equity is defined as the sum of the value of the warrants and the value of the common stock, divided by twice the number of outstanding shares of common stock. If we take this point of view, then we will take v^2 in equation (13) to be the variance rate of the return on the company's equity, rather than the variance rate of the return on the company's common stock.

A similar modification in the parameters of equation (13) can be made if the number of shares of stock outstanding after exercise of the warrants will be other than twice the number of shares outstanding before exercise of the warrants.

Common Stock and Bond Valuation

It is not generally realized that corporate liabilities other than warrants may be viewed as options. Consider, for example, a company that has common stock and bonds outstanding and whose only asset is shares of common stock of a second company. Suppose that the bonds are "pure discount bonds" with no coupon, giving the holder the right to a fixed sum of money, if the corporation can pay it, with a maturity of 10 years. Suppose that the bonds contain no restrictions on the company except a restriction that the company cannot pay any dividends until after the bonds are paid off. Finally, suppose that the company plans to sell all the stock it holds at the end of 10 years, pay off the bond holders if possible, and pay any remaining money to the stockholders as a liquidating dividend.

Under these conditions, it is clear that the stockholders have the equivalent of an option on their company's assets. In effect, the bond holders own the company's assets, but they have given options to the stockholders to buy the assets back. The value of the common stock at the end of 10 years will be the value of the company's assets minus the face value of the bonds, or zero, whichever is greater.

Thus, the value of the common stock will be $w(x, t)$, as given by equation (13), where we take v^2 to be the variance rate of the return on the shares held by the company, c to be the total face value of the outstanding bonds, and x to be the total value of the shares held by the company. The value of the bonds will simply be $x - w(x, t)$.

By subtracting the value of the bonds given by this formula from the value they would have if there were no default risk, we can figure the discount that should be applied to the bonds due to the existence of default risk.

Suppose, more generally, that the corporation holds business assets rather than financial assets. Suppose that at the end of the 10 year period, it will recapitalize by selling an entirely new class of common stock, using the proceeds to pay off the bond holders, and paying any money that is left to the old stockholders to retire their stock. In the absence of taxes, it is clear that the value of the corporation can be taken to be the sum of the total value of the debt and the total value of the common stock.[12] The amount of debt outstanding will not affect the total value of the corporation, but will affect the division of that value between the bonds and the stock. The formula for $w(x, t)$ will again describe the total value of the common stock, where x is taken to be the sum of the value of the bonds and the value of the stock. The formula for $x - w(x, t)$ will again describe the total value of the bonds. It can be shown that, as the face value c of the bonds increases, the market value $x - w(x, t)$ increases by a smaller percentage. An increase in the corporation's debt, keeping the total value of the corporation constant, will increase the probability of default and will thus reduce the market value of one of the corporation's bonds. If the company changes its capital structure by issuing more bonds and using the proceeds to retire common stock, it will hurt the existing bond holders, and help the existing stockholders. The bond price will fall, and the stock price will rise. In this sense, changes in the capital structure of a firm may affect the price of its common stock.[13] The price changes will occur when the change in the capital structure becomes certain, not when the actual change takes place.

Because of this possibility, the bond indenture may prohibit the sale of additional debt of the same or higher priority in the event that the firm is recapitalized. If the corporation issues new bonds that are subordinated to the existing bonds and uses the proceeds to retire common stock, the price of the existing bonds and the common stock price will be unaffected. Similarly, if the company issues new common stock and uses the proceeds to retire completely the most junior outstanding issue of bonds, neither the common stock price nor the price of any other issue of bonds will be affected.

The corporation's dividend policy will also affect the division of its total value between the bonds and the stock.[14] To take an extreme example, suppose again that the corporation's only assets are the shares of another company, and suppose that it sells all these shares and uses the proceeds to pay a dividend to its common stockholders. Then the value of the firm will go to zero, and the value of the bonds will go to zero. The common stockholders will have "stolen" the company out from under the bond

[12]The fact that the total value of a corporation is not affected by its capital structure, in the absence of taxes and other imperfections, was first shown by Modigliani and Miller (1958).
[13]For a discussion of this point, see Fama and Miller (1972, pp. 151-52).
[14]Miller and Modigliani (1961) show that the total value of a firm, in the absence of taxes and other imperfections, is not affected by its dividend policy. They also note that the price of the common stock and the value of the bonds will not be affected by a change in dividend policy if the funds for a higher dividend are raised by issuing common stock or if the money released by a lower dividend is used to repurchase common stock.

holders. Even for dividends of modest size, a higher dividend always favors the stockholders at the expense of the bond holders. A liberalization of dividend policy will increase the common stock price and decrease the bond price.[15] Because of this possibility, bond indentures contain restrictions on dividend policy, and the common stockholders have an incentive to pay themselves the largest dividend allowed by the terms of the bond indenture. However, it should be noted that the size of the effect of changing dividend policy will normally be very small.

If the company has coupon bonds rather than pure discount bonds outstanding, then we can view the common stock as a "compound option." The common stock is an option on an option on . . . an option on the firm. After making the last interest payment, the stockholders have an option to buy the company from the bond holders for the face value of the bonds. Call this "option 1." After making the next-to-the-last interest payment, but before making the last interest payment, the stockholders have an option to buy option 1 by making the last interest payment. Call this "option 2." Before making the next-to-the-last interest payment, the stockholders have an option to buy option 2 by making that interest payment. This is "option 3." The value of the stockholders' claim at any point in time is equal to the value of option $n + 1$, where n is the number of interest payments remaining in the life of the bond.

If payments to a sinking fund are required along with interest payments, then a similar analysis can be made. In this case, there is no "balloon payment" at the end of the life of the bond. The sinking fund will have a final value equal to the face value of the bond. Option 1 gives the stockholders the right to buy the company from the bond holders by making the last sinking fund and interest payment. Option 2 gives the stockholders the right to buy option 1 by making the next-to-the-last sinking fund and interest payment. And the value of the stockholders' claim at any point in time is equal to the value of option n, where n is the number of sinking fund and interest payments remaining in the life of the bond. It is

[15]This is true assuming that the liberalization of dividend policy is not accompanied by a change in the company's current and planned financial structure. Since the issue of common stock or junior debt will hurt the common shareholders (holding dividend policy constant), they will normally try to liberalize dividend policy without issuing new securities. They may be able to do this by selling some of the firm's financial assets, such as ownership claims on other firms. Or they may be able to do it by adding to the company's short-term bank debt, which is normally senior to its long-term debt. Finally, the company may be able to finance a higher dividend by selling off a division. Assuming that it receives a fair price for the division, and that there were no economies of combination, this need not involve any loss to the firm as a whole. If the firm issues new common stock or junior debt in exactly the amounts needed to finance the liberalization of dividend policy, then the common stock and bond prices will not be affected. If the liberalization of dividend policy is associated with a decision to issue more common stock or junior debt than is needed to pay the higher dividends, the common stock price will fall and the bond price will rise. But these actions are unlikely, since they are not in the stockholders' best interests.

clear that the value of a bond for which sinking fund payments are required is greater than the value of a bond for which they are not required.

If the company has callable bonds, then the stockholders have more than one option. They can buy the next option by making the next interest or sinking fund and interest payment, or they can exercise their option to retire the bonds before maturity at prices specified by the terms of the call feature. Under our assumption of a constant short-term interest rate, the bonds would never sell above face value, and the usual kind of call option would never be exercised. Under more general assumptions, however, the call feature would have value to the stockholders and would have to be taken into account in deciding how the value of the company is divided between the stockholders and the bond holders.

Similarly, if the bonds are convertible, we simply add another option to the package. It is an option that the bond holders have to buy part of the company from the stockholders.

Unfortunately, these more complicated options cannot be handled by using the valuation formula (13). The valuation formula assumes that the variance rate of the return on the optioned asset is constant. But the variance of the return on an option is certainly not constant: it depends on the price of the stock and the maturity of the option. Thus the formula cannot be used, even as an approximation, to give the value of an option on an option. It is possible, however, that an analysis in the same spirit as the one that led to equation (13) would allow at least a numerical solution to the valuation of certain more complicated options.

Empirical Tests   We have done empirical tests of the valuation formula on a large body of call-option data (Black and Scholes 1972). These tests indicate that the actual prices at which options are bought and sold deviate in certain systematic ways from the values predicted by the formula. Option buyers pay prices that are consistently higher than those predicted by the formula. Option writers, however, receive prices that are at about the level predicted by the formula. There are large transaction costs in the option market, all of which are effectively paid by option buyers.

Also, the difference between the price paid by option buyers and the value given by the formula is greater for options on low-risk stocks than for options on high-risk stocks. The market appears to underestimate the effect of differences in variance rate on the value of an option. Given the magnitude of the transaction costs in this market, however, this systematic misestimation of value does not imply profit opportunities for a speculator in the option market.

References

Ayres, Herbert F. "Risk Aversion in the Warrants Market." *Indus. Management Rev.* 4 (Fall 1963): 497-505. Reprinted in Cootner (1967), pp. 497-505.

Baumol, William J.; Malkiel, Burton G.; and Quandt, Richard E. "The Valuation of Convertible Securities." *Q. J. E.* 80 (February 1966): 48-59.

Black, Fischer, and Scholes, Myron. "The Valuation of Option Contracts and a Test of Market Efficiency." *J. Finance* 27 (May 1972): 399-417.

Boness, A. James. "Elements of a Theory of Stock-Option Values." *J. P. E.* 72 (April 1964): 163-75.

Chen, Andrew H. Y. "A Model of Warrant Pricing in a Dynamic Market." *J. Finance* 25 (December 1970): 1041-60.

Churchill, R. V. *Fourier Series and Boundary Value Problems,* 2d ed. New York: McGraw-Hill, 1963.

Cootner, Paul A. *The Random Character of Stock Market Prices.* Cambridge, Mass.: M. I. T. Press, 1967.

Fama, Eugene F. "Multiperiod Consumption-Investment Decisions." *A. E. R.* 60 (March 1970): 163-74.

Fama, Eugene F., and Miller, Merton H. *The Theory of Finance.* New York: Holt, Rinehart & Winston, 1972.

Lintner, John. "The Valuation of Risk Assets and the Selection of Risky Investments in Stock Portfolios and Capital Budgets." *Rev. Econ. and Statis.* 47 (February 1965): 768-83.

McKean, H. P., Jr. *Stochastic Integrals.* New York: Academic Press, 1969.

Merton, Robert C. "Theory of Rational Option Pricing." *Bell J. Econ. and Management Sci.* (1973): in press.

Miller, Merton H., and Modigliani, Franco. "Dividend Policy, Growth, and the Valuation of Shares." *J. Bus* 34 (October 1961): 411-33.

Modigliani, Franco, and Miller, Merton H. "The Cost of Capital, Corporation Finance, and the Theory of Investment." *A. E. R.* 48 (June 1958): 261-97.

Mossin, Jan. "Equilibrium in a Capital Asset Market." *Econometrica* 34 (October 1966): 768-83.

Samuelson, Paul A. "Rational Theory of Warrant Pricing." *Indus. Management Rev.* 6 (Spring 1965): 13-31. Reprinted in Cootner (1967), pp. 506-32.

Samuelson, Paul A., and Merton, Robert C. "A Complete Model of Warrant Pricing that Maximizes Utility." *Indus. Management Rev.* 10 (Winter 1969): 17-46.

Sharpe, William F. "Capital Asset Prices: A Theory of Market Equilibrium Under Conditions of Risk." *J. Finance* 19 (September 1964): 425-42.

———. *Portfolio Theory and Capital Markets:* New York: McGraw-Hill, 1970.

Sprenkle, Case. "Warrant Prices as Indications of Expectations." *Yale Econ. Essays* 1 (1961): 179-232. Reprinted in Cootner (1967), 412-74.

Stoll, Hans R. "The Relationship Between Put and Call Option Prices." *J. Finance* 24 (December 1969): 802-24.

Thorp, Edward O., and Kassouf, Sheen T. *Beat the Market.* New York: Random House, 1967.

Treynor, Jack L. "Implications for the Theory of Finance." Unpublished memorandum, 1961. (*a*)

———. "Toward a Theory of Market Value of Risky Assets. " Unpublished memorandum, 1961. (*b*)

3

The Theory of Rational Option Pricing

Robert C. Merton

The long history of the theory of option pricing began in 1900 when the French mathematician Louis Bachelier deduced an option pricing formula based on the assumption that stock prices follow a Brownian motion with zero drift. Since that time, numerous researchers have contributed to the theory. The present paper begins by deducing a set of restrictions on option pricing formulas from the assumption that investors prefer more to less. These restrictions are necessary conditions for a formula to be consistent with a rational pricing theory. Attention is given to the problems created when dividends are paid on the underlying common stock and when the terms of the option contract can be changed explicitly by a change in exercise price or implicitly by a shift in the investment or capital structure policy of the firm. Since the deduced restrictions are not sufficient to uniquely determine an option pricing formula, additional assumptions are introduced to examine and extend the seminal Black-Scholes theory of option pricing. Explicit formulas for pricing both call and put options as well as for warrants and the new "down-and-out" option are derived. The effects of dividends and call provisions on the warrant price are examined. The possibilities for further extension of the theory to the pricing of corporate liabilities are discussed.

Robert C. Merton received the B.S. in engineering mathematics from Columbia University's School of Engineering and Applied Science (1966), the M.S. in applied mathematics from the California Institute of Technology (1967), and the Ph.D. from the Massachusetts Institute of Technology (1970). Currently he is Assistant Professor of Finance at M.I.T., where he is conducting research in capital theory under uncertainty.

The paper is a substantial revision of sections of Merton [34] and [29]. I am particularly grateful to Myron Scholes for reading an earlier draft and for his comments. I have benefited from discussion with P. A. Samuelson and F. Black. I thank Robert K. Merton for editorial assistance. Any errors remaining are mine. Aid from the National Science Foundation is gratefully acknowledged.

1. Introduction   The theory of warrant and option pricing has been studied extensively in both the academic and trade literature.[1] The approaches taken range from sophisticated general equilibrium models to ad hoc statistical fits. Because options are specialized and relatively unimportant financial securities, the amount of time and space devoted to the development of a pricing theory might be questioned. One justification is that, since the option is a particularly simple type of contingent-claim asset, a theory of option pricing may lead to a general theory of contingent-claims pricing. Some have argued that all such securities can be expressed as combinations of basic option contracts, and, as such, a theory of option pricing constitutes a theory of contingent-claims pricing.[2] Hence, the development of an option pricing theory is, at least, an intermediate step toward a unified theory to answer questions about the pricing of a firm's liabilities, the term and risk structure of interest rates, and the theory of speculative markets. Further, there exist large quantities of data for testing the option pricing theory.

The first part of the paper concentrates on laying the foundations for a rational theory of option pricing. It is an attempt to derive theorems about the properties of option prices based on assumptions sufficiently weak to gain universal support. To the extent it is successful, the resulting theorems become necessary conditions to be satisfied by any rational option pricing theory.

As one might expect, assumptions weak enough to be accepted by all are not sufficient to determine uniquely a rational theory of option pricing. To do so, more structure must be added to the problem through additional assumptions at the expense of losing some agreement. The Black and Scholes (henceforth, referred to as B-S) formulation[3] is a significant "break-through" in attacking the option problem. The second part of the paper examines their model in detail. An alternative derivation of their formula shows that it is valid under weaker assumptions than they postulate. Several extensions to their theory are derived.

2. Restrictions on rational option pricing[4]   An "American"-type warrant is a security, issued by a company, giving its owner the right to purchase a share of stock at a given ("exercise") price on or before a given date. An "American"-type call option has the same terms as the warrant except that it is issued by an individual instead of a company. An "American"-type put option gives its owner the right to sell a share of stock at a given exercise price on or before a given date. A "European"-type option has the same terms as its "American" counterpart except that it cannot be surrendered ("exercised") before the

---

[1] See the bibliography for a substantial, but partial, listing of papers.
[2] See Black and Scholes [4] and Merton [29].
[3] In [4].
[4] This section is based on Merton [34] cited in Samuelson and Merton [43], p. 43, footnote 6.

last date of the contract. Samuelson[5] has demonstrated that the two types of contracts may not have the same value. All the contracts may differ with respect to other provisions such as antidilution clauses, exercise price changes, etc. Other option contracts such as strips, straps, and straddles, are combinations of put and call options.

The principal difference between valuing the call option and the warrant is that the aggregate supply of call options is zero, while the aggregate supply of warrants is generally positive. The "bucket shop" or "incipient" assumption of zero aggregate supply[6] is useful because the probability distribution of the stock price return is unaffected by the creation of these options, which is not in general the case when they are issued by firms in positive amounts.[7] The "bucket-shop" assumption is made throughout the paper although many of the results derived hold independently of this assumption.

The notation used throughout is: $F(S, \tau; E)$ — the value of an American warrant with exercise price E and τ years before expiration, when the price per share of the common stock is S; $f(S, \tau; E)$ — the value of its European counterpart; $G(S, \tau; E)$ — the value of an American put option; and $g(S, \tau; E)$ — the value of its European counterpart.

From the definition of a warrant and limited liability, we have that

$$F(S, \tau; E) \geqq 0; \quad f(S, \tau; E) \geqq 0 \tag{1}$$

and when $\tau = 0$, at expiration, both contracts must satisfy

$$F(S, 0; E) = f(S, 0; E) = \text{Max}[0, S - E]. \tag{2}$$

Further, it follows from conditions of arbitrage that

$$F(S, \tau; E) \geqq \text{Max}[0, S - E]. \tag{3}$$

In general, a relation like (3) need not hold for a European warrant.

[5] In [42].
[6] See Samuelson and Merton [43], p. 26 for a discussion of "incipient" analysis. Essentially, the incipient price is such that a slightly higher price would induce a positive supply. In this context, the term "bucket shop" was coined in oral conversation by Paul Samuelson and is based on the (now illegal) 1920's practice of side-bets on the stock market.

Myron Scholes has pointed out that if a company sells a warrant against stock already *outstanding* (not just authorized), then the incipient analysis is valid as well. (E.g., Amerada Hess selling warrants against shares of Louisiana Land and Exploration stock it owns and City Investing selling warrants against shares of General Development Corporation stock it owns.)
[7] See Merton [29], Section 2.

Definition: Security (portfolio) *A* is *dominant* over security (portfolio) *B*, if on some known date in the future, the return on *A* will exceed the return on *B* for some possible states of the world, and will be at least as large as on *B*, in all possible states of the world.

Note that in perfect markets with no transactions costs and the ability to borrow and short-sell without restriction, the existence of a dominated security would be equivalent to the existence of an arbitrage situation. However, it is possible to have dominated securities exist without arbitrage in imperfect markets. If one assumes something like "symmetric market rationality" and assumes further that investors prefer more wealth to less,[8] then any investor willing to purchase security *B* would prefer to purchase *A*.

Assumption 1: A necessary condition for a rational option pricing theory is that the option be priced such that it is neither a dominant nor a dominated security.

Given two American warrants on the same stock and with the same exercise price, it follows from Assumption 1, that

$$F(S, \tau_1; E) \geq F(S, \tau_2; E) \text{ if } \tau_1 > \tau_2, \tag{4}$$

and that

$$F(S, \tau; E) \geq f(S, \tau; E). \tag{5}$$

Further, two warrants, identical in every way except that one has a larger exercise price than the other, must satisfy

$$F(S, \tau; E_1) \leq F(S, \tau; E_2)$$

$$f(S, \tau; E_1) \leq f(S, \tau; E_2) \text{ if } E_1 > E_2. \tag{6}$$

Because the common stock is equivalent to a perpetual ($\tau = \infty$) American warrant with a zero exercise price ($E = 0$), it follows from (4) and (6) that

$$S \geq F(S, \tau; E), \tag{7}$$

and from (1) and (7), the warrant must be worthless if the stock is, i.e.,

$$F(0, \tau; E) = f(0, \tau; E) = 0. \tag{8}$$

Let $P(\tau)$ be the price of a riskless (in terms of default), discounted loan (or "bond") which pays one dollar, τ years from now. If it is assumed that current and future interest rates are positive, then

[8] See Modigliani and Miller [35], p. 427, for a definition of "symmetric market rationality."

$$1 = P(0) > P(\tau_1) > P(\tau_2) > \cdots > P(\tau_n)$$

$$\text{for } 0 < \tau_1 < \tau_2 < \cdots < \tau_n, \tag{9}$$

at a given point in calendar time.

Theorem 1: If the exercise price of a European warrant is E and if no payouts (e.g. dividends) are made to the common stock over the life of the warrant (or alternatively, if the warrant is protected against such payments), then f $(S, \tau; E) \geqq \text{Max}[0, S - EP(\tau)]$.

Proof: Consider the following two investments:

A: Purchase the warrant for $f(S, \tau; E)$;
    Purchase E bonds at price $P(\tau)$ per bond.
       Total investment: $f(S, \tau; E) + EP(\tau)$.
B: Purchase the common stock for S.
       Total investment: S.

Suppose at the end of τ years, the common stock has value S^*. Then, the value of B will be S^*. If $S^* \leq E$, then the warrant is worthless and the value of A will be $0 + E = E$. If $S^* > E$, then the A will be $(S^* - E) + E = S^*$. Therefore, unless the current value of A is at least as large as B, A will dominate B. Hence, by Assumption 1, $f(S, \tau; E) + EP(\tau) \geq S$, which together with (1), implies that $f(S, \tau; E) \geqq \text{Max}[0, S - EP(\tau)]$. Q. E. D.

From (5), it follows directly that Theorem 1 holds for American warrants with a fixed exercise price over the life of the contract. The right to exercise an option prior to the expiration date always has nonnegative value. It is important to know when this right has zero value, since in that case, the values of an European and American option are the same. In practice, almost all options are of the American type while it is always easier to solve analytically for the value of an European option. Theorem 1 significantly tightens the bounds for rational warrant prices over (3). In addition, it leads to the following two theorems.

Theorem 2. If the hypothesized conditions for Theorem 1 hold, an American warrant will never be exercised prior to expiration, and hence, it has the same value as a European warrant.

Proof: If the warrant is exercised, its value will be $\text{Max}[0, S - E]$. But from Theorem 1, $F(S, \tau; E) \geq \text{Max}[0, S - EP(\tau)]$, which is larger than $\text{Max}[0, S - E]$ for $\tau > 0$ because, from (9), $P(\tau) < 1$. Hence, the warrant is always worth more "alive" than "dead." Q.E.D.

Theorem 2 suggests that if there is a difference between the American and European warrant prices which implies a positive probability of a premature exercise, it must be due to unfavorable changes in the exercise price or to lack of protection against payouts to the common stocks. This result is consistent with the findings of Samuelson and Merton.[9]

It is a common practice to refer to Max $[0, S - E]$ as the *intrinsic value* of the warrant and to state that the warrant must always sell for at least its intrinsic value [condition (3)]. In light of Theorems 1 and 2, it makes more sense to define Max $[0, S - EP(\tau)]$ as the intrinsic value. The latter definition reflects the fact that the amount of the exercise price need not be paid until the expiration date, and $EP(\tau)$ is just the present value of that payment. The difference between the two values can be large, particularly for long-lived warrants, as the following theorem demonstrates.

Theorem 3. If the hypothesized conditions for Theorem 1 hold, the value of a perpetual $(\tau = \infty)$ warrant must equal the value of the common stock.

Proof: From Theorem 1, $F(S, \infty; E) \geq$ Max $[0, S - EP(\infty)]$. But, $P(\infty) = 0$, since, for positive interest rates, the value of a discounted loan payable at infinity is zero. Therefore, $F(S, \infty; E) \geq S$. But from (7), $S \geq F(S, \infty; E)$. Hence, $F(S, \infty; E) = S$. Q.E.D.

Samuelson, Samuelson and Merton, and Black and Scholes[10] have shown that the price of a perpetual warrant equals the price of the common stock for their particular models. Theorem 3 demonstrates that it holds independent of any stock price distribution or risk-averse behavioral assumptions.[11]

The inequality of Theorem 1 demonstrates that a finite-lived, rationally-determined warrant price must be a function of $P(\tau)$. For if it were not, then, for some sufficiently small $P(\tau)$ (i.e., large interest rate), the inequality of Theorem 1 would be violated. From the form of the inequality and previous discussion, this direct dependence on the interest rate seems to be "induced" by using as a variable, the exercise price instead of the present value of the exercise price (i.e., I conjecture that the pricing function, $F[S, \tau; E, P(\tau)]$, can be written as $W(S, \tau; e)$, where $e = EP(\tau)$.[12] If this is so, then the qualitative effect of a change in P on the warrant price would be similar to a change in the exercise price, which, from (6), is negative.

[9] In [43], p. 29 and Appendix 2.

[10] In [42], [43], and [4], respectively.

[11] It is a bit of a paradox that a perpetual warrant with a positive exercise price should sell for the same price as the common stock (a "perpetual warrant" with a zero exercise price), and, in fact, the few such outstanding warrants do not sell for this price. However, it must be remembered that one assumption for the theorem to obtain is that no payouts to the common stock will be made over the life of the contract which is almost never true in practice. See Samuelson and Merton [43], pp. 30-31, for further discussion of the paradox.

[12] The only case where the warrant price does not depend on the exercise price is the perpetuity, and the only case where the warrant price does not depend on $P(\tau)$ is when the exercise price is zero. Note that in both cases, $e = 0$, (the former because $P(\infty) = 0$, and the latter because $E = 0$), which is consistent with our conjecture.

Therefore, the warrant price should be an increasing function of the interest rate. This finding is consistent with the theoretical models of Samuelson and Merton and Black and Scholes and with the empirical study by Van Horne.[13]

Another argument for the reasonableness of this result comes from recognizing that a European warrant is equivalent to a long position in the common stock levered by a limited-liability, discount loan, where the borrower promises to pay E dollars at the end of τ periods, but in the event of default, is only liable to the extent of the value of the common stock at that time.[14] If the present value of such a loan is a decreasing function of the interest rate, then, for a given stock price, the warrant price will be an increasing function of the interest rate.

We now establish two theorems about the effect of a change in exercise price on the price of the warrant.

Theorem 4. If $F(S, \tau; E)$ is a rationally determined warrant price, then F is a convex function of its exercise price, E.

Proof: To prove convexity, we must show that if

$$E_3 \equiv \lambda E_1 + (1 - \lambda) E_2,$$

then for every λ, $0 \le \lambda \le 1$,

$$F(S, \tau; E_3) \leqq \lambda F(S, \tau; E_1) + (1 - \lambda) F(S, \tau; E_2).$$

We do so by a dominance argument similar to the proof of Theorem 1. Let portfolio A contain λ warrants with exercise price E_1 and $(1 - \lambda)$ warrants with exercise price E_2 where by convention, $E_2 > E_1$. Let portfolio B contain one warrant with exercise price E_3. If S^* is the stock price on the date of expiration, then by the convexity of Max $[0, S^* - E]$, the value of portfolio A,

$$\lambda \, \text{Max} \, [0, S^* - E_1] + (1 - \lambda) \, \text{Max} \, [0, S^* - E_2],$$

will be greater than or equal to the value of portfolio B,

$$\text{Max} \, [0, S^* - \lambda E_1 - (1 - \lambda) E_2].$$

Hence, to avoid dominance, the current value of portfolio B must be less than or equal to the current value of portfolio A. Thus, the theorem is

[13] In [43], [4], and [54], respectively.
[14] Stiglitz [51], p. 788, introduces this same type loan as a sufficient condition for the Modigliani-Miller Theorem to obtain when there is a positive probability of bankruptcy.

proved for a European warrant. Since nowhere in the argument is any factor involving τ used, the same results would obtain if the warrants in the two portfolios were exercised prematurely. Hence, the theorem holds for American warrants. Q.E.D.

Theorem 5. If $f(S, \tau; E)$ is a rationally determined European warrant price, then for $E_1 < E_2$, $-P(\tau)(E_2 - E_1) \leqq f(S, \tau; E_2) - f(S, \tau; E_1) \leq 0$. Further, if f is a differentiable function of its exercise price, $-P(\tau) \leq \partial f(S, \tau; E)/\partial E \leq 0$.

Proof: The right-hand inequality follows directly from (6). The left-hand inequality follows from a dominance argument. Let portfolio A contain a warrant to purchase the stock at E_2 and $(E_2 - E_1)$ bonds at price $P(\tau)$ per bond. Let portfolio B contain a warrant to purchase the stock at E_1. If S^* is the stock price on the date of expiration, then the terminal value of portfolio A,

$$\text{Max}\,[0, S^* - E_2] + (E_2 - E_1),$$

will be greater than the terminal value of portfolio B, $\text{Max}\,[0, S^* - E_1]$, when $S^* < E_2$, and equal to it when $S^* \geq E_2$. So, to avoid dominance, $f(S, \tau; E_1) \leqq f(S, \tau; E_2) + P(\tau)(E_2 - E_1)$. The inequality on the derivative follows by dividing the discrete-change inequalities by $(E_2 - E_1)$ and taking the limit as E_2 tends to E_1. Q.E.D.

If the hypothesized conditions for Theorem 1 hold, then the inequalities of Theorem 5 hold for American warrants. Otherwise, we only have the weaker inequalities, $-(E_2 - E_1) \leq F(S, \tau; E_2) - F(S, \tau; E_1) \leq 0$ and $-1 \leq \partial F(S, \tau; E)/\partial E \leq 0$.

Let $Q(t)$ be the price per share on a common stock at time t and $F_Q(Q, \tau; E_Q)$ be the price of a warrant to purchase one share of stock at price E_Q on or before a given date τ years in the future, when the current price of the common stock is Q.

Theorem 6. If k is a positive constant; $Q(t) = kS(t)$; $E_Q = kE$, then $F_Q(Q, \tau; E_Q) \equiv kF(S, \tau; E)$ for all S, τ; E and each k.

Proof: Let S^* be the value of the common stock with initial value S when both warrants either are exercised or expire. Then, by the hypothesized conditions of the theorem, $Q = Q^* \equiv kS^*$ and $E_Q = kE$. The value of the warrant on Q will be $\text{Max}\,[0, Q^* - E_Q] = k\,\text{Max}\,[0, S^* - E]$ which is k times the value of the warrant on S. Hence, to avoid dominance of one over the other, the value of the warrant on Q must sell for exactly k times the value of the warrant on S. Q.E.D.

The implications of Theorem 6 for restrictions on rational warrant pricing depend on what assumptions are required to produce the hypothesized conditions of the theorem. In its weakest form, it is a dimensional theorem where k is the proportionality factor between two units of account (e.g., $k = 100$ cents/dollar). If the stock and warrant markets are purely competitive, then it can be interpreted as a scale theorem. Namely, if there are no economies of scale with respect to transactions costs and no problems with indivisibilities, then k shares of stock will always sell for exactly k times the value of one share of stock. Under these conditions, the theorem states that a warrant to buy k shares of stock for a total of (kE) dollars when the stock price per share is S dollars, is equal in value to k times the price of a warrant to buy one share of the stock for E dollars, all other terms the same. Thus, the rational warrant pricing function is homogeneous of degree one in S and E with respect to scale, which reflects the usual constant returns to scale results of competition.

Hence, one can always work in standardized units of $E = 1$ where the stock price and warrant price are quoted in units of exercise price by choosing $k = 1/E$. Not only does this change of units eliminate a variable from the problem, but it is also a useful operation to perform prior to making empirical comparisons across different warrants where the dollar amounts may be of considerably different magnitudes.

Let $F_i(S_i, \tau_i; E_i)$ be the value of a warrant on the common stock of firm i with current price per share S_i, when τ_i is the time to expiration and E_i is the exercise price.

Assumption 2. If $S_i = S_j = S$; $\tau_i = \tau_j = \tau$; $E_i = E_j = E$, and the returns per dollar on the stocks i and j are identically distributed, then $F_i(S, \tau; E) = F_j(S, \tau; E)$.

Assumption 2 implies that, from the point of view of the warrant holder, the only identifying feature of the common stock is its (*ex ante*) distribution of returns.

Define $z(t)$ to be the one-period random variable return per dollar invested in the common stock in period t. Let $Z(\tau) \equiv \prod_{t=1}^{\tau} z(t)$ be the τ-period return per dollar.

Theorem 7. If $S_i = S_j = S$, $i, j = 1, 2, \ldots, n$;

$$Z_{n+1}(\tau) \equiv \Sigma_1^n \lambda_i Z_i(\tau)$$

for $\lambda_i \in [0, 1]$ and $\Sigma_1^n \lambda_i = 1$, then

$$F_{n+1}(S, \tau; E) \le \Sigma_1^n \lambda_i F_i(S, \tau; E).$$

Proof: By construction, one share of the $(n + 1)$st security contains λ_i shares of the common stock of firm i, and by hypothesis, the price per share, $S_{n+1} = \Sigma_1^n \lambda_i S_i = S \Sigma_1^n \lambda_i = S$. The proof follows from a dominance argument. Let portfolio A contain λ_i warrants on the common stock of firm i, $i = 1, 2, \ldots, n$. Let portfolio B contain one warrant on the $(n + 1)$st security. Let S_i^* denote the price per share on the common stock of the ith firm, on the date of expiration, $i = 1, 2, \ldots, n$. By definition, $S_{n+1}^* = \Sigma_1^n \lambda_i S_i^*$. On the expiration date, the value of portfolio A, $\Sigma_1^n \lambda_i \mathrm{Max} [0, S_i^* - E]$, is greater than or equal to the value of portfolio B, $\mathrm{Max} [0, \Sigma_1^n \lambda_i S_i^* - E]$, by the convexity of $\mathrm{Max} [0, S - E]$. Hence, to avoid dominance,

$$F_{n+1}(S, \tau; E) \leq \Sigma_1^n \lambda_i F_i(S, \tau; E). \text{ Q.E.D.}$$

Loosely, Theorem 7 states that a warrant on a portfolio is less valuable than a portfolio of warrants. Thus, from the point of view of warrant value, diversification "hurts," as the following special case of Theorem 7 demonstrates:

Corollary. If the hypothesized conditions of Theorem 7 hold and if, in addition, the $z_i(t)$ are identically distributed, then

$$F_{n+1}(S, \tau; E) \leq F_i(S, \tau; E)$$

for $i = 1, 2, \ldots, n$.

Proof: From Theorem 7, $F_{n+1}(S, \tau; E) \leq \Sigma_1^n \lambda_i F_i(S, \tau; E)$. By hypothesis, the $z_i(t)$ are identically distributed, and hence, so are the $Z_i(\tau)$. Therefore, by Assumption 2, $F_i(S, \tau; E) = F_j(S, \tau; E)$ for $i, j = 1, 2, \ldots n$. Since $\Sigma_1^n \lambda_i = 1$, it then follows that $F_{n+1}(S, \tau; E) \leq F_i(S, \tau; E), i = 1, 2, \ldots n$. Q.E.D.

Theorem 7 and its Corollary suggest the more general proposition that the more risky the common stock, the more valuable the warrant. In order to prove the proposition, one must establish a careful definition of "riskiness" or "volatility."

Definition: Security one is *more risky* than security two if $Z_1(\tau) = Z_2(\tau) + \epsilon$ where ϵ is a random variable with the property

$$E[\epsilon \mid Z_2(\tau)] = 0.$$

This definition of more risky is essentially one of the three (equivalent) definitions used by Rothschild and Stiglitz.[15]

---

[15] The two other equivalent definitions are: (1) every risk averter prefers X to Y (i. e., $EU(X) \geq EU(Y)$, for all concave U); (2) Y has more weight in the tails than X. In addition, they

Theorem 8. The rationally determined warrant price is a nondecreasing function of the riskiness of its associated common stock.

Proof: Let $Z(\tau)$ be the τ-period return on a common stock with warrant price, $F_Z(S, \tau; E)$. Let $Z_i(\tau) = Z(\tau) + \epsilon_i, i = 1, \ldots, n$, where the ϵ_i are independently and identically distributed random variables satisfying $E[\epsilon_i \mid Z(\tau)] = 0$. By definition, security i is more risky than security Z, for $i = 1, \ldots, n$. Define the random variable return $Z_{n+1}(\tau) \equiv \frac{1}{n} \Sigma_1^n Z_i(\tau) = Z(\tau) + \frac{1}{n} \Sigma_1^n \epsilon_i$. Note that, by construction, the $Z_i(\tau)$ are identically distributed. Hence, by the Corollary to Theorem 7 with $\lambda_i = 1/n$, $F_{n+1}(S, \tau; E) \leq F_i(S, \tau; E)$ for $i = 1, 2, \ldots, n$. By the law of large numbers, $Z_{n+1}(\tau)$ converges in probability to $Z(\tau)$ as $n \to \infty$, and hence, by Assumption 2, limit $F_{n+1}(S, \tau; E) = F_Z(S, \tau; E)$. Therefore, $F_Z(S, \tau; E) \leq F_i(S, \tau; E)$ for $i = 1, 2, \ldots, n$. Q.E.D.

Thus, the more uncertain one is about the outcomes on the common stock, the more valuable is the warrant. This finding is consistent with the empirical study by Van Horne.[16]

To this point in the paper, no assumptions have been made about the properties of the distribution of returns on the common stock. If it is assumed that the $\{z(t)\}$ are independently distributed,[17] then the distribution of the returns per dollar invested in the stock is independent of the initial level of the stock price, and we have the following theorem:

Theorem 9. If the distribution of the returns per dollar invested in the common stock is independent of the level of the stock price, then $F(S, \tau; E)$ is homogeneous of degree one in the stock price per share and exercise price.

Proof: Let $z_i(t)$ be the return per dollar if the initial stock price is $S_i, i = 1, 2$. Define $k = (S_2/S_1)$ and $E_2 = kE_1$. Then, by Theorem 6, $F_2(S_2, \tau; E_2) \equiv kF_2(S_1, \tau; E_1)$. By hypothesis, $z_1(t)$ and $z_2(t)$ are identically distributed. Hence, by Assumption 2, $F_2(S_1, \tau; E_1) = F_1(S_1, \tau; E_1)$. Therefore, $F_2(kS_1, \tau; kE_1) \equiv kF_1(S_1, \tau; E_1)$ and the theorem is proved. Q.E.D.

Although similar in a formal sense, Theorem 9 is considerably stronger than Theorem 6, in terms of restrictions on the warrant pricing function. Namely, given the hypothesized conditions of Theorem 9, one would expect to find in a table of rational warrant values for a given maturity, that the value of a warrant with exercise price E when the common stock is at S will

---

show that if Y has greater variance than X, then it need not be more risky in the sense of the other three definitions. It should also be noted that it is the *total* risk, and not the *systematic* or portfolio risk, of the common stock which is important to warrant pricing. In [39], p. 225.

[16] In [54].

[17] Cf. Samuelson [42].

be exactly k times as valuable as a warrant on the same stock with exercise price E/k when the common stock is selling for S/k. In general, this result will not obtain if the distribution of returns depends on the level of the stock price as is shown by a counter example in Appendix 1.

Theorem 10. If the distribution of the returns per dollar invested in the common stock is independent of the level of the stock price, then $F(S, \tau; E)$ is a convex function of the stock price.

Proof: To prove convexity, we must show that if

$$S_3 \equiv \lambda S_1 + (1 - \lambda) S_2,$$

then, for every λ, $0 \leq \lambda \leq 1$,

$$F(S_3, \tau; E) \leq \lambda F(S_1, \tau; E) + (1 - \lambda) F(S_2, \tau; E).$$

From Theorem 4,

$$F(1, \tau; E_3) \leq \gamma F(1, \tau; E_1) + (1 - \gamma) F(1, \tau; E_2),$$

for $0 \leq \gamma \leq 1$ and $E_3 = \gamma E_1 + (1 - \gamma) E_2$. Take $\gamma \equiv \lambda S_1/S_3, E_1 \equiv E/S_1$, and $E_2 \equiv E/S_2$. Mutiplying both sides of the inequality by S_3, we have that

$$S_3 F(1, \tau; E_3) \leq \lambda S_1 F(1, \tau; E_1) + (1 - \lambda) S_2 F(1, \tau; E_2).$$

From Theorem 9, F is homogeneous of degree one in S and E. Hence,

$$F(S_3, \tau; S_3 E_3) \leq \lambda F(S_1, \tau; S_1 E_1) + (1 - \lambda) F(S_2, \tau; S_2 E_2).$$

By the definition of E_1, E_2, and E_3, this inequality can be rewritten as $F(S_3, \tau; E) \leq \lambda F(S_1, \tau; E) + (1 - \lambda) F(S_2, \tau; E)$. Q.E.D.

Although convexity is usually assumed to be a property which always holds for warrants, and while the hypothesized conditions of Theorem 10 are by no means necessary, Appendix 1 provides an example where the distribution of future returns on the common stock is sufficiently dependent on the level of the stock price, to cause perverse local concavity.

Based on the analysis so far, Figure 1 illustrates the general shape that the rational warrant price should satisfy as a function of the stock price and time.

3. Effects of dividends and changing exercise price

A number of the theorems of the previous section depend upon the assumption that either no payouts are made to the common stock over the life of the contract or that the contract is protected against such payments. In this section, the adjustments required in the contracts to protect them against payouts are derived, and the effects of payouts on the valuation of

Figure 1.

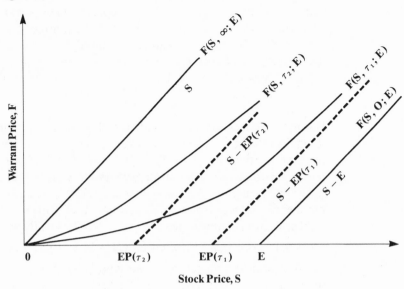

Stock Price, S

unprotected contracts are investigated. The two most common types of payouts are stock dividends (splits) and cash dividends.

In general, the value of an option will be affected by unanticipated changes in the firm's investment policy, capital structure (e.g., debt-equity ratio), and payout policy. For example, if the firm should change its investment policy so as to lower the riskiness of its cash flow (and hence, the riskiness of outcomes on the common stock), then, by Theorem 8, the value of the warrant would decline for a given level of the stock price. Similarly, if the firm changed its capital structure by raising the debt-equity ratio, then the riskiness of the common stock would increase, and the warrant would become more valuable. If that part of the total return received by shareholders in the form of dividends is increased by a change in payout policy, then the value of an unprotected warrant would decline since the warrant-holder has no claim on the dividends.[18]

While it is difficult to provide a set of adjustments to the warrant contract to protect it against changes in investment or capital structure policies without severely restricting the management of the firm, there do exist a set of adjustments to protect the warrant holders against payouts.

Definition: An option is said to be *payout protected* if, for a fixed investment policy and fixed capital structure, the value of the option is invariant to the choice of payout policy.

[18] This is an important point to remember when valuing unprotected warrants of companies such as A. T. & T. where a substantial fraction of the total return to shareholders comes in the form of dividends.

Theorem 11. If the total return per dollar invested in the common stock is invariant to the fraction of the return represented by payouts and if, on each expayout date during the life of a warrant, the contract is adjusted so that the number of shares which can be purchased for a total of E dollars is increased by (d/S^x) percent where d is the dollar amount of the payout and S^x is the expayout price per share of the stock, then the warrant will be payout protected.

Proof: Consider two firms with identically distributed total returns per dollar invested in the common stock, $z_i(t)$, $i = 1, 2$, and whose initial prices per share are the same ($S_1 = S_2 = S$). For firm i, let $\lambda_i(t)$ ($t \geq 1$) be the return per dollar in period t from payouts and $x_i(t)$ be the return per dollar in period t from capital gains, such that $z_i(t) \equiv \lambda_i(t) x_i(t)$. Let $N_i(t)$ be the number of shares of firm i which the warrant of firm i has claim on for a total price of E, at time t where $N_1(0) = N_2(0) = 1$. By definition, $\lambda_i(t) \equiv 1 + d_i(t)/S_i^x(t)$, where $S_i^x(t) = \prod_{k=1}^{t} x_i(k) S$ is the expayout price per share at time t. Therefore, by the hypothesized conditions of the theorem, $N_i(t) = \lambda_i(t) N_i(t - 1)$. On the date when the warrants are either exercised or expire, the value of the warrant on firm i will be

$$\text{Max}\,[0, N_i(t) S_i^x(t) - E].$$

But, $N_i(t) S_i^x(t) = [\prod_{k=1}^{t} \lambda_i(t)] [\prod_{k=1}^{t} x_i(t) S] = \prod_{k=1}^{t} z_i(t) S$. Since, by hypothesis, the $z_i(t)$ are identically distributed, the distribution of outcomes on the warrants of the two firms will be identical. Therefore, by Assumption 2, $F_1(S, \tau; E) = F_2(S, \tau; E)$, independent of the particular pattern chosen for the $\lambda_i(t)$. Q.E.D.

Note that if the hypothesized conditions of Theorem 11 hold, then the value of a protected warrant will be equal to the value of a warrant which restricts management from making any payouts to the common stock over the life of the warrant (i.e., $\lambda_i(t) \equiv 1$). Hence, a protected warrant will satisfy all the theorems of Section 2 which depend on the assumption of no payouts over the life of the warrant.

Corollary. If the total return per dollar invested in the common stock is invariant to the fraction of the return represented by payouts; if there are no economies of scale; and if, on each expayout date during the life of a warrant, each warrant to purchase one share of stock for exercise price E, is exchanged for $\lambda (\equiv 1 + d/S^x)$ warrants to purchase one share of stock for exercise price E/λ, then the warrant will be payout protected.

Proof: By Theorem 11, on the first expayout date, a protected warrant will have claim on λ shares of stock at a total exercise price of E. By hypothesis, there are no economies of scale. Hence, the scale interpretation of Theorem 6 is valid which implies that the value of a warrant on λ shares at a total price of E must be identically (in λ) equal to the value of λ warrants to purchase one share at an exercise price of E/λ. Proceeding inductively, we can show that this equality holds on each payout date. Hence, a warrant with the adjustment provision of the Corollary will be payout protected. Q.E.D.

If there are no economies of scale, it is generally agreed that a stock split or dividend will not affect the distribution of future per dollar returns on the common stock. Hence, the hypothesized adjustments will protect the warrant holder against stock splits where λ is the number of postsplit shares per presplit share.[19]

The case for cash dividend protection is more subtle. In the absence of taxes and transactions costs, Miller and Modigliani[20] have shown that for a fixed investment policy and capital structure, dividend policy does not affect the value of the firm. Under their hypothesized conditions, it is a necessary result of their analysis that the total return per dollar invested in the common stock will be invariant to payout policy. Therefore, warrants adjusted according to either Theorem 11 or its Corollary, will be payout protected in the same sense that Miller and Modigliani mean when they say that dividend policy "doesn't matter."

The principal cause for confusion is different definitions of payout protected. Black and Scholes[21] give an example to illustrate "that there may not be any adjustment in the terms of the option that will give adequate protection against a large dividend." Suppose that the firm liquidates all its assets and pays them out in the form of a cash dividend. Clearly, $S^x = 0$, and hence, the value of the warrant must be zero no matter what adjustment is made to the number of shares it has claim on or to its exercise price.

While their argument is correct, it also suggests a much stronger definition of payout protection. Namely, since their example involves changes in investment policy and if there is a positive supply of warrants (the nonincipient case), a change in the capital structure, in addition to a payout, their definition would seem to require protection against all three.

To illustrate, consider the firm in their example, but where management is prohibited against making any payouts to the shareholders prior to expiration of the warrant. It seems that such a warrant would be called payout protected by any reasonable definition. It is further assumed that the

---

[19] For any particular function, $F(S, \tau; E)$, there are many other adjustments which could leave value the same. However, the adjustment suggestions of Theorem 11 and its Corollary are the only ones which do so for every such function. In practice, both adjustments are used to protect warrants against stock splits. See Braniff Airways 1986 warrants for an example of the former and Leasco 1987 warrants for the latter. λ could be less than one in the case of a reverse split.
[20] In [35].
[21] In [4].

firm has only equity outstanding (i.e., the incipient case for the warrant) to rule out any capital structure effects.[22]

Suppose the firm sells all its assets for a fair price (so that the share price remains unchanged) and uses the proceeds to buy riskless, τ-period bonds. As a result of this investment policy change, the stock becomes a riskless asset and the warrant price will fall to Max $[0, S - EP]$. Note that if $S < EP$, the warrant will be worthless even though it is payout protected. Now lift the restriction against payouts and replace it with the adjustments of the Corollary to Theorem 11. Given that the shift in investment policy has taken place, suppose the firm makes a payment of γ percent of the value of the firm to the shareholders. Then, $S^x = (1 - \gamma) S$ and

$$\lambda = 1 + \gamma / (1 - \gamma) = 1/ (1 - \gamma).$$

The value of the warrant after the payout will be

$$\lambda \operatorname{Max} [0, S^x - EP/ \lambda] = \operatorname{Max} [0, S - EP],$$

which is the same as the value of the warrant when the company was restricted from making payouts. In the B-S example, $\gamma = 1$ and so, $\lambda = \infty$ and $E/ \lambda = 0$. Hence, there is the indeterminacy of multiplying zero by infinity. However, for every $\gamma < 1$, the analysis is correct, and therefore, it is reasonable to suspect that it holds in the limit.

A similar analysis in the nonincipient case would show that both investment policy and the capital structure were changed. For in this case, the firm would have to purchase γ percent of the warrants outstanding to keep the capital structure unchanged without issuing new stock. In the B-S example where $\gamma = 1$, this would require purchasing the entire issue, after which the analysis reduces to the incipient case. The B-S emphasis on protection against a "large" dividend is further evidence that they really have in mind protection against investment policy and capital structure shifts as well, since large payouts are more likely to be associated with nontrivial changes in either or both.

It should be noted that calls and puts that satisfy the incipient assumption have in practice been the only options issued with cash dividend protection clauses, and the typical adjustment has been to reduce the exercise price by the amount of the cash dividend which has been demonstrated to be incorrect.[23]

---

[22] The incipient case is a particularly important example since in practice, the only contracts that are adjusted for cash payouts are options. The incipient assumption also rules out "capital structure induced" changes in investment policy by malevolent management. For an example, see Stiglitz [50].

[23] By Taylor series approximation, we can compute the loss to the warrant holder of the standard adjustment for dividends: namely, $F(S - d, \tau; E - d) - F(S, \tau; E) = - dF_S(S, \tau; E) - dF_E(S, \tau; E) + o(d) = - [F(S, \tau; E) - (S - E)F_S(S, \tau; E)](d/E) +$

To this point it has been assumed that the exercise price remains constant over the life of the contract (except for the before-mentioned adjustments for payouts). A variable exercise price is meaningless for a European warrant since the contract is not exercisable prior to expiration. However, a number of American warrants do have variable exercise prices as a function of the length of time until expiration. Typically, the exercise price increases as time approaches the expiration date.

Consider the case where there are n changes of the exercise price during the life of an American warrant, represented by the following schedule:

Exercise Price	Time until Expiration (τ)
E_0	$0 \leq \tau \leq \tau_1$
E_1	$\tau_1 \leq \tau \leq \tau_2$
$\vdots$	$\vdots$
E_n	$\tau_n \leq \tau$,

where it is assumed that $E_{j+i} < E_j$ for $j = 0, 1, \ldots, n-1$. If, otherwise the conditions for Theorems 1 - 11 hold, it is easy to show that, if premature exercising takes place, it will occur only at points in time just prior to an exercise price change, i.e., at $\tau = \tau_j{}^+$, $j = 1, 2, \ldots, n$. Hence, the American warrant is equivalent to a *modified European warrant* which allows its owner to exercise the warrant at discrete times, just prior to an exercise price change. Given a technique for finding the price of a European warrant, there is a systematic method for valuing a modified European warrant. Namely, solve the standard problem for $F_0 (S, \tau; E_0)$ subject to the boundary conditions $F_0 (S, 0; E_0) = \text{Max} [0, S - E_0]$ and $\tau \leq \tau_1$. Then, by the same technique, solve for $F_1 (S, \tau; E_1)$ subject to the boundary conditions $F_1 (S, \tau_1; E_1) = \text{Max} [0, S - E_1, F_0 (S, \tau_1; E_0)]$ and $\tau_1 \leq \tau \leq \tau_2$. Proceed inductively by this dynamic-programming-like technique, until the current value of the modified European warrant is determined. Typically, the number of exercise price changes is small, so the technique is computationally feasible.

Often the contract conditions are such that the warrant will never be prematurely exercised, in which case, the correct valuation will be the standard European warrant treatment using the exercise price at expiration, E_0. If it can be demonstrated that

$$F_j (S, \tau_{j+1}; E_j) \geq S - E_{j+1}$$
$$\text{for all } S \geq 0 \text{ and } j = 0, 1, \ldots, N - 1, \tag{10}$$

then the warrant will always be worth more ''alive'' than ''dead,'' and the no-premature exercising result will obtain. From Theorem 1, $F_j (S, \tau_{j+1}; E_j)$

$\sigma (d)$, by the first-degree homogeneity of F in (S, E). Hence, to a first approximation, for $S = E$, the warrant will lose (d/S) percent of its value by this adjustment. Clearly, for $S > E$, the percentage loss will be smaller and for $S < E$, it will be larger.

$\geqq \text{Max}\,[0, S - P(\tau_{j+1} - \tau_j)E_j]$. Hence, from (10), a sufficient condition for no early exercising is that

$$E_{j+1}/E_j > P(\tau_{j+1} - \tau_j).\tag{11}$$

The economic reasoning behind (11) is identical to that used to derive Theorem 1. If by continuing to hold the warrant and investing the dollars which would have been paid for the stock if the warrant were exercised, the investor can with certainty earn enough to overcome the increased cost of exercising the warrant later, then the warrant should not be exercised.

Condition (11) is not as simple as it may first appear, because in valuing the warrant today, one must know for certain that (11) will be satisfied at some future date, which in general will not be possible if interest rates are stochastic. Often, as a practical matter, the size of the exercise price change versus the length of time between changes is such that for almost any reasonable rate of interest, (11) will be satisfied. For example, if the increase in exercise price is 10 percent and the length of time before the next exercise price change is five years, the yield to maturity on riskless securities would have to be less than 2 percent before (11) would not hold.

As a footnote to the analysis, we have the following Corollary.

Corollary. If there is a finite number of changes in the exercise price of a payout-protected, perpetual warrant, then it will not be exercised and its price will equal the common stock price.

Proof: applying the previous analysis, consider the value of the warrant if it survives past the last exercise price change, $F_0(S, \infty; E_0)$. By Theorem 3, $F_0(S, \infty; E_0) = S$. Now consider the value just prior to the last change in exercise price, $F_1(S, \infty; E_1)$. It must satisfy the boundary condition,

$$\begin{aligned}F_1(S, \infty; E_1) &= \text{Max}\,[0, S - E_1, F_0(S, \infty; E_0)]\\ &= \text{Max}\,[0, S - E_1, S] = S.\end{aligned}$$

Proceeding inductively, the warrant will never be exercised, and by Theorem 3, its value is equal to the common stock. Q.E.D.

The analysis of the effect on unprotected warrants when future dividends or dividend policy is known,[24] follows exactly the analysis of a changing exercise price. The arguments that no one will prematurely exercise his warrant except possibly at the discrete points in time just prior to a dividend

---

[24] The distinction is made between knowing future dividends and dividend policy. With the former, one knows, currently, the actual amounts of future payments while, with the latter, one knows the conditional future payments, conditional on (currently unknown) future values, such as the stock price.

payment, go through, and hence, the modified European warrant approach works where now the boundary conditions are $F_j (S, \tau_j; E) = \text{Max} [0, S - E, F_{j-1} (S - d_j, \tau_j; E)]$ where d_j equals the dividend per share paid at τ_j years prior to expiration, for $j = 1, 2, \ldots, n$.

In the special case, where future dividends and rates of interest are known with certainty, a sufficient condition for no premature exercising is that[25]

$$E > \sum_{t=0}^{\tau} d(t) P(\tau - t) / [1 - P(\tau)]. \tag{12}$$

I.e., the net present value of future dividends is less than the present value of earnings from investing E dollars for τ periods. If dividends are paid continuously at the constant rate of d dollars per unit time and if the interest rate, r, is the same over time, then (12) can be rewritten in its continuous form as

$$E > \frac{d}{r}. \tag{13}$$

Samuelson suggests the use of discrete recursive relationships, similar to our modified European warrant analysis, as an approximation to the mathematically difficult continuous-time model when there is some chance for premature exercising.[26] We have shown that the only reasons for premature exercising are lack of protection against dividends or sufficiently unfavorable exercise price changes. Further, such exercising will never take place except at boundary points. Since dividends are paid quarterly and exercise price changes are less frequent, the Samuelson recursive formulation with the discrete-time spacing matching the intervals between dividends or exercise price changes is actually the correct one, and the continuous solution is the approximation, even if warrant and stock prices change continuously!

Based on the relatively weak Assumption 1, we have shown that dividends and unfavorable exercise price changes are the only rational reasons for premature exercising, and hence, the only reasons for an American warrant to sell for a premium over its European counterpart. In those cases where early exercising is possible, a computationally feasible, general algorithm for modifying a European warrant valuation scheme has been derived. A number of theorems were proved putting restrictions on the structure of rational European warrant pricing theory.

[25] The interpretation of (12) is similar to the explanation given for (11). Namely, if the losses from dividends are smaller than the gains which can be earned risklessly, from investing the extra funds required to exercise the warrant and hold the stock, then the warrant is worth more "alive" than "dead."

[26] See [42], pp. 25-26, especially equation [42]. Samuelson had in mind small, discrete-time intervals, while in the context of the current application, the intervals would be large. Chen [8] also used this recursive relationship in his empirical testing of the Samuelson model.

4. Restrictions on rational put option pricing

The put option, defined at the beginning of Section 2, has received relatively little analysis in the literature because it is a less popular option than the call and because it is commonly believed [27] that, given the price of a call option and the common stock, the value of a put is uniquely determined. This belief is false for American put options, and the mathematics of put options pricing is more difficult than that of the corresponding call option.

Using the notation defined in Section 2, we have that, at expiration,

$$G(S, 0; E) = g(S, 0; E) = \text{Max} [0, E - S]. \tag{14}$$

To determine the rational European put option price, two portfolio positions are examined. Consider taking a long position in the common stock at S dollars, a long position in a τ-year European put at $g(S, \tau; E)$ dollars, and borrowing $[EP'(\tau)]$ dollars where $P'(\tau)$ is the current value of a dollar payable τ-years from now at the borrowing rate [28] (i.e., $P'(\tau)$ may not equal $P(\tau)$ if the borrowing and lending rates differ). The value of the portfolio τ years from now with the stock price at S^* will be: $S^* + (E - S^*) - E = 0$, if $S^* \leq E$, and $S^* + 0 - E = S^* - E$, if $S^* > E$. The pay-off structure is identical in every state to a European call option with the same exercise price and duration. Hence, to avoid the call option from being a dominated security, [29] the put and call must be priced so that

$$g(S, \tau; E) + S - EP'(\tau) \geq f(S, \tau; E). \tag{15}$$

As was the case in the similar analysis leading to Theorem 1, the values of the portfolio prior to expiration were not computed because the call option is European and cannot be prematurely exercised.

Consider taking a long position in a τ-year European call, a short position in the common stock at price S, and ending $EP(\tau)$ dollars. The value of the portfolio τ years from now with the stock price at S^* will be: $0 - S^* + E = E - S^*$, if $S^* \leq E$, and $(S^* - E) - S^* + E = 0$, if $S^* > E$. The pay-off structure is identical in every state to a European put option with the same exercise price and duration. If the put is not to be a dominated security, [30]

---

[27] See, for example, Black and Scholes [4] and Stoll [52].

[28] The borrowing rate is the rate on a τ-year, noncallable, discounted loan. To avoid arbitrage, $P'(\tau) \leq P(\tau)$.

[29] Due to the existent market structure, (15) must hold for the stronger reason of arbitrage. The portfolio did not require short-sales and it is institutionally possible for an investor to issue (sell) call options and reinvest the proceeds from the sale. If (15) did not hold, an investor, acting unilaterally, could make immediate, positive profits with no investment and no risk.

[30] In this case, we do not have the stronger condition of arbitrage discussed in footnote (29) because the portfolio requires a short sale of shares, and, under current regulations, the proceeds cannot be reinvested. Again, intermediate values of the portfolio are not examined because the put option is European.

then

$$f(S, \tau; E) - S + EP(\tau) \geqq g(S, \tau; E) \tag{16}$$

must hold.

Theorem 12. If Assumption 1 holds and if the borrowing and lending rates are equal [i.e., $P(\tau) = P'(\tau)$], then

$$g(S, \tau; E) = f(S, \tau; E) - S + EP(\tau).$$

Proof: the proof follows directly from the simultaneous application of (15) and (16) when $P'(\tau) = P(\tau)$. Q.E.D.

Thus, the value of a rationally priced European put option is determined once one has a rational theory of the call option value. The formula derived in Theorem 12 is identical to B-S's equation (26), when the riskless rate, r, is constant (i.e., $P(\tau) = e^{-r\tau}$). Note that no distributional assumptions about the stock price or future interest rates were required to prove Theorem 12.

Two corollaries to Theorem 12 follow directly from the above analysis.

Corollary 1. $EP(\tau) \geqq g(S, \tau; E)$.

Proof: from (5) and (7), $f(S, \tau; E) - S \leqq 0$ and from (16), $EP(\tau) \geqq g(S, \tau; E)$. Q.E.D.

The intuition of this result is immediate. Because of limited liability on the common stock, the maximum value of the put option is E, and because the option is European, the proceeds cannot be collected for τ years. The option cannot be worth more than the present value of a sure payment of its maximum value.

Corollary 2. The value of a perpetual ($\tau = \infty$) European put option is zero.

Proof: the put is a limited liability security [$g(S, \tau; E) \geqq 0$]. From Corollary 1 and the condition that $P(\infty) = 0, 0 \geqq g(S, \infty; E)$. Q.E.D.

Using the relationship $g(S, \tau; E) = f(S, \tau; E) - S + EP(\tau)$, it is straightforward to derive theorems for rational European put pricing which are analogous to the theorems for warrants in Section 2. In particular, whenever f is homogeneous of degree one or convex in S and E, so g will be also. The correct adjustment for stock and cash dividends is the same as prescribed for warrants in Theorem 11 and its Corollary.[31]

---

[31] While such adjustments for stock or cash payouts add to the value of a warrant or call option, the put option owner would prefer not to have them since lowering the exercise price on a put decreases its value. For simplicity, the effects of payouts are not considered, and it is assumed that no dividends are paid on the stock, and there are no exercise price changes.

Since the American put option can be exercised at any time, its price must satisfy the arbitrage condition

$$G(S, \tau; E) \geqq \text{Max}[0, E - S].$$ (17)

By the same argument used to derive (5), it can be shown that

$$G(S, \tau; E) \geqq g(S, \tau; E),$$ (18)

where the strict inequality holds only if there is a positive probability of premature exercising.

As shown in Section 2, the European and American warrant have the same value if the exercise price is constant and they are protected against payouts to the common stock. Even under these assumptions, there is almost always a positive probability of premature exercising of an American put, and hence, the American put will sell for more than its European counterpart. A hint that this must be so comes from Corollary 2 and arbitrage condition (17). Unlike European options, the value of an American option is always a nondecreasing function of its expiration date. If there is no possibility of premature exercising, the value of an American option will equal the value of its European counterpart. By the Corollary to Theorem 11, the value of a perpetual American put would be zero, and by the monotonicity argument on length of time to maturity, all American puts would have zero value. This absurd result clearly violates the arbitrage condition (17) for $S < E$.

To clarify this point, reconsider the two portfolios examined in the European put analysis, but with American puts instead. The first portfolio contained a long position in the common stock at price S, a long position in an American put at price $G(S, \tau; E)$, and borrowings of $[EP'(\tau)]$. As was previously shown, if held until maturity, the outcome of the portfolio will be identical to those of an American (European) warrant held until maturity. Because we are now using American options with the right to exercise prior to expiration, the interim values of the portfolio must be examined as well. If, for all times prior to expiration, the portfolio has value greater than the exercise value of the American warrant, $S - E$, then to avoid dominance of the warrant, the current value of the portfolio must exceed or equal the current value of the warrant.

The interim value of the portfolio at T years until expiration when the stock price is S^*, is

$$S^* + G(S^*, T; E) - EP'(T)$$
$$= G(S^*, T; E) + (S^* - E) + E[1 - P'(T)] > (S^* - E).$$

Hence, condition (15) holds for its American counterparts to avoid dominance of the warrant, i.e.,

$$G(S, \tau; E) + S - EP'(\tau) \geq F(S, \tau; E). \tag{19}$$

The second portfolio has a long position in an American call at price $F(S, \tau; E)$, a short position in the common stock at price S, and a loan of $[EP(\tau)]$ dollars. If held until maturity, this portfolio replicates the outcome of a European put, and hence, must be at least as valuable at any interim point in time. The interim value of the portfolio, at T years to go and with the stock price at S^*, is

$$\begin{aligned} F(S^*, T; E) &- S^* + EP(T) \\ &= (E - S^*) + F(S^*, T; E) - E[1 - P(T)] < E - S^*, \end{aligned}$$

if $F(S^*, T; E) < E[1 - P(T)]$, which is possible for small enough S^*. From (17), $G(S^*, T; E) \geq E - S^*$. So, the interim value of the portfolio will be less than the value of an American put for sufficiently small S^*. Hence, if an American put was sold against this portfolio, and if the put owner decided to exercise his put prematurely, the value of the portfolio could be less than the value of the exercised put. This result would certainly obtain if $S^* < E | 1 - P(T) |$. So, the portfolio will not dominate the put if inequality (16) does not hold, and an analog theorem to Theorem 12, which uniquely determines the value of an American put in terms of a call, does not exist. Analysis of the second portfolio does lead to the weaker inequality that

$$G(S, \tau; E) \leq E - S + F(S, \tau; E). \tag{20}$$

Theorem 13. If, for some $T < \tau$, there is a positive probability that $f(S, T; E) < E | 1 - P(T) |$, then there is a positive probability that a τ-year, American put option will be exercised prematurely and the value of the American put will strictly exceed the value of its European counterpart.

Proof: the only reason that an American put will sell for a premium over its European counterpart is that there is a positive probability of exercising prior to expiration. Hence, it is sufficient to prove that $g(S, \tau; E) < G(S, \tau; E)$. From Assumption 1, if for some $T \leq \tau$, $g(S^*, T; E) < G(S^*, T; E)$ for some possible value(s) of S^*, then $g(S, \tau; E) < G(S, \tau; E)$. From Theorem 12, $g(S^*, T; E) = f(S^*, T; E) - S^* + EP(T)$. From (17), $G(S^*, T; E) \geq \text{Max}[0, E - S^*]$. But $g(S^*, T; E) < G(S^*, T; E)$ is implied if $E - S^* > f(S^*, T; E) - S^* + EP(T)$, which holds if $f(S^*, T; E) < E[1 - P(T)]$. By hypothesis of the theorem, such an S^* is a possible value. Q.E.D.

Since almost always there will be a chance of premature exercising, the formula of Theorem 12 or B-S equation (26) will not lead to a correct valuation of an American put and, as mentioned in Section 3, the valuation of such options is a more difficult analytical task than valuing their European counterparts.

5. Rational option pricing along Black-Scholes lines

A number of option pricing theories satisfy the general restrictions on a rational theory as derived in the previous sections. One such theory developed by B-S[32] is particularly attractive because it is a complete general equilibrium formulation of the problem and because the final formula is a function of "observable" variables, making the model subject to direct empirical tests.

B-S assume that: (1) the standard form of the Sharpe-Lintner-Mossin capital asset pricing model holds for intertemporal trading, and that trading takes place continuously in time; (2) the market rate of interest, r, is known and fixed over time; and (3) there are no dividends or exercise price changes over the life of the contract.

To derive the formula, they assume that the option price is a function of the stock price and time to expiration, and note that, over "short" time intervals, the stochastic part of the change in the option price will be perfectly correlated with changes in the stock price. A hedged portfolio containing the common stock, the option, and a short-term, riskless security, is constructed where the portfolio weights are chosen to eliminate all "market risk." By the assumption of the capital asset pricing model, any portfolio with a zero ("beta") market risk must have an expected return equal to the risk-free rate. Hence, an equilibrium condition is established between the expected return on the option, the expected return on the stock, and the riskless rate.

Because of the distributional assumptions and because the option price is a function of the common stock price, B-S in effect make use of the Samuelson[33] application to warrant pricing of the Bachelier-Einstein-Dynkin derivation of the Fokker-Planck equation, to express the expected return on the option in terms of the option price function and its partial derivatives. From the equilibrium condition on the option yield, such a partial differential equation for the option price is derived. The solution to this equation for a European call option is

$$f(S, \tau; E) = S\phi(d_1) - Ee^{-r\tau}\phi(d_2), \tag{21}$$

where ϕ is the cumulative normal distribution function, σ^2 is the instantaneous variance of the return on the common stock,

$$d_1 \equiv [\log(S/E) + (r + \tfrac{1}{2}\sigma^2)\tau]/\sigma\sqrt{\tau},$$

and $d_2 \equiv d_1 - \sigma\sqrt{\tau}$.

An exact formula for an asset price, based on observable variables only, is a rare finding from a general equilibrium model, and care should be taken to

---

[32] In [4].
[33] In [42].

analyze the assumptions with Occam's razor to determine which ones are necessary to derive the formula. Some hints are to be found by inspection of their final formula (21) and a comparison with an alternative general equilibrium development.

The manifest characteristic of (21) is the number of variables that it does *not* depend on. The option price does not depend on the expected return on the common stock, [34] risk preferences of investors, or on the aggregate supplies of assets. It does depend on the rate of interest (an "observable") and the *total* variance of the return on the common stock which is often a stable number and hence, accurate estimates are possible from time series data.

The Samuelson and Merton[35] model is a complete, although very simple (three assets and one investor) general equilibrium formulation. Their formula[36] is

$$f(S, \tau; E) = e^{-r\tau} \int_{E/S}^{\infty} (ZS - E)\, dQ(Z; \tau), \tag{22}$$

where dQ is a probability density function with the expected value of Z over the dQ distribution equal to $e^{r\tau}$. Equations (22) and (21) will be the same only in the special case when dQ is a log-normal density with the variance of $\log(Z)$ equal to $\sigma^2 \tau$.[37] However, dQ is a risk-adjusted ("util-prob") distribution, dependent on both risk-preferences and aggregate supplies, while the distribution in (21) is the objective distribution of returns on the common stock. B-S claim that one reason that Samuelson and Merton did not arrive at formula (21) was because they did not consider other assets. If a result does not obtain for a simple, three asset case, it is unlikely that it would in a more general example. More to the point, it is only necessary to consider three assets to derive the B-S formula. In connection with this point, although B-S claim that their central assumption is the capital asset pricing model (emphasizing this over their hedging argument), their final formula, (21), depends only on the interest rate (which is exogenous to the capital asset pricing model) and on the *total* variance of the return on the common stock. It does not depend on the betas (covariances with the market) or other assets' characteristics. Hence, this assumption may be a "red herring."

Although their derivation of (21) is intuitively appealing, such an important result deserves a rigorous derivation. In this case, the rigorous derivation is

[34] This is an important result because the expected return is not directly observable and estimates from past data are poor because of nonstationarity. It also implies that attempts to use the option price to estimate expected returns on the stock or risk-preferences of investors are doomed to failure (e. g., see Sprenkle [49]).

[35] In [43].

[36] *Ibid.*, p. 29, equation 30.

[37] This will occur only if: (1) the objective returns on the stock are log-normally distributed; (2) the investor's utility function is iso-elastic (i.e., homothetic indifference curves); and (3) the supplies of *both* options and bonds are at the incipient level.

not only for the satisfaction of the "purist," but also to give insight into the necessary conditions for the formula to obtain. The reader should be alerted that because B-S consider only terminal boundary conditions, their analysis is strictly applicable to European options, although as shown in Sections 2 through 4, the European valuation is often equal to the American one.

Finally, although their model is based on a different economic structure, the formal analytical content is identical to Samuelson's "linear, $\alpha = \beta$" model when the returns on the common stock are log-normal.[38] Hence, with different interpretation of the parameters, theorems proved in Samuelson and in the difficult McKean appendix[39] are directly applicable to the B-S model, and vice versa.

6. An alternative derivation of the Black-Scholes model[40]

Initially, we consider the case of a European option where no payouts are made to the common stock over the life of the contract. We make the following further assumptions.

(1) *"Frictionless"* markets: there are no transactions costs or differential taxes. Trading takes place continuously and borrowing and short-selling are allowed without restriction.[41] The borrowing rate equals the lending rate.

(2) *Stock price dynamics:* the instantaneous return on the common stock is described by the stochastic differential equation[42]

$$\frac{dS}{S} = \alpha dt + \sigma dz, \tag{23}$$

where α is the instantaneous expected return on the common stock, σ^2 is the instantaneous variance of the return, and dz is a standard Gauss-Wiener

[38] In [42]. See Merton [28] for a brief description of the relationship between the Samuelson and B-S models.

[39] In [26].

[40] Although the derivation presented here is based on assumptions and techniques different from the original B-S model, it is in the spirit of their formulation, and yields the same formula when their assumptions are applied.

[41] The assumptions of unrestricted borrowing and short-selling can be weakened and still have the results obtained by splitting the created portfolio of the text into two portfolios: one containing the common stock and the other containing the warrant plus a long position in bonds. Then, as was done in Section 2, if we accept Assumption 1, the formulas of the current section follow immediately.

[42] For a general description of the theory of stochastic differential equations of the Itô type, see McKean [27] and Kushner [24]. For a description of their application to the consumption-portfolio problem, see Merton [32], [33], and [31]. Briefly, Itô processes follow immediately from the assumption of a continuous-time stochastic process which results in continuous price changes (with finite moments) and some level of independent increments. If the process for price changes were functions of stable Paretian distributions with infinite moments, it is conjectured that the only equilibrium value for a warrant would be the stock price itself, independent of the length of time to maturity. This implication is grossly inconsistent with all empirical observations.

process. α may be a stochastic variable of quite general type including being dependent on the level of the stock price or other assets' returns. Therefore, no presumption is made that dS/S is an independent increments process or stationary, although dz clearly is. However, σ is restricted to be nonstochastic and, at most, a known function of time.

(3) *Bond price dynamics*: $P(\tau)$ is as defined in previous sections and the dynamics of its returns are described by

$$\frac{dP}{P} = \mu(\tau)dt + \delta(\tau)dq(t;\tau), \tag{24}$$

where μ is the instantaneous expected return, δ^2 is the instantaneous variance, and $dq(t;\tau)$ is a standard Gauss-Wiener process for maturity τ. Allowing for the possibility of habitat and other term structure effects, it is not assumed that dq for one maturity is perfectly correlated with dq for another, i.e.,

$$dq(t;\tau)dq(t;T) = \varrho_{\tau T}dt, \tag{24a}$$

where $\varrho_{\tau T}$ may be less than one for $\tau \neq T$. However, it is assumed that there is no serial correlation[43] among the (unanticipated) returns on any of the assets, i.e.,

$$\begin{aligned} dq(s;\tau)dq(t;T) &= 0 \ \text{ for } \ s \neq t \\ dq(s;\tau)dz(t) &= 0 \ \text{ for } \ s \neq t, \end{aligned} \tag{24b}$$

which is consistent with the general efficient market hypothesis of Fama and Samuelson.[44] $\mu(\tau)$ may be stochastic through dependence on the level of bond prices, etc., and different for different maturities. Because $P(\tau)$ is

---

[43] The reader should be careful to note that it is assumed only that the *unanticipated* returns on the bonds are not serially correlated. Cootner [11] and others have pointed out that since the bond price will equal its redemption price at maturity, the total returns over time cannot be uncorrelated. In no way does this negate the specification of (24), although it does imply that the variance of the unanticipated returns must be a function of time to maturity. An example to illustrate that the two are not inconsistent can be found in Merton [29]. Suppose that bond prices for all maturities are only a function of the current (and future) short-term interest rates. Further, assume that the short-rate, r, follows a Gauss-Wiener process with (possibly) some drift, i.e., $dr = adt + gdz$, where a and g are constants. Although this process is not realistic because it implies a positive probability of negative interest rates, it will still illustrate the point. Suppose that all bonds are priced so as to yield an expected rate of return over the next period equal to r (i.e., a form of the expectations hypothesis):

$$P(\tau;r) = \exp\left[-r\tau - \frac{a}{2}\tau^2 + \frac{g^2\tau^3}{6} \right]$$

and

$$\frac{dP}{P} = rdt - g\tau dz.$$

By construction, dz is not serially correlated and in the notation of (24), $\delta(\tau) = -g\tau$.

[44] In [13] and [41], respectively.

the price of a discounted loan with no risk of default, $P(0) = 1$ with certainty and $\delta(\tau)$ will definitely depend on τ with $\delta(0) = 0$. However, δ is otherwise assumed to be nonstochastic and independent of the level of P. In the special case when the interest rate is nonstochastic and constant over time, $\delta \equiv 0$, $\mu = r$, and $P(\tau) = e^{-r\tau}$.

(4) *Investor preferences and expectations:* no assumptions are necessary about investor preferences other than that they satisfy Assumption 1 of Section 2. All investors agree on the values of σ and δ, and on the distributional characteristics of dz and dq. It is *not* assumed that they agree on either α or μ.[45]

From the analysis in Section 2, it is reasonable to assume that the option price is a function of the stock price, the riskless bond price, and the length of time to expiration. If $H(S, P, \tau; E)$ is the option price function, then, given the distributional assumptions on S and P, we have, by Itô's Lemma,[46] that the change in the option price over time satisfies the stochastic differential equation,

$$
\begin{aligned}
dH = H_1 dS + H_2 dP + H_3 d\tau \\
+ \tfrac{1}{2} [H_{11}(dS)^2 + 2H_{12}(dSdP) + H_{22}(dP)^2],
\end{aligned} \tag{25}
$$

where subscripts denote partial derivatives, and $(dS)^2 \equiv \sigma^2 S^2 dt$, $(dP)^2 \equiv \delta^2 P^2 dt$, $d\tau = -dt$, and $(dSdP) \equiv \varrho\sigma\delta SP dt$ with ϱ, the instantaneous correlation coefficient between the (unanticipated) returns on the stock and on the bond. Substituting from (23) and (24) and rearranging terms, we can rewrite (25) as

$$
dH = \beta H dt + \gamma H dz + \eta H dq, \tag{26}
$$

where the instantaneous expected return on the warrant, β, equals $[\tfrac{1}{2}\sigma^2 S^2 H_{11} + \varrho\sigma\delta SP H_{12} + \tfrac{1}{2}\delta^2 P^2 H_{22} + \alpha S H_1 + \mu P H_2 - H_3]/H$, $\gamma \equiv \sigma S H_1/H$, and $\eta \equiv \delta P H_2/H$.

In the spirit of the Black-Scholes formulation and the analysis in Sections 2 thru 4, consider forming a portfolio containing the common stock, the option, and riskless bonds with time to maturity, τ, equal to the expiration date of the option, such that the aggregate investment in the portfolio is zero. This is achieved by using the proceeds of short-sales and borrowing to finance long positions. Let W_1 be the (instantaneous) number of dollars of

[45] This assumption is much more acceptable than the usual homogeneous expectations. It is quite reasonable to expect that investors may have quite different estimates for current (and future) expected returns due to different levels of information, techniques of analysis, etc. However, most analysts calculate estimates of variances and covariances in the same way: namely, by using previous price data. Since all have access to the same price history, it is also reasonable to assume that their variance-covariance estimates may be the same.

[46] Itô's Lemma is the stochastic-analog to the fundamental theorem of the calculus because it states how to differentiate functions of Wiener processes. For a complete description and proof, see McKean [27]. A brief discussion can be found in Merton [33].

the portfolio invested in the common stock, W_2 be the number of dollars invested in the option, and W_3 be the number of dollars invested in bonds. Then, the condition of zero aggregate investment can be written as $W_1 + W_2 + W_3 = 0$. If dY is the instantaneous dollar return to the portfolio, it can be shown[47] that

$$dY = W_1 \frac{dS}{S} + W_2 \frac{dH}{H} + W_3 \frac{dP}{P}$$

$$= [W_1(\alpha - \mu) + W_2(\beta - \mu)]\,dt + [W_1\sigma + W_2\gamma]\,dz$$

$$+ [W_2\eta - (W_1 + W_2)\delta]\,dq, \quad (27)$$

where $W_3 \equiv -(W_1 + W_2)$ has been substituted out.

Suppose a strategy, $W_j = W_j^*$, can be chosen such that the coefficients of dz and dq in (27) are always zero. Then, the dollar return on that portfolio, dY^*, would be nonstochastic. Since the portfolio requires zero investment, it must be that to avoid "arbitrage"[48] profits, the expected (and realized) return on the portfolio with this strategy is zero. The two portfolio and one equilibrium conditions can be written as a 3 x 2 linear system,

$$(\alpha - \mu)\,W_1^* + (\beta - \mu)\,W_2^* = 0$$

$$\sigma\,W_1^* + \gamma\,W_2^* = 0 \quad (28)$$

$$-\delta\,W_1^* + (\eta - \delta)\,W_2^* = 0.$$

A nontrivial solution ($W_1^* \neq 0;\ W_2^* \neq 0$) to (28) exists if and only if

$$\frac{\beta - \mu}{\alpha - \mu} = \frac{\gamma}{\sigma} = \frac{\delta - \eta}{\delta}. \quad (29)$$

Because we make the "bucket shop" assumption, μ, α, δ, and σ are legitimate exogenous variables (relative to the option price), and β, γ, and η are to be determined so as to avoid dominance of any of the three securities. If (29) holds, then $\gamma/\sigma = 1 - \eta/\delta$, which implies from the definition of γ and in (26), that

$$\frac{SH_1}{H} = 1 - \frac{PH_2}{H} \quad (30)$$

or

$$H = SH_1 + PH_2. \quad (31)$$

[47] See Merton [32] or [33].
[48] "Arbitrage" is used in the qualified sense that the distributional and other assumptions are known to hold with certainty. A weaker form would say that if the return on the portfolio is nonzero, either the option or the common stock would be a dominated security. See Samuelson [44] or [45] for a discussion of this distinction.

Although it is not a sufficient condition, by Euler's theorem, (31) is a necessary condition for H to be first degree homogeneous in (S, P) as was conjectured in Section 2.

The second condition from (29) is that $\beta - \mu = \gamma(\alpha - \mu)/\sigma$, which implies from the definition of β and γ in (26) that

$$\tfrac{1}{2}\sigma^2 S^2 H_{11} + \varrho\,\sigma\,\delta\,SPH_{12} + \tfrac{1}{2}\delta^2 P^2 H_{22}$$

$$+ \alpha\,SH_1 + \mu\,PH_2 - H_3 - \mu H = SH_1(\alpha - \mu), \qquad (32)$$

or, by combining terms, that

$$\tfrac{1}{2}\sigma^2 S^2 H_{11} + \varrho\,\sigma\,\delta\,SPH_{12} + \tfrac{1}{2}\delta^2 P^2 H_{22} + \mu\,SH_1$$

$$+ \mu\,PH_2 - H_3 - \mu H = 0. \qquad (33)$$

Substituting for H from (31) and combining terms, (33) can be rewritten as

$$\tfrac{1}{2}\left[\sigma^2 S^2 H_{11} + 2\varrho\sigma\delta\,SPH_{12} + \delta^2 P^2 H_{22}\right] - H_3 = 0, \qquad (34)$$

which is a second-order, linear partial differential equation of the parabolic type.

If H is the price of a European warrant, then H must satisfy (34) subject to the boundary conditions:

$$H(0, P, \tau; E) = 0 \qquad (34a)$$

$$H(S, 1, 0; E) = \text{Max}\,[0, S - E], \qquad (34b)$$

since by construction, $P(0) = 1$.

Define the variable $x \equiv S/EP(\tau)$, which is the price per share of stock in units of exercise price-dollars payable at a *fixed date* in the future (the expiration date of the warrant). The variable x is a well-defined price for $\tau \geq 0$, and from (23), (24), and Itô's Lemma, the dynamics of x are described by the stochastic differential equation,

$$\frac{dx}{x} = [\alpha - \mu + \delta^2 - \varrho\sigma\delta]\,dt + \sigma\,dz - \delta\,dq. \qquad (35)$$

From (35), the expected return on x will be a function of S, P, etc., through α and μ, but the instantaneous variance of the return on x, $V^2(\tau)$, is equal to $\sigma^2 + \delta^2 - 2\varrho\sigma\delta$, and will depend only on τ.

Motivated by the possible homogeneity properties of H, we try the change in variables, $h(x, \tau; E) \equiv H(S, P, \tau; E)/EP$ where h is assumed to be independent of P and is the warrant price evaluated in the same units as x.

Substituting (h, x) for (H, S) in (34), (34a) and (34b), leads to the partial differential equation for h,

$$\tfrac{1}{2} V^2 x^2 h_{11} - h_2 = 0, \tag{36}$$

subject to the boundary conditions, $h(0, \tau; E) = 0$, and $h(x, 0; E) = \mathrm{Max}$ $[0, x - 1]$. From inspection of (36) and its boundary conditions, h is only a function of x and τ, since V^2 is only a function of τ. Hence, the assumed homogeneity property of H is verified. Further, h does not depend on E, and so, H is actually homogeneous of degree one in $[S, EP(\tau)]$.

Consider a new time variable, $T \equiv \int_0^\tau V^2(s)\, ds$. Then, if we define $y(x, T) \equiv h(x, \tau)$ and substitute into (36), y must satisfy

$$\tfrac{1}{2} x^2 y_{11} - y_2 = 0, \tag{37}$$

subject to the boundary conditions, $y(0, T) = 0$ and $y(x, 0) = \mathrm{Max}$ $[0, x - 1]$. Suppose we wrote the warrant price in its "full functional form," $H(S, P, \tau; E, \sigma^2, \delta^2, \varrho)$. Then,

$$y = H(x, 1, T; 1, 1, 0, 0),$$

and is the price of a warrant with T years to expiration and exercise price of one dollar, on a stock with unit instantaneous variance of return, when the market rate of interest is zero over the life of the contract.

Once we solve (37) for the price of this "standard" warrant, we have, by a change of variables, the price for any European warrant. Namely,

$$H(S, P, \tau; E) = EP(\tau)\, y\left[S/EP(\tau), \int_0^\tau V^2(s)\, ds \right]. \tag{38}$$

Hence, for empirical testing or applications, one need only compute tables for the "standard" warrant price as a function of two variables, stock price and time to expiration, to be able to compute warrant prices in general.

To solve (37), we first put it in standard form by the change in variables $Z \equiv \log(x) + T/2$ and $\phi(Z, T) \equiv y(x, T)/x$, and then substitute in (37) to arrive at

$$0 = \tfrac{1}{2}\phi_{11} - \phi_2, \tag{39}$$

subject to the boundary conditions: $|\phi(Z, T)| \leq 1$ and $\phi(Z, 0) = \mathrm{Max}$ $[0, 1 - e^{-z}]$. Equation (39) is a standard free-boundary problem to be solved by separation of variables or Fourier transforms.[49] Its solution is

---

[49] For a separation of variables solution, see Churchill [9], pp. 154-156, and for the transform technique, see Dettman [12], p. 390. Also see McKean [26].

$$y(x, T) = x\phi(Z, T) = [x erfc(h_1) - erfc(h_2)]/2, \qquad (40)$$

where *erfc* is the error complement function which is tabulated, $h_1 \equiv -[\log x + \frac{1}{2}T]/\sqrt{2T}$, and $h_2 \equiv -[\log x - \frac{1}{2}T]/\sqrt{2T}$. Equation (40) is identical to (21) with $r = 0$, $\sigma^2 = 1$, and $E = 1$. Hence, (38) will be identical to (21) the B-S formula, in the special case of a nonstochastic and constant interest rate (i.e., $\delta = 0$, $\mu = r$, $P = e^{-rr}$, and $T \equiv \sigma^2 \tau$).

Equation (37) corresponds exactly to Samuelson's equation[50] for the warrant price in his "linear" model when the stock price is log-normally distributed, with his parameters $\alpha = \beta = 0$, and $\sigma^2 = 1$. Hence, tables generated from (40) could be used with (38) for valuations of the Samuelson formula where $e^{-\alpha\tau}$ is substituted for $P(\tau)$ in (38).[51] Since α in his theory is the expected rate of return on a risky security, one would expect that $e^{-\alpha\tau} < P(\tau)$. As a consequence of the following theorem, $e^{-\alpha\tau} < P(\tau)$ would imply that Samuelson's forecasted values for the warrants would be higher than those forecasted by B-S or the model presented here.

Theorem 14. For a given stock price, the warrant price is a nonincreasing function of $P(\tau)$, and hence, a nondecreasing function of the τ-year interest rate.

Proof: it follows immediately, since an increase in P is equivalent to an increase in E which never increases the value of the warrant. Formally, H is a convex function of S and passes through the origin. Hence, $H - SH_1 \leq 0$. But from (31), $H - SH_1 = PH_2$, and since $P \geq 0$, $H_2 \leq 0$. By definition, $P(\tau)$ is a decreasing function of the τ-year interest rate. Q.E.D.

Because we applied only the terminal boundary condition to (34), the price function derived is for a European warrant. The correct boundary conditions for an American warrant would also include the arbitrage-boundary inequality

$$H(S, P, \tau; E) \geq \text{Max}[0, S - E]. \qquad (34c)$$

Since it was assumed that no dividend payments or exercise price changes occur over the life of the contract, we know from Theorem 1, that if the formulation of this section is a "rational" theory, then it will satisfy the stronger inequality $H \geq \text{Max}[0, S - EP(\tau)]$ [which is homogeneous in S and $EP(\tau)$], and the American warrant will have the same value as its European counterpart. Samuelson argued that solutions to equations like (21) and (38) will always have values at least as large as $\text{Max}[0, S - E]$, and

[50] In [42], p.27.
[51] The tables could also be used to evaluate warrants priced by the Sprenkle [49] formula. Warning: while the Samuelson interpretation of the "$\beta = \alpha$" case implies that expected returns are equated on the warrant and the stock, the B-S interpretation does not. Namely, from [29], the expected return on the warrant satisfies $\beta = r + H_1 S(\alpha - r)/H$, where H_1 can be computed from (21) by differentiation.

Samuelson and Merton[52] proved it under more general conditions. Hence, there is no need for formal verification here. Further, it can be shown that (38) satisfies all the theorems of Section 2.

As a direct result of the equal values of the European and American warrants, we have:

Theorem 15. The warrant price is a nondecreasing function of the variance of the stock price return.

Proof: from (38), the change in H with respect to a change in variance will be proportional to y_2. But, y is the price of a legitimate American warrant and hence, must be a nondecreasing function of time to expiration, i.e., $y_2 \geqq 0$. Q.E.D.

Actually, Theorem 15 is a special case of the general proposition (Theorem 8) proved in Section 2, that the more risky is the stock, the more valuable is the warrant. Although Rothschild and Stiglitz[53] have shown that, in general, increasing variance may not imply increasing risk, it is shown in Appendix 2 that variance is a valid measure of risk for this model.

We have derived the B-S warrant pricing formula rigorously under assumptions weaker than they postulate, and have extended the analysis to include the possibility of stochastic interest rates.

Because the original B-S derivation assumed constant interest rates in forming their hedge positions, it did not matter whether they borrowed or lent long or short maturities. The derivation here clearly demonstrates that the correct maturity to use in the hedge is the one which matches the maturity date of the option. "Correct" is used in the sense that if the price $P(\tau)$ remains fixed while the price of other maturities changes, the price of a τ-year option will remain unchanged.

The capital asset pricing model is a sufficient assumption to derive the formula. While the assumptions of this section are necessary for the intertemporal use of the capital asset pricing model,[54] they are not sufficient, e.g., we do not assume that interest rates are nonstochastic, that price dynamics are stationary, nor that investors have homogeneous expectations. All are required for the capital asset pricing model. Further, since we consider only the properties of three securities, we do not assume that the capital market is in full general equilibrium. Since the final formula is independent of α or μ, it will hold even if the observed stock or bond prices are transient, nonequilibrium prices.

---

[52] In [42] and [43], respectively.
[53] In [39].
[54] See Merton [31] for a discussion of necessary and sufficient conditions for a Sharpe-Lintner-Mossin type model to obtain in an intertemporal context. The sufficient conditions are rather restrictive.

The key to the derivation is that any one of the securities' returns over time can be perfectly replicated by continuous portfolio combinations of the other two. A complete analysis would require that all three securities' prices be solved for simultaneously which, in general, would require the examination of all other assets, knowledge of preferences, etc. However, because of "perfect substitutability" of the securities and the "bucket shop" assumption, supply effects can be neglected, and we can apply "partial equilibrium" analysis resulting in a "causal-type" formula for the option price as a function of the stock and bond prices.

This "perfect substitutability" of the common stock and borrowing for the warrant or the warrant and lending for the common stock explains why the formula is independent of the expected return on the common stock or preferences. The expected return on the stock and the investor's preferences will determine how much capital to invest (long or short) in a given company. The decision as to whether to take the position by buying warrants or by leveraging the stock depends only on their relative prices and the cost of borrowing. As B-S point out, the argument is similar to an intertemporal Modigliani-Miller theorem. The reason that the B-S assumption of the capital asset pricing model leads to the correct formula is that because it is an equilibrium model, it must necessarily rule out "sure-thing" profits among perfectly correlated securities, which is exactly condition (29). Careful study of both their derivations shows that (29) is the only part of the capital asset pricing model ever used.

The assumptions of this section are necessary for (38) and (40) to hold.[55] The continuous-trading assumption is necessary to establish perfect correlation among nonlinear functions which is required to form the "perfect hedge" portfolio mix. The Samuelson and Merton model[56] is an immediate counter-example to the validity of the formula for discrete-trading intervals.

The assumption of Itô processes for the assets' returns dynamics was necessary to apply Itô's Lemma. The further restriction that σ and δ be nonstochastic and independent of the price levels is required so that the option price change is due only to changes in the stock or bond prices, which was necessary to establish a perfect hedge and to establish the homogeneity property (31).[57] Clearly if investors did not agree on the value of $V^2(\tau)$, they would arrive at different values for the same warrant.

The B-S claim that (21) or (38) is the only formula consistent with capital market equilibrium is a bit too strong. It is not true that if the market prices

[55] If most of the "frictionless" market assumptions are dropped, it may be possible to show that, by substituting current institutional conditions, (38) and (40) will give lower bounds for the warrant's value.
[56] In [43].
[57] In the special case when interest rates are nonstochastic, the variance of the stock price return can be a function of the price level and the derivation still goes through. However, the resulting partial differential equation will not have a simple closed-form solution.

options differently, then arbitrage profits are ensured. It is a "rational" option pricing theory relative to the assumptions of this section. If these assumptions held with certainty, then the B-S formula is the only one which all investors could agree on, and no deviant member could prove them wrong.[58]

7. Extension of the model to include dividend payments and exercise price changes

To analyze the effect of dividends on unprotected warrants, it is helpful to assume a constant and known interest rate r. Under this assumption, $\delta = 0$, $\mu = r$, and $P(\tau) = e^{-r\tau}$. Condition (29) simplifies to

$$\beta - r = \gamma(\alpha - r)/\sigma. \tag{41}$$

Let $D(S, \tau)$ be the dividend per share unit time when the stock price is S and the warrant has τ years to expiration. If α is the instantaneous, *total* expected return as defined in (23), then the instantaneous expected return from price appreciation is $[\alpha - D(S, \tau)/S]$. Because $P(\tau)$ is no longer stochastic, we suppress it and write the warrant price function as $W(S, \tau; E)$. As was done in (25) and (26), we apply Itô's Lemma to derive the stochastic differential equation for the warrant price to be

$$dW = W_1(dS - D(S, \tau)dt) + W_2 d\tau + \tfrac{1}{2} W_{11}(dS)^2$$

$$= [\tfrac{1}{2}\sigma^2 S^2 W_{11} + (\alpha S - D)W_1 - W_2]\,dt + \sigma S W_1\,dz. \tag{42}$$

Note: since the warrant owner is not entitled to any part of the dividend return, he only considers that part of the expected dollar return to the common stock due to price appreciation. From (42) and the definition of β and γ, we have that

$$\beta W = \tfrac{1}{2}\sigma^2 S^2 W_{11} + (\alpha S - D)W_1 - W_2 \tag{43}$$

$$\gamma W = \sigma S W_1.$$

Applying (41) to (43), we arrive at the partial differential equation for the warrant price,

$$\tfrac{1}{2}\sigma^2 S^2 W_{11} + (rS - D)W_1 - W_2 - rW = 0, \tag{44}$$

subject to the boundary conditions, $W(0, \tau; E) = 0$, $W(S, 0; E) = \text{Max}[0, S - E]$ for a European warrant, and to the additional arbitrage boundary condition, $W(S, \tau; E) \geq \text{Max}[0, S - E]$ for an American warrant.

Equation (44) will not have a simple solution, even for the European warrant and relatively simple functional forms for D. In evaluating the American warrant in the "no-dividend" case ($D = 0$), the arbitrage

---

[58] This point is emphasized in a critique of Thorp and Kassouf's [53] "sure-thing" arbitrage techniques by Samuelson [45] and again, in Samuelson [44], footnote 6.

boundary inequalities were not considered explicitly in arriving at a solution, because it was shown that the European warrant price never violated the inequality, and the American and European warrant prices were equal. For many dividend policies, the solution for the European warrant price will violate the inequality, and for those policies, there will be a positive probability of premature exercising of the American warrant. Hence, to obtain a correct value for the American warrant from (44), we must explicitly consider the boundary inequality, and transform it into a suitable form for solution.

If there exists a positive probability of premature exercising, then, for every τ, there exists a level of stock price, $C[\tau]$, such that for all $S > C[\tau]$, the warrant would be worth more exercised than if held. Since the value of an exercised warrant is always $(S - E)$, we have the appended boundary condition for (44),

$$W(C[\tau], \tau; E) = C[\tau] - E, \tag{44a}$$

where W satisfies (44) for $0 \leq S \leq C[\tau]$.

If $C[\tau]$ were a known function, then, after the appropriate change of variables, (44) with the European boundary conditions and (44a) appended, would be a semiinfinite boundary value problem with a time-dependent boundary. However, $C[\tau]$ is not known, and must be determined as part of the solution. Therefore, an additional boundary condition is required for the problem to be well-posed.

Fortunately, the economics of the problem are sufficiently rich to provide this extra condition. Because the warrant holder is not contractually obliged to exercise his warrant prematurely, he chooses to do so only in his own best interest (i.e., when the warrant is worth more "dead" than "alive"). Hence, the only rational choice for $C[\tau]$ is that time-pattern which maximizes the value of the warrant. Let $f(S, \tau; E, C[\tau])$ be a solution to (44)-(44a) for a given $C[\tau]$ function. Then, the value of a τ-year American warrant will be

$$W(S, \tau; E) = \underset{[c]}{\text{Max}} f(S, \tau; E, C). \tag{45}$$

Further, the structure of the problem makes it clear that the optimal $C[\tau]$ will be independent of the current level of the stock price. In attacking this difficult problem, Samuelson[59] postulated that the extra condition was "high-contact" at the boundary, i.e.,

$$W_1(C[\tau], \tau; E) = 1. \tag{44b}$$

It can be shown[60] that (44b) is implied by the maximizing behavior

---

[59] In [42].
[60] Let $f(x, c)$ be a differentiable function, concave in its second argument, for $0 \leq x \leq c$. Require that $f(c, c) = h(c)$, a differentiable function of c. Let $c = c^*$ be the c which

described by (45). So the correct specification for the American warrant price is (44) with the European boundary conditions plus (44a) and (44b).

Samuelson and Samuelson and Merton[61] have shown that for a proportional dividend policy where $D(S, \tau) = \varrho S, \varrho > 0$, there is always a positive probability of premature exercising, and hence, the arbitrage boundary condition will be binding for sufficiently large stock prices.[62] With $D = \varrho S$, (44) is mathematically identical to Samuelson's[63] "nonlinear" ("$\beta > \alpha$") case where his $\beta = r$ and his $\alpha = r - \varrho$. Samuelson and McKean[64] analyze this problem in great detail. Although there are no simple closed-form solutions for finite-lived warrants, they did derive solutions for perpetual warrants which are power functions, tangent to the "$S - E$" line at finite values of S.[65]

A second example of a simple dividend policy is the constant one where $D = d$, a constant. Unlike the previous proportional policy, premature exercising may or may not occur, depending upon the values for d, r, E, and τ. In particular, a sufficient condition for no premature exercising was derived in Section 3. Namely,

$$E > \frac{d}{r}. \tag{13}$$

If (13) obtains, then the solution for the European warrant price will be the solution for the American warrant. Although a closed-form solution has

---

maximizes f, i.e.,

$$f_2(x, c^*) = 0,$$

where subscripts denote partial derivatives. Consider the total derivative of f with respect to c along the boundary $x = c$. Then,

$$df/dc = dh/dc = f_1(c, c) + f_2(c, c).$$

For $c = c^*, f_2 = 0$. Hence, $f_1(c^*, c^*) = dh/dc$. In the case of the text, $h = c - E$, and the "high-contact" solution, $f_1(c^*, c^*) = 1$, is proved.

[61] In [42] and [43], respectively.

[62] For $D = \varrho S$, the solution to (44) for the European warrant is

$$W = [e^{-\varrho\tau} S \phi(d_1) - E e^{-r\tau} \phi(d_2)]$$

where ϕ, d_1, and d_2 are as defined in (21). For large S,

$$W \sim [e^{-\varrho\tau} S - E e^{-r\tau}]$$

which will be less than $(S - E)$ for large S and $\varrho > 0$. Hence, the American warrant can be worth more "dead" than "alive."

[63] In [42].

[64] *Ibid.* In the appendix.

[65] *Ibid.*, p. 28.

not yet been found for finite τ, a solution for the perpetual warrant when $E > d/r$, is [66]

$$W(S, \infty; E)$$

$$= S - \frac{d}{r} \left[1 - \frac{\left(\frac{2d}{\sigma^2 S} \right)^{2r/\sigma^2}}{\Gamma \left(2 + \frac{2r}{\sigma^2} \right)} M \left(\frac{2r}{\sigma^2}, 2 + \frac{2r}{\sigma^2}, \frac{-2d}{\sigma^2 S} \right) \right] \tag{46}$$

where M is the confluent hypergeometric function, and W is plotted in Figure 2.

Figure 2.

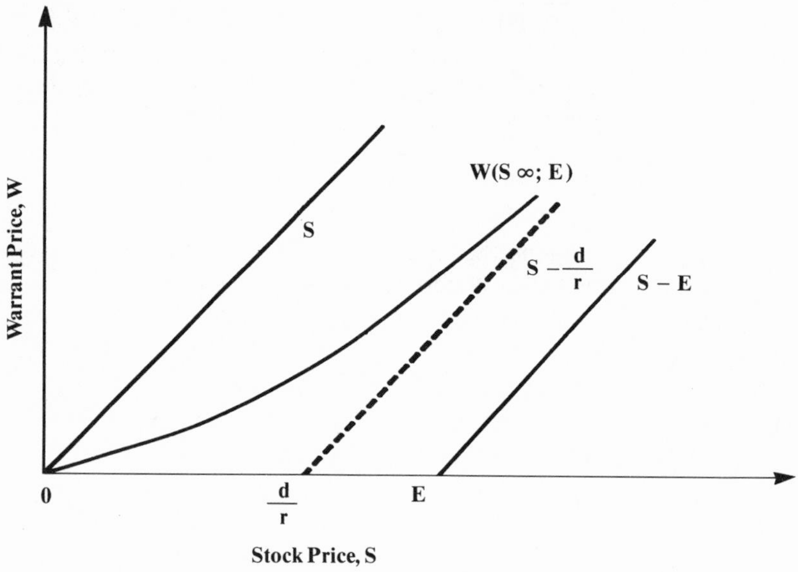

[66] Make the change in variables: $Z \equiv \delta / S$ and

$$h(Z) \equiv \exp[Z] Z^{-\gamma} W$$

where

$$\delta \equiv 2d / \sigma^2$$

and

$$\gamma \equiv 2r / \sigma^2.$$

Then, substituting in (44), we have the differential equation for h:

$$Zh'' + (\gamma + 2 - Z)h' - 2h = 0,$$

whose general solution is $h = c_1 M(2, 2 + \gamma, Z) + c_2 Z^{-(\gamma+1)} M(1 - \gamma, -\gamma, Z)$ which becomes (46) when the boundary conditions are applied. Analysis of (46) shows that W passes through the origin, is convex, and is asymptotic to the line $(S - d/r)$ for large S, i.e., it approaches the common stock value less the present discounted value of all future dividends forgone by holding the warrant.

Consider the case of a continuously changing exercise price, $E(\tau)$, where E is assumed to be differentiable and a decreasing function of the length of time to maturity, i.e., $dE/d\tau = -dE/dt = -E < 0$. The warrant price will satisfy (44) with $D = 0$, but subject to the boundary conditions,

$$W[S, 0; E(0)] = \text{Max}[0, S - E(0)]$$

and

$$W[S, \tau; E(\tau)] \geqq \text{Max}[0, S - E(\tau)].$$

Make the change in variables $X \equiv S/E(\tau)$ and

$$F(X, \tau) \equiv W[S, \tau; E(\tau)]/E(\tau).$$

Then, F satisfies

$$\tfrac{1}{2}\sigma^2 X^2 F_{11} + \eta(\tau) X F_1 - \eta(\tau) F - F_2 = 0, \tag{47}$$

subject to $F(X, 0) = \text{Max}[0, X - 1]$ and $F(X, \tau) \geq \text{Max}[0, X - 1]$ where $\eta(\tau) \equiv r - \dot{E}/E$. Notice that the structure of (47) is identical to the pricing of a warrant with a fixed exercise price and a variable, but nonstochastic, "interest rate" $\eta(\tau)$. (I.e., substitute in the analysis of the previous section for $P(\tau)$, $\exp[-\int_0^\tau \eta(s)\,ds]$, except $\eta(\tau)$ can be negative for sufficiently large changes in exercise price.) We have already shown that for $\int_0^\tau \eta(s)\,ds \geq 0$, there will be no premature exercising of the warrant, and only the terminal exercise price should matter. Noting that $\int_0^\tau \eta(s)\,ds = \int_0^\tau [r + dE/d\tau]\,ds = r\tau + \log[E(\tau)/E(0)]$, formal substitution for $P(\tau)$ in (38) verifies that the value of the warrant is the same as for a warrant with a fixed exercise price, $E(0)$, and interest rate r. We also have agreement of the current model with (11) of Section 3, because $\int_0^\tau \eta(s)\,ds \geq 0$ implies $E(\tau) \geqq E(0)\exp[-r\tau]$, which is a general sufficient condition for no premature exercising.

8. Valuing an American put option

As the first example of an application of the model to other types of options, we now consider the rational pricing of the put option, relative to the assumptions in Section 7. In Section 4, it was demonstrated that the value of a European put option was completely determined once the value of the call option is known (Theorem 12). B-S give the solution for their model in equation (26). It was also demonstrated in Section 4 that the European valuation is not valid for the American put option because of the positive probability of premature exercising. If $G(S, \tau; E)$ is the rational put price, then, by the same technique used to derive (44) with $D = 0$, G satisfies

$$\tfrac{1}{2}\sigma^2 S^2 G_{11} + rSG_1 - rG - G_2 = 0, \tag{48}$$

subject to $G(\infty, \tau; E) = 0$, $G(S, 0; E) = \text{Max}[0, E - S]$, and $G(S, \tau; E) \geq \text{Max}[0, E - S]$.

From the analysis by Samuelson and McKean[67] on warrants, there is no closed-form solution to (48) for finite τ. However, using their techniques, it is possible to obtain a solution for the perpetual put option (i.e., $\tau = \infty$). For a sufficiently low stock price, it will be advantageous to exercise the put. Define C to be the largest value of the stock such that the put holder is better off exercising than continuing to hold it. For the perpetual put, (48) reduces to the ordinary differential equation,

$$\tfrac{1}{2}\, \sigma^2 S^2 G_{11} + rSG_1 - rG = 0, \tag{49}$$

which is valid for the range of stock prices $C \leqq S \leqq \infty$. The boundary conditions for (49) are:

$$G(\infty, \infty; E) = 0, \tag{49a}$$

$$G(C, \infty; E) = E - C, \text{ and} \tag{49b}$$

choose C so as to maximize the value of the option, which follows from the maximizing behavior arguments of the previous section. (49c)

From the theory of linear ordinary differential equations, solutions to (49) involve two constants, a_1 and a_2. Boundary conditions (49a), (49b), and (49c) will determine these constants along with the unknown lower-bound, stock price, C. The general solution to (49) is

$$G(S, \infty; E) = a_1 S + a_2 S^{-\gamma}, \tag{50}$$

where $\gamma \equiv 2r/\sigma^2 > 0$. Equation (49a) requires that $a_1 = 0$, and (49b) requires that $a_2 = (E - C)C^\gamma$. Hence, as a function of C,

$$G(S, \infty; E) = (E - C)(S/C)^{-\gamma}. \tag{51}$$

To determine C, we apply (49c) and choose that value of C which maximizes (51), i.e., choose $C = C^*$ such that $\partial G/\partial C = 0$. Solving this condition, we have that $C^* = \gamma E/(1 + \gamma)$, and the put option price is,

$$G(S, \infty; E) = \frac{E}{(1 + \gamma)} \left[(1 + \gamma) S/\gamma E \right]^{-\gamma}. \tag{52}$$

The Samuelson "high-contact" boundary condition

$$G_1(C^*, \infty; E) = -1,$$

as an alternative specification of boundary condition (49c), can be verified by differentiating (52) with respect to S and evaluating at $S = C^*$. Figure 3

---

[67] In [42].

illustrates the American put price as a function of the stock price and time to expiration.

9. Valuing the "down-and-out" call option

As a second example of the application of the model to other types of options, we consider the rational pricing of a new type of call option called the "down-and-outer."[68] This option has the same terms with respect to exercise price, antidilution clauses, etc., as the standard call option, but with the additional feature that if the stock price falls below a stated level, the option contract is nullified, i.e., the option becomes worthless.[69] Typically, the "knock-out" price is a function of the time to expiration, increasing as the expiration date nears.

Figure 3.

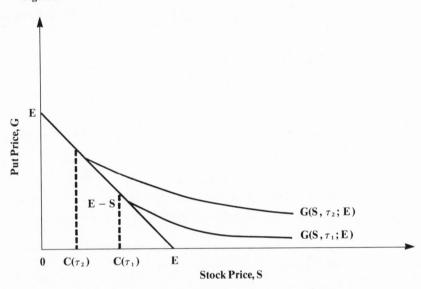

Let $f(S, \tau; E)$ be the value of a European "down-and-out" call option, and $B[\tau] = bE \exp[-\eta\tau]$ be the "knock-out" price as a function of time to expiration where it is assumed that $\eta \geq 0$ and $0 \leq b \leq 1$. Then f will satisfy the fundamental partial differential equation,

$$\tfrac{1}{2}\sigma^2 S^2 f_{11} + rSf_1 - rf - f_2 = 0, \tag{53}$$

[68]See Snyder [48] for a complete description. A number of Wall Street houses are beginning to deal in this option. See *Fortune,* November, 1971, p. 213.

[69] In some versions of the "down-and-outer," the option owner receives a positive rebate, $R(\tau)$, if the stock price hits the "knock-out" price. Typically, $R(\tau)$ is an increasing function of the time until expiration [i.e., $R'(\tau) > 0$] with $R(0) = 0$. Let $g(S, \tau)$ satisfy (53) for $B(\tau) \leq S < \infty$, subject to the boundary conditions (a) $g(B[\tau], \tau) = R(\tau)$ and (b) $g(S, 0) = 0$. Then, $F(S, \tau; E) \equiv g(S, \tau) + f(S, \tau; E)$ will satisfy (53) subject to the boundary conditions (a) $F(B[\tau], \tau; E) = R(\tau)$ and (b) $F(S, 0; E) = \text{Max}[0, S - E]$. Hence, F is the value of a "down-and-out" call option with rebate payments $R(\tau)$, and $g(S, \tau)$ is the additional value for the rebate feature. See Dettman [12], p. 391, for a transform solution for $g(S, \tau)$.

subject to the boundary conditions,

$$f(B[\tau], \tau; E) = 0$$

$$f(S, 0; E) = \text{Max}[0, S - E].$$

Note: if $B(\tau) = 0$, then (53) would be the equation for a standard European call option.

Make the change in variables, $x \equiv \log[S/B(\tau)]$; $T \equiv \sigma^2 \tau$;

$$H(x, T) \equiv \exp[ax + \gamma\tau] f(S, \tau; E)/E,$$

and $a \equiv [r - \eta - \sigma^2/2]/\sigma^2$ and $\gamma \equiv r + a^2\sigma^2/2$. Then, by substituting into (53), we arrive at the equation for H,

$$\tfrac{1}{2} H_{11} - H_2 = 0 \tag{54}$$

subject to

$$H(0, T) = 0$$

$$\text{H}(x, 0) = e^{ax} \text{Max}[0, be^x - 1],$$

which is a standard, semiinfinite boundary value problem to be solved by separation of variables or Fourier transforms.[70]

Solving (54) and substituting back, we arrive at the solution for the "down-and-out" option,

$$f(S, \tau; E) = [S\, erfc(h_1) - Ee^{-r\tau} erfc(h_2)]/2$$

$$- (S/B[\tau])^{-\delta}[B[\tau]\, erfc(h_3) - (S/B[\tau])Ee^{-r\tau} erfc(h_4)]/2, \tag{55}$$

where

$$h_1 \equiv -[\log(S/E) + (r + \sigma^2/2)\tau]/\sqrt{2\sigma^2\tau},$$

$$h_2 \equiv -[\log(S/E) + (r - \sigma^2/2)\tau]/\sqrt{2\sigma^2\tau},$$

$$h_3 \equiv -[2\log(B[\tau]/E) - \log(S/E) + (r + \sigma^2/2)\tau]/\sqrt{2\sigma^2\tau},$$

$$h_4 \equiv -[2\log(B[\tau]/E) - \log(S/E) + (r - \sigma^2/2)\tau]/\sqrt{2\sigma^2\tau},$$

and $\delta \equiv 2(r - \eta)/\sigma.^2$ Inspection of (55) and (21) reveals that the first bracketed set of terms in (55) is the value of a standard call option, and

[70] See Churchill [9], p. 152, for a separation of variables solution and Dettman [12], p. 391, for a transform solution.

hence, the second bracket is the "discount" due to the "down-and-out" feature.

To gain a better perspective on the qualitative differences between the standard call option and the "down-and-outer," it is useful to go to the limit of a perpetual option where the "knock-out" price is constant (i.e., $\eta = 0$). In this case, (53) reduces to the ordinary differential equation

$$\tfrac{1}{2}\sigma^2 S^2 f'' + rSf' - rf = 0 \tag{56}$$

subject to

$$f(bE) = 0 \tag{56a}$$

$$f(S) \leqq S, \tag{56b}$$

where primes denote derivatives and $f(S)$ is short for $f(S, \infty; E)$. By standard methods, we solve (56) to obtain

$$f(S) = S - bE(S/bE)^{-\gamma}, \tag{57}$$

where $\gamma \equiv 2r/\sigma^2$. Remembering that the value of a standard perpetual call option equals the value of the stock, we may interpret $bE(S/bE)^{-\gamma}$ as the "discount" for the "down-and-out" feature. Both (55) and (57) are homogeneous of degree one in (S, E) as are the standard options. Further, it is easy to show that $f(S) \geq \text{Max}\,[0, S - E]$, and although a tedious exercise, it also can be shown that $f(S, \tau; E) \geq \text{Max}\,[0, S - E]$. Hence, the option is worth more "alive" than "dead," and therefore, (55) and (57) are the correct valuation functions for the American "down-and-outer."

Figure 4.

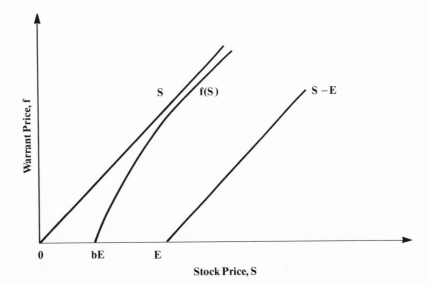

From (57), the elasticity of the option price with respect to the stock price $[Sf'(S)/f(S)]$ is greater than one, and so it is a "levered" security. However, unlike the standard call option, it is a concave function of the stock price, as illustrated in Figure 4.

10. Valuing a callable warrant

As our third and last example of an application of the model to other types of options, we consider the rational pricing of a callable American warrant. Although warrants are rarely issued as callable, this is an important example because the analysis is readily carried over to the valuation of other types of securities such as convertible bonds which are almost always issued as callable.

We assume the standard conditions for an American warrant except that the issuing company has the right to ("call") buy back the warrant at any time for a fixed price. Because the warrant is of the American type, in the event of a call, the warrant holder has the option of exercising his warrant rather than selling it back to the company at the call price. If this occurs, it is called "forced conversion," because the warrant holder is "forced" to exercise, if the value of the warrant exercised exceeds the call price.

The value of a callable warrant will be equal to the value of an equivalent noncallable warrant less some "discount." This discount will be the value of the call provision to the company. One can think of the callable warrant as the resultant of two transactions: the company sells a noncallable warrant to an investor and simultaneously, purchases from the investor an option to either "force" earlier conversion or to retire the issue at a fixed price.

Let $F(S, \tau; E)$ be the value of a callable American warrant; $H(S, \tau; E)$ the value of an equivalent noncallable warrant as obtained from equation (21), $C(S, \tau; E)$ the value of the call provision. Then $H = F + C$. F will satisfy the fundamental partial differential equation,

$$\tfrac{1}{2}\sigma^2 S^2 F_{11} + rSF_1 - rF - F_2 = 0 \tag{58}$$

for $0 \leqq S \leqq \overline{S}$ and subject to

$$F(0, \tau; E) = 0,$$

$$F(S, 0; E) = \text{Max}\,[0, S - E]$$

$$F(\overline{S}, \tau; E) = \text{Max}\,[K, \overline{S} - E],$$

where K is the call price and $\overline{S}$ is the (yet to be determined) level of the stock price where the company will call the warrant. Unlike the case of "voluntary" conversion of the warrant because of unfavorable dividend protection analyzed in Section 7, $\overline{S}$ is not the choice of the warrant owner, but of the company, and hence will not be selected to maximize the value of the warrant.

Because $C = H - F$ and H and F satisfy (58), C will satisfy (58) subject to the boundary conditions,

$$C(0, \tau; E) = 0$$

$$C(S, 0; E) = 0$$

$$C(\bar{S}, \tau; E) = H(\bar{S}, \tau; E) - \text{Max}\,[K, \bar{S} - E].$$

Because $\bar{S}$ is the company's choice, we append the maximizing condition that $\bar{S}$ be chosen so as to maximize $C(S, \tau;\ E)$ making (58) a well-posed problem. Since $C = H - F$ and H is not a function of $\bar{S}$, the maximizing condition on C can be rewritten as a minimizing condition on F.

In general, it will not be possible to obtain a closed-form solution to (58). However, a solution can be found for the perpetual warrant. In this case, we know that $H(S, \tau;\ E) = S$, and (58) reduces to the ordinary differential equation

$$\tfrac{1}{2}\,\sigma^2 S^2 C'' + rSC' - rC = 0 \tag{59}$$

for $0 \leq S \leq \bar{S}$ and subject to

$$C(0) = 0$$

$$C(\bar{S}) = \bar{S} - \text{Max}\,(K, \bar{S} - E)$$

Choose $\bar{S}$ so as to maximize C,

where $C(S)$ is short for $C(S,\ \infty;\ E)$ and primes denote derivatives. Solving (59) and applying the first two conditions, we have

$$C(S) = (1 - \text{Max}\,[K/\bar{S}, 1 - E/\bar{S}])S. \tag{60}$$

Although we cannot apply the simple calculus technique for finding the maximizing $\bar{S}$, it is obviously $\bar{S} = K + E$, since for $\bar{S} < K + E$, C is an increasing function of $\bar{S}$ and for $\bar{S} > K + E$, it is a decreasing function. Hence, the value of the call provision is

$$C(S) = \left(\frac{E}{K + E}\right)S, \tag{61}$$

and because $F = H - C$, the value of the callable perpetual warrant is

$$F(S) = \left(\frac{K}{K + E}\right)S. \tag{62}$$

11. Conclusion It has been shown that a B-S type model can be derived from weaker assumptions than in their original formulation. The main attractions of the model are: (1) the derivation is based on the relatively weak condition of avoiding dominance; (2) the final formula is a function of "observable" variables; and (3) the model can be extended in a straightforward fashion to determine the rational price of any type option.

The model has been applied with some success to empirical investigations of the option market by Black and Scholes and to warrants by Leonard.[71]

As suggested by Black and Scholes and Merton,[72] the model can be used to price the various elements of the firm's capital structure. Essentially, under conditions when the Modigliani-Miller theorem obtains, we can use the total value of the firm as a "basic" security (replacing the common stock in the formulation of this paper) and the individual securities within the capital structure (e.g., debt, convertible bonds, common stock, etc.) can be viewed as "options" or "contingent claims" on the firm and priced accordingly. So, for example, one can derive in a systematic fashion a risk-structure of interest rates as a function of the debt-equity ratio, the risk-class of the firm, and the riskless (in terms of default) debt rates.

Using the techniques developed here, it should be possible to develop a theory of the term structure of interest rates along the lines of Cootner and Merton.[73] The approach would also have application in the theory of speculative markets.

Appendix 1[74]

Theorems 9 and 10 state that warrants whose common stock per dollar returns possess *distributions* that are independent of *stock price* levels (henceforth, referred to as D.I.S.P.) are: (1) homogeneous of degree one in stock price S and exercise price E—Theorem 9 and (2) convex in S—Theorem 10. This appendix exhibits via counterexample the insufficiency of the posited assumptions *sans* D.I.S.P. for the proof of Theorems 9 and 10.

First, we posit a very simple, noncontroversial, one-period European warrant pricing function, W:

$$W(S, \lambda) = K \int_{E/S}^{\infty} (S\hat{Z} - E) \, dP(\hat{Z}; S, \lambda), \tag{A1}$$

wherein: $1 > K > 0$ is a discounting factor which is deemed (somewhat erroneously) to be constant at this point in time (i.e., independent of S),

$\lambda \in [0, 1]$ is a parameter of the distribution, dP,

$$\hat{Z} \equiv Z + \lambda g(S)\epsilon \equiv Z + U(S, \lambda) \equiv \text{Common stock per dollar return,} \tag{A2}$$

Z and ϵ are independent random variables such that $E(\epsilon|Z) = 0$.

---

[71] In [5] and [25], respectively.

[72] In [4] and [29], respectively.

[73] In [11] and [29], respectively.

[74] I thank B. Goldman of M. I. T. for constructing this example and writing the appendix.

The function $g(S)$ has the following properties for our example:

$g(S) \epsilon (0,1)$, $\dfrac{dg(S)}{ds} < 0$, $dP(\hat{Z}; S, \lambda)$ is the Stieltjes integral representation of the probability density which is equivalent to the convolution of the probability densities of Z and U.

In constructing the counterexample, we choose the following uniform distributions for Z and U:

$$f(\epsilon) = (1/2)\,\text{for} - 1 \le \epsilon \le 1 \tag{A3}$$

$$= 0\,\text{elsewhere}$$

$$\rightarrow f(U) = \frac{1}{2\lambda g(S)}\ \text{for} - \lambda g(S) \le U \le \lambda g(S)$$

$$= 0\,\text{elsewhere}$$

$$h(Z) = (1/2)\,\text{for}\ 1 \le Z \le 3$$

$$= 0\,\text{elsewhere.} \tag{A4}$$

The convoluted density would then be:

$$\frac{dP}{d\hat{Z}}(\hat{Z}; S, \lambda) = \frac{\hat{Z} - 1 + \lambda g(S)}{4\lambda g(S)}$$

$$\text{for}\ 1 - \lambda g(S) \le \hat{Z} \le 1 + \lambda g(S) \tag{A5}$$

$$= (1/2)\,\text{for}\ 1 + \lambda g(S) \le \hat{Z} \le 3 - \lambda g(S)$$

$$= \frac{3 + \lambda g(S) - \hat{Z}}{4\lambda g(S)}$$

$$\text{for}\ 3 - \lambda g(S) \le \hat{Z} \le 3 + \lambda g(S)$$

$$= 0\,\text{elsewhere.}$$

As a further convenience, we choose the exercise price, E, to be in the neighborhood of twice the stock price, S, and evaluate (A1):

$$W(S, \lambda) = K[E^2/4S - 3E/2 + 9S/4 + \lambda^2 g(S)^2 S/12]. \tag{A6}$$

By inspection of (A6), we notice that W is not homogeneous of degree one in S and E. Moreover, the convexity of W can be violated (locally) $\left(\text{i.e., } \dfrac{d^2 W}{dS^2}\ \text{can become negative}\right)$ by choosing a sufficiently negative

$$\frac{d^2g(S)}{dS^2}:$$

$$\frac{d^2W}{dS^2} =$$

$$K\left(E^2/2S^3 + \lambda^2/6\left[2g(S)\,dg/ds + \frac{S(dg)^2}{(dS)} + Sg(S)\frac{d^2g(S)}{dS^2}\right]\right) \gtreqless 0. \tag{A7}$$

Thus, our example has shown Theorems 9 and 10 to be not generally consistent with a non-D.I.S.P. environment; however, we can verify Theorems 9 and 10 for the D.I.S.P. subcase of our example, since by construction setting $\lambda = 0$ reinstates the D.I.S.P. character of the probability distribution. By inspection, we observe that when $\lambda = 0$, the right-hand side of (A6) is homogeneous of degree one in S and E, while the right-hand side of (A7) is $KE^2/2S^3 > 0$, verifying the convexity theorem.

Appendix 2

It was stated in the text that Theorem 15 is really a special case of Theorem 8, i.e., variance is a constant measure of risk in the B-S model. To prove consistency, we use the equivalent, alternative definition (Rothschild and Stiglitz')[75] of more risky that X is more risky than Y if $E[X] = E[Y]$ and $EU(X) \le EU(Y)$ for every concave function U.

Since the B-S formula for warrant price, (21), is independent of the expected return on the stock and since the stock returns are assumed to be log normally distributed, different securities are distinguished by the single parameter, σ^2. Therefore, without loss of generality, we can assume that $\alpha = 0$, and prove the result by showing that for every concave U, $EU(Z)$ is a decreasing function of σ, where Z is a log-normal variate with $E[Z] = 1$ and the variance of $\log(Z)$ equal to σ^2:

$$EU(Z) = \frac{1}{\sqrt{2\pi\sigma^2}} \int_0^\infty U(Z)\exp\{-[\log Z + (1/2)\sigma^2]^2/2\sigma^2\}\,dZ/Z$$

$$= \frac{1}{\sqrt{2\pi}} \int_{-\infty}^\infty U(e^{\sigma x - (1/2)\sigma^2})e^{(-1/2)x^2}\,dx,$$

$$\text{for } x \equiv [\log Z + (1/2)\sigma^2]/\sigma;$$

[75] In [39].

$$\partial EU(Z)/\partial\sigma = \frac{1}{\sqrt{2\pi}} \int_{-\infty}^{\infty} U'(\quad)\exp[-(1/2)(x-\sigma)^2](x-\sigma)\,dx$$

$$= \frac{1}{\sqrt{2\pi}} \int_{-\infty}^{\infty} U'(e^{\sigma y + (1/2)\sigma^2})ye^{-1/2y^2}\,dy, \ \text{ for } y \equiv x - \sigma$$

$$\equiv \text{Convariance}\,[U'(e^{\sigma y + (1/2)\sigma^2}), y].$$

But, $U'(\quad)$ is a decreasing function of y by the concavity of U. Hence, by Theorem 236, Hardy et al.,[76] Cov $[U', y] < 0$. Therefore, $\partial EU/\partial\sigma < 0$ for all concave U.

[76] In [16], p. 168.

References

1. Ayres, R.F. "Risk Aversion in the Warrant Markets." *Industrial Management Review,* Vol. 50, No. 1 (Fall 1963), pp. 45-53; reprinted in Cootner [10], pp. 497-505.

2. Bachelier, L. *Theory of Speculation* (translation of 1900 French edition), in Cootner [10], pp. 17-78.

3. Baumol, W. J., Malkiel, B. G., and Quandt, R. E. "The Valuation of Convertible Securities." *Quarterly Journal of Economics,* Vol. 80, No. 1 (February 1966), pp. 48-59.

4. Black, F. and Scholes, M. "The Pricing of Options and Corporate Liabilities," forthcoming in *Journal of Political Economy.*

5. ———. "The Valuation of Option Contracts and a Test of Market Efficiency." *Journal of Finance,* Vol. 27, No. 2 (May 1972).

6. ———. "Some Evidence on the Profitability of Trading in Put and Call Options," in Cootner [10], pp. 475-496.

7. Boness, A.J. "Elements of a Theory of Stock-Option Value, " *Journal of Political Economy,* Vol. 72, No. 2 (April 1964), pp. 163-175.

8. Chen, A.H.Y. "A Model of Warrant Pricing in a Dynamic Market," *Journal of Finance,* Vol. 25, No. 5 (December 1970).

9. Churchill, R.V. *Fourier Series and Boundary Value Problems,* 2nd ed. New York: McGraw-Hill, 1963.

10. Cootner, P.H., ed. *The Random Character of Stock Market Prices.* Cambridge: M.I.T. Press, 1964.

11. ———. "The Stochastic Theory of Bond Prices." Mimeographed. Massachusetts Institute of Technology, December 1966.

12. Dettman, J.W. *Mathematical Methods in Physics and Engineering.* 2nd ed. New York: McGraw-Hill, 1969.

13. Fama, E.F. "Efficient Capital Markets: A Review of Theory and Empirical Work." *Journal of Finance,* Vol. 25, No. 2 (May 1970).

14. Giguere, G. "Warrants: A Mathematical Method of Evaluation." *Analysts Journal,* Vol. 14, No. 5 (November 1958), pp. 17-25.

15. Hallingby, P., Jr. "Speculative Opportunities in Stock Purchase Warrants." *Analysts Journal,* Vol. 3, No. 3 (1947).

16. Hardy, G.H., Littlewood, J.E. and Pölya, G. *Inequalities.* Cambridge: The University Press, 1959.

17. Hausman, W.H. and White, W.L. "Theory of Option Strategy under Risk Aversion." *Journal of Financial and Quantitative Analysis,* Vol. 3, No. 3 (September 1968).

18. Kassouf, S.T. *Evaluation of Convertible Securities.* Maspeth, N. Y.: Analytic Investors Inc., 1962.

19. ———. "Stock Price Random Walks: Some Supporting Evidence." *Review of Economics and Statistics.* Vol. 50, No. 2 (May 1968). pp. 275-278.

20. ———. *A Theory and an Econometric Model for Common Stock Purchase Warrants.* Ph.D. dissertation, Columbia University. New York: Analytical Publishers Co., 1965.

21. Kruizenga, R.J. "Introduction to the Option Contract," in Cootner [10], pp. 277-391.

22. ———. "Profit Returns from Purchasing Puts and Calls," in Cootner [10], pp. 392-411.

23. ———. *Put and Call Options: A Theoretical and Market Analysis.* Unpublished Ph.D. dissertation. M.I.T., 1956.

24. Kushner, H.J. *Stochastic Stability and Control.* New York: Academic Press, 1967.

25. Leonard, R.J. "An Empirical Examination of a New General Equilibrium Model for Warrant Pricing." Unpublished M. S. thesis, M.I.T., September 1971.

26. McKean, H.P., Jr. "Appendix: A Free Boundary Problem for the Heat Equation Arising from a Problem in Mathematical Economics." *Industrial Management Review,* Vol. 6, No. 2 (Spring 1965), pp. 32-39; reprinted in [40], Chapter 199.

27. Merton, R.C. *Stochastic Integrals.* New York: Academic Press, 1969.

28. ——. "Appendix: Continuous-Time Speculative Processes." (Appendix to Samuelson [45]), in *Mathematical Topics in Economic Theory and Computation,* SIAM, Philadelphia, 1972.

29. ——. "A Dynamic General Equilibrium Model of the Asset Market and its Application to the Pricing of the Capital Structure of the Firm." Sloan School of Management Working Paper #497-70, M.I.T., (December 1970).

30. ——. "An Empirical Investigation of the Samuelson Rational Warrant Pricing Theory," Chapter V in *Analytical Optimal Control Theory as Applied to Stochastic and Non-Stochastic Economics,* unpublished Ph.D. dissertation, M.I.T., 1970.

31. ——. "An Intertemporal Capital Asset Pricing Model," forthcoming in *Econometrica.*

32. ——. "Lifetime Portfolio Selection under Uncertainty: The Continuous-Time Case," *Review of Economics and Statistics,* Vol. 51, No. 3 (August 1969).

33. ——. "Optimum Consumption and Portfolio Rules in a Continuous-Time Model." *Journal of Economic Theory,* Vol. 3, No. 4 (December 1971).

34. ——. "Restrictions on Rational Option Pricing: A Set of Arbitrage Conditions." Mimeographed. Massachusetts Institute of Technology, August 1968.

35. Miller, M. and Modigliani, F. "Dividend Policy, Growth, and the Valuation of Shares," *Journal of Business,* Vol. 34, No. 4(October 1961).

36. Morrison, R.J. "The Warrants or the Stock?" *Analysts Journal,* Vol. 13, No. 5 (November 1957).

37. Pease, F. "The Warrant—Its Powers and Its Hazards." *Financial Analysts Journal,* Vol. 19, No. 1(January-February 1963).

38. Plum, V.L. and Martin, T.J. "The Significance of Conversion Parity in Valuing Common Stock Warrants." *The Financial Review* (February 1966).

39. Rothschild, M. and Stiglitz, J.E. "Increasing Risk: I. A Definition." *Journal of Economic Theory,* Vol. 2, No. 3 (September 1970).

40. Samuelson, P.A. *The Collected Scientific Papers of Paul A. Samuelson.* Vol. 3. R. C. Merton, ed. Cambridge: M.I.T. Press, 1972.

41. ——. "Proof That Properly Anticipated Prices Fluctuate Randomly." *Industrial Management Review,* Vol. 6, No. 2 (Spring 1965), pp. 41-50; reprinted in [40], Chapter 198.

42. ——. "Rational Theory of Warrant Pricing." *Industrial Management Review,* Vol. 6, No. 2 (Spring 1965), pp. 13-31; reprinted in [40], Chapter 199.

43. —— and Merton, R.C. "A Complete Model of Warrant Pricing That Maximizes Utility." *Industrial Management Review,* Vol. 10, No. 2 (Winter 1969), pp. 17-46; reprinted in [40], Chapter 200.

44. ——. "Mathematics of Speculative Price ," in *Mathematical Topics in Economic Theory and Computation,* SIAM, Philadelphia, 1972.

45. ——. Review of [53]. *Journal of American Statistical Association,* Vol. 63, No. 323 (September 1968), pp. 1049-1051.

46. Shelton, J.P. "The Relation of the Pricing of a Warrant to the Price of Its Associated Stock." *Financial Analysts Journal,* Vol. 23, Nos. 3-4 (Part I: May-June 1967) and (Part II: July-August 1967).

47. Slater, L.J. "Confluent Hypergeometric Functions," Chapter 13 in *Handbook of Mathematical Functions.* National Bureau of Standards, Applied Mathematics Series, 55, August, 1966.

48. Snyder, G. L., "Alternative Forms of Options." *Financial Analysts Journal,* Vol. 25, No. 1 (September-October 1969), pp. 93-99.

49. Sprenkle, C.M. "Warrant Prices as Indicators of Expectations and Preferences." *Yale Economic Essays* I, pp. 172-231; reprinted in Cootner [10], pp. 412-474.

50. Stiglitz, J.E. "On Some Aspects of the Pure Theory of Corporate Finance: Bankruptcies and Take-Overs." *The Bell Journal of Economics and Management Science,* Vol. 3, No. 2 (Autumn 1972), pp. 458-482.

51. ———. "A Re-Examination of the Modigliani-Miller Theorem." *The American Economic Review,* Vol. 59, No. 5 (December 1969).

52. Stoll, H.R. "The Relationship between Put and Call Option Prices." *Journal of Finance,* Vol. 24, No. 4 (December 1969), pp. 802-824.

53. Thorp, E.O. and Kassouf, S.T. *Beat the Market.* New York: Random House, 1967.

54. Van Horne, J.C. "Warrant Valuation in Relation to Volatility and Opportunity Costs." *Industrial Management Review,* Vol. 10, No. 3 (Spring 1969), pp. 17-32.

4

The Valuation of Options for Alternative Stochastic Processes*

John C. Cox and Stephen A. Ross

This paper examines the structure of option valuation problems and develops a new technique for their solution. It also introduces several jump and diffusion processes which have not been used in previous models. The technique is applied to these processes to find explicit option valuation formulas, and solutions to some previously unsolved problems involving the pricing of securities with payouts and potential bankruptcy.

1. Introduction

One of the central problems of modern finance is that of valuing claims to assets. The major result in this area is the insight of Modigliani and Miller (1958) that, in equilibrium, packages of financial claims which are, in essence, equivalent must command the same price. Modigliani and Miller recognized that in the absence of market imperfections these claims were simply financial tools for offering alternative modes of ownership of the same economic stream of returns. As a consequence, the aggregate value of the claims against the returns of a firm, for example, should be independent of the types of claims issued. Simultaneously with work on the Modigliani-Miller theorems and somewhat independently of it considerable progress was made by Samuelson (1965) and others [see Cootner (1964)] in evaluating stock options, a specialized form of

John C. Cox, Stanford University, Stanford, Calif. 94305, U.S.A.
Stephen A. Ross, University of Pennsylvania, Philadelphia, Penn. 19174, U.S.A.

*The authors are grateful for the research support of the Rodney L. White Center for Financial Research at the University of Pennsylvania and the National Science Foundation Grant No. 20292. We also wish to thank Fischer Black, Michael Jensen, John Long, and Robert Merton for helpful comments.

Received July 1975, revised version received July 1975

John C. Cox and Stephen A. Ross, "The Valuation of Options for Alternative Stochastic Processes." Reprinted with permission from the *Journal of Financial Economics*, Vol. 3, Winter 1976.

financial claim. This work came to a focus in the major paper by Black and Scholes (1973) in which a complete option pricing model depending only on observable variables was derived. The Black and Scholes option pricing results can in some ways be viewed as an intertemporal analogue of the Modigliani-Miller theory. Although subsequent research has achieved greater generality and has been distinctly different in important ways, the underlying theme remains Black and Scholes' observation that in an intertemporal as well as a static setting two things which can be shown to be equivalent must sell for the same price.

It is useful to pursue this a bit further. Modigliani and Miller argue that the financial instruments issued by a firm span the returns stream, i.e., that the total package of claims on a firm, no matter how complex, is equivalent to a simple equity claim on the returns stream. A similar spanning situation is apparent in the Black and Scholes analysis. Black and Scholes assume that the value of the stock follows a particular diffusion process which will be discussed below and, as a consequence, locally in time, a stock and any option written on it will be perfectly correlated and combined with borrowing or lending at the riskless rate a position in one will be a perfect substitute for, or span, a position in the other. In this way the option is, locally, spanned by riskless bonds and the stock, and knowing the value of the stock permits us to value the option (globally by an integration argument). The critical factor in this argument and in any contingent claims valuation model is the precise description of the stochastic process governing the behavior of the basic asset. It is the characteristics of this process that determine the exact nature of the equivalence between packages of claims. The main contribution of this paper is the consideration of some alternative forms of the stochastic process governing stock prices, and the development of an approach to the option valuation problem that connects it directly to the structure of the underlying stochastic process. It will be useful, then, to give a brief and informal discussion of the stochastic processes that have previously been used.

The basic assumption employed by Black and Scholes was that the stock value followed a log-normal diffusion process,

$$dS/S = \mu dt + \sigma dz, \tag{1}$$

where S is the value of the stock, μ is the drift term and z is a Wiener process. Eq. (1) is a short-hand notation for the following stochastic process. Let S_t be the value of the stock at time t. The percentage change in this value in the next instant, from t to $t + dt$, is

$$dS/S = (S_{t+dt} - S_t)/St.$$

By (1) this percentage change is made up of two components, a drift term, μdt, which is certain as viewed from time t and a normally distributed stochastic term σdz. The stochastic term is independent of its values in other periods and has mean zero and variance $\sigma^2 dt$. Put simply, eq. (1) says that the percentage change in stock value from t to $t + dt$ is normally distributed with mean μdt and variance $\sigma^2 dt$. As dt gets small, then, $S_{t + dt}$ will not differ much from S_t. This is the hallmark of a diffusion process; it represents a continuous frictional sort of random walk around a trend term and, in the short run, offers no surprises.

The diffusion processes, though, are only one of two general classes of continuous time stochastic processes. The second type of stochastic process in continuous time is the jump process. A simple jump process can be written in analogy with (1) as

$$dS/S = \mu dt + (k - 1) d\pi$$

$$= \mu dt + \left\langle \begin{array}{l} \overline{\quad\lambda dt \quad} \quad k - 1, \\[2ex] \underline{\quad\quad\quad} \quad 0. \\ 1 - \lambda dt \end{array} \right. \tag{2}$$

In eq. (2) π is a continuous time Poisson process, λ is referred to as the intensity of the process and $k - 1$ is the jump amplitude. As with (1), eq. (2) is a shorthand notation for the stochastic process that governs the percentage change in the value of the stock on the interval from t to $t + dt$. Eq. (2) says that this percentage change is composed of a drift term, μdt, and a term, $d\pi$, which with probability λdt will jump the percentage stock change to $k - 1$, possibly random itself, and with probability $1 - \lambda dt$ will do nothing. One possible interpretation is that λdt represents the instantaneous probability of receiving a packet of information that will cause S to jump.

In contrast to the diffusion process, the jump process (2) follows a deterministic movement upon which are superimposed discrete jumps. Formally, a jump process has sample paths which are discontinuous with probability one, while those of the diffusion process are continuous with probability one. In addition, the jump processes we consider are continuous from the right almost surely, i.e., their discontinuities are simple jumps. Because of the jumps in value the local analysis of Black and Scholes for valuing options does not carry directly over to eq. (2). By assuming that k was fixed, though, Cox and Ross (1975a) showed that a riskless hedge could be formed and used to value options on jump processes.

The intent of this paper is two fold. First, we examine the rationale for assuming that stock value follows (1) or (2) and propose some plausible alternative forms. This will allow us to examine the relationships between the choice of process and the solutions to option problems, while at the same time providing additional models for empirical testing. The second central feature of this paper is the development and application of an intuitive technique, introduced in Cox and Ross (1975a), for finding the solution to option valuation problems. This approach provides new insights into the structure of option valuation problems and its application allows us to solve a previously unresolved problem, the valuation of coupon paying bonds of arbitrary finite maturity, and the complementary problem of valuing an option on a stock with constant dividend payouts. Section 2 introduces the new stochastic processes studied in this paper. Section 3 studies the general option valuation problem and develops the solution technique. Section 4 applies the technique to the processes of section 1, and section 5 briefly summarizes and concludes the paper.

2. Some alternative stochastic processes

In exploring alternative forms it is useful to construct them as jump processes. Aside from the question of whether the 'real world' follows a diffusion or a jump process, even if we use diffusion processes for their analytic conveniences, much of our intuition can be formalized with jump processes. Eq. (2), for example, describes an equity whose value drifts deterministically until a unit of information arrives. Information arrives with probability $\lambda \, dt$ and, when it does, the stock value jumps discontinuously by $k - 1$ per cent. The diffusion in (1) is the limit of such a process, where information arrives continuously and has only a differential impact.

Eq. (2) is a very special case of the general form for Markov jump processes. If x denotes the current state of the world, then a general jump process is of the form

$$dS = \mu(x)\,dt + \begin{cases} \overline{}^{\;\lambda(x)dt} & \tilde{k}(x) - 1, \\[2mm] \underline{}_{\;1-\lambda(x)dt} & 0, \end{cases} \tag{3}$$

where $\tilde{k}(x)$ has a distribution dependent on the current world state, x. We will assume that $x = S$, i.e., all state information is contained in the current stock value, S. We could, of course, also add a Wiener diffusion term, $\sigma(x)\,dz$, to (3) to obtain a more general process, but (3) actually contains the diffusion as a limiting case (see below). The motivation for specializing (3) to (1) or (2), is that they capture two notions. First, they are in relative or percentage terms and there is some intuitive rationale for specifying the stochastic mechanism in percentage terms since this is the form of the returns. Second, by putting the process in percentage terms we can naturally include as the limited liability constraint, $S \geq 0$. Both (1) and (2) obey this boundary condition. Beyond these not entirely compelling arguments though there does not seem to be terribly much reason for the exclusive use of (1) or (2) and doing so would overlook a number of interesting and equally defensible forms.

Suppose, for example, that in (3) we specialize the intensity, $\lambda(S)$ and the drift, $\mu(S)$, to be proportional to value, λS and μS, and choose the distribution, $k - 1$, to be independent of value. Thus,

$$dS = \mu S\,dt + \begin{cases} \overline{}^{\;\lambda Sdt} & k - 1, \\[2mm] \underline{}_{\;1-\lambda Sdt} & 0. \end{cases} \tag{4}$$

With the drift term eq. (4) is a generalization of a class of stochastic processes known as birth and death processes. The local mean and variance of (4) are given by

$$E\{dS\} = [\mu + \lambda E\{k - 1\}]\, S dt, \tag{5}$$

and

$$V\{dS\} = \lambda E\{(k - 1)^2\}\, S dt.$$

To construct a pure birth and death process we ignore the drift in (4) and let k take on two values, $k^+ > 1$ and $k^- < 1$ with respective (conditional) probabilities π^+ and π^-,

$$dS = \left\langle \begin{array}{l} \xrightarrow{\lambda\,Sdt} \left\langle \begin{array}{l} \xrightarrow{\pi^+} k^+ - 1, \\ \xrightarrow{\pi^-} k^- - 1 = \left\langle \begin{array}{l} \xrightarrow{\pi\,+\,\lambda\,Sdt} k^+ - 1, \\ \xrightarrow{\pi\,-\,\lambda\,Sdt} k^- - 1, \\ \xrightarrow{1 - \lambda\,Sdt} 0. \end{array}\right. \end{array}\right. \\ \xrightarrow{1 - \lambda\,Sdt} \end{array}\right. \tag{6}$$

Eq. (6) is now an example of a simple birth and death process for a population. Imagine a firm made up of individual units (members of the population) whose sum value (population size) is S. If these units are stochastically independent of each other, we can let λdt represent the probability of an event occurring for any one unit. An event is, with probability π^+, the 'birth' of $k^+ - 1$ additional units and with probabilty π^- the 'death' of $1 - k^-$ units. For the whole firm (population), then, (6) describes its local movement. If $\mu = 0$ and if $\pi^+ = 1$, then (6) describes a pure birth process and if $\pi^- = 1$, (6) is called a pure death process. Eq. (2) in contrast to (6) describes the stochastic movement of a firm (population) all of whose members are perfectly dependent, that is, when one moves they all move, and the probability of such an event, λdt, is independent of the firm value (population size) although the magnitude is simply proportional.

Another interesting difference between (2) and (6) can be seen by passing to the diffusion limit in (6). The diffusion limit of (2) is the relative process (1) [see Cox and Ross (1975a)]. The limit of (6), though, as $k^+ \to 1$ and $k^- \to 1$ and $\lambda \to \infty$ in the fashion indicated in footnote 1 is a diffusion with instantaneous mean μS and variance $\sigma^2 S$, where μ and σ are given by (5), and μ is not the same as the drift in (4).[1] We could write this in the formalism of the stochastic differential as

$$dS = \mu S dt + \sigma\sqrt{S}\,dz. \tag{7}$$

---

[1] To derive the diffusion limit (7) it is sufficient to demonstrate that the Kolmogorov backward equation (see discussion below in section 3) for the probability transition function

$$P_{x,y}(t, \tau) \equiv \text{Prob}\{S_\tau = y \mid S_\tau = x\}, \quad \tau > t;$$

Although it is useful to consider this type of diffusion as a limiting case of an economy where firms are compositions of independent units, this interpretation is by no means necessary. Other forms of causation could lead to the same probabilistic description of events. We could in fact consider this diffusion process solely on its own merits as a description of a situation in which changes in state are small and in which the variance of price changes increases with the stock price, but more slowly than (1) so that the variance of the rate of return decreases rather than remaining constant. Considered in this way the process can certainly not be rejected on an a priori basis, and may in many situations be preferable to (1). Unlike (1) it should be noted that the diffusion process represented by (7) does permit $S = 0$, i.e., bankruptcy, to occur with positive probability (even in the absence of stock payouts).

---

for the birth and death process (6) converges to that for the diffusion (7) under an appropriate limiting argument. The backward equation for (6) is

$$-(\partial P_{x,y} / \partial t) = -\lambda x P_{x,y} + \lambda x \pi^+ P_{x+\Delta x, y} + \lambda x \pi^- P_{x-\Delta x, y},$$

where we have set $k^+ - 1 = \Delta x$ and $k^- - 1 = -\Delta x$.

Now, to maintain the instantaneous mean and variance of the diffusion process (7) in the passage to the limit we alter the intensities as $\Delta x \to 0$ in such a fashion as to maintain

$$\lambda x (\Delta x)^2 = \sigma^2 x \ \text{and} \ \lambda x (\pi^+ - \pi^-) \Delta x = \mu x; \ \text{or}$$

$$\lambda = \sigma^2 / (\Delta x)^2, \ \lambda \pi^+ = \tfrac{1}{2} [\sigma^2 / (\Delta x)^2 + \mu / \Delta x], \ \lambda \pi^- = \tfrac{1}{2} [\sigma^2 / (\Delta x)^2 - \mu / \Delta x].$$

Passing to the limit as $\Delta x \to 0$ in the backward equation we have the backward equation for the diffusion (7),

$$-\partial P_{x,y} / \partial t \ = -\lambda x P_{x,y} + \lambda x \pi^+ [P_{x,y} + (\partial P_{x,y} / \partial x) \Delta x +$$

$$\tfrac{1}{2} (\partial^2 P_{x,y} / \partial x^2 (\Delta x)^2)]$$

$$+ \lambda x \pi^- [P_{x,y} - (\partial P_{x,y} / \partial x) \Delta x + \tfrac{1}{2} (\partial^2 P_{x,y} / \partial x^2)(\Delta x)^2]$$

$$= \mu x (\partial P_{x,y} / \partial x) + \tfrac{1}{2} \sigma^2 x (\partial^2 P_{x,y} / \partial x^2).$$

The derivation of the absolute process (10) from the absolute jump (8) is nearly identical, but in that case we need the drift term. For the absolute process (8) the backward equation is given by

$$-\partial P_{x,y} / \partial t = -\lambda P_{x,y} + \lambda \pi^+ P_{x+\Delta x, y} + \lambda \pi^- P_{x-\Delta x, y} + \mu x (\partial P_{x,y} / \partial x).$$

Using the limiting process $\lambda \pi^+ = \lambda \pi^- = \tfrac{1}{2} (\sigma^2 / (\Delta x)^2)$, we can show, as above, that the backward equation converges to the backward equation for the absolute process (10),

$$-\partial P_{x,y} / \partial t = \mu x (\partial P_{x,y} / \partial x) + \tfrac{1}{2} \sigma^2 (\partial^2 P_{x,y} / \partial x^2).$$

These derivations are intended to be heuristic and only prove pointwise convergence, but they can be rigorously extended to show uniform convergence. A detailed treatment of a similar argument can be found in Feller (1951a). We should also add that since S is considered to be a value we append to (7) and (10) an absorbing barrier at $S = 0$. This recognizes that both (7) and (10) will drive a positive S to zero with positive probability.

Another specialization of (3) that is of interest is one where the firm is composed of dependent units as in (2), so that intensity, λ, is constant, and where the value increment is also constant. In this case

$$dS = \mu S dt + \begin{cases} \dfrac{\lambda\,dt}{} & \begin{cases} \dfrac{\pi^+}{} & k^+ - 1, \\[2mm] \dfrac{\pi^-}{} & k^- - 1, \end{cases} \\[4mm] \dfrac{1 - \lambda\,dt}{} & 0, \end{cases} \tag{8}$$

and we have jettisoned proportionality altogether. This is a case where value grows endogenously at the exponential rate μ, and where lump exogenous increments to value of size, $k - 1$, occur with intensity λ. For reference we can call this the absolute process.

The local mean and variance of the absolute process are given by

$$E\{dS\} = \{\mu S + \lambda\,[\,\pi^+(k^+ - 1) + \pi^-(k^- - 1)]\}\,dt,$$

and

$$V\{dS\} = \lambda\,[\,\pi^+(k^+ - 1)^2 + \pi^-(k^- - 1)^2]\,dt, \tag{9}$$

in the case where k is constant. If $\pi^- = 0$ the process has limited liability, but if $\pi^- > 0$ there is a positive probability that it will go into default. To preserve limited liability we would, therefore, also have to specify a non-negative lower barrier for S. Taking the diffusion limit of (8) as with (6) (see footnote 1), we obtain

$$dS = \mu S dt + \sigma\,dz, \tag{10}$$

where μ and σ are given by (9). This process would thus characterize a firm whose increments in value have a constant variance. To impose limited liability, we let the origin be an absorbing barrier, and consider (10) as governing the stock value only as long as this point is not reached. There would again be a positive probability of bankruptcy during any period.

3. Option valuation theory

The structure of the hedging arguments used to obtain valuation formulas for options can be illustrated in a fairly general setting. The first step is to choose a particular stochastic process to govern the price movement of the underlying asset, say a stock with price, S. Let us assume that we can write the random differential movement in S as

$$dS = \mu_S\,dt + \sigma_S\,dx_S. \tag{11}$$

As in the examples of section 2, μ_S and σ_S are taken to be functions of the current state of the world, which for simplicity is supposed to be summarized by S and t alone. The (non-anticipating) stochastic term dx_S is assumed to be either a Wiener diffusion term, dz, or a unit Poisson variable $d\pi$. If dx_S is a Poisson term, then we interpret σ_S in (11) to be the random jump amplitude given a jump.

The next step in the argument is to take an instrument whose value is dependent on S, say an option written on the stock, and assume that a sufficiently regular price function exists, $P(S, t)$, which is the option value at time t, given that the stock price at t is equal to S. Postulating such a function permits us (given that μ_S, σ_S and P are sufficiently well behaved mathematically) to derive the differential movement in the option value,

$$dP = \mu_P\,dt + \sigma_P\,dx_S. \qquad (12)$$

The functions of μ_P and σ_P now depend on the unknown function P and the known values of S and t. If dx_S follows a unit Poisson process σ_P may be a random function whose values depend on the function P and the jump size, σ_S, and it need not be proportional to σ_S.

The economic argument that leads to a formula for pricing the option is based on the presence of a third asset that earns a riskless instantaneous interest rate, r, which we will take to be a constant rate at which individuals can borrow and lend freely. We also will assume that the stock, S, can be sold short with the seller receiving the proceeds, and that there are no transactions costs or taxes. Most importantly, we make the competitive assumption that agents act as though they cannot influence r or any price. Under these assumptions it is easy to show that all riskless assets must earn the riskless rate, r, to prevent arbitrage.

While it is possible to solve option problems for random jumps to more than one value as in the birth and death process of (6) when π^+, $\pi^- \neq 0$, to do so requires the introduction of additional stocks either to support the hedging argument as in Cox and Ross (1975b), or the use of Ross's (1973) arbitrage argument to obtain an approximate formula as in Merton (1975). To avoid either of these possibilities we will further assume that if dx_S is a Poisson process, the jump amplitude σ_S (and σ_P) is a non-random function at a jump. It follows that there is a hedge portfolio of the stock, S, and its option, P, such that

$$\alpha_S\,\sigma_S\,(dx_S/S) + \alpha_P\,\sigma_P\,(dx_S/P) = 0,$$

or

$$\alpha_S\,(\sigma_S/S) + \alpha_P\,(\sigma_P/P) = 0, \qquad (13)$$

where α_S and α_P are the portfolio weights in the stock and the option respectively. Such a hedge portfolio is riskless and must have a rate of return

$$\alpha_S\,(\mu_S/S) + \alpha_P\,(\mu_P/P) = (\alpha_S + \alpha_P)r, \qquad (14)$$

the return at the riskless rate. From (13) and (14) we obtain the fundamental option valuation equation

$$(\mu_P - rP) / \sigma_P = (\mu_S - rS) / \sigma_S . \tag{15}$$

The valuation equation, thus, reduces to the familiar statement that the risk premium divided by the scale of risk has to be the same for the stock and its option. As a mathematical matter, eq. (15) is usually a differential-difference equation and together with the terms of the option we can hopefully apply some available mathematical techniques to solve it.

For example, with the Black and Scholes log-normal diffusion (1), the valuation eq. (15) takes the form

$$\frac{1}{2}\sigma^2 S^2 P_{SS} + rSP_S - rP = -P_t . \tag{16}$$

Using the boundary condition for a European call option

$$P(S, T) = \max\{S - E, 0\},$$

where E is the exercise price, Black and Scholes were able to transform (16) to the heat equation of physics and solve it in closed form.

In Cox and Ross (1975a), however, a systematic technique for solving the valuation equation was introduced that exploits the economic structure of the problem and provides further insight into the structure of option valuation problems in general. The fact that we could use a hedging argument to derive (15) and the argument that $P(S, t)$ exists uniquely means that given S and t the value of the option, P, does not depend directly on the structure of investors' preferences. Investors' preferences and demand conditions in general enter the valuation problem only in so far as they determine the equilibrium parameter values. No matter what preferences are, as long as they determine the same relevant parameter values, they will also value the option identically. In the Black and Scholes case, for example, (16) does not depend on μ and the only relevant parameters for the pricing problem are r and σ. To solve (15), then, we need only find the equilibrium solution for P in some world where preferences are given and consistent with the specified parameter values; the solution obtained will then be preference free.

A convenient choice of preferences for many problems (although one can envision problems where another preference structure might be more suitable) is risk neutrality. In such a world equilibrium requires that the expected returns on both the stock and the option must equal the riskless rate. For the stock, then

$$E\left\{\frac{S_T}{S_t} \,\Big|\, S_t\right\} = e^{r(T-t)} . \tag{17}$$

Similarly, if we are considering a general European option with boundary value,

$$P(S, T) = h(S), \tag{18}$$

then, at time t,

$$E\left\{\frac{P(S_T, T)}{P} \,\bigg|\, S_t\right\} = \frac{1}{P} E\{h(S_T) \mid S_t\} = e^{r(T-t)},$$

or

$$P(S, t) = e^{-r(T-t)} E\{h(S_T) \mid S_t\} \tag{19}$$

$$= e^{-r(T-t)} \int h(S_T) \, dF(S_T, T \mid S_t, t),$$

where $F(S_T, T \mid S_t, t)$ is the probability distribution of the stock price at time T, S_T, given the stock price at time $t < T$, S_t. Eq. (19), with (17), provides the solution to the option valuation problem. Eq. (17) is used to satisfy any special features of the parameter set that are implied by the hedging equation.[2]

From (19) it is apparent that if we know the cumulative probability distribution of the stock process we can value the option. The converse is generally true as well. In the case of European calls, for example, the general option pricing formula (19) for arbitrary exercise prices, E, involves knowing all of the right semi-moments of the terminal stock distribution, given that (17) is satisfied. This is, however, equivalent to knowing the distribution itself.[3] In other words, the option valuation problem is really equivalent to the problem of determining the distribution of the stock variable, S, whose movement is governed by the postulated process (11). This establishes an important link between the option valuation problem and the fundamentals of stochastic processes.

It is well known that the probability transition functions, $F(S_T, T \mid S_t, t)$, satisfy two central equations, the forward (or Fokker-Planck) equation and the Kolomogorov backward equations [see Feller (1966)]. The backward equations describe the way in which $F(S_T, T \mid S_t, t)$ is altered as the initial

---

[2]Some awareness of this technique appears in previous work. Black and Scholes, in an earlier version of their seminal paper, first found the solution to (16) by setting $\mu = r$ in Sprenkle's (1961) formula for the option value. Merton, in Samuelson (1973), also noted that setting $\alpha = \beta = r$ in Samuelson's $\alpha - \beta$ model gave the Black and Scholes solution.

[3]We can sketch a formal proof of this proposition. We only need to show that the semi-moments determine the distribution. Suppose that two distributions, F and G, have the same semimoments, or equivalently, the same option values for all exercise prices, E. The family of functions, $f_E(S) = \max\{S - E, 0\}$, generates a lattice, K (closed under addition and multiplication by constants), on compact sets on the line which contains the constant functions and separates points. The lattice structure is immediate and for $E' > E$, $f_E(S) - f_{E'}(S) = E' - E$, $S \geq E'$, i.e., a constant. By the Stone-Weierstrass theorem, then, on compact sets, the lattice, K, is dense in the continuous functions and since F and G agree on K, it follows from the Helly-Brey lemma that they agree on all continuous functions.

time, t, is changed. For example, the backward equation for the diffusion process (1) is given by

$$\frac{1}{2} \sigma^2 S^2 F_{SS} + \mu S F_S + F_t = 0,$$

(20)

where $S_t = S$, and $F(S_T, T \mid S, t)$ must satisfy (20) for all values of (S_T, T). In a risk-neutral world, from (17), the drift on the stock $\mu = r$. Suppose, then, we consider the backward equation (20) with $\mu = r$. Transforming this equation by substituting (19) we obtain (16), the Black and Scholes option valuation equation. In general, if (17) can be satisfied, the option valuation equation (15), is the transform (19) of the Kolmogorov backward equation for the transition probability function, F. The operational significance of these observations is simply that we can solve the option valuation problem only for those cases where we know the probability distribution of the terminal stock value.

The next sections illustrate these techniques by applying them to the option valuation problems for the stochastic processes introduced above. In the final section we are able to obtain an important new result, the valuation of options on stocks paying dividends, by the application of these techniques to the square root process (7).

4. Option valuation problems

In this section we will explore the option valuation problem for some of the jump processes considered in section 2. As in section 3 we restrict the general form (3) to the case of a single post jump value, $k(S, t)$.

4.1. Alternative jump processes

Our problem is to value a call option on S with an expiration date T at which time the holder receives $\max\{S_T - E, 0\}$. We will initially assume that the stock pays no dividends so that it would never be optimal to exercise an American call before the expiration date T and it will, therefore, be valued as a European call [see Merton (1973)]. To solve this problem we specialize the hedging argument to the jump case. The local return on the stock is given by (3) and the option follows a perfectly dependent process

$$dP = \Bigg\langle \begin{array}{c} \xrightarrow{\lambda S dt} \quad P(S + k - 1, t) - P(S, t), \\ \xrightarrow[1 - \lambda S dt]{} \quad P_t dt + \mu P_S dt, \end{array}$$

(21)

where λ is an arbitrary function.

By forming a hedge portfolio of the stock and the option with weights α_S and α_P respectively chosen so that

$$\alpha_S \left[\frac{k-1}{S}\right] + \alpha_P \left[\frac{P(S + k - 1, t) - P(S, t)}{P(S, t)}\right] = 0,$$

(22)

the hedge position will be riskless. It follows that if r is the (instantaneous) riskless rate of interest, then

$$\alpha_S\left(\frac{\mu}{S}\right) + \alpha_P\left(\frac{P_t + \mu P_S}{P}\right) = (\alpha_S + \alpha_P)r, \qquad (23)$$

i.e., the hedge must be equivalent to a riskless short bond to prevent arbitrage possibilities. Combining (22) and (23) we have that $P(S, t)$ must satisfy the difference-differential equation version of (15),

$$\mu P_S + \left[\frac{\mu - rS}{1 - k}\right] P(S + k - 1, t) + \left[\frac{r[k - 1 + S] - \mu}{1 - k}\right] P = -P_t, \qquad (24)$$

where μ and k are functions of S and t.

An important feature of (24) and, consequently, the resulting option formulas is that they are independent of the choice of λ, the process intensity. This characteristic feature of option valuation formulas for jump processes was first shown for process (2) [see Cox and Ross (1975a)], and it is easy to see by the hedging argument that the intensity, quite generally, plays no role in the valuation since the hedge position depends only on the jump size. In fact, by setting $\mu(S, t) = \mu S$ and $k(S, t) = S(k - 1) + 1$, (24) becomes the option pricing relation [equation (10) in Cox and Ross (1975a)] for process (2). We can, now, use (24) to study a variety of alternative jump processes.

Example 1

Consider, first, a pure birth process without drift,

$$dS = \left\langle \begin{array}{cc} \overline{\lambda\,Sdt} & k - 1, \\[6pt] \underline{1 - \lambda\,Sdt} & 0. \end{array}\right. \qquad (25)$$

In this case eq. (24) specializes to

$$r(k - 1)^{-1}S[P(S + (k - 1), t) - P(S, t)] - rP(S, t) \qquad (26)$$

$$= -P_t(S, t),$$

with

$$P(S, T) = \max\{S - E, 0\}.$$

To solve (26) we use the technique described in section 3. [As a check, it is not difficult to verify that (26) is the transformed backward equation for the process (25).] In a risk-neutral world the expected returns on both the stock and the option must equal the riskless rate, and (17) becomes

$$E\left[\frac{S_T}{S_0}\right] = e^{\lambda(k-1)(T-1)} = e^{r(T-1)}, \tag{27}$$

or

$$\lambda(k-1) = r,$$

where we have used a familiar result from the theory of birth processes. To obtain the expected return on the option we have to use the distribution function for S_T, which is simply the distribution for a scaled pure birth process [see, e.g., Feller (1966)]. It follows that,

$$E\left[\frac{P_T}{P}\right] = \frac{1}{P}E[\max\{S_T - E, 0\}]$$

$$= \frac{1}{P}\sum_{S_T \geq E}(S_T - E)\begin{bmatrix}\dfrac{S_t}{k-1} - 1 \\[2mm] \dfrac{S_t}{k-1} - 1\end{bmatrix}(e^{-r(T-t)})^{S_t/(k-1)}$$

$$\times (1 - e^{-r(T-t)})^{(S_T - S_t)/(k-1)}, \tag{28}$$

and using (27) and the required equality with the riskless return, we obtain

$$P(S, t) = S\sum_{j \geq [E/(k-1)+2]}B\left(j; \frac{S}{k-1} + 1, e^{-r(T-t)}\right)$$

$$- Ee^{-r(T-t)}\sum_{j \geq [E/(k-1)+1]}B\left(j; \frac{S}{k-1}, e^{-r(T-t)}\right), \tag{29}$$

where

$$B(j; x, q) = \binom{j-1}{x-1}q^x(1-q)^{j-x},$$

the negative binomial density, $\binom{j-1}{x-1}$ denotes $\Gamma(j)/\Gamma(x)\Gamma(j-x+1)$, and $[y]$ is the largest integer not exceeding y. This example illustrates the way in which (17) is used in the solution technique. From the hedging argument the intensity λ does not affect the option valuation. In a risk-neutral market $\lambda = r/(k-1)$, which allows us to eliminate λ from the option valuation (29). It is important to realize that this does not imply that we are only solving the valuation problem when (27) is satisfied. On the contrary, for a given r and k the solution is independent of λ and for any λ the solution will be identical to the solution when (27) holds.

This example also reveals an important feature of solutions to valuation problems in general and jump problems in particular. At points where (29) and the solutions below are not differentiable they cannot, of course, satisfy differential equations of the form of (26). The paradox is resolved by modifying (26) appropriately. At points of non-differentiability, P_t, for example, will not in general capture the true time component of the change, or gradient, in option value. The hedging argument, on the other hand, will use this time gradient and the result is a slight generalization of the differential equations. Our solutions are everywhere correct for these generalized equations. This point is discussed in greater detail in Cox and Ross (1975a and b).

Unfortunately, though, there is no general solution for (24) available, and our technique of evaluating the solution for a risk-neutral world cannot avoid this difficulty. As a consequence, even seemingly straightforward generalizations of the results we do have can become formidable.

Example 2

Suppose we try to extend our option valuation results to the case of the pure jump process, (25), augmented by a proportional drift term, μS, as in (4). This is an important extension because by the techniques employed in footnote 1, (4), like a birth and death process, can be made to converge to the square root diffusion, (7).

To apply our technique to obtain the solution for the differential valuation equation, (24), requires us to know the distribution of S_T/S_t so as to be able to calculate the semi-moment $E\{\max\{S_T - E, 0\}\}$, which gives the option value. Unfortunately, though, the addition of the deterministic drift term greatly complicates this problem. The reason is that the process is now non-homogeneous in time in the sense that the probability of a jump in the next instant depends not only on the number of past jumps, but also on when they occurred, i.e., their timing. Without going into the messy details it can be shown, though, that, given (4), the density function of S_T is

$$\text{Prob}\{S_T \epsilon (x, x + dx)\} = \sum_{n=0}^{\infty} \left(\frac{\lambda(k-1)}{\mu} \right)^n e^{(\lambda/\mu)[S_t + n(k-1) - x]}$$

$$\times \int_{A_n} \prod_{i=1}^{n} \left(S_t - \sum_{j=1}^{i=1} x_j \right) x_i^{-2} dx_{ij},$$

where   (30)

$$A_n \equiv \{(x_1, \ldots, x_n) \mid \sum_i x_i = S_t - xe^{-\mu(T-t)},$$

$$-(k-1) \leqq x_1 \leqq \ldots \leqq x_n \leqq$$

$$-(k-1)e^{-\mu(T-1)}\}.$$

We can now use (19) and (30) to evaluate the option value, but we will no longer have a closed form solution. [The integrals in (30) do not appear to be readily available in closed form, but (30) can be approximated for computation purposes.]

Example 3

As a final jump example that illustrates one of the hazards of applying the solution technique consider applying it to the option valuation problem for the absolute process (8) without drift. To avoid limited liability problems and to permit one stock hedging suppose that $\Pi^+ = 1$, so that this is a pure growth jump. Simply solving (17), and using the fact that the number of jumps in $[t, T]$ is Poisson distributed, would give

$$E\left\{\frac{S_T}{S_t}\right\} = \frac{\lambda(k-1)}{S_t}(T-t) = e^{r(T-t)},$$

which solves for the omitted parameter, λ, as a function of S_t, the current stock value. This, however, violates the originally postulated absolute process with λ independent of current stock value. In other words, the assumed process is inconsistent in a risk neutral market. Nevertheless, we can still value an option on such a process by noting that the hedging differential equation is given by (26) just as for the pure birth process. This must be the case, since the intensity parameter plays no role in the valuation, other than through (27). It follows, then, that the solution to this problem will be the same as that for the birth process, (29) without drift, and can be found from (30) with a drift term. Even though the absolute process is inconsistent in a risk-neutral market, the differential valuation equation is the same as that for the birth process which is consistent with risk neutrality. This permits us to value the absolute process given whatever structure of market preferences and other assets which will support it in equilibrium. This inconsistency with risk neutrality does not apply to an absolute process with a symmetric two point jump and proportional drift, but consideration of this two jump case cannot be done in the context of single stock hedging.

We now turn to the option problems for the diffusion limits introduced in section 3.

4.2. Alternative diffusion processes

The first step is to derive the differential equation which the option value must follow for all diffusion processes and then specialize for our two cases.[4] In this section we will explicitly consider a stock or firm which makes payouts.[5]

Suppose that the stock price is governed by

$$dS = \mu(S, t)\,dt + \sigma(S, t)\,dz, \tag{31}$$

where $\mu(S, t)$ and $\sigma^2(S, t)$ are, respectively, the instantaneous mean and variance of the diffusion process. Applying Ito's lemma [see McKean

---

[4]This development follows along the lines given by Black and Scholes and Merton (1974) for the diffusion process (1).
[5]Payouts can also be readily introduced into the jump processes, but this may in some cases greatly complicate the solution.

(1969)], the option price will follow,

$$dP = [P_t + \mu(S, t)P_S + \frac{1}{2}\sigma^2(S, t)P_{SS}] dt + P_S \sigma(S, t) dz. \qquad (32)$$

Suppose also that each unit of the stock pays out in dividends the continuous stream $b(S, t)$. Consider a portfolio in which we hold a unit of the option, some fraction α_S of a unit of stock, and some amount of borrowing or lending such that the aggregate investment is zero. If we choose α_S to be $-P_S$ then the portfolio will have no stochastic component and to prevent arbitrage its local mean must be zero.

This means that in each instant the three sources of change in the portfolio, the deterministic part of the price changes in the stock and option, the risk-free return on the lending (or borrowing), and payouts received (or made in restitution in the case of short sales) must exactly offset each other. From the above we have that the net deterministic price change component is $\frac{1}{2}\sigma^2(S, t)P_{SS} + P_t$, the return on the bond position in $rSP_S - rP$, and the restitution required for dividend payments made to the stock while held short is $-b(S, t)P_S$. Collecting these terms yields the differential equation form of (15),

$$\frac{1}{2}\sigma^2(S, t)P_{SS} + [rS - b(S, t)]P_S - rP = -P_t. \qquad (33)$$

With the diffusion processes, then, the stochastic assumptions enter the valuation equation only in the determination of the coefficient of the second derivative term, as would be expected from the earlier discussion about the relation between the valuation equation and the Kolmogorov backward equation for the process in question. Also we can note the convenience of the choice of risk-neutral preferences is not affected by payouts, since the risk neutrality would simply require that the instantaneous mean total return on the stock be rS, so that the required mean price change would be $\mu(S, t) = rS - b(S, t)$.

In the following we will consider only payout functions of the form $b(S, t) = aS + c$ since this will provide a satisfactory representation for most problems. Also we will consider only European options, although for many constant dividend policies equivalent American options would have the same value, since premature exercising would never be optimal.

Example 4

Let us first examine the case (7) where the variance is proportional to the stock price. From (23), the differential valuation equation becomes

$$\frac{1}{2}\sigma^2 SP_{SS} + [(r - a)S - c]P_S - rP = -P_t. \qquad (34)$$

We could attack this problem directly by standard analytic methods but it is easier to apply the solution technique used above if the terminal density (in a risk-neutral setting) is already known. Fortunately, this is the case since Feller (1951a, b), in his work on birth and death processes, was led to studying the limiting diffusion case. The density of S_T conditional on S_t is given for $S_T > 0$ by

$$f(S_T, T; S_t, t) = \left(\frac{2(r-a)}{\sigma^2 (e^{(r-a)(T-t)} - 1)} \right) \left(\frac{S_t e^{(r-a)(T-t)}}{S_T} \right)^{\frac{1}{2}(1+2c/\sigma^2)}$$

$$\times \exp \left[- \frac{2(r-a)(S_t e^{(r-a)(T-t)} + S_T)}{\sigma^2 (e^{(r-a)(T-t)} - 1)} \right]$$

$$\times I_{1+2c/\sigma^2} \left[\frac{4(r-a)(S_T S_t e^{(r-a)(T-t)})^{\frac{1}{2}}}{\sigma^2 (e^{(r-a)(T-t)} - 1)} \right], \quad (35)$$

where $I_q(\bullet)$ is the modified Bessel function of the first kind of order q.[6]

Integrating (35) over the range $S_T > 0$ results in a probability of less than unity. The remaining mass is the probability that $S_t = 0$ for some $t \leq T$, in which case S was 'absorbed' and remains at zero. Applying our technique we take the expectation of $\max(S_T - E, 0)$ and discount it to time t as in (19) to obtain the valuation formula

$$P(S, t) = S e^{-a(T-t)} \sum_{n=0}^{\infty} \frac{(n+1) e^{-y} y^{n+2c/\sigma^2} G(n+2, \theta E)}{\Gamma[n+2+2c/\sigma^2]}$$

$$- E e^{-r(T-t)} \sum_{n=0}^{\infty} \frac{e^{-y} y^{n+1+2c/\sigma^2} G(n+1, \theta E)}{\Gamma[n+2+2c/\sigma^2]}, \quad (36)$$

where

$$\theta = \frac{2(r-a)}{\sigma^2 [e^{(r-a)(T-t)} - 1]},$$

$$y = \theta S e^{(r-a)(T-t)}, \quad G(m, x) = [\Gamma(m)]^{-1} \int_x^\infty e^{-z} z^{m-1} dz,$$

the complimentary standard gamma distribution function. The value of an option at $S = 0$ is implied by the description of the process and no additional restrictions need to be made. For a process with an absorbing barrier at zero we will obviously have $P(0, t) = 0$.

Example 5

Turning now to (10) where the variance is independent of the price, eq. (33) is specialized to

$$\frac{1}{2} \sigma^2 P_{SS} + (r-a) S P_S - rP = -P_t. \quad (37)$$

[6] It is a difficult mathematical question to decide whether a stochastic differential equation can be solved for a non-trivial stochastic process in cases where the coefficents do not have bounded derivatives. In this case, however, (7) was actually derived from the stochastic process given by (35) and no such problems arise. More generally, if we are given the process

As with (34) this problem could be handled directly, for example by transformation to the heat equation. It is again easier and more illuminating however to make use of knowledge of the terminal stock distribution. Inspecting the equation we note that it is analogous to the backward equation of the Ornstein-Uhlenbeck process, whose physical origins lay in the study of particles in Brownian motion in the presence of an elastic force. It makes little economic sense for a price with limited liability to reach zero if it can subsequently become positive, so we would wish to use the Ornstein-Uhlenbeck process with an absorbing barrier at zero as with the square root process. In the above we have looked only at the specialization $c = 0$, i.e., only at proportional payouts, since otherwise the corresponding density is not known (and the transformation to the heat equation leads to an as yet unsolved time-dependent boundary problem). For the case considered, the density of S_T conditional on S_t is, for $S_T > 0$,

$$f(S_T, T; S_t, t) = (2\pi Z)^{-\frac{1}{2}} \left[\exp\left(- \frac{[S_T - S_t e^{(r-a)(T-t)}]^2}{2Z} \right) \right.$$
$$\left. - \exp\left(- \frac{-[S_T + S_t e^{(r-a)(T-t)}]^2}{2Z} \right) \right],$$

where

$$Z = \left[\frac{\sigma^2}{2(r-a)} \right] [e^{2(r-a)(T-t)} - 1]. \tag{38}$$

Applying (19) yields the valuation formula,

$$P(S, t) = (S e^{-a(T-t)} - E e^{-r(T-t)}) N(y_1)$$
$$+ (S e^{-a(T-t)} + E e^{-r(T-t)}) N(y_2)$$
$$+ v[n(y_1) - n(y_2)], \tag{39}$$

where $N(\cdot)$ is the cumulative unit normal distribution function, $n(\cdot)$ is the unit normal density function, and

$$v = \sigma \left(\frac{e^{-2a(T-t)} - e^{-2r(T-t)}}{2(r-a)} \right)^{\frac{1}{2}},$$
$$y_1 = \frac{S e^{-a(T-t)} - E e^{-r(T-t)}}{v},$$
$$y_2 = \frac{-S e^{-a(T-t)} - E e^{-r(T-t)}}{v}.$$

---

itself, any increasing transform of it (like P) will itself be a well-defined process with instantaneous mean, $\mu(S, t) P_S + \frac{1}{2} \sigma^2(S, t) P_{SS} + P_t$, and instantaneous variance, $\sigma^2(S, t) P_S^2$, if it is C^2, and derivable even if it is not [see Feller (1966, p. 326)]. This approach permits us to bypass the Ito processes and any additional regularity conditions they might require.

The comparative statics associated with parameter changes in (36) and (39) are tedious, but fairly intuitive, and we defer then to subsequent work.

4.3.
Applications to
other securities

While we have focused on options above these same techniques can be applied to a wide range of financial instruments. A convenient approach to valuing corporate securities is to assume that the total value of the firm, V, follows a particular stochastic process and then consider individual securities as functions of the value of the firm and time. The value of the individual securities of any firm whose total value follows a diffusion process, for example, must, then, satisfy an equation of the same form as (33). Unlike options, though, most corporate securities, F, receive payouts, $b'(V, t)$, and eq. (33) must be modified to include this return,

$$\frac{1}{2} \sigma^2(V, t) F_{VV} + [rV - b(V, t)] F_V - rF + b'(V, t) = -F_t. \quad (40)$$

The securities of a given firm can be distinguished by their terminal conditions and payouts received. As a concrete example, consider a firm with one stock issue and one bond issue. The bond would have a terminal value of $\min(B, V)$, where B is the maturity value of the bond, and would receive a constant payout, say c'. The stock would have a terminal condition of $\max(V - B, 0)$ and would receive in dividends $aV + c''$, where $c' + c'' = c$, the total constant portion of payouts.[7]

To value such securities it will be useful to think of the total value of any security as being the value the security would have if it received no payouts, i.e., it only received its terminal return, plus the value of the payouts it will potentially receive. In terms of eq. (40) these two components would correspond, respectively, to (i) the solution of (40) without the inhomogeneous term $b'(V, t)$ but with the proper terminal conditions for the security, and (ii) the solution of the full eq. (40) with a zero terminal condition $[F(V, T) = 0]$. If we restrict our attention to payout policies of the form $aV + c$, then we can further break down (ii) into the value of the proportional payout and the value of the constant payout. It is easy to see that the sum of these solutions is the complete value of the security.

Applying our technique, the solution to (i) for any security is simply given by eqs. (19) and (17). Having found the solution to (i) for all securities, by the Modigliani-Miller theorem we can find the value of the total payout stream, $aV + c$, by subtracting the sum of these solutions from V. If the payout received by each security j can be written as a proportion of the total payout $k_j(aV + c)$, $(\Sigma k_j = 1)$, then it is evident from (40) that the value of (ii) for each security j will be k_j times the value of the total payout to all securities. We can then obtain a complete solution without having to solve (ii) separately. This technique can be used, for example, if $a = 0$, which would

---

[7]For the log-normal process (1), Merton (1974) has studied the problem of valuing the pure discount funds of a firm which makes no payouts ($a = c = 0$) and Ingersoll (1975) has discussed a model with proportional payouts ($c = 0$).

be the case of a stock that received constant dividends, or $c = 0$, i.e., the bond was a pure discount bond. In general, though, the securities of the firm receive different proportions of the constant payout, c, and the proportional payout, aV, and it is necessary to have a direct solution to (ii) to value such securities. However, we would only need to value separately the total proportional component and the total constant component, since from (40) the value of the payouts to individual securities can be written as a linear combination of these two terms.

To solve problem (ii) by our techniques note that the value of each point in a payout stream in a risk-neutral world must be its expected value discounted to the present. The total value of the stream can then be obtained in the usual way by integrating over all points in the stream. Once again, since we have established the hedging eq. (40), this solution will be the correct solution in general, not simply in a risk-neutral world. The expected value of any point in the constant stream, say, at time q, will be c times the probability that the payment will be received. This will be the probability, conditional on the current ($t < q$) value of the firm, that the firm will not be bankrupt at time q. We get this probability by replacing T with q in the terminal density of the value of the firm and then integrating this density with respect to $V_q > 0$. For our process (7), this probability can be obtained from (35) as

$$\sum_{n=0}^{\infty} \frac{e^{-y} y^{n+1+2c/\sigma^2}}{\Gamma[n+2+2c/\sigma^2]} = 1 - G[1 + 2c/\sigma^2, y], \tag{41}$$

where in y, q replaces T and V replaces S. The value of the entire stream will then be given by integration from t to T, giving

$$\int_t^T c e^{-r(q-t)} [1 - G(1 + 2c/\sigma^2, \theta V e^{(r-a)(q-t)})] \, dq. \tag{42}$$

If we knew the solution to (i) for all securities and the solution to (ii) for the constant component, we could value the proportional component by simply subtracting these from V. It is instructive, though, to value the proportional part of the payout stream directly. The expected value of the stream aV_q at each point q can again be obtained from the density and then discounted back to the present. Alternatively, the discounted expected value could be obtained directly in each of our cases from (36) or (39) by replacing S with V and T with q, and setting the price, $E = 0$. We could then find the total value of the proportional component of the stream at time t by integration with respect to q from t to T.

For the case with variance proportional to value, the solution for the proportionate payout is

$$\int_t^T aV e^{-a(q-t)} \left[\sum_{n=0}^{\infty} \frac{(n+1)e^{-y} y^{n+2c/\sigma^2}}{\Gamma[n+2+2c/\sigma^2]} \right] dq, \tag{43}$$

where, again, in y, V replaces S and q replaces T. When $c = 0$ the expression in square brackets equals one, and (43) reduces to simply

$$\int_t^T aVe^{-a(q-t)}dq = V[1 - e^{-a(T-t)}]. \tag{44}$$

Applying the analysis to the absolute diffusion (10) where $c = 0$, we find that (44) solves this case as well. In fact, inspection of (40) shows that when only proportional payouts are being made, (44) is the proper valuation for the payout stream for any diffusion process. However, as we have seen, when constant payouts are being made, the valuation of the proportional component will depend on the process being considered.

5. Summary and conclusion

The type of stochastic process determining the movement of the stock is of prime importance in option valuation. At present the workhorse of the option pricing literature has been the log-normal diffusion process. This paper introduced several alternative jump and diffusion processes, and provided solutions for the limiting diffusion cases and for the single-stage forms of the jump processes. The explicit solutions presented have potential empirical applications and a comparative study of them should give additional insight into the structure of security valuation. Aside from the intrinsic value of studying alternative admissible processes, though, a number of important problems involving payouts and bankruptcy which remain intractable for the log-normal are, nevertheless, solvable for some other processes. Throughout, the paper developed and used an economically interpretable technique for solving option problems which has intuitive appeal and should facilitate the solution of other problems in this field.

References

Black, F. and M. J. Scholes, 1973, The pricing of options and corporate liabilities, Journal of Political Economy 81, no. 3, 637-654.

Cootner, P. H., ed., 1964, The random character of stock market prices (M.I.T. Press, Cambridge, Mass.).

Cox, J. C. and S. A. Ross, 1975a, The pricing of options for jump processes, Rodney L. White Center Working Paper no. 2-75 (University of Pennsylvania, Philadelphia, Penn.).

Cox, J. C. and S. A. Ross, 1975b, The general structure of contingent claim pricing, mimeo. (University of Pennsylvania, Philadelphia, Penn.).

Feller, W., 1951a, Diffusion processes in genetics, Proceedings of the Second Berkeley Symposium on Mathematical Statistics and Probability, 227-246.

Feller, W., 1951b, Two singular diffusion problems, Annals of Mathematics 54, 173-182.

Feller, W., 1966, An introduction to probability theory and its applications, vols. I and II (Wiley, New York).

Ingersoll, Jr., J., 1975, A theoretical and empirical investigation of the dual purpose funds: An application of contingent-claims analysis, M.I.T. Working Paper no. 782-75 (M.I.T., Cambridge, Mass.).

McKean, H. P., 1969, Stochastic integrals (Academic Press, New York).

Merton, R. C., 1973, The theory of rational option pricing, Bell Journal of Economics and Management Science 4, no. 1, 141-183.

Merton, R. C., 1974, On the pricing of corporate debt: The risk structure of interest rates, The Journal of Finance 29, no. 2, 449-470.

Merton, R. C., 1975, Option pricing when underlying stock returns are discontinuous, M.I.T. Working Paper no. 787-75 (M.I.T., Cambridge, Mass.).

Modigliani, F. and M. H. Miller, 1958, The cost of capital, corporation finance, and the theory of investment, American Economic Review 48, no. 3, 261-297.

Ross, S. A., 1973, The arbitrage theory of capital asset pricing, Rodney L. White Center Working Paper no. 2-73, forthcoming in the Journal of Economic Theory.

Samuelson, P. A., 1965, Rational theory of warrant pricing, Industrial Management Review 6, no. 2, 13-31.

Samuelson, P., 1973, Mathematics of speculative price, with Appendix: R. C. Merton, Continuous time speculative prices, SIAM Review 15, no. 1.

Sprenkle, C. M., 1961, Warrant prices as indicators of expectations and preferences, Yale Economic Essays 1, no. 2, 178-231.

Section 2
Extensions

In the introduction to this book, a description of the Black-Scholes framework was provided. The essential elements of this framework are that the underlying commodity price follows geometric Brownian motion and that a riskless hedge may be formed between the option and the underlying commodity. This section contains four articles that derive other types of option pricing models within the Black-Scholes framework. The models are for nonstandard types of options, but these options are interesting and important nonetheless. In general, these options fall under the heading *exotic options*.[1]

One important extension of the Black-Scholes model is the valuation of compound options. Geske [1979], reprinted first in this section, derives the valuation equation for a call on a call. Compound option valuation results are important for at least three reasons. First, certain exchange-traded options can be viewed as compound options. For example, a call option on a stock may be

viewed as a call option (the exchange-traded security) on a call option on the value of the firm (the common stock of the firm). Second, the compound option valuation formula can provide useful insights on the value of the early exercise premium embedded in American-style options. Third, compound option markets are beginning to emerge. Calls on calls, calls on puts, puts on calls, and puts on puts are actively traded in OTC markets.

Margrabe [1978] extends the Black-Scholes model in yet another way. He derives a valuation equation for an exchange option, that is, the right to exchange one asset or commodity for another.[2] While, on face appearance, this type of option may seem to have little practical significance, its role in pricing the options embedded in futures contracts is extremely important. For example, Stulz [1982] and Johnson [1987], based on the work of Margrabe [1978], derive pricing equations for options on the maximum and the minimum of two or more risky assets. Conceptually, many of the

---

[1] For a partial listing of the exotic options that are traded in the OTC markets, see Stoll and Whaley [1992, Ch.16].

[2] Margrabe [1982] extends his model to the case on n underlying assets.

futures contracts that currently trade are options on the minimum. With the CBOT's Treasury bond futures, for example, the short holds the right to deliver the cheapest of a number of deliverable T-bond issues and, therefore, has an option on the minimum. Such options, called *quality options*, are also embedded in many of the CBOT's grain futures contracts where a number of grades are eligible for delivery.

Other research articles complement those that are reprinted here. For example, Fischer [1978] develops an option pricing model with an uncertain exercise price. This development is very similar to Margrabe [1978]. The Goldman, Sosin, and Gatto [1979] article develops an option pricing model that sets the exercise price of the call (put) equal to the lowest (highest) price that the commodity reaches during the life of the option. This option has come to be known as a *lookback option*.

Yet other research has attempted to relax certain of the Black-Scholes assumptions. One important issue that remains at the center of investigation is stochastic volatility. The Black-Scholes model assumes that the return volatility of the underlying commodity is constant through time. One needs only to recall the October 1987 stock market crash to understand that this assumption may be violated. Among the researchers who have investigated the implications of stochastic volatility on option pricing are Hull and White [1987], Scott [1987], and Wiggins [1987].

References and Bibliography

Geske, R., 1978, "Pricing of Options with Stochastic Dividend Yields," *Journal of Finance* 33, 617-25.

——, 1979, "The Valuation of Compound Options," *Journal of Financial Economics* 7 (March), 63-81.

Goldman, M.B., H.B. Sosin, and M.A. Gatto, 1979, "Path Dependent Options: Buy at the Low, Sell at the High," *Journal of Finance* 34 (December), 1111-27.

Fischer, S., 1978, "Call Option Pricing When the Exercise Price Is Uncertain and the Valuation of Index Bonds," *Journal of Finance* 33, 169-76.

Hull, J.C., and A. White, 1987, "The Pricing of Options on Assets with Stochastic Volatilities," *Journal of Finance* 42 (June), 281-300.

Johnson, H.E., 1987, "Options on the Maximum or the Minimum of Several Assets," *Journal of Financial and Quantitative Analysis* 22 (September), 277-84.

Margrabe, W., 1978, "The Value of an Option to Exchange One Asset for Another," *Journal of Finance* (March), 177-86.

——, 1982, "A Theory of the Price of a Contingent Claim on *N* Asset Prices," Working paper, School of Government and Business Administration, George Washington University.

Merton, R.C., 1976a, "Option Pricing When Underlying Stock Returns Are Discontinuous," *Journal of Financial Economics* 3, 125-44.

——, 1976b, "The Impact on Option Pricing of Specification Error in the Underlying Stock Price Returns," *Journal of Finance* 31, 333-50.

Scott, L.O., 1987, "Option Pricing When the Variance Changes Randomly: Theory, Estimation, and an Application," *Journal of Financial and Quantitative Analysis* 22 (December), 419-38.

Stoll, H.R., and R.E. Whaley, 1992, *Futures and Options*, Cincinnati, OH: Southwestern Publishing Company.

Stulz, R., 1982, "Options on the Minimum or the Maximum of Two Risky Assets: Analysis and Applications," *Journal of Financial Economics* 10 (July), 161-85.

Wiggins, J.B., 1987, "Option Values Under Stochastic Volatility: Theory and Empirical Estimates," *Journal of Financial Economics* 19, 351-72.

1

The Valuation of Compound Options*

Robert Geske

This paper presents a theory for pricing options on options, or compound options. The method can be generalized to value many corporate liabilities. The compound call option formula derived herein considers a call option on stock which is itself an option on the assets of the firm. This perspective incorporates leverage effects into option pricing and consequently the variance of the rate of return on the stock is not constant as Black-Scholes assumed, but is instead a function of the level of the stock price. The Black-Scholes formula is shown to be a special case of the compound option formula. This new model for puts and calls corrects some important biases of the Black-Scholes model.

1. Introduction

Almost any opportunity with a choice whose value depends on an underlying asset can be viewed as an option. A contract specifies the terms of the opportunity, or details what financial economists call the option's boundary conditions. Many opportunities have a sequential nature, where latter opportunities are available only if earlier opportunities are

University of California, Los Angeles, CA 90024, USA

*This work was completed as a part of *The Valuation of Complex Options,* the author's unpublished Ph.D. dissertation at the University of California, Berkeley. It was presented at the Fifth Annual Meetings (1978) of the European Finance Association in Bergamo, Italy. I thank Mark Rubinstein for originally suggesting this topic and for abundant help along the way. I also thank Vijay Bawa, John Cox, and Barry Goldman for beneficial discussions, Hayne Leland and Mark Garman for comments, and Stoddard Vandersteel for computer simulations. Finally and most recently I would like to thank Jon Ingersoll and Cliff Smith for their suggestions. Typing services were provided by a grant from the Dean Witter Foundation under the auspices of the Institute of Business and Economic Research, University of California, Berkeley.

Received November 1977, revised version received November 1978

Robert Geske, "The Valuation of Compound Options." Reprinted with permission from *Journal of Financial Economics,* 7, 1979.

undertaken. Such is the nature of the compound option or option on an option. Black and Scholes (1973) indicated in their seminal paper that most corporate liabilities may be viewed as options. After deriving a formula for the value of a call option, they discussed the pricing of a firm's common stock and bonds when the stock is viewed as an option on the value of the firm. In this setting, an option on the common stock is an option on an option. They also suggested that when a company has coupon bonds outstanding, the common stock and coupon bonds can be viewed as a compound option, and warrants and stocks that pay constant dividends can also be considered compound options. Geske (1977) has derived formulas for valuing coupon bonds and subordinated debt as compound options, while Roll (1977) has used this technique to value American options on stocks paying constant dividends. Recently, Myers (1977) has suggested that corporate investment opportunities may be represented as options. In that setting, common stock is again a compound option. Insurance policies with sequential premiums offer another application of the compound option technique. This paper develops the theory for dealing with compound option problems.

The main difficulty in using the Black-Scholes differential equation when dealing with compound options is that it assumes that the variance rate of the return on the stock is constant. However, with compound options this variance is not constant, but depends on the level of the stock price, or more fundamentally, on the value of the firm.

In section 2, the valuation equation for a call as a compound option is derived in continuous time, using a hedging argument. The solution contains an additional term than the Black-Scholes (1973) solution, which reflects the firm's debt position. It is this financial leverage which alters the total risk or volatility of the stockholder's equity as the market continuously revalues the firm's prospective cash flows. The derived formula has the desirable attributes of the Black-Scholes model in that it does not depend on knowledge of the expected return on either the stock or the firm's assets. It is shown that an alternate hedging approach, a risk neutral approach, and a discrete time approach all lead to the same result, and some similarities and differences of these approaches are offered. Comparative statics are also presented here. In section 3, a comparison to the Black-Scholes model shows it to be a special case of the compound option model. Changes in the equity value change the firm's leverage, and the stock's return variance is shown to be monotonic increasing with leverage in the compound option model. Thus, this model has the potential to correct several important biases of the Black-Scholes model. It is shown that the hedge ratio between the option and the stock is different for these two models, and that the Black-Scholes hedge is not riskless for any levered firm but instead leads to overinvestment in calls or under investment in stock. Section 4 considers relationships to other option pricing results. Here it is shown that the lognormal distribution for stock returns assumed by Black-Scholes/Merton is not consistent with the Modigliani-Miller theorem (M-M) and risky debt. However, in the compound option setting, the induced return distribution of stock prices, which cannot be lognormal, is consistent. Also, the compound option model's relation to the Cox-Ross (1975) constant elasticity of variance model and warrants as compound options are discussed.

2. The valuation equation

A formula for the value of a call option, C, as a compound option can be derived as a function of the value of the firm, V, if the firm's stock, S, can be viewed as an option on the value of the firm. The following setting describes this perspective. Consider a corporation that has common stock and bonds outstanding. Suppose the bonds are pure discount bonds, giving the holder the right to the face value, M, if the corporation can pay it, with a maturity of T years. Suppose the indenture of the bond stipulates that the firm cannot issue any new senior or equivalent rank claims on the firm, nor pay cash dividends or repurchase shares prior to the maturity of the bonds. Finally, suppose the firm plans to liquidate in T years, pay off the bonds, if possible, and pay any remaining value to the stockholders as a liquidating dividend.[1] Here the bondholders own the firm's assets and have given the stockholders the option to buy the assets back when the bonds mature. Now a call on the firm's stock is an option on an option or a compound option. This situation can be represented functionally as $C = f(S, t) = f(g(V, t), t)$, where t is current time. Therefore, changes in the value of the call can be expressed as a function of changes in the value of the firm and changes in time. If the value of the firm follows a continuous sample path, and if investors can continuously adjust their positions, a riskless hedge can be formed by choosing an appropriate mixture of the firm and call options on the firm's stock.

Merton (1973a) has shown that an American call option will not be exercised early if the underlying asset has no payouts. Thus, the stock depicted as an option on the value of the firm, will not be exercised early because the firm by assumption makes no dividend or coupon payments. Since Merton's proof does not rely on any distributional assumptions the compound call option on the stock will not be prematurely exercised either.

To derive the compound option formula for a call in continuous time, assume that security markets are perfect and competitive, unrestricted short sales of all assets with full use of proceeds is allowed, the risk-free rate of interest is known and constant over time, trading takes place continuously in time, and changes in the value of the firm follow a random walk in continuous time with a variance rate proportional to the square of the value of the firm. Thus, the return on the firm follows a diffusion described by the following stochastic differential equation formalized by Itô:

$$dV/V = \alpha_V dt + \sigma_V dZ_V,$$

---

[1] Most of these restrictions can be relaxed. In particular, the firm does not have to liquidate at date T, but could pay off the bonds and refinance.

where α_V is the instantaneous expected rate of return on the firm per unit time, σ_V^2 is the instantaneous variance of the return on the firm per unit time, and dZ_V is a mean zero normal random variable with variance dt, or a standard Gauss-Weiner process.

Since the call option is a function of the value of the firm and time, $C(V, t)$, its return also follows a diffusion process that can be described by a related stochastic differential equation,

$$dC/C = \alpha_C dt + \sigma_C dZ_C,$$

where α_C is the instantaneous expected rate of return per unit time on the call, σ_C^2 is the instantaneous variance of the return per unit time, and dZ_C is also a standard Gauss-Weiner process. Because of the functional relationship between C and V, α_C, σ_C, and dZ_C are explicitly related to α_V, σ_V, and dZ_V, and by employing either Itô's lemma or a Taylor's series expansion, the dynamics of the call option can be re-expressed as

$$dC = \frac{\partial C}{\partial t}\, dt + \frac{\partial C}{\partial V}\, dV + \frac{1}{2}\, \frac{\partial^2 C}{\partial V^2}\, V^2 \sigma_V^2 dt.$$

As Black-Scholes (1973) demonstrated, a riskless hedge can be created and maintained with two securities, in this case the firm and a call, which requires a net investment that earns the riskless rate of interest. Alternatively, Merton (1973a) showed that a three security riskless hedge portfolio containing an additional risk-free instrument can be created for zero net investment by using the proceeds from short sales and borrowings to finance the long position. Following this alternative, let n_1 be the instantaneous number of dollars invested in the firm, n_2 the instantaneous number of dollars invested in the call, and $n_3 \equiv -(n_1 + n_2)$ the instantaneous number of dollars invested in riskless debt. Now if dH is the instantaneous dollar return to the hedge portfolio, then

$$dH = n_1\left(dV/V\right) + n_2\left(dC/C\right) + n_3 r_F\, dt.$$

Substituting for the stochastic return on the firm and the call yields

$$dH = \left[n_1\left(\alpha_V - r_F\right) + n_2\left(\alpha_C - r_F\right)\right] dt + \left[n_1 \sigma_V + n_2 \sigma_C\right] dZ_V.$$

Since this portfolio requires zero net investment, if it could be made nonstochastic ($dZ_V = 0$), then to avoid arbitrage profits, the expected and realized return on this portfolio must be zero. Therefore, a strategy of choosing n_j^* so that $dZ_V = 0$ implies that $dH = 0$. A non-trivial solution $(n_j^* \neq 0)$ exists if and only if $(\alpha_V - r_F)/\sigma_V = (\alpha_C - r_F)/\sigma_C$. Substituting for α_C and σ_C, and then simplifying yields the familiar partial differential equation,

$$\frac{\partial C}{\partial t} = r_F C - r_F V \frac{\partial C}{\partial V} - \frac{1}{2}\sigma_V^2 V^2 \frac{\partial^2 C}{\partial V^2}. \tag{1}$$

Eq. (1) for a call option on the firm's stock as a function of V and t is subject to a boundary condition at $t = t^*$, the expiration date of this option. The value of the call at expiration is either zero if the stock price, $\tilde{S}_{t*}$, is less than or equal to the exercise price, K, or is equal to the difference between the stock price and the exercise price if the stock price is greater than the exercise price. Algebraically $C_{t*} = \max(0, S_{t*} - K)$. From the perspective of the stock as an option of the value of the firm, this boundary poses a problem not previously encountered in option pricing. The stochastic variable determining the option's value in (1) is not the stock price, $\tilde{S}$, which enters the boundary condition, but instead is the value of the firm. However, since the stock is an option on the value of the firm, it follows a related diffusion and by again using either Itô's lemma or a Taylor's series expansion its dynamics can be expressed as a function of $\tilde{V}$ and t as

$$dS = \frac{\partial S}{\partial t}\, dt + \frac{\partial S}{\partial V}\, dV + \frac{1}{2}\, \frac{\partial^2 S}{\partial V^2}\, V^2 \sigma_V^2\, dt.$$

By constructing a similar hedge between the stock, the firm, and a riskless security, the stock's equilibrium path can be described by the following similar partial differential equation:

$$\frac{\partial S}{\partial t} = r_F S - r_F V \frac{\partial S}{\partial V} - \frac{1}{2} \sigma_V^2 V^2 \frac{\partial^2 S}{\partial V^2}. \tag{2}$$

The boundary condition for eq. (2) at date T, the date the firm's pure discount bonds mature, is that $S_T = 0$ if the value of the firm is less than or equal to the face value of the debt, or if the value of the firm is greater than the face value of the debt, S_T is equal to the difference between the value of the firm and the face value of the debt. The solution to eq. (2) subject to this boundary condition that $S_T = \max(0, V_T - M)$ is independent of eq. (1) and is the well known Black-Scholes equation

$$S = VN_1(k + \sigma_V\sqrt{T-t}) - Me^{-r_F(T-t)}N_1(k), \tag{3}$$

where

$$k = \frac{\ln(V/M) + (r_F - 1/2\sigma_V^2)(T - t)}{\sigma_V\sqrt{T-t}},$$

S = current market value of the stock,
V = current market value of the firm,
M = face value of the debt,
r_F = the risk-free rate of interest,
σ_V^2 = the instantaneous variance of the return on the assets of the firm,
t = current time,
T = maturity date of the debt,
$N_1(\cdot)$ = univariate cumulative normal distribution function.

Eq. (1) is more difficult to solve than (2) because its boundary condition depends on the solution to eq. (2). Essentially both partial differential eqs. (1) and (2) describing the equilibrium paths of the call option and the stock, subject to their respective boundary conditions, must hold simultaneously in the solution to eq. (1). The exercise decision at expiration of the call option on the stock, which depends on the relationship between the stock and the exercise price, can be characterized by a relationship between the value of the firm and the exercise price. Thus, at date $t = t^*$, the value of the firm that makes the holder of an option on the stock indifferent between exercising and not exercising the option is the solution to the integral equation $S_{t*} - K = 0$, where $\tilde{S}_{t*}$ is given in eq. (3) and $\tau = T - t^*$. This partitions the probability measure over the value of the firm at $\overline{V}$, which is defined as that value of the firm which solves the integral equation $S_{t*} - K = 0$. For values of the firm less than $\overline{V}$ the call option on the stock will remain unexercised, while if the value of the firm is greater than $\overline{V}$, the option will be exercised. Given these two partial differential eqs. (1) and (2), and their boundary conditions, the following solution for the value of the compound call option can be found either by Fourier transforms or by separation of variables.[2]

Theorem. Assume that investors are unsatiated, that security markets are perfect and competitive, that unrestricted short sales with full use of proceeds is allowed, that the risk-free rate of interest is known and constant over time, that trading takes place continuously in time, that the firm has no payouts, that changes in the value of the firm follow a random walk in continuous time with a variance rate proportional to the square root of the value of the firm, and that investors agree on this variance σ_V^2, then

$$C = VN_2(h + \sigma_v\sqrt{\tau_1},\ k + \sigma_v\sqrt{\tau_2};\sqrt{\tau_1/\tau_2})$$
$$- Me^{-r_F T_2}N_2(h, k;\sqrt{\tau_1/\tau_2}) - Ke^{-r_F T_1}N_1(h), \tag{4}$$

where

$$h = \frac{\ln(V/\overline{V}) + (r_F - \frac{1}{2}\sigma_V^2)\tau_1}{\sigma_V\sqrt{\tau_1}},$$

$$k = \frac{\ln(V/M) + (r_F - \frac{1}{2}\sigma_V^2)\tau_2}{\sigma_V\sqrt{\tau_2}},$$

$\overline{V}$ = *that value of V such that*

$$S_\tau - K = VN_1(k + \sigma_V\sqrt{\tau}) - Me^{-r_F\tau}N_1(k) - K = 0$$
where $\tau = T - t^*$,

[2]This problem can also be solved by the Cox-Ross (1975) technique of assuming a risk-neutral set of preferences, or by Rubinstein's (1976) approach to discounting uncertain income streams. For a third general approach to these valuation problems see Garman (1976).

and the notation not previously specified is: C = current value of the call option, and N₂ (·) = bivariate cumulative normal distribution function with h and k as upper integral limits and $\sqrt{\tau_1/\tau_2}$ as the correlation coefficient, where $\tau_1 = t^* - t$ and $\tau_2 = T - t$.

Proof. See appendix.

There are several alternate ways to derive the formula for the compound call option. All approaches are conceptually valuation by duplication. The essence of duplication as noted by Ross (1978) is that any asset of unknown value can be comparatively priced by finding or creating an 'identical' asset whose value is either known or can be determined.[3] An option can be readily valued by duplication because it is a derivative asset, or an asset whose value is derived from the optioned asset. The cash flows of the option can be duplicated by a hedge containing the optioned asset and a riskless security. An alternative to the previous hedge between the call and the firm for deriving the compound option formula would be the more traditional hedge between the call and the stock. If the stock follows a diffusion process, then the maintenance of a riskless hedge leads to the familiar Black-Scholes (1973) partial differential equation

$$\frac{\partial C}{\partial t} = r_F C - r_F S \frac{\partial C}{\partial S} - \frac{1}{2} \sigma_S^2 S^2 \frac{\partial^2 C}{\partial S^2}. \tag{5}$$

However, if the stock is considered to be an option on the value of the firm, then with the previous assumptions eq. (3) relating S and V results. This equation implies that both S and σ_S are functions of V and t, and that $\sigma_S(V, t) = \{(\partial S/\partial V)(V/S)\} \sigma_V$. Thus, σ_S is not constant as Black-Scholes/Merton assumed,[4] but instead is a particular function of $S(V, t)$. Solving eq. (5) subject to the boundary condition for the option at $t = t^*$ and using the functional relationship between $S(V, t)$ and $\sigma_S(S(V), t)$ also yields eq. (4).[5]

Later Cox-Ross (1975) recognized that if a riskless hedge could be created and maintained then the transformation solution to the partial differential equation was not necessary. They argued that since no explicit use was made of preferences by Black-Scholes/Merton any set of preferences consistent with the distributional assumptions would be satisfactory. In particular, in a risk-neutral world where all assets earn the same expected rate of return, the riskless rate, the current value of an option is the following riskless discounted expected value of the option at expiration:

---

[3] An obvious dilemma occurs when valuing the most basic set of securities.
[4] See section 3 of this paper for elaboration about $\sigma_s(V, t)$.
[5] This result implies that the Black-Scholes equation with the 'proper' variance and stock price yields the compound option equation, a fact which enhances the significance of implicit volatility estimates.

$$C = \mathrm{e}^{-rF(t^*-t)} E\{\max(S_{t^*} - K, 0)\}. \tag{6}$$

Given the assumed relation between the stock and the firm, if the conditional distribution for the value of the firm at the option's expiration date is known, $F(V_{t^*}|V)$, then substituting from eq.(3) for $S(V, t^*)$, eq. (6) becomes

$$C = \mathrm{e}^{-rF\,T_1}\left\{ \int_K^\infty VN_1(k + \sigma_V\sqrt{\tau_1 - \tau_2})F(V_{t^*}|V)\,\mathrm{d}V \right.$$

$$\left. - \int_K^\infty Me^{-rF(T_2 - T_1)}N_1(k)F(V_{t^*}|V)\,\mathrm{d}V - \int_K^\infty KF(V_{t^*}|V)\,\mathrm{d}V \right\}. \tag{7}$$

Evaluating these integrals yields the compound option eq. (4).

Recently Rubinstein (1976) developed a discrete time, preference specific, general equilibrium approach to valuing uncertain income streams and then used this to show that the Black-Scholes/Merton option pricing equation does not depend on the maintenance of a riskless hedge. He demonstrates that under certain conditions individual's demands can be aggregated so that the market's return space is spanned by an identifiable linear operator or vector of contingent claims which allows valuation by duplication. Letting $P(s(t))$ be a set of continuous random variables, not necessarily unique but containing the same price and probability information for all securities, Rubinstein shows that the value of a European call option on stock with the previous boundary condition is equal to the conditional expectation

$$C = E[(S_{t^*} - K)P(s(t))|S_{t^*} > K]. \tag{8}$$

When stock is considered an option on the firm, its value is the conditional expectation $S = E[V_T - M)P(s(t))|\tilde{V}_T > M]$. With the major assumptions on tastes and beliefs of Constant Proportional Risk-Averse utility functions (CPRA) and joint lognormality between $\tilde{P}$ and $\tilde{V}$, and with proper stationarity conditions, eq. (3) for S obtains.[6] Substituting this result into eq. (8) yields the following integral equation:

$$C = \int_K^\infty VN_1(k + \sigma_V\sqrt{\tau_2 - \tau_1})PF(P, V)\,\mathrm{d}P\,\mathrm{d}V$$

$$- \int_K^\infty Mr_F^{-(T_2 - T_1)}N_1(k)PF(P, V)\,\mathrm{d}P\,\mathrm{d}V - \int_K^\infty KPF(P, V)\,\mathrm{d}P\,\mathrm{d}V, \tag{9}$$

where $F(P, V)$ is the joint probability distribution function of $\tilde{P}$ and $\tilde{V}$. Evaluating these integrals yields the discrete version of the compound option eq. (4).

---

[6]See Rubinstein (1976) for further details. Although individuals are not required to have identical beliefs, a representative individual must exist. Here $P(s(t))$ is shortened to P. The discrete version of eq. (3) is similar except e^{-rFt} is replaced by r_F^{-t}. The joint lognormality assumption is not uncommon in finance. See Merton (1973b) for another example of this assumption.

One important distinction between the discrete time and continuous time derivations of option valuation formulas pertains to investor's expectations of the variance. Agreement about σ^2 is necessary in the continuous time models but not in the discrete time version if heterogeneous investor's beliefs can be meaningfully aggregated. The continuous time model collapses if there is the slightest disagreement about the variance. The ability to create a riskless hedge will induce those in disagreement to take infinite positions, and no market price equilibrium can be achieved. It is true that if by assumption all investors use the same past data the same way to estimate the variance there will be no disagreement. However, in the discrete formulation, as long as a representative individual exists, instead of using past price changes, investors may have possibly different priors about the variance which on 'average' are exactly correct, and the discrete model will be correct. This is because the discrete time approach does not depend on the formation and maintenance of a riskless hedge.[7]

The response of the compound option model to changes in the value of its arguments conforms to some but not all of the restrictions placed on the option price by the arguments of Merton.[8]

(1) As the value of the firm rises so does the call value

$$\partial C / \partial V = N_2(h + \sigma_V \sqrt{\tau_1}, \ k + \sigma_V \sqrt{\tau_2}; \sqrt{\tau_1/\tau_2}) \equiv N_2(\cdot) > 0. \qquad (10)$$

Although increases in the value of the firm are divided, but not usually proportionally, between the debt and the equity, any increase in V increases the expected payoff to the option.

(2) As the face value of the debt increases, the call value falls,

$$\partial C / \partial M = -\mathrm{e}^{-r_F T_2} N_2(h; k; \sqrt{\tau_1/\tau_2}) < 0. \qquad (11)$$

Even though the increased leverage raises the variance of the stock, σ_s^2, which increases the call price, the reduced equity value lowers the call price, and this first order equity effect dominates the second order variance effect.

(3) As the time to maturity of the debt increases, the call price increases,

$$\frac{\partial C}{\partial T} = \frac{N_2(\cdot)}{N_1(k + \sigma_V \sqrt{\tau_2})} M \mathrm{e}^{-r_F T_2} \left[N_1'(k) \frac{\sigma_V}{2\sqrt{\tau_2}} + r_F N_1(k) \right] > 0. \qquad (12)$$

[7] If individuals are Bayesian and realize there is estimation risk in $\bar{\sigma}$ then they would not take infinite positions, but this is not consistent with the continuous time assumptions.
[8] See Merton (1973a, pp. 143-150). Use Liebnitz's rule for differentiation of an integral equation here. The intuition of these partial derivatives works through the stock price, S, which is not an explicit argument of eq. (4).

This reduces the present value of the debt, reducing the leverage and again the increased equity value dominates the reduced equity risk.[9]

(4) As the riskless rate of interest rises, the call price rises,

$$\frac{\partial C}{\partial r_F} = \frac{N_2(\cdot)}{N_1(k + \sigma_V \sqrt{\tau_2})} \, M\tau_2 e^{-r_F \tau_2} N_1(k) > 0. \tag{13}$$

When the riskless interest rate rises the present value of the debt and of the option's exercise price fall, both increasing C. Even though σ_s falls as S rises, which should decrease C, the first order equity effect again dominates.

(5) As the variance rate of the firm rises, so does the call price,

$$\frac{\partial C}{\partial \sigma_V^2} = \frac{N_2(\cdot)}{N_1(k + \sigma_V \sqrt{\tau_2})} \, M e^{-r_F \tau_2} N_1'(k) \frac{\sqrt{\tau_2}}{2\sigma_V} > 0. \tag{14}$$

The increased variance rate of the firm raises the value of the equity as an option on the firm, which increases the call value.

(6) As the call's exercise price rises, the call price falls,

$$\partial C/\partial K = -e^{-r_F \tau_1} N_1(h) < 0. \tag{15}$$

By dominance the value of the call in every state after K increases is less than or equal to its value before the exercise price change.

(7) As the time to expiration increases, the value of the call rises,

$$\partial C/\partial t^* > 0. \tag{16}$$

This reflects the decreased present value of the future exercise price as t^* increases.

3. Comparison to the Black-Scholes model

The Black-Scholes model is a special case of the compound option model. To see this note that eq. (4) for valuing a call option as a compound option reduces to the Black-Scholes equation whenever the call is written on the equity of an unlevered firm. This occurs in eq. (4) whenever the present value of the firm's debt is zero, or when $T = \infty$ or $M = 0$. In either case the stockholder's option to repurchase the firm from the bondholders disappears. Furthermore, if the option on the stock expires coincident with the maturity of the debt ($t^* = T$), the second option merges with the first, and the exercise price of this then simple option is the sum of the face value of the debt and the striking price of the option ($M + K$).

This result for pricing compound options incorporates the effects of short

---

[9]$N'(k) \equiv (1/\sqrt{2\pi}) e^{-k^2}/2 =$ the standard normal density at k.

or long term changes in the firm's capital structure on the value of a call option. To see this notice that as the stock price changes, if the firm does not react, the debt-equity ratio of the firm changes, which should affect the riskiness of the firm's stock.[10] Whereas the Black-Scholes model assumes that the variance of the stock's return is not a function of the stock price, in the compound option model the variance of the return on the stock is inversely related to the stock price. As the stock price falls (rises), the firm's debt-equity ratio rises (falls), and this increased (decreased) risk is reflected by a rise (fall) in the variance of the returns on the stock. This can be demonstrated explicitly by taking the instantaneous covariance of the instantaneous return on the stock with itself and noting that changes in the stock price are perfectly correlated with changes in the value of the firm. So the instantaneous standard deviation of the return on the stock is, as given previously,

$$\sigma_S = \left(\frac{\partial S}{\partial V} \frac{V}{S} \right) \sigma_V = \epsilon_S \sigma_V, \tag{17}$$

where $\epsilon_S \equiv ((\partial S/\partial V)(V/S))$ is the elasticity of the stock price with respect to the value of the firm. The partial derivative of the instantaneous standard deviation of the stock's return with respect to the stock price is

$$\frac{\partial \sigma_s}{\partial S} = - \frac{V}{S^2} \left(\frac{\partial S}{\partial V} \right) \sigma_V = - \frac{V}{S^2} N_1(k + \sigma_V \sqrt{\tau_2}) \sigma_V < 0.$$

Thus, in the short run, when fluctuations in the stock price are the main determinants of variations in the debt-equity ratio, percentage changes in the stock's return will be larger when prices have fallen than when they have risen. Since the value of an option is monotonic increasing in the volatility of the optioned asset, if the stock price has fallen (risen), the increased (decreased) variance of the returns on the stock will act to raise (lower) the price of the option on the stock. Thus, variations in the firm's capital structure induced by changes in the value of the firm as the market continuously revalues the firm's prospective cash flows are transmitted through the variance of the stock to affect the price of an option on the stock.

Since the variance of the stock is a function of the stock price in the compound option model, it is accordingly a function of all of the variables which determine the price of the stock, including T, the maturity date of the firm's debt. As the time to expiration of the option on the stock decreases, the life of the stock as an option on the value of the firm is also decreasing. Because the price of any call option is monotonic increasing in time to

[10] For expositional purposes of this argument, assume throughout that the firm does not react to stock price changes. Also M does not equal zero even if the firm has no long term debt because the liability side of most firms' balance sheets includes short term debt.

expiration, as T decreases, S does also.[11] This decrease of S causes an increase in the firm's debt-equity ratio, increasing the riskiness of the return on the firm's stock. The increase in the variance of the stock will act to increase the value of an option on the stock.

These leverage effects introduced into option pricing by the compound option model are not without empirical costs. One advantage of the Black-Scholes option pricing model is that only five input variables are required to predict option prices: $C^{BS} = f(S, \sigma_s, r_F, t^*, K)$. All of these variables are either known or directly observable except σ_s, the instantaneous variance of the stock return. The compound option formula requires seven input variables: $C^{CO} = g(V, \sigma_V, r_F, t^*, T, K, M)$. The two extra variables necessary to capture the leverage effects are M, the face value of the debt, and T, the maturity date of the debt. Three of these variables, r_F, t^*, and K, are directly observable and the other four can be computed. V and σ_V can be found either by defining $V = S + B$, where B is the market value of the firm's debt, and using empirical data, or by solving for V and σ_V from past stock price data, using $S(V, \sigma_V)$ and $\sigma_s(V, \sigma_V)$.[12] The face value of the firm's debt, M, and the maturity of the debt, T, can be read directly from the balance sheet, or for firms with more complex capital structures, surrogates can be constructed.[13] As in the Black-Scholes model, the significant unobservable variables not necessary for pricing compound options are the expected rates of return on the firm, the stock, and the option, and any measure of market risk aversion.

Merton (1973a) proved two theorems which depended on the assumption that the return distribution of the stock is independent of the stock price level. The first theorem was that options are homogeneous of degree one in stock price and exercise price, and the second theorem showed that options are convex in the stock price. Although the stock price does not directly enter eq. (4) for the value of a call option, neither of these theorems is necessarily valid in the compound option model, since the distribution of stock returns is dependent on the level of stock prices. However, an analog to these theorems is valid if the distribution of changes in the value of the firm is independent of the level of the firm value. Following Merton (1973a) it is straightforward to show first that the value of the call is homogeneous of degree one in the value of the firm, V, the face value of the debt, M,

[11]The $\partial S/\partial T = M e^{-r_F \tau_2} \{ (\sigma_V/2\sqrt{\tau_2}) N_1'(k) + N_1(k) r_F \} > 0$. Unlike all American options, European puts are not monotonic increasing in time to expiration.

[12]It may be better to estimate r_F since it does change stochastically. In addition, estimating the variance implicitly from yesterday's option price would be a biased way to test either option formula. This bias may be diminished by using a different option. Recall that the Black-Scholes model economizes on the leverage parameters by assuming they are zero.

[13]All the firm's debt could be moved to a point in time which is the average maturity for that firm's industry, or possibly this critical time could be found using duration. Morris (1975) found the average maturity for 159 industrial firms, using both short term and long term debt weighted by a percent of total value to be about 6.4 years.

and the call's exercise price, K, and second that options are convex in the value of the firm.[14] Since this linear homogeneity can be demonstrated without knowledge of the solution for the compound call option given in eq. (4), this property can assist in the solution by establishing its form. By Euler's theorem, since C is linearly homogeneous in V, M, and K, the solution to eq. (1) subject to eq. (2) and both boundary conditions must be of the following form:

$$C(V, t) = V\frac{\partial C}{\partial V} + M\frac{\partial C}{\partial M} + K\frac{\partial C}{\partial K}. \tag{18}$$

The solution given in eq. (4) complies with this form.

An important concept in option pricing models is the hedge ratio, defined as the partial derivative of the option price with respect to the stock price. The hedge ratio indicates the number of call contracts written (bought) against round lots of stock bought (shorted) to maintain a riskless hedge. In the compound option model this hedge ratio between the stock and the option can be found by multiplying the partial derivative of the option price with respect to the value of the firm by the reciprocal of the partial derivative of the stock price, given by eq. (3), with respect to the value of the firm, so

$$\frac{\partial C}{\partial S} = \frac{\partial C}{\partial V}\bigg/\frac{\partial S}{\partial V} = \frac{N_2(h + \sigma_V\sqrt{\tau_1},\ k + \sigma_V\sqrt{\tau_2};\sqrt{\tau_1/\tau_2})}{N_1(k + \sigma_V\sqrt{\tau_2})}. \tag{19}$$

This differs from the hedge ratio in the Black-Scholes model,[15] which is N_1 $(h + \sigma_V\sqrt{\tau_1})$, and the two are only equal when the firm has no leverage. Thus for options written on the equity of levered firms, if the compound option model is correct, a Black-Scholes hedge will not be riskless. It is easily verified that whenever the firm has leverage, the stock-option hedge ratio from the compound option model is greater than the Black-Scholes hedge ratio. Therefore, fewer call contracts must be written (bought) to offset long (short) round lot positions in the stock. To see this, first note that, given the value of the firm at a particular point in time, t, $N_2(\cdot)$ may be loosely interpreted as a measure of the joint probability that at t^* the value of the firm will be greater than $\overline{V}$ so that $S_{t^*} > K$ and the option is exercised, and at T the value of the firm will be greater than the face value of the debt so that the firm is not bankrupt. Since the correlation between these two events, $\sqrt{\tau_1/\tau_2}$, is always positive or zero, $N_2(\cdot) \geqq N_1(h + \sigma_V\sqrt{\tau_1})N_1(k + \sigma_V\sqrt{\tau_2})$, and the result is established. Thus if the compound option model is

[14]The proofs of these two theorems, given in Merton (1973a, pp. 149-150), are not repeated here. It follows that the stock is linearly homogeneous in V and M, and thus that the compound call option is also implicitly linearly homogeneous in the stock price, even though the stock's return distribution is dependent on the level of S.

[15]See Black-Scholes (1973) for a description of their hedge ratio. In h, (the integral limit of their hedge ratio), $V/\overline{V}$ is replaced by S/K and σ_V by σ_S, which is the case for an unlevered firm since $V = S$, $\overline{V} = K$, and $\sigma_V = \sigma_S$.

the correct way to capture the leverage effects and subsequent non-stationarity in the stock's instantaneous return variance, then hedgers using the Black-Scholes hedge ratio do not have riskless positions.[16] Such hedgers would be systematically over-investing in calls or under-investing in stock, depending on the hedge.

The introduction of these leverage effects adds a new dimension to theoretical option pricing. Any change in the stock price will cause a discrepancy between the compound option value and the Black-Scholes value. The qualitative discrepancies between these two formulas corresponds to what practitioners and empiricists observe in the market—namely, that the Black-Scholes formula underprices deep-out-of-the-money options and near-maturity options, and it overprices deep-in-the-money options.[17] Since options are issued near-the-money, the stock price must undergo a considerable rise or fall before either deep-in or deep-out-of-the-money options will exist. The change in the firm's leverage as the stock price changes will cause the variance of the stock in the compound option model to change in the direction necessary to alleviate these biases. This same leverage effect also acts in the proper direction to correct the time to maturity bias.

Since both the compound option and Black-Scholes models assume that the stock follows a diffusion process, the probability of deep-in and deep-out-of-the-money options existing simultaneously on one stock is small. Casual empiricism of quoted option prices substantiates this view and also offers a possible check on the frequency of stocks that may exhibit a jump process. The near-to-expiration bias complicates the problem because if the diffusion assumption is correct then the probable time elapsed before a stock price could diffuse along the path required for the existence of either deep-in or deep-out-of-the-money biases may also make these options 'near-to-expiration'. Furthermore, the nature of the actual conditions under which these biases are observed by market makers and empiricists is important to understanding the problem.[18] Also tests using closing prices which are possibly invalid due to market makers manipulating their margin requirements may cause these biases.

The key to whether the compound option model dominates the Black-Scholes model depends upon both models' variance assumptions. If the variance of the firm is more stationary than the variance of the firm's

[16]See Rosenberg (1972), Blume (1971), Black (1975), and more recently Schmalensee and Trippi (1978) for evidence on the non-stationarity of σ_S. In particular Black and Schmalensee and Trippi document the inverse relationship between S and σ_S.
[17]See Black (1975). He discusses some of the biases observed when comparing the Black-Scholes model to actual prices. Also see Black and Scholes (1972). Merton (1976) claims the model underprices deep-in-the-money options.
[18]Discussions in September 1976 with market makers at the Chicago Board Options Exchange (CBOE) who use the Black-Scholes model as one guide for trading decisions revealed no consensus about how these deep-in and out-of-the-money biases are observed.

equity, which the compound option model predicts, then the compound option model is probably a more fundamental model.

Although the compound option model offers an explanation for these observed biases of the Black-Scholes model, it is not the only explanation. Merton (1976) showed that jump processes might explain some biases, while Geske (1978) showed that a stochastic dividend yield might explain the deep-out-of-the-money bias, and Roll (1977) showed that the dividend effect on American options might explain the deep-in-the-money bias.

4. On relationships to other option pricing results

The assumption that stock price changes follow a stationary random walk in continuous time, and thus the stock price distribution at the end of any finite interval is lognormal, is a frequent assumption in finance, especially in option pricing models. However, if the M-M theorem is correct, and if the firm is financed with risky debt, then the implication is that future stock price changes cannot be lognormal, regardless of the probability distribution for changes in the value of the firm. The reason is that with risky debt there must be some future values of V such that the firm must liquidate to pay off a portion of the debt, and for these low V's the value of the equity must be zero, which is not allowable for standard lognormal random variables. *A fortiori*, future stock price changes cannot be standard lognormal if changes in the value of the firm are assumed stationary lognormal as in the compound option model, even if the debt is riskless.

In the compound option model, the stock's return distribution depends on the stock price. Notice that since changes in the value of the firm are assumed to be stationary, it is evident from eq. (17) that the variance of stock price changes will generally be non-stationary.[19] This elasticity of the stock price with respect to the value of the firm, $\epsilon_S = (\partial S/\partial V)(V/S)$, is always greater than or equal to one, and as V approaches zero ($S \rightarrow 0$ also), this elasticity approaches infinity. Thus, the instantaneous variance of the value of the equity is always greater than the instantaneous variance of the value of the firm.[20]

The compound option model can be related to the Cox-Ross (1975) constant elasticity of variance models.[21] In these diffusion models, the instantaneous variance of the stock price is assumed to be given by $\sigma_S^2 = S^\beta \sigma^2$, where σ^2 is the instantaneous diffusion coefficient of the Weiner process and $0 \leq \beta \leq 2$. Thus the elasticity of the variance with respect to the stock price is bounded. Since $\beta = 2$ implies the diffusion process is lognormal, the Black-Scholes model is one special case of these constant elasticity of variance models. In the compound option model the elasticity of the instantanteous variance of stock returns with respect to the stock price is not a constant. However, if the

[19]Galai and Masulis (1976) reason that the firm's systematic risk, β_S is not stationary when the stock is an option on the value of the firm.

[20]Repeated use of l'Hopital's rule confirms that $\lim_{V \rightarrow 0} \epsilon_s = \infty$.

[21]For a discussion of these models, see Cox-Ross (1975) and Cox (1975).

elasticity of the stock price with respect to the value of the firm, ϵ_S, is assumed to equal a power function of S, then the compound option model reduces to a form of the constant elasticity of variance models. In particular, if $\epsilon_s = (\partial S/\partial V)(V/S) = S^{-\gamma(V)}$, where $0 < \gamma(V) < 1$, then the compound option model becomes a constant elasticity of variance model,[22] where $dS = \psi_s dt + S^{\beta(V)/2}\sigma_V dZ$ and $\beta(V) \equiv 2(1 - \gamma(V))$, and the instantaneous variance of the stock price, S, is $\sigma_s^2 = S^{\beta(V)} \sigma_V^2$.

Under certain situations, warrants can be treated as compound options. Since a warrant generally has a longer life than a call option, the valuation adjustments of the compound option model may be more significant for warrants than for options. Here the requirement that the expiration of the warrant be less than or equal to the maturity of the bonds may be more restricted, particularly if an average T is used. The parameter T may cause an additional measurement problem, since it could conceivably change over time as the firm pays off old or issues new debt. Such changes in T would change the value of the firm's stock and would thus change the value of an option on the stock. If we assume that the firm matches the life of its assets with the maturity of its liabilities, replacing old with new debt so that average T remains constant over time, this remedies the problem unless shifts in technology cause changes in the average life of the firm's assets.

5. Summary

An extension to the theory for valuing contingent claims has been developed, and a new formula was derived for the value of a call option as a compound option which introduces leverage effects into put-call option pricing. Since many corporate liabilities with sequential opportunities fit this compound option mold, their solutions can also be approached in this fashion. Thus, the theory of compound options can be used to price out the capital structure of the firm.

[22]The assumption that $\epsilon_s = S^{-\gamma}$ follows from Thorpe (1976). Since $(\partial S/\partial V)V = S^{\beta(V)/2} = N_1(k + \sigma_V\sqrt{\tau_2})$, then the elasticity of the variance is $\beta(V) = 2\ln(N_1(k + \sigma_V\sqrt{\tau_2}))V/\ln S$. Thorpe simulates this for various intervals of V and finds that $\beta(V)$ does vary with V and is less than 2 for the ranges tested.

Appendix

Proof. In order to solve eqs. (1) and (2), subject to their boundary conditions, separate the variables and obtain equations with known Fourier integrals.[23] Thus, define $j(a, b)$ such that

$$C(V, t) \equiv e^{-r_F \tau_1} j(a,b),$$

where

$$a \equiv (2/\sigma_V^2)(r_F - 1/2\sigma_V^2)(\ln(V/\bar{V}) + (r_F - 1/2\sigma_V^2)\tau_1),$$

and

$$b \equiv (2/\sigma_V^2)(r_F - 1/2\sigma_V^2)\tau_1,$$

and define $d(u, p)$ such that

$$S(V, t) \equiv e^{-r_F \tau_2} d(u, p),$$

where

$$u \equiv (2/\sigma_V^2)(r_F - 1/2\sigma_V^2)(\ln(V/M) + (r_F - 1/2\sigma_V^2)\tau_2),$$

and

$$p \equiv (2/\sigma_V^2)(r_F - 1/2\sigma_V^2)\tau_2.$$

Substituting these definitions into eqs. (1) and (2), respectively, changes (1) into $\partial j(a,b)/\partial b = \partial^2 j(a,b)/\partial a^2$ subject to the boundary condition $j(a, 0)$ equals zero if $a \leq 0$ or $j(a, 0)$ equals $K[e^{a(1/2\sigma_V^2)/(r_F - 1/2\sigma_V^2)} - 1]$ if $a > 0$, and changes (2) into $\partial d(u, p)/\partial p = \partial^2 d(u, p)/\partial u^2$ subject to the boundary condition $d(u, 0) = 0$ if $u \leq 0$ or $d(u, 0)$ equals $M[e^{u(1/2\sigma_V^2)/(r_F - 1/2\sigma_V^2)} - 1]$ if $u > 0$. Implementing the Fourier integrals, rechanging the variables, and substituting the solution given in eq. (3) for $S(V, t)$ into $C(V, t)$ yields the following equation:

$$C(V, t) = V \int_{a\sqrt{2b}}^{\infty} \int_{-u/\sqrt{2p}}^{\infty} \frac{e^{-\frac{1}{2}(q - \sigma_V \sqrt{\tau_2})^2}}{\sqrt{2\pi}} \frac{e^{-\frac{1}{2}(z - \sigma_V \sqrt{\tau_1})^2}}{\sqrt{2\pi}} dq \, dz$$

$$-Me^{-r_F \tau_2} \int_{-a/\sqrt{2b}}^{\infty} \int_{b/\sqrt{2p}}^{\infty} \frac{e^{-\frac{1}{2}q^2}}{\sqrt{2\pi}} \frac{e^{-\frac{1}{2}(z - \sigma_V \sqrt{\tau_1})^2}}{\sqrt{2\pi}} dq \, dz$$

$$-Ke^{-r_F \tau_1} \int_{-a/\sqrt{2b}}^{\infty} \frac{e^{-z^2/2}}{\sqrt{2\pi}} dz.$$

[23]See Churchill (1963, pp. 152-156) for reference.

To evaluate these three integrals, note that the bivariate normal distribution function is the definite integral solution to the following density function, where x and y are any two bivariate normal random variables and ϱ is their correlation:

$$N_2(h, k; \varrho) = \int\limits_{-\infty}^{h} \int\limits_{-\infty}^{k} f(x, y)\, dx\, dy = \int\limits_{-\infty}^{h} \int\limits_{-\infty}^{k} f(y|x)f(x)\, dy\, dx$$

$$= \frac{1}{2\pi\sqrt{1-\varrho^2}} \int\limits_{-\infty}^{h} \int\limits_{-\infty}^{k} \exp\left\{-\frac{1}{2}\left(\frac{x^2 - 2\varrho xy + y^2}{1-\varrho^2}\right)\right\} dx\, dy.$$

Defining $y = w\sqrt{1-\varrho^2} + \varrho x$ and changing variables yields

$$N_2(h, k; \varrho) = \int\limits_{-\infty}^{h} \frac{1}{\sqrt{2\pi}} e^{-x^2/2} \left[\int\limits_{-\infty}^{\lambda-\varrho x/\sqrt{1-\varrho^2}} \frac{1}{\sqrt{2\pi}} e^{-w^2/2}\, dw\right] dx$$

$$= \int\limits_{-\infty}^{h} f(x) N_1\left(\frac{k-\varrho x}{\sqrt{1-\varrho^2}}\right) dx.$$

Thus, evaluating the above three integrals[24] yields eq. (4). Q.E.D.

[24]For reference see Abramowitz and Stegum (1970) or Owen (1957).

References

Abramowitz, M. and I. Stegum, 1970, Handbook of mathematical functions, NBS Applied Mathematical Series 55, 9th printing, Nov. (National Bureau of Standards, Washington, DC).

Black, F., 1975, Fact and fantasy in the use of options, Financial Analysts Journal, July-Aug.

Black, F., 1976, Studies of stock price volatility changes, Proceedings of the Journal of American Statistical Association.

Black, F. and J. Cox, 1976, Valuing corporate securities: Some effects of bond indenture conditions, Journal of Finance, May.

Black, F. and M. Scholes, 1972, The valuation of option contracts and a test of market efficiency, Journal of Finance, May.

Black, F. and M. Scholes, 1973, The pricing of options and corporate liabilities, Journal of Political Economy, May-June.

Blume, M., 1971, On the assessment of risk, The Journal of Finance, March.

Churchill, R., 1963, Fourier series and boundary value problems (McGraw-Hill, New York).

Cox, J., 1975, Notes on option pricing I: Constant elasticity of variance diffusions, Unpublished preliminary draft (Stanford, CA).

Cox, J. and R. Ross, 1975, The pricing of options for jump processes, Rodney L. White working paper no. 2-75 (University of Pennsylvania, Philadelphia, PA).

Cox, J. and S. Ross, 1976, The valuation of options for alternative stochastic processes, Journal of Financial Economics, Jan.-March.

Galai, D. and R. Masulis, 1976, The option pricing model and the risk factor of stock, Journal of Financial Economics, Jan.-March.

Garman, M., 1976, A general theory of asset valuation under diffusion state processes, Research Program in Finance working paper no. 50 (Institute of Business and Economic Research, University of California, Berkeley, CA).

Geske, R., 1977, The valuation of corporate liabilities as compound options, Journal of Financial and Quantitative Analysis, Nov.

Geske, R., 1978, The pricing of options with stochastic dividend yield, Journal of Finance, May.

Merton, R. C., 1973a, Theory of rational option pricing, Bell Journal of Economics and Management Science, Spring.

Merton, R. C., 1973b, An intertemporal capital asset pricing model, Econometrica, Sept.

Merton, R. C., 1976, Option pricing when underlying stock returns are discontinuous, Journal of Financial Economics, Jan.-March.

Morris, J., 1975, An empirical investigation of the corporate debt maturity structure, Rodney L. White working paper no. 5-75 (University of Pennsylvania, Philadelphia, PA).

Myers, S., 1977, Determinants of corporate borrowing, Journal of Financial Economics, Nov.

Owen, D. B., 1957, The bivariate normal probability distribution, Research report (Sandia Corporation).

Roll, R., 1977, An analytical valuation formula for unprotected American call options on stocks with known dividends, Journal of Financial Economics, Nov.

Rosenberg, B., 1972, The behavior of random variables and the distribution of security prices, Research Program in Finance working paper no. 11 (Institute of Business and Economic Research, University of California, Berkeley, CA).

Ross, S., 1978, A simple approach to the valuation of risky streams, Journal of Business, July.

Rubinstein, M., 1976, The valuation of uncertain income streams and the pricing of options. Bell Journal of Economics, Autumn.

Schmalensee, R. and R. Trippi, 1978, Common stock volatility expectations implied by option premia, Journal of Finance, March.

Thorpe, E., 1976, Common stock volatilities in option formulas. Paper presented at the Seminar on the Analysis of Security Prices, May (University of Chicago, Chicago, IL).

2

The Value of an Option to Exchange One Asset for Another

William Margrabe*

I. Introduction

Some common financial arrangements are equivalent to options to exchange one risky asset for another: the investment adviser's performance incentive fee, the general margin account, the exchange offer, and the standby commitment. Yet the literature does not discuss the theory of such an option.[1] In this paper, I develop an equation for the value of the option to exchange one risky asset for another. My theory grows out of the brilliant Black-Scholes (1973) solution to the longstanding call option pricing problem—which assumes that the price of a riskless discount bond grew exponentially at the riskless interest rate—and Merton's (1973) extension—in which the discount bond's value is stochastic until maturity.

In section II, I develop the pricing equation for a European-type option to exchange one asset for another. In section III, I show that such an option is worth more alive than dead, which implies that its owner will not exercise it until the last possible moment. Thus, the formula for the European option is also valid for its American counterpart. Since such an option is not only a call, but also a put, the formula is a closed-form expression for the value of a special sort of American put option. I derive the put-call parity theorem for American options of this sort. Section IV contains applications of the

*Lecturer, Department of Finance, The Wharton School, University of Pennsylvania. The author thanks Stephen Ross, Jeffrey Jaffe, and Randolph Westerfield for helpful discussions; Sudipto Bhattacharya, a referee for this *Journal,* for useful comments; and the Rodney L. White Center for Financial Research for assistance in preparing the manuscript.

[1] The Black-Scholes (1973) breakthrough spawned a burgeoning literature on the theory of option pricing—with applications. Smith (1976) comprehensively reviews these articles.

William Margrabe, "The Value of an Option to Exchange One Asset for Another."
Reprinted with permission from *The Journal of Finance,* Vol. XXXIII, No. 1, March 1978.

model to financial arrangements commonplace in the real world: the investment adviser's performance incentive fee, the general margin account, the exchange offer, and the standby commitment. In the last section, I summarize the findings.

II. The Mathematical Problem and Solution

Since this problem and its solution are extensions of the Black-Scholes work, I will use their notation and assumptions as much as possible. The capital market is perfect, of course. Let x_1 and x_2 be the prices of assets one and two. Assume there are no dividends: all returns come from capital gains. The rate of return on each asset is given by

$$dx_i = x_i [\alpha_i dt + v_i dz_i] \quad (i = 1, 2),$$

where dz_i is a Wiener process. That is, the rate of return is an "Ito process."[2] The correlation between the Wiener processes dz_1 and dz_2 is ϱ_{12}. Further assume that α_i and v_i are constants.

We want the equation for the value $w(x_1, x_2, t)$ of a European-type option which can be exercised only at t^*, when it will yield $x_1 - x_2$ if exercised or nothing if not exercised. This option is simultaneously a call option on asset one with exercise price x_2 and a put option on asset two with exercise price x_1. Of course, the owner exercises his option if and only if this brings him a positive return. This implies the initial condition

$$w(x_1, x_2, t^*) = \max(0, x_1 - x_2). \tag{1}$$

The option is worth at least zero, and no more than x_1, if assets one and two are worth at least zero:

$$0 \le w(x_1, x_2, t) \le x_1. \tag{2}$$

The option buyer can hedge his position by selling $w_1 \equiv \partial w / \partial x_1$ units of asset one short and buying $- w_2 \equiv - \partial w / \partial x_2$ units of asset two. The pricing formula $w(\cdot)$ must be linear homogeneous in x_1 and x_2,[3] so the hedger's investment will be

$$w - w_1 x_1 - w_2 x_2 = 0, \tag{3}$$

by Euler's Theorem.

[2] See McKean (1969) for a discussion of the theory of Ito processes and Merton (1973a) and Fischer (1975) for applications.

[3] First, consider the distribution of returns on an option to exchange asset two for asset one. This distribution of returns sells for $w(x_1, x_2, t)$.

Second, the distribution of returns on λ options to exchange asset two for asset one sells for $\lambda w(x_1, x_2, t)$ in a perfect market (where all participants are price takers).

Third, consider the distribution of returns of the option to exchange asset two for asset one, when both assets sell for λ times what they sold for in the first case. Denote this market value by $w(\lambda x_2, \lambda x_2, t)$.

That investment equals zero may seem puzzling. But in this hedge, to eliminate risk we eliminate the entire return. Thus, the value of the hedged position must be nil.

The return on this investment over a short interval is nil:

$$dw - w_1 \, dx_1 - w_2 \, dx_2 = 0. \tag{4}$$

Black and Scholes (1973, p. 642) eliminate all risk, but not all the return. They convert a long position in the stock and a short position in the option into a riskless investment.[4] From the stochastic calculus,[5] the return on the option is

$$dw = w_1 \, dx_1 + w_2 \, dx_2 + w_3 \, dt$$

$$+ \frac{1}{2} \, [\, w_{11} \, v_1^2 \, x_1^2 + 2 \, w_{12} \, v_1 \, v_2 \, \varrho_{12} \, x_1 \, x_2 + w_{22} \, v_2^2 \, x_2^2] \, dt, \tag{5}$$

where $w_3 = \partial w / \partial t$.

Equations (3) and (5) imply

$$w_3 + \frac{1}{2} \, [\, w_{11} \, v_1^2 \, x_1^2 + 2 \, w_{12} \, v_1 \, v_2 \, \varrho_{12} \, x_1 \, x_2 + w_{22} \, v_2^2 \, x_2^2] = 0. \tag{6}$$

The function $w(x_1, x_2, t)$ is the solution to the differential equation (6), subject to the boundary conditions (2) and the initial condition (1):

$$w(x_1, x_2, t) = x_1 N(d_1) - x_2 N(d_2)$$

$$d_1 = \frac{\ln(x_1/x_2) + \frac{1}{2} \, v^2(t^* - t)}{v \sqrt{t^* - t}} \tag{7}$$

$$d_2 = d_1 - v \sqrt{t^* - t}.$$

The distribution of returns in the third case is identical to that given in the second case, given the Ito processes (described in paragraph one of section II) which generate prices x_1 and x_2. Thus, the returns in the second case must sell for the same as those in the third case:

$$\lambda w(x_1, x_2, t) = w(\lambda x_1, \lambda x_2, t).$$

Thus $w(\cdot)$ is linear homogeneous in x_1 and x_2. See also Merton (1973c, p. 149) on this point.
[4]We can create a long (short) position in either underlying asset out of a short (long) position in the other asset and an appropriate position in the option to exchange the assets. According to equation (3):

$$x_1 = (w - w_2 x_2) / w_1$$
and
$$x_2 = (w - w_1 x_1) / w_2.$$

[5]See McKean (1969). Merton (1973c, sec. 6) develops the same differential equation en route to his alternative derivation of the Black-Scholes model.

Here, N(·) is the cumulative standard normal density function and $v^2 = v_1^2 - 2v_1 v_2 \varrho_{12} + v_2^2$ is the variance of $(x_1/x_2)^{-1} d(x_1/x_2)$. ($v^2 = v_1^2$ if $v_2 = 0$, the Black-Scholes case.)

Equations (7) satisfy (6), (2), and (1), and are unique. The easiest way to prove this is to transform the problem at hand into the Black-Scholes problem. Let asset two be the numeraire.[6] Then the price of asset two in terms of itself is unity. The price of asset one is $x \equiv x_1/x_2$. The option sells for

$$w(x_1, x_2, t)/x_1 = w(x_1/x_2, 1, t).$$

The interest rate on a riskless loan denominated in units of asset two is zero in a perfect market. A lender of one unit of asset two demands one unit of asset two back as repayment of principle. He charges no interest on the loan, because asset two's appreciation over the loan period is equilibrium compensation for the investment and risk.

Taking asset two as numeraire, the option to exchange asset two for asset one is a call option on asset one, with exercise price equal to unity and interest rate equal to zero. This is a special case of the Black-Scholes problem. Thus,

$$w(x_1, x_2, t)/x_2 = w(x, t)$$

$$\equiv (x_1/x_2) N(d_1) - 1 \cdot e^{0(t - t^*)} N(d_2),$$

where $w(x, t)$ is the Black-Scholes formula. Equations (7) follow immediately.

The Black-Scholes model is also a special case of (7), where $x_2 = ce^{r(t - t^*)}$. The Merton (1973) model, which allows a stochastic interest rate, is also a special case, where $x_2 = cP(t^* - t)$, $P(t^* - t)$ is the stochastic value of a default-free discount bond maturing at t^*, and $P(0) = 1$. Thus, in Merton's model as in the Black-Scholes model, $x_2 = c$ at $t = t^*$.

III. Some Extensions

Equations (7) also give the value for American options, if x_1 and x_2 are equilibrium asset prices. The proof is simple. Consider two portfolios:

A: purchase a European option to exchange asset one for asset two;

B: purchase asset one and sell two short.

---

[6]Stephen Ross suggested this lucid approach, which emphasizes the Black-Scholes heritage of this problem and its solution, and which lets us avoid much tedious mathematics. The student who wants to see all the mathematics can follow Merton's (1973c, sec. 6) solution to an isomorphic problem.

The values of the portfolios at any time t are

A: $w(x_1, x_2, t)$

B: $x_1 - x_2$.

The returns at t^* are

A: $\max(0, x_1^* - x_2^*)$

B: $x_1^* - x_2^*$.

The return on Portfolio A dominates that on B, so A must sell for at least as much as B:

$$w(x_1, x_2, t) \geq x_1 - x_2.$$

Thus, the value of a European option exceeds what you would get if you exercised a similar American option. So you will not exercise the American option early, and its value $W(x_1, x_2, t)$ will be exactly the same as that of a similar European option: $W(x_1, x_2, t) = w(x_1, x_2, t)$.

Recall that the option to exchange two assets can be viewed as a call on x_1 or a put on x_2, and that such an option is worth more alive than dead for $t < t^*$. This does not contradict Merton's (1973) conclusion that it may pay to exercise the ordinary American put option early. The exercise price for the ordinary American put is constant, not an asset price.

For the moment, assume as Black and Scholes did that the interest rate is known and constant. Then $ce^{r(t - t^*)}$ is the value of a default-free discount bond paying c at t^*. We know that an American option (whether a put or a call) with such an exercise price is worth more alive than dead. Then, equation (7) gives the formula for an American option (put or call) whose exercise price grows exponentially at the riskless interest rate and equals c at t^*.

Now, let $E(t)$ be the deterministic exercise price of the option, a function of time. Stipulate that $E(t^*) = c$. Any American call option with an exercise price $E(t) \geq ce^{r(t - t^*)}$ for $t < t^*$, must be worth the same as a European call option with exercise price c.[7] We know that an American call option with exercise price $E(t) = ce^{r(t - t^*)}$ is worth the same as the similar European option. Increasing the exercise price cannot increase the call option's value. Nor can increasing the exercise price decrease the option's value. The European call option has, in effect, an infinite exercise price until t^*. Yet, this option sells for as much as the American call option with exercise price growing exponentially at the instantaneous interest rate.

[7]Merton (1973c, p. 155) proves a similar theorem for discrete changes in the exercise price.

Similarly, an American put option with exercise price growing exponentially at the market interest rate until it reaches c at t^* will sell for the same as a European put option with exercise price c at t^*. If the American put option's exercise price is always less than or equal to $ce^{r(t-t^*)}$, then that American option is worth the same as a similar European option.

The preceding arguments imply a parity theorem[8] for European- and American-type put and call options whose common exercise price is the price of some asset. Consider two portfolios. The first portfolio contains an American call option on asset one with exercise price equal to the price of asset two, a short position in an American put on asset one with the same exercise price as the call, and asset two. The second portfolio contains asset one. We know that an American option is worth more alive than dead, if its exercise price is an asset price. So the American options are worth the same as European options and will not be exercised before the expiration date t^*. The holder of portfolio one will exchange asset two for asset one at t^*, in any event. Thus, portfolios one and two will have the same value at t^*. They must be worth the same at any time $t < t^*$, or arbitrage would occur. Hence, the usual put-call parity theorem holds for these options to exchange two assets. The reader can confirm that

$$w(x_1, x_2, t) - w(x_2, x_1, t) + x_2 = x_1$$

and

$$W(x_1, x_2, t) - W(x_2, x_1, t) + x_2 = x_1.$$

IV. Applications   The performance incentive fee, the margin account, the exchange offer, and the standby commitment are common arrangements which are also options to exchange one risky asset for another.

A. The
Performance
Incentive Fee

Modigliani and Pogue (1975) opened the discussion of performance incentive fees of the form

$$\text{Fee} = \delta(R_1 - R_2) \tag{8}$$

for portfolio managers, where R_1 is the rate of return on the managed portfolio, R_2 is the rate of return on the standard against which performance is measured, and δ is a number of dollars. The number δ will usually fall between zero and the total that investors have invested in the managed portfolio. Margrabe (1976) proves that such a fee is worth nothing when entered into, in Sharpe-Lintner equilibrium.

---

[8]Stoll (1969) states the theorem. Merton (1973b) shows that the theorem does not hold for ordinary American options.

This fee arrangement is valuable to the adviser if he can default on his obligation under the arrangement. The adviser could declare personal bankruptcy in case the fee were so negative that his net worth was negative. Or an investment adviser might form a corporation to handle his business and collect the fee. He would have the protection of limited liability in case the fee were negative. In such cases, the portfolio management fee is equivalent to an option. We can compute its value using equations (7).

For example, suppose the management corporation receives $10 million from its clients and invests it all. Management has no other assets. Management collects 10% of any superior performance of the managed portfolio over the standard and promises to pay its clients 10% of any inferior performance. (That is, $\delta = 1$ million.) Management plans to default if the managed portfolio does worse than the standard, and its clients know this. The fee arrangement lasts for six months. The monthly standard deviation of rate of return is 5% for the managed portfolio and 5% for the standard. The rates of return on the two portfolios are uncorrelated. Under these assumptions, the management corporation's option would be worth $690 thousand, and management would have to pay its investors for it to get their business.[9]

If management put up collateral to ensure its compliance with the fee agreement, it would be less likely to default and its option would be worth less. Equations (7) would still give the option value, though the calculations would be more tedious.

In order to prohibit abuse, the management contract may specify that the management cannot change the nature of the managed portfolio, without compensating the investors for the change. Management would never unilaterally end the contract, because its option is always worth more alive than dead. Investors may find it desirable to withdraw their funds early, if that is allowed. But, this would void the manager's option, so he would either rule out this possibility by contract or refuse to pay anything for the performance incentive fee.

B. The Margin Account

Suppose an investor buys securities worth x_1 on margin. (He borrows a fraction of the securities' cost from his broker, securing the loan with the portfolio of securities.) When the sum c of the principal amount and accrued interest is payable, he can either repay his debt and claim the collateral or default. If the margin loan is his only liability and the collateral includes all his assets, he has an option on the collateral, where the striking price is c. Below, I discuss mainly this simple case.

One may not think of this as an option, because its life is so brief. When the securities markets are open, the broker monitors the value of the collateral for the margin loan. He may ask for more collateral if its value shrinks (this

---

[9]Evaluate equations (7) for $x_1 = x_2 = \$10$ million, $t^* - t = 6$, $v_1 = v_2 = .05$, and $\varrho_{12} = 0$.

is the margin call). If the investor fails to put up more collateral immediately, the broker may sell off some of the collateral and reduce the investor's debit balance, until the remaining debit balance is adequately secured. If the collateral is dangerously small, the broker may sell some of it without notifying the investor.

If the broker measures the value of the collateral every $t^* - t$ months, he has issued an option with a life of $t^* - t$. In this application $t^* - t$ can grow arbitrarily small, at the broker's discretion. As $t^* - t$ approaches zero, the option value approaches the net asset value of the account, $x_1 - c$.

At the market's daily close the margin trader has a European option which expires when the markets reopen. He ordinarily exercises this option by borrowing the exercise price from the broker if the collateral is adequate. He may have to meet a margin call if the collateral is poor. He might let the option expire if the collateral were inadequate.

Sometimes the option lasts longer than the eighteen hours from the New York Stock Exchange's daily close at 4:00 p.m. until the 10:00 a.m. reopening. When a holiday interrupts the business week, the option is for 42 hours. Over a normal weekend the option is for 66 hours. Over a three-day weekend the option is for 90 hours.

An investor might not exercise his option under exactly the circumstances implied by my analysis. I assume the investor holds all his non-human capital in his margin account. If the investor has other assets and liabilities, he may default when his net worth is negative. An investor might not default even if his net worth, as usually measured, was negative, if he thought the stigma of personal bankruptcy was horrible enough or would cause him sufficient future inconvenience.

If the margin trader sells a risky security short, his option is to exchange his risky short position for his risky long position. Equations (7) can tell us what this option is worth.

For example, consider two closed-end funds with the same systematic and nonsystematic risk ($\varrho_{12} = 1$ and $v_1 = v_2 = .05$, for monthly rates of return). An investor wants to finance the purchase of $100,000 worth of shares in the first fund with a short sale of shares in the second.[10] The broker arranging this transaction will find it less risky than making a margin loan. In fact, the investor's option is worthless. In equilibrium the broker will demand less compensation for this sort of transaction than he would for selling securities on margin.

For other values of ϱ_{12}, v_1 and v_2, the broker may find a short sale riskier. Suppose in the above example $\varrho_{12} = -1$. Then the short sale and purchase

---

[10]Here we assume away regulations on short sales.

would together be twice as risky as either one alone ($v = 2v_1 = 2v_2$). The margin trader would be willing to pay some $1433 for this option over a three-day weekend and the broker would not sell it for less.

C. The Exchange Offer [11]

An exchange offer of shares in one unlevered corporation for shares in another presents shareholders in the offeree corporation with an option to exchange one type of share for another. For simplicity, let the price of a share in firm one, z_1, equal the price of a share in firm two, z_2. Firm one has N shares; firm two has n. Suppose firm one, the much larger firm, announces it will trade one of its shares for one of firm two's. [12] The offer, firm and uncontested by firm two's management, expires at t^*.

Further, assume this offer conveys no information about the prospects of either firm. Then the offer may increase the price of shares in the second firm, because these shareholders now have an option to exchange their shares for something else. This option is worth at least zero.

We can compute the *increase in* the value of a share in firm two, after the exchange offer is made, but before it expires: substitute the value of what a shareholder in firm two gets if he exercises his option,

$$x_1 = [(N - n)z_1 + nz_2]/N,$$

and the value of what he gives up,

$$x_2 = z_2$$

into equations (7). As usual, this option's value depends on the characteristics of the joint distribution of x_1 and x_2 and on the length of time until the option expires.

Under these circumstances, the management of firm one is acting against the best interest of its shareholder. Any gain to shareholders of firm two is a loss to shareholders in firm one, which grants the option. For, firm one is giving up this option in return for nothing. In a perfect market, a cash tender offer would be a similarly unwise move. (This says more about the stringent assumptions in this paper than about managerial irrationality.)

Management of the offering firm could charge shareholders of the offeree firm a premium for the right to tender a share of the offeree's stock. It would compensate the shareholders of the offering firm for the option they give up. This right would be valuable and might even trade apart from the stock to be tendered.

---

[11] Ron Masulis suggested this application of the model.
[12] Firm one will sell n/N of its (homogeneous) assets, use the proceeds to repurchase n shares, and trade the n shares for n shares in firm two.

D. The Standby Commitment

The standby commitment is a put option on a forward contract in mortgage notes.[13] The buyer gets the option to sell a bundle of mortgage notes at a predetermined price. He must exercise his option on or before the notification date, some month(s) before the delivery date: if he exercises his option, he sells his mortgages in the forward market. Thus, the option is on a forward sale of mortgage notes. The commitment fee is the option premium.

We want to find the value at t of an option expiring at t^* on a forward contract calling for delivery at some later date t^{**}. Buyer will exercise his option at t^* (he won't exercise it earlier) if the value at t^* of his profit at t^{**} is positive. Define C as the striking price. $P(t) = P(t^{**}, t)$ is the price at t of a riskless, discount bond maturing at t^{**}. Let $X(t)$ be the spot price for the underlying mortgage notes. Thus buyer will exercise his option if $CP(t^*) - X(t^*) > 0$, and the option value at t^* is

$$\max[0, PC - X].$$

Assume that percentage changes in the spot price X are an Ito process with constant drift α_x and dispersion $V_x : dX/X = \alpha_x \, dt + V_x \, dz_x$. As Merton (1973c) proposes, assume the riskless discount bond will be worth unity when it matures. Until then changes in its prices are given by the stochastic differential

$$dP/P = \alpha_p \, dt + v_p \, dz_p.$$

Let $x_1 = PC$ and $x_2 = X$, both asset prices. Then for all $t \leq t^*$ this option is worth

$$w(x_1, x_2, t)$$

$$= w(PC, X, t)$$

$$= PCN(d_1) - XN(d_2),$$

where

$$d_1 = [\ln(PC/X) + v^2(t^* - t) \div 2] \div v\sqrt{t^* - t},$$

$$d_2 = d_1 - v\sqrt{t^* - t},$$

and

$$v^2 = v_p^2 - 2v_p v_x \varrho_{px} + v_x^2.$$

[13]Several types of standbys exist. This section refers to the easiest type to analyze. The Federal National Mortgage Association offers types which do not fit this model. In this section we assume away problems associated with coupons on the mortgage notes. One can handle them as one handles dividend payments on stock.

V. Summary

In this paper I develop an equation for the value of an option to exchange one asset for another within a stated period. The formula applies to American options, as well as European ones; to puts, as well as calls. Thus, I found a closed-form expression for this sort of American put option and a put-call parity theorem for such American options.

One can apply the equation to options that investors create when they enter into certain common financial arrangements. The investment adviser, who receives a fee which depends at least in part on how well his managed portfolio does relative to some standard, has an option to refuse the fee and declare bankruptcy if the fee is extremely negative. The short-seller has the option to similarly escape his obligations, at the expense of his broker. The offeree in an exchange offer may have the opportunity to exchange one company's securities for those of another. The buyer of a standby commitment has the (put) option to trade mortgage notes for dollars in the forward market. In each case the value of the option depends not only on the current values of the assets which might be exchanged, but also on the variance-covariance matrix for the rates of return on the two assets, and on the life of the option.

References

1. Fischer Black. "The Pricing of Commodity Contracts," *Journal of Financial Economics,* Volume 3 (January/March 1976).

2. ———. "The Pricing of Complex Options and Corporate Liabilities," Graduate School of Business, University of Chicago, 1975.

3. ——— and Myron Scholes. "The Pricing of Options and Corporate Liabilities," *Journal of Political Economy,* Volume 81 (May/June 1973), pp. 637-654.

4. Ruel Vance Churchill. *Fourier Series and Boundary Value Problems,* 2nd ed. New York, McGraw-Hill, 1963.

5. Stanley Fischer. "The Demand for Index Bonds," *Journal of Political Economy,* Volume 83 (June 1975), pp. 509-534.

6. Jonathan E. Ingersoll, Jr. "A Theoretical and Empirical Investigation of the Dual Purpose Funds," *Journal of Financial Economics,* Volume 3 (January/March 1976), pp. 83-123.

7. Fritz John. *Partial Differential Equations,* 2nd ed. New York, Springer Verlag, 1975.

8. William Margrabe. "Alternative Investment Performance Fee Arrangements and Implications for SEC Regulatory Policy: A Comment," *Bell Journal of Economics,* Volume 7 (Autumn 1976), pp. 716-718.

9. H. P. McKean, Jr., *Stochastic Integrals,* New York, Academic Press, 1969.

10. Robert C. Merton. "An Intertemporal Capital Asset Pricing Model," *Econometrica,* Volume 41 (September 1973a), pp. 867-887.

11. ———. "The Relationship between Put and Call Option Prices: Comment," *Journal of Finance,* Volume 28 (March 1973b), pp. 183-184.

12. ———. "The Theory of Rational Option Pricing," *The Bell Journal of Economics and Management Science,* Volume 4 (Spring 1973c), pp. 141-183.

13. Franco Modigliani and Gerald A. Pogue. "Alternative Investment Performance Fee Arrangements and Implications for SEC Regulatory Policy," *Bell Journal of Economics,* Volume 6 (Spring 1975), pp. 127-160.

14. Clifford W. Smith, Jr. "Option Pricing: A Review," *Journal of Financial Economics,* Volume 3 (January/March 1976), pp. 3-51.

15. Hans R. Stoll. "The Relationship between Put and Call Option Prices," *Journal of Finance,* Volume 24 (December 1969), pp. 802-824.

3

Options on the Minimum or the Maximum of Two Risky Assets: Analysis and Applications

René M. Stulz*

This paper provides analytical formulas for European put and call options on the minimum or the maximum of two risky assets. The properties of these formulas are discussed in detail. Options on the minimum or the maximum of two risky assets are useful to price a wide variety of contingent claims of interest to financial economists. Applications discussed in this paper include the valuation of foreign currency debt, option-bonds, compensation plans, risk-sharing contracts, secured debt and growth opportunities involving mutually exclusive investments.

1. Introduction

This paper provides formulas for (European) put and call options on the maximum or the minimum of two risky assets and discusses the properties of these options. This analysis provides an important tool because a wide variety of contingent claims of interest to financial economists have a payoff function which includes the payoff function of a put or a call option on the minimum or the maximum of two risky assets.

University of Rochester, Rochester, NY 14677, USA

*I am especially grateful to John Long for generous and substantial help in the process of writing this paper. I thank Lee Wakeman for suggesting the problem of pricing option-bonds and for useful discussions. The referee, Jon Ingersoll, provided useful comments and pointed out a mistake in an earlier draft. I am also grateful to Fischer Black, Andrew Christie, Michael Jensen, Pat Reagan, Bill Schwert, Cliff Smith, Jerry Warner and Jerry Zimmerman for useful discussions and comments, and to the Center for Research in Government Policy and Business for financial support. Johnson (1981) has independently derived some of the results of this paper.

Received October 1981, final version received February 1982

Options on the minimum of two risky assets enter the payoff function of some traded assets in a straightforward way. An important example of traded assets whose value depends on the value of an option on the minimum of two risky assets is given by option-bonds. Option-bonds are financial instruments which are primarily sold on the Euro-bond market.[1] On the Euro-bond market, when the issuer of an option-bond makes a payment to the bearer, the bearer has a choice of two or more currencies in which the payment is to be made.[2] The exchange rate among these currencies is written in the indenture of the bond. For example, a discount option-bond could let the bearer choose at maturity between U. S. dollars and British pounds at a predetermined exchange rate of two dollars per pound. If the firm is solvent at maturity, the bearer chooses to be paid in pounds only if the price of a pound in dollars is larger than two dollars. However, at maturity, the firm may be able to pay the amount due in dollars but not the amount due in pounds.[3] In this case the bondholders get the whole firm in payment. In this example, the bearers of the option-bond hold a straight dollar bond plus an option on the minimum of the value of the firm and the dollar value of the amount to be paid in pounds. The exercise price of this option is equal to the amount to be paid in dollars.

Other examples of applications of options on the minimum or the maximum of two risky assets are given in the paper. It is shown that compensation plans, risk-sharing contracts, collateralized loans and secured debt, indexed wages and some growth opportunities are contingent claims whose payoff function includes the payoff function of options on the minimum or the maximum of two risky assets.

The plan of the paper is as follows. In section 2, an analytical solution for the pricing of a European call option on the minimum of two risky assets is obtained. The price of a European call option on the maximum of two risky assets can be obtained by using the price of an option on the minimum of two risky assets and the price of two conventional call options. This relationship between options on the minimum of two risky assets and options on the maximum of two risky assets is discussed in section 3. Other properties of options on the minimum or the maximum of two risky assets are also discussed in section 3. Some applications of options on the minimum or the maximum of two risky assets to the study of problems in

[1] For information on the Euro-bond market, see Park (1974) and Feiger and Jacquillat (1981). Fisher (1979) provides good information on the Euro-dollar bond market. Many Euro-bonds are listed on the Luxembourg, London or Singapore stock exchanges. *Euromoney* provides a description of new offerings in each of its monthly issues.
[2] A growing number of option-bonds involve the choice of a commodity numeraire. E.g., the July 1981 issue of *Euromoney* describes a bond which offers a barrel of oil as a numeraire.
[3] Feiger and Jacquillat (1979) discuss the pricing of *default-free* option-bonds using an option-theoretic approach. They do not present an analytical formula and are, therefore, unable to shed much light on the properties of those bonds. Furthermore, in general, option-bonds are issued by firms and involve a default-risk.

the theory of corporate finance are discussed in section 4. Section 5 provides a summary of the results of the paper.

2. The pricing of a call option on the minimum of two risky assets

In this section, a European call option[4] on the minimum of two risky assets is priced. If V and H are the prices of two risky assets, the European call to be priced has a payoff at maturity equal to $\max\{\min(V, H) - F, 0\}$, where F is the exercise price. The following assumptions are made:[5]

(A.1) Markets are 'frictionless,' in the sense that there are no transactions costs, no taxes, no restrictions on short-sales and no difference between the borrowing rate and the lending rate. Trading takes place continuously.

(A.2) Prices V and H satisfy, respectively, the following stochastic differential equations:[6]

$$dV/V = \mu_V \, dt + \sigma_V \, dZ_V, \tag{1}$$

$$dH/H = \mu_H \, dt + \sigma_H \, dZ_H. \tag{2}$$

It is assumed that σ_V^2 and σ_H^2, which are, respectively, the instantaneous variances of the rates of return of assets V and H, are constant. μ_V and μ_H, i.e., the instantaneous expected rate of return of, respectively, assets V and H, can change through time, but must be such that (1) and (2) have solutions. dZ_V and dZ_H are standard Wiener processes whose coefficient of correlation is written ϱ_{VH}. ϱ_{VH} is assumed to be constant through time.

(A.3) The instantaneous rate of interest R is constant through time.

Let $M(V, H, F, T - t)$ be the price of a European call option on $\min(V, H)$ with maturity at date T and exercise price F. To find M, it is sufficient to find the value of a self-financing portfolio whose value at date T is equal to the value of the option at date T.[7] If such a portfolio can be found, its value at date t must be equal to the value of the option at date t, $\forall t \leq T$, to prevent the possibility of arbitrage profits. Let τ be equal to $T - t$, i.e., the time to maturity of the option, and P be equal to the value of the self-financing portfolio. With the assumptions stated in (A.1)-(A.3), it is natural to conjecture that P is a function of V, H and τ only, i.e., $P = P(V, H, \tau)$. Using Ito's Formula, the dynamics for P can be obtained.

---

[4] A review of early developments in the option pricing literature is given by Smith (1976). The seminal contributions to that literature are Black and Scholes (1973) and Merton (1973).
[5] Some of these assumptions could be relaxed. In particular, it would be possible to let the interest rate change over time in the same way as in Merton (1973). The added complexity would not add significant insights to the present paper.
[6] See Merton (1971) for an introduction to those equations.
[7] See Harrison and Kreps (1979) for a rigorous discussion of self-financing portfolios. A self-financing portfolio is a portfolio which does not yield or does not require any cash payments until its maturity. Dynamics for the value of a self-financing portfolio are given in Merton (1971).

$$dP = P_V \, dV + P_H \, dH - P_\tau \, dt$$

$$+ \tfrac{1}{2} \{ P_{VV} \, V^2 \, \sigma_V^2 + P_{HH} \, H^2 \, \sigma_H^2 + 2 P_{VH} \, VH \varrho_{VH} \, \sigma_V \, \sigma_H \} \, dt. \quad (3)$$

If the portfolio is self-financing and if it consists of investments in V, H and the safe asset, its dynamics can also be written

$$dP = x(dV/V)P + y(dH/H)P + (1 - x - y)RP \, dt, \quad (4)$$

where x is the fraction of the portfolio invested in asset V and y is the fraction of the portfolio invested in asset H. x and y are functions of V, H and τ. Setting (4) equal to (3), it follows that x and y must satisfy at each point in time

$$P_V V = x P, \quad (5)$$

$$P_H H = y P. \quad (6)$$

Using (4), (5) and (6), the stochastic terms in (4) can be eliminated to yield (after dividing by dt)

$$- P_\tau = RP - RP_V \, V - RP_H \, H$$

$$- \tfrac{1}{2} \{ P_{VV} \, V^2 \, \sigma_V^2 + P_{HH} \, H^2 \, \sigma_H^2 + 2 P_{HV} \, VH \varrho_{VH} \, \sigma_V \, \sigma_H \}. \quad (7)$$

The portfolio whose value is P is self-financing if it satisfies the partial differential equation given by (7). For P to be equal to the value of the option, the self-financing portfolio must satisfy the boundary conditions specified in the contract which defines the option,

$$P(V, H, 0) = \max \{ \min (V, H) - F, 0 \}, \quad (8)$$

$$P(0, H, \tau) = 0, \quad (9)$$

$$P(V, 0, \tau) = 0. \quad (10)$$

To obtain a solution to (7) which satisfies (8), (9) and (10), note that (7) does not depend on the instantaneous expected rate of return of V and H. This means that the value of the option does not depend on the attitude of investors towards risk. It is therefore possible to assume that investors are risk-neutral without thereby changing the value of the option, provided that the dynamics of asset prices are adjusted so that all assets have the same expected instantaneous rate of return, i.e., R, as they would in a risk-neutral world. The value of the call option today is, consequently, equal to its expected value at maturity discounted at the interest rate R, where the expectation is taken with respect to risk-neutral dynamics for assets V and

H. Using this approach to find a solution to (7) which satisfies (8), (9) and (10), it follows that the value of the option is given by[8]

$$
\begin{aligned}
M = \; & HN_2(\gamma_1 + \sigma_H\sqrt{\tau}, (\ln(V/H) \\
& - \tfrac{1}{2}\sigma^2\tau)/\sigma\sqrt{\tau}, (\varrho_{VH}\sigma_V - \sigma_H)/\sigma) \\
& + VN_2(\gamma_2 + \sigma_V\sqrt{\tau}, (\ln(H/V) \\
& - \tfrac{1}{2}\sigma^2\tau)/\sigma\sqrt{\tau}, (\varrho_{VH}\sigma_H - \sigma_V)/\sigma) \\
& - Fe^{-R t}N_2(\gamma_1, \gamma_2, \varrho_{VH}),
\end{aligned}
\tag{11}
$$

where $N_2(\alpha, \beta, \theta)$ is the bivariate cumulative standard normal distribution with upper limits of integration α and β, and coefficient of correlation θ, and

$$
\gamma_1 = (\ln(H/F) + (R - \tfrac{1}{2}\sigma_H^2)\tau)/\sigma_H\sqrt{\tau},
$$

$$
\gamma_2 = (\ln(V/F) + (R - \tfrac{1}{2}\sigma_V^2)\tau)/\sigma_V\sqrt{\tau},
$$

$$
\sigma^2 = \sigma_V^2 + \sigma_H^2 - 2\varrho_{VH}\sigma_V\sigma_H.
$$

It can be verified by substitution that (11) satisfies the partial differential equation given by (7) and its boundary conditions. Appendix 1 sketches the derivation of (11).

If the exercise price of the option on the minimum of two risky assets is equal to zero, the formula for the price of the option takes a simpler form than the formula given by eq. (11). Let $E(V, H, 1, \tau)$ be the price of an option to exchange one unit of asset H for one unit of asset V at maturity. Margrabe (1978) prices such an option. Using his results, it follows that

$$
M(V, H, 0, \tau) = V - E(V, H, 1, \tau) = V - VN(d_1) + HN(d_2), \tag{11$'$}
$$

where

$$
d_1 = (\ln(V/H) + \tfrac{1}{2}\sigma^2\tau)/\sigma\sqrt{\tau},
$$

$$
d_2 = d_1 - \sigma\sqrt{\tau}.
$$

To prove that eq. (11$'$) is correct, remember that the payoff of an option to exchange one unit of asset H for one unit of asset V is equal to $\max\{V - H, 0\}$. Let W be the value of a portfolio which consists of holding one unit of

[8]The method used here is presented in Cox and Ross (1976) and in Harrison and Kreps (1979).

asset V and writing one option to exchange one unit of asset H for one unit of asset V at maturity $T = t + \tau$. The value of portfolio W at maturity if V is greater than H is $V - (V - H) = H$. The value of a call option on $\min(V, H)$ with an exercise price of zero and maturity at date $T = t + \tau$ is also equal to H at maturity if V is greater than H at that time. If V is smaller than H at maturity, the portfolio W is worth V at that date and $M(V, H, 0, 0) = V$. This completes the proof.

3. Properties of call options on the minimum of two risky assets

This section presents comparative static results for call options on the minimum of two risky assets and shows that call options on the minimum of two risky assets can be used to price other options. The comparative static results can be extended in a natural way to the other options priced in this section. The following compact notation is adopted for the price of a call option on the minimum of two risky assets V and H, with exercise price F, and time to maturity τ:

$$M(V, H, F, \tau) = HN_2(\alpha_1, \alpha_2, \varrho_c) + VN_2(\beta_1, \beta_2, \varrho_c)$$

$$- Fe^{-Rt}N_2(\gamma_1, \gamma_2, \varrho_{VH}).$$

3.1. Some parity relationships

From the price of a call option on the minimum of two risky assets and the price of assets V, H and the interest rate R, it is possible to obtain the price of a call option on the maximum of two risky assets, the price of a put option on the minimum of two risky assets and the price of a put option on the maximum of two risky assets.

3.1.1. Pricing a call option on the maximum of two risky assets

Let $MX(V, H, F, \tau)$ be the price of a European call option whose pay-off at maturity is given by

$$\max \{ \max (V, H) - F, 0 \}.$$

The value of this option is

$$MX(V, H, F, \tau) = C(V, F, \tau) + C(H, F, \tau) - M(V, H, F, \tau), \quad (12)$$

where $C(A, F, \tau)$ is a European call option on asset A with exercise price F and time to expiration τ. To verify this result, note that if V, $V \geqq F$, is the maximum of V and H at maturity, the option on the maximum of two risky assets pays $V - F$. A portfolio which consists of holding a call option on V and a call option on H, and writing a call option on the minimum of V and H (with exercise price F for each of the three call options) pays $V - F$ also, as $M(V, H, F, 0)$ is equal to $C(H, F, 0)$. A similar reasoning holds if H is the maximum of V and H.

3.1.2. Pricing a put option on the minimum of two risky assets

If $PM(V, H, F, \tau)$ is the price of a European put option on the minimum of V and H with exercise price F and time to maturity τ, then

$$PM(V, H, F, \tau) = e^{-Rt}F - M(V, H, 0, \tau) + M(V, H, F, \tau). \quad (13)$$

To verify this result consider the following two investments:

Portfolio A. Purchase one put option on the minimum of V and H with exercise price F.

Portfolio B. Purchase one discount bond which pays F at maturity. Write one option on the minimum of V and H with an exercise price of zero.
Purchase one option on the minimum of V and H with exercise price F.

At maturity, if $\min(V, H) \geq F$, Portfolio A pays zero whereas Portfolio B pays $F - \min(V, H) + \min(V, H) - F = 0$. If $\min(V, H) = V < F$, then Portfolio A pays $F - V$, whereas Portfolio B pays $F - V + 0 = F - V$. If $\min(V, H) = H < F$, then Portfolio A pays $F - H$, whereas Portfolio B pays $F - H + 0 = F - H$. It follows that in all states of the world, Portfolio A pays the same as Portfolio B at maturity and therefore must have the same value as Portfolio B at time $T - \tau$. This completes the proof that a European put option on the minimum of two risky assets is indeed priced as in eq. (13).

3.1.3. Pricing a put option on the maximum of two risky assets

If $PX(V, H, F, \tau)$ is a European put option on the maximum of assets V and H with exercise price F and time to maturity τ, then $PX(V, H, F, \tau)$ is given by

$$PX(V, H, F, \tau) = e^{-Rt} F - MX(V, H, 0, \tau) + MX(V, H, F, \tau). \quad (14)$$

The proof of this result is similar to the proof for the pricing of a put option on the minimum of two risky assets.

3.2. A simple dominance result

It is possible to find upper and lower bounds for the option on the minimum of two risky assets which are easy to compute. Let $E(B, A, 1, \tau)$ be an option to exchange one unit of asset A for one unit of asset B at maturity of the option. The following result holds:

$$\min\{C(V, F, \tau), \; C(H, F, \tau)\} \geq M(V, H, F, \tau)$$

$$\geq \max\{C(V, F, \tau) - E(VH, 1, \tau)$$

$$C(H, F, \tau) - E(H, V, 1, \tau), 0\}.$$

Clearly, there is no state of the world in which a European call option on the minimum of two risky assets has a payoff which exceeds the payoff of a call option on any of the two risky assets. If $CE(H, V, 1, F, \tau)$ is a call option to exchange one unit of asset V for one unit of asset H if and only if $V \geq F$, then a portfolio which consists of holding one call option $C(H, F, \tau)$ and writing one call option $CE(H, V, 1, F, \tau)$ has payoffs which match exactly the payoffs of $E(H, V, F, \tau)$. Similarly, a portfolio which consists of holding one call option $C(V, F, \tau)$ and writing one call option $CE(H, V, 1, F, \tau)$ has payoffs which match exactly the payoffs of $M(V, H, F, \tau)$. However, it must be true that

$$E(H, V, 1, \tau) \geqq CE(H, V, 1, F, \tau),$$

$$E(H, V, 1, \tau) \geqq CE(H, V, 1, F, \tau).$$

This completes the proof of the dominance result.

Notice that the Black and Scholes (1973) formula can be used to compute $C(V, F, \tau)$ and $C(H, F, \tau)$. Margrabe (1978) has shown that $E(H, V, 1, \tau)$ is given by $HC(V/H, 1, \tau)$, with $R = 0$. The instantaneous variance of the rate of return on V/H is $\sigma_V^2 + \sigma_H^2 - 2 \varrho_{VH} \sigma_V \sigma_H$. Note finally that if $F = 0$, then $C(V, F, \tau) = V$, $CE(H, V, 1, F, \tau) = E(H, V, 1, \tau)$ and $M(V, H, F, \tau) = H - E(H, V, 1, \tau)$.

3.3.
Comparative
statics of the
price of the call
option on the
minimum of
two risky assets
with respect to
V, H, F and R

To simplify the analysis, it is useful to define two artificial assets. Let $A(V, H, \tau)$ be the value at time t of receiving the larger of H or V at time $T = t + \tau$. Furthermore, let $a(V, H, \tau)$ be the value at time t of receiving the smaller of H or V at time $T = t + \tau$. It follows that $A(H, V, \tau) = H + E(V, H, 1, \tau)$ and $a(H, V, \tau) = H - E(V, H, 1, \tau)$. A call option on the minimum of two risky assets with an exercise price F is a call option on asset $a(H, V, \tau)$ with the same exercise price, i.e., $M(V, H, F, \tau) = C(a, F, \tau)$. [Note also that $MX(V, H, F, \tau) = C(A, F, \tau)$.] Since A and a can be treated as assets, it is possible to use Merton's (1973) distribution-free results to obtain

$$\partial M / \partial H = C_a(\partial a / \partial H) > 0, \tag{15}$$

$$\partial M / \partial V = C_a(\partial a / \partial V) > 0, \tag{16}$$

$$\partial M / \partial F = C_F < 0. \tag{17}$$

Merton (1973) shows that $C_a > 0$ and $C_F < 0$. $\partial a / \partial H$ is positive because an asset which pays $\min(V, \lambda H)$ at maturity T, with $\lambda > 1$, must be worth more than an asset which pays $\min(V, H)$ at the same maturity, provided that the probability that $\min(V, H) = H < V$ is positive. Eq. (11') shows that the value of $a(V, H, \tau)$ does not depend on the interest rate R. This implies that Merton's (1973) result that the value of a call option is an increasing function of the rate of interest applies here in a straightforward way. It also implies that the value of a call option on the minimum of two risky assets is an increasing function of the rate of interest. Appendix 2 verifies these results for the formula developed in this paper. These results also hold for an option on the maximum of two risky assets.

3.4.
Comparative
statics of the
price of the call
option on the
minimum of two
risky assets with
respect to σ_V^2,
σ_H^2, ϱ_{VH} and τ

3.4.1. Effect of a
change in σ_V^2
and σ_H^2

Black and Scholes (1973) show that an increase in the instantaneous variance of the risky asset always increases the price of the option. In the case of an option on the minimum of two risky assets, it is not true, however, that an increase in the instantaneous variance of one of the risky assets always increases the price of the option. The sign of the partial derivative of the option price with respect to the variance of either one of the risky assets is ambiguous.

The ambiguity in the sign of this partial derivative arises from the fact that an increase in the instantaneous variance of a risky asset's return can either increase or decrease the expected payoff of the option, assuming that the expectation is taken with respect to risk-neutral price dynamics. The following argument supports this point. Suppose that for large (small) values of H, the probability that V is larger (smaller) than H at maturity is very small. An increase in the instantaneous variance of the return of asset H puts more weight in the tails of the distribution of H at maturity. If the expected value of H at maturity is higher than F, an increase in the instantaneous variance of the return of H simultaneously increases the probability that H is smaller than F at maturity and increases the probability of large values of H. The increase in the probability that H is smaller than F at maturity decreases the expected payoff of the option. The increase in the probability of H taking a large value at maturity has a negligible effect on the expected payoff of the option, because it is assumed that the probability that a large value of H is equal to $\min(V, H)$ is very small and that the distribution of V is left unchanged. It follows that an increase in the instantaneous variance of the return of asset H decreases the value of the option. An increase in the instantaneous variance of the return of asset V simultaneously increases the probability of a large payoff for the option at maturity and increases the probability that V is smaller than F at maturity. The increase in the probability of low values of V does not affect the expected payoff of the option very much as the probability that V is smaller than H, for low values of H, is very small by assumption. It follows that an increase in the instantaneous variance of the return of asset V increases the value of the option.

An example may be useful to understand the above discussion. Suppose that the option has an exercise price equal to zero. It has been shown earlier that in this case:

$$M(V, H, 0, \tau) = H - E(H, V, 1, \tau). \tag{18}$$

It immediately follows that

$$\frac{\partial M(V, H, 0, \tau)}{\partial \sigma_V^2} = -He^{-Rt}N_1'\left(\frac{\ln(V/H) + (R - \frac{1}{2}\sigma^2)\tau}{\sigma\sqrt{\tau}}\right)$$

$$* \frac{\sqrt{\tau}}{\sigma}\left(1 - \varrho_{VH}\frac{\sigma_V}{\sigma_H}\right), \tag{19}$$

where $\sigma^2 = (\sigma_V^2 + \sigma_H^2 - 2\varrho_{VH}\sigma_V\sigma_H)$ and $N_1'(Q)$ is the derivative of the cumulative standard normal distribution $N_1(Q)$ with respect to Q. The partial derivative given by (19) is negative when $\sigma_H > \varrho_{VH}\sigma_V$. If (a) the instantaneous variance of H is large, (b) the instantaneous variance of V is small, and (c) H and V are positively correlated, an increase in σ_V^2 can make the payoffs of V 'closer' to those of H than they were before in most states of the world and consequently decrease the expected payoff of exchanging one unit of asset V for one unit of asset H.

Merton (1973) shows that an increase in the Rothschild-Stiglitz measure of risk of asset a implies an increase in the value of a call option on asset a, irrespectively of the distribution of the return on asset a. It follows from this result that an increase in the Rothschild-Stiglitz measure of risk of asset $a(V, H, \tau)$ increases the value of the option on the minimum of two risky assets. Similarly, an increase in the Rothschild-Stiglitz measure of risk of the artificial asset $A(V, H, \tau)$ increases the value of the option on the maximum of two risky assets.

3.4.2. Effect of a change in ϱ_{VH}

The partial derivative of the price of the option with respect to the coefficient of correlation between the two risky assets is given by

$$\partial C/\partial \varrho_{VH} = HN_1\left(\frac{\alpha_1 - \varrho_c\alpha_2}{\sqrt{1 - \varrho_c^2}}\right)\frac{e^{-\frac{1}{2}\alpha_2^2}}{\sqrt{2\pi}}\left[\frac{\sigma_V\sigma_H\sqrt{\tau}}{\sigma} + \frac{\sigma_V\sigma_H}{\sigma^2}\alpha_2\right]$$

$$+ VN_1\left(\frac{\beta_1 - \varrho_c\beta_2}{\sqrt{1 - \varrho_c^2}}\right)\frac{e^{-\frac{1}{2}\beta_2^2}}{\sqrt{2\pi}}\left[\frac{\sigma_V\sigma_H\sqrt{\tau}}{\sigma} + \frac{\sigma_V\sigma_H}{\sigma^2}\beta_2\right]. \quad (20)$$

It is proved in the appendix 3 that (20) is positive everywhere for $-1 \leqq \varrho_{VH} \leqq 1$. This means that the value of the option is the highest if the two risky assets have a correlation coefficient of one.[9] Intuitively, as ϱ_{VH} increases, the probability that the payoff of V will be 'close' to the payoff of H increases. This implies that V is more likely to be high when H is high. It follows that the probability of asset H being above F when asset V is above F increases. Consequently, the expected payoff of the option is higher.

Contrary to the option studied by Black and Scholes (1973), it is possible for an option on the minimum of two risky assets to be worthless when the two risky assets have a positive value. Indeed, if $\gamma_1 + \gamma_2 \leqq 0$, the option is worthless for $\varrho_{VH} = -1$.[10] To understand this, suppose that $R = \frac{1}{2}\sigma_H^2 = \frac{1}{2}\sigma_V^2$, with $\gamma_1 < 0$ and $\gamma_2 < 0$. It is obviously true that the sum of γ_1 and γ_2 is negative with these assumptions. These assumptions also imply that $H < F$ and $V < F$. Because $\varrho_{VH} = -1$, if $V > F$ at maturity,

---

[9] If $\sigma_V = \sigma_H$, (17) may be indefinite. A dominance argument or taking the appropriate limits verifies the claim in the text.
[10] Abramowitz and Stegun (1970) show that $N_2(a, b, -1) = 0$ for $a + b \leqq 0$.

it must be true that $H < F$. It follows that since the option is worthless, it is never possible for both H and V to be larger than the exercise price F.

3.4.3. Effect of a change in τ

Merton (1973) shows that the value of a call option on an asset which pays no dividends is an increasing function of time to maturity, irrespectively of the distribution of the return on the optioned asset. The price of the artificial asset $a(V, H, \tau)$ is a decreasing function of the time to maturity, as it is equal to H minus V times the price of a European call option. It follows therefore that

$$\partial M/\partial \tau = C_a(\partial a/\partial \tau) + C_\tau \gtreqless 0.$$

To understand why the value of asset $a(V, H, \tau)$ is a decreasing function of time to maturity, it is useful to notice that $a(V, H, \tau) < \min(V, H)$. This is true because it is always possible to buy the asset whose price is the lowest at time $T - \tau$, hold it until time T, and sell it at time T for a price which is at least as high as the price of asset $a(V, H, \tau)$ at maturity of this asset. At time $\tau = 0$, however, it must be true that $a(V, H, 0) = \min(V, H)$. It follows that the price of asset $a(V, H, \tau)$ must be a decreasing function of time to maturity. The partial derivative of the price of the call option on the minimum of two risky assets given by the formula developed in this paper is lengthy and is not reproduced here. Its sign is ambiguous.

Whereas the price of asset $a(V, H, \tau)$ is a decreasing function of time to maturity, the price of asset $A(V, H, \tau)$ is an increasing function of time to maturity. [Notice that the price of asset $A(V, H, \tau)$, i.e., of the asset which pays the maximum of V and H at maturity, is equal to H plus V times the price of a European call option.] Because the price of asset $A(V, H, \tau)$ is an increasing function of time to maturity, it follows that the value of an option on the maximum of two risky assets is unambiguously an increasing function of time to maturity, irrespectively of the distribution of the returns of the two risky assets.

One important implication of this discussion is that the price of a European call option on the minimum of two risky assets is not in general the same as the price of an American call option on the minimum of two risky assets. The formula for the price of a call option on the minimum of two risky assets developed here is correct, in general, only for a European call option on the minimum of two risky assets.

3.5. A comparison with other option pricing formulas

It has already been shown that the formula for the pricing of a call option on the minimum of two risky assets reduces to a formula which involves only the univariate normal distribution in some special cases. In particular, an option on the minimum of two risky assets whose exercise price is equal to zero has a price given by $M(V, H, 0, \tau) = V - E(V, H, 1, \tau)$, where $E(V, H, 1, \tau)$ is the price of an option to exchange one unit of asset H for one unit of asset V at date $T = t + \tau$ and is given in eq. (11′).

In general, an option on the minimum of two risky assets is an option on $M(V, H, 0, \tau)$ with an exercise price equal to F. Geske (1979) has priced an option on an option. The optioned asset in the case of Geske's formula is a call option on the value of the firm with maturity at date $T^* \geq T$, where T is the maturity of the option he prices. The problem Geske addresses involves pricing the promise of a payment at date T of an option on an asset whose price is V, with maturity at date T^*, $T^* \geq T$, when the promise is contingent on V being larger than some number $\overline{V}$ at date T. The problem addressed in this paper involves pricing the promise of a payment at date T of an option on an asset V with exercise price F and maturity at date T, when the promise is contingent on V being smaller than some variable H at date T. An extension of the present analysis would be to price the promise of a payment at date T of an option on an asset V with exercise price F and maturity at date T^*, when the promise is contingent on V being smaller than some variable H at date T. This extension would lead to a formula which would reduce either to the formula developed by Geske or to the formula developed here in some special cases.

4. Applications

In this section, the results obtained earlier are used to price a variety of contingent claims. The section is divided into two parts. The first part analyses the pricing of bonds involving one or more foreign currencies. These bonds could be used for empirical tests of the results of this paper. The second part of this section shows that the formulas developed earlier can be usefully applied to a wide range of problems in the theory of corporate finance.

4.1. Pricing bonds whose value depends on exchange rates

The most interesting question about the bonds priced here is how their value depends on the stochastic properties of the risky assets which affect their payoff at maturity. The fairly restrictive assumptions made in this section make it possible to focus the discussion on this question. It is assumed that the term structure of interest rates is flat, that the instantaneous rate of return on the safe asset is constant, and that international markets are frictionless.[11,12] Furthermore, only discount bonds are priced.

[11] It is important to notice that 'fixed but adjustable' exchange rates do not have a continuous sample path. It follows that the discussion of this section is more relevant for a regime of flexible exchange rates than for the exchange rate regime which prevailed before 1973.

[12] Schwartz (1982) prices bonds which have a payoff similar to the payoff of the bonds priced here, except that the value of the bonds depends on the price of commodities instead of the price of foreign currencies. The formula obtained in this paper could be used to price the bonds studied by Schwartz (1982), but one should take into account the fact that commodities are not assets, whereas default-free foreign currency bonds are assets. Ingersoll (1982) also points out that stocks of commodities have a convenience yield and that the assumptions required to use option-pricing techniques may be too strong to provide a realistic characterization of commodity markets.

4.1.1. Foreign currency bonds

For simplicity, define a foreign currency bond as a bond denominated in a different currency from the currency in which the common stock of the firm is traded. A foreign currency bond is the easiest option-bond to price and therefore is useful as an introduction to a discussion of the pricing of more complex bonds. Let V be the value of the firm in terms of the domestic currency, i.e., the currency in which the common stock is traded, and let F^* be the face value of the bond in foreign currency. Define x to be the domestic price of one unit of foreign currency. The payoff in domestic currency of the bond at maturity is

$$\min (V, xF^*),$$

where xF^* is stochastic. The value at date t of a discount bond which pays xF^* at date T is equal to $x(t)e^{-R^*(T-t)}F^*$, where $x(t)$ is the exchange rate at date t and R^* is the instantaneous rate of return of the safe asset in foreign currency. Let $H(t) = x(t)e^{-R^*\tau}F^*$ and $B^*(V/x, F^*, \tau)$ be the value of the foreign currency bond in foreign currency. It can be verified that

$$B^*(V/x, F^*, \tau) = (1/x) M(V, H, 0, \tau). \tag{21}$$

In section 3, $M(V, H, 0, \tau)$ is evaluated. It is stated that $M(V, H, 0, \tau)$ can be obtained by computing the value of a conventional European call option, with V/H as the stock price, 1 as the exercise price, $R = 0$, and an instantaneous variance given by $\sigma^2 = \sigma_H^2 + \sigma_V^2 - 2\varrho_{VH}\sigma_V\sigma_H$.[13]

$M(V, H, 0, \tau)$ is a decreasing function of σ^2. Therefore a bond whose face value is denominated in foreign currency is a decreasing function of the standard deviation of the instantaneous percentage rate of change of the value of the firm and of the value of the exchange rate (holding constant the covariance between the instantaneous percentage rate of change of the value of firm and of the exchange rate). Furthermore, the value of the bond is an increasing function of the covariance between the instantaneous percentage rate of change of the value of the firm and of the exchange rate.

H can be shown to depend on the forward exchange rate. Let $X(t, T)$ be the forward exchange rate on date t on a contract maturing at date T. The interest rate parity theorem[14] states that

$$X(t, T) = x(t)e^{(R-R^*)\tau}. \tag{22}$$

[13]Fischer (1978) prices indexed-bonds using the formula for the valuation of an option to exchange one asset for another. Note that one can also price $xB^*(V/x, F^*, \tau)$ by using the fact that $B^*(V/x, F^*, \tau) = (1/x)V - C(V/x, F^*, \tau)$.

[14]See Officer and Willet (1970). Frenkel and Levich (1977), among others, show that interest rate parity holds well on Euro-markets.

Note that (22) just means that the price today of a dollar to be delivered at date T must be the same whether that dollar is invested at home in a default-free bond or abroad in a default-free bond with the proceeds at maturity of the foreign investment sold on the forward exchange market. H can now be rewritten as

$$H = X(t, T) e^{-R\tau} F^*. \tag{23}$$

It follows that, *ceteris paribus*, the higher the forward exchange rate of the foreign currency, the higher the value of the bond. This also means that, *ceteris paribus*, the higher the expected future spot exchange rate, the higher the value of the bond.[15] To understand this result, it is useful to think about the case in which changes in the exchange rate are not stochastic. In this case, the bond is equivalent to a bond in domestic currency with an exercise price equal to $X(t, T)F^*$, where $X(t, T)F^*$ is not stochastic. Any increase in $X(t, T)$ means an increase in the face value of the bond in domestic currency. Introducing uncertainty does not change that fact.

4.1.2.
Default-free
option-bonds

Feiger and Jacquillat (1979) discuss the pricing of default-free option-bonds. The analytical formulas developed in this paper make it possible to price default-free option-bonds which let the bearer choose among payments in three different currencies. Let $B(x_A F_A^*, x_B F_B^*, F, \tau)$ be the price of a discount bond which at maturity pays, at the choice of the bearer, either F units of domestic currency, F_A^* units of currency of country A or F_B^* units of currency of country B. x_A (x_B) is the current price of one unit of currency of country A (B). The payoffs of the option-bond are equal to the payoffs of a portfolio that consists of holding one safe domestic discount bond, one option on $x_A F_A^*$ with exercise price F, one option on $x_B F_B^*$, with exercise price F, and of writing an option on the minimum of $x_A F_A^*$ and $x_B F_B^*$ with the same exercise price, F. Let H be the value today of an asset which will be worth $x_A F_A^*$ at maturity and let V be the value today of an asset which will be worth $x_B F_B^*$ at maturity. If R_A^* and R_B^* are respectively the instantaneous rates of return of the safe nominal asset in country A and B, then

$$H = x_A e^{-R_A^* \tau} F_A^*, \tag{24}$$

$$V = x_B e^{-R_B^* \tau} F_B^*. \tag{25}$$

With this notation,

$$B(x_A F_A^*, x_B F_B^*, F, \tau) = MX(V, H, F, \tau) + e^{-R\tau} F, \tag{26}$$

---

[15]Stulz (1981) discusses the relationship between the forward exchange rate and the future spot exchange rate.

where $MX(V, H, F, \tau)$ is the price of an option on the maximum of V and H with exercise price F and time to maturity τ given in section 3. The default-free option-bond is a decreasing function of the coefficient of correlation between the two exchange rates. This is due to the fact that a call option on the maximum of two risky assets is the least valuable when those risky assets have a correlation coefficient of one. An option on the maximum of two risky assets will always pay at least as much as an option on the minimum of two risky assets, but the only case in which the options are the same is when $V = H, \sigma_V = \sigma_H, \varrho_{VH} = 1$, i.e., when the two risky assets are perfect substitutes.

4.1.3. Option-bonds issued by firms

Foreign currency bonds are the risky assets which are the most popular among the risky assets involving foreign currencies priced here. However, currency option-bonds issued by firms are the most interesting. For instance, very little—if anything—is known about why such bonds exist. While an analysis of why such bonds exist is beyond the purpose of this paper, knowing how these bonds are priced could be helpful for such an analysis.

Define $B(V, xF^*, F, \tau)$ to be the price of an option-bond issued by a firm whose value is V, which promises to pay at maturity either F^* units of the foreign currency or F units of the domestic currency, at the choice of the bearer of the bond. To reproduce the payoff of such a bond, one can form a portfolio which consists of holding one safe discount bond with face value F, one option on the minimum of V and H, where $H = xe^{-R^*\tau}F^*$, with exercise price F, and of writing a put on V with exercise price F. Let $P(V, F, \tau)$ be the price of a European put option on V with exercise price F. The price of the bond is given by

$$B(V, F, xF^*, \tau) = Fe^{-R\tau} - P(V, F, \tau) + M(V, H, F, \tau). \tag{27}$$

At maturity, if the value of the firm is smaller than F, the currency option included in the bond is irrelevant, since the payment to the bondholder cannot be more than the value of the firm. If, at maturity, $V > xF^* > F$, the option on the minimum of V and H pays $xF^* - F$, whereas it pays zero if $V > F > xF^*$. The total payoff of the portfolio on the right-hand side of (27) or of the option-bond is, in those cases, either xF^* or F. Finally, if $xF^* > V > F$, the bondholder receives V and the holder of the portfolio receives $F + \{\min(V, H) - F\} = V$.

The value of the option-bond is an increasing function of V, H, F and ϱ_{VH}. This means that, *ceteris paribus*, an investor is always better off buying an option-bond of a firm whose value is positively as opposed to negatively correlated with the exchange rate when the bonds have identical prices. The fact that the value of the option-bond is an increasing function of H means that, *ceteris paribus*, the higher the forward exchange rate with respect to the spot exchange rate the more valuable is the option-bond.

4.2. Some other applications in the theory of corporate finance

This section illustrates a number of other applications of the previous analysis to problems in corporate finance. The goal of this section is to emphasize the usefulness of the results developed earlier rather than to provide a complete analysis of these problems.

4.2.1. Incentive and/or risk-sharing contracts

Many contracts entered into by corporations and individuals involve the promise of a payment at date T of a fixed fee and of a variable amount which depends on the realization of some random variable Z at date T. A special case of such contracts occurs when the total promised payment at date T is equal to $F + \max\{\lambda Z - F, 0\}$. If Z is equal to the value of the firm, the payoff of the contract, at date T, written $Q(V, Z, F, 0)$, is equal to the payoff at that date of a discount bond issued by the firm with face value F and maturity T and of λ times a call option on the value of the firm with exercise price $(1/\lambda)F$ and maturity T. However, in general, such contracts have a payoff at maturity which depends on a random variable which is not perfectly correlated with the value of the firm. If the firm has no debt except for the promised payment considered here and pays no dividends until date T, the creditor of the firm receives at maturity either the promised payment or the value of the firm, V. It follows that if V and Z are jointly lognormally distributed and correspond to the prices of traded assets,[16] the formula for the pricing of an option on the minimum of two risky assets can be used to find $Q(V, \lambda Z, F, \tau)$, i.e., the value of the contract at date $t = T - \tau$,

$$Q(V, \lambda Z, F, \tau) = Fe^{-R\tau} - P(V, F, \tau) + M(V, \lambda Z, F, \tau), \tag{28}$$

where $P(V, F, \tau)$ is the price of a European put option on V with exercise price F and maturity T.

Examples of contracts in which Z corresponds to the price of a traded asset can be given. In a number of countries, there exist default-free index-bonds, i.e., bonds whose real return is not affected by unanticipated changes in the price-level. (Israel is such a country.) In such a country, a wage contract with a cost-of-living adjustment clause (COLA) can be valued using the formula for an option on the minimum of two risky assets. Let P be the price-level. COLAs generally imply that the nominal wage, F, is adjusted by an amount proportional to $\max\{P - \bar{P}, 0\}$, where $\bar{P}$ is some price-level chosen at the time the worker enters into the contract. If the value of the firm is lower than the promised payment, the worker receives the value of the firm. If $W(V, P, F, 0)$ is the payment made at date T and if this payment is the last and only payment the worker receives, it follows that

[16]The assumption that Z corresponds to the price of a traded asset is made to simplify the discussion, so that it can be focused on the usefulness of the formula for the pricing of an option on the minimum of two risky assets. It is possible to price assets in which Z does not correspond to the price of a traded asset. Cox, Ingersoll and Ross (1978) develop a methodology which can be used to price such assets and Dothan and Williams (1980) show how such a methodology can be used for capital budgeting purposes.

$$W(V, P, F, 0) = F - \max\{F - V, 0\} + \max\{\min(V, \delta FP) - F, 0\},$$
(29)

where δ is a coefficient determined in the wage contract and V is the value of the firm. As, by assumption, there exist traded assets whose value at date T is equal, respectively, to V and δFP, $W(V, P, F, \tau)$ can be computed using eq. (29) with H equal to the current value of a discount bond which pays δFP at date T. [17]

An interesting implication of this example is that the value of a COLA is an increasing function of the coefficient of correlation between the dynamics of the value of the firm and the dynamics of the price-level. Furthermore, an increase in the variance of the rate of inflation could decrease the value of a COLA. In general, one would expect an increase in the variance of the rate of growth of the firm to decrease the value of the wage contract.

A COLA is a risk-sharing arrangement between an employer and an employee. There exists a wide variety of risk-sharing arrangements whose payoff at maturity takes the same form as the payoff at maturity of a wage contract with a COLA. For instance, many contracts for the delivery of some commodity at some future date involve a risk-sharing arrangement similar to a COLA, except that the price-level P is replaced by the spot price of the commodity to be delivered. Many contracts whereby a firm produces a commodity to order for a buyer involve the payment at some date T^*, of a fixed amount, and of a variable amount which depends on the costs of some inputs, if these costs exceed some given number specified in the contract.[18] It follows from this discussion that potentially a wide variety of risk-sharing contracts could be priced by using the formula for an option on the minimum of two risky assets.

Compensation plans for managers often have a payoff at maturity similar to the payoff at maturity of a wage contract with a COLA.[19] As an example, some compensation plans include a variable payment which depends on a comparison of the performance of the firm for which the managers work and the performance of some competing firm (or the performance of the industry). For simplicity, it is assumed here that the performance of the firms is measured by their value at maturity of the contract. Let V be the value of the managers' firm and S be the value of the competing firm. Both firms pay no dividends until date T. The firm whose value is S has no debt.

[17]It is also necessary that H and V are jointly lognormally distributed, that the firm pays no dividends until date T and has no debt of higher or equal priority.
[18]See Rodriguez and Carter (1979, p. 501) for an example of a contract where P is replaced by the spot price of a commodity. For examples of industrial contracts which have a payment which depends on the cost of inputs if it exceeds some number, see Cummins (1977).
[19]See Smith and Watts (1981) for a description and analysis of compensation plans. See also Miller and Scholes (1980).

The only debt of the firm whose value is V is the promised payment to its managers, which is assumed to be equal to

$$F + \min\{\max\{\gamma V - \delta S, 0\}, \max\{\gamma V - F, 0\}\},$$

where γ and δ are positive constants, $\gamma < 1$, and F is the fixed component of the managers' compensation at date T. No variable payment is made if the firm does poorly, i.e., if $\gamma V < F$. It can be verified that the value of the compensation plan at maturity, i.e., $L(V, S, F, 0)$, is equal to

$$L(V, S, F, 0) = F - P(V, F, 0) + C(\gamma V, F, 0) - M(\gamma V, \delta S, F, 0). \quad (30)$$

If V and S are prices of traded assets and are jointly lognormally distributed, $L(V, S, F, \tau)$ is given by the following equation:

$$L(V, S, F, \tau) = Fe^{-R\tau} - P(V, F, \tau) + C(\gamma V, F, \tau) - M(\gamma V, \delta S, F, \tau). \quad (31)$$

No clear statement can be made about the effect of a change in the variance of the rate of change of the value of the firm on the value of the compensation plan. In other words, for different values of the parameters of the plan, it might well happen that an increase in the variance of the rate of change of the value of the firm has effects of opposite signs on the value of the compensation plan. However, a compensation plan like the one discussed here induces managers to choose projects which reduce the coefficient of correlation between the rates of change of V and S.

4.2.2. The valuation of investment opportunities

The formula for a call option on the maximum of two risky assets can be used to value complex projects in which the firm chooses among various streams of cash-flows at a future date. Myers (1977) shows that an investment opportunity to which a firm has exclusive access can be regarded as a call option where the exercise price is the future outlay required to undertake the investment. In many cases, when the future outlay is made, the firm can choose among two mutually exclusive risky streams of cash-flows. Such an investment opportunity can be valued using the formula for an option on the minimum of two risky assets.

As an example, suppose that an all-equity firm has the opportunity to buy a parcel of land at date t which it can use for two mutually exclusive purposes at some future date T. The firm can use the parcel of land to build either a residential property or an office-building. The cost of each building, to be paid at date T, is known and equal to F. For simplicity, assume that $V(H)$ is the price of an asset which pays no dividends and that $V(H)$ is equal to the value of the residential property (office building) at date T.[20] It is assumed that V and H are jointly lognormally distributed. If an outlay is made at date T, the firm cannot change its use of the parcel of land ever again. If no outlay is made, the firm cannot use the parcel of land after date T. Construction takes a negligible amount of time. Taxes and transaction costs are neglected. With these assumptions, the firm buys the parcel of land if its price is no greater than $MX(V, H, F, \tau)$, i.e., the price of a call option on the maximum of V and H, with exercise price F and time to maturity τ. The approach used here offers three interesting insights: (1) The lower the coefficient of correlation between the value of the alternative uses of the parcel of land, the more valuable the parcel of land is to the firm. (2) The parcel of land is always more valuable if it has two possible uses than if it has only one of these two possible uses, as $MX(V, H, F, \tau) \geqq C(V, F, \tau)$ and $MX(V, H, F, \tau) \geqq C(H, F, \tau)$. (3) The loss suffered by the firm if a zoning restriction is approved (after it has bought the land) which forbids it from building an office-building is equal to $MX(V, H, F, \tau') - C(V, F, \tau')$, where $\tau' = T - t'$ and $t' < T$ is the time at which the zoning restriction is approved.

4.2.3. The valuation of secured debt	The formula for a call option on the minimum of two risky assets makes it possible to obtain some new insights into the problem of valuing secured debt.[21] Let $D(V, S, F, \tau)$ be the value of a discount bond with maturity at date T and facevalue F, secured by a collateral which pays no dividends and whose price is S. The value of the firm's assets, which include the collateral, is equal to W. There exist claims which mature at date T and have priority over the claim of the holders of the secured bond over the assets of the firm whose value is given by $W - S$. These claims have a facevalue equal to G. Define $W - G$ to be equal to V. The firm pays no dividends until date T and has no other claimants than those already discussed. At date T, the holders of the secured bond receive $\min\{F, \max\{V, S\}\}$. This implies that the holders of the secured bond receive at least the value of the collateral in the event of default; they receive the value of the assets of the firm if, after all claimants of higher priority have been paid off, that value exceeds the value of the collateral. The value of the secured bond at maturity can be written as

$$D(V, S, F, 0) = F - \max\{F - \max(V, S), 0\}. \tag{32}$$

It follows from eq. (32) that the value of the secured debt at maturity is equal to the value of a default-free discount-bond with maturity T and facevalue F minus the value at maturity T of a put option on the maximum of V and S with exercise price F. In section 3, a formula for a put option on the

---

[20]The assumption that the assets whose price is, respectively, V and H, do not pay dividends could be relaxed to allow for a dividend paid continuously and proportional to the value of the firm. See Merton (1973) for such an adjustment. (A dividend adjustment would allow these assets to be existing buildings which are perfect substitutes for those which could be constructed on the parcel of land.)

[21]For earlier work on secured debt, see Smith and Warner (1979) and Scott (1978).

maximum of two risky assets is given. To apply this formula to value $D(V, S, F, \tau)$, it is necessary that V and S are jointly lognormally distributed. It does not seem realistic to assume that V is lognormally distributed when S is lognormally distributed, because V is equal to $W - G$ and W is a sum of random variables, one of which is S. Should one assume that V is lognormally distributed, however, one would obtain the interesting result that the lower the coefficient of correlation between the dynamics of the price of the collateral and the dynamics of the value of the firm, the more valuable is the secured debt.

5. Conclusion and summary

This paper presents analytical formulas for the pricing of a European put and call option on the maximum or the minimum of two risky assets. It is shown that a call option on the minimum of two risky assets with an exercise price equal to zero can be evaluated by using the formula for the pricing of an option to exchange one asset for another. A call option on the minimum of two risky assets is an increasing function of the price of each risky asset and a decreasing function of the exercise price. It is an increasing function of the coefficient of correlation between the dynamics of the two risky assets. An increase in time to maturity or in the standard deviation of the return on one of the risky assets has an ambiguous effect on the value of the option.

This paper contains a number of applications of options on the minimum or the maximum of two risky assets. Foreign currency bonds, default-free currency option-bonds and risky currency option-bonds are priced. It is shown that a wide variety of risk-sharing and incentive contracts have a payoff at maturity which contains the payoff at maturity of an option on the minimum or maximum of two risky assets. Investment opportunities which correspond to complex projects in which a firm chooses among various cash-flows at a future date can also be valued using the techniques developed in this paper. Finally, secured debt has a payoff at maturity which corresponds to the payoff of a default-free discount bond minus the payoff of a put option on the maximum of two risky assets.

Appendix 1

In this appendix, the derivation of eq. (11) is sketched. For the purpose of computing the expected value of the option at maturity in a risk-neutral world, there is no loss in generality if it is assumed that V and H each follow a lognormal distribution. Let $v = \ln V$ and $h = \ln H$. Define $k = \min(v, h)$. The probability that k is smaller than some value K is

$$F(K) = 1 - \int_K^\infty \int_K^\infty n_2(v,h)\,dh\,dv, \tag{A.1}$$

where $n_2(v, h)$ is the bivariate normal density function. To obtain the density function of the minimum, take the derivative of (A.1) with respect to K. Let $\bar{v}$ be the expected value of v, $\sigma(v)$ the standard deviation of v, $\sigma(h)$ the standard deviation of h and ϱ the coefficient of correlation between v and h. If $f(k)$ is the probability density function of k, then

$$f(k) = N_1\left(\frac{-k + \bar{v} + \varrho(\sigma(v)/\sigma(h))(k - \bar{h})}{\sqrt{1 - \varrho^2}\,\sigma(v)}\right) n_1\left(\frac{k - \bar{h}}{\sigma(h)}\right)$$
$$+ N_1\left(\frac{-k + \bar{h} + \varrho(\sigma(h)/\sigma(v))(k - \bar{v})}{\sqrt{1 - \varrho^2}\,\sigma(h)}\right) n_1\left(\frac{k - \bar{v}}{\sigma(v)}\right). \tag{A.2}$$

$N_1(a)$ is the cumulative standard normal distribution evaluated at a and $n_1(a)$ is the standard normal density function evaluated at a.

The expected payoff of the option at maturity is

$$E(C(V, H, F, 0)) = \int_{\ln F}^\infty e^k f(k)\,dk - \int_{\ln F}^\infty F f(k)\,dk. \tag{A.3}$$

(A.3) can be rewritten as the sum of three terms. The first term is the expected value of H at maturity if H is the maximum and exceeds F. The second term is the expected value of V at maturity if V is the minimum and exceeds F. The third term is minus F times the probability that the option will be exercised at maturity. The first term can be written as

$$A = \int_{\ln(F/H)}^\infty e^{R\tau} H N_1\left(\frac{-a + \ln(V/H) + (R - \frac{1}{2}\sigma_V^2)\tau}{\sigma_V\sqrt{\tau}\sqrt{1 - \varrho_{VH}^2}}\right.$$
$$\left. + \frac{\varrho_{VH}(\sigma_V/\sigma_H)(a - (R - \frac{1}{2}\sigma_H^2)\tau)}{\sigma_V\sqrt{\tau}\sqrt{1 - \varrho_{VH}^2}}\right) n_1\left(\frac{a - (R + \frac{1}{2}\sigma_H^2)\tau}{\sigma_H\sqrt{\tau}}\right)da. \tag{A.4}$$

Rewrite this in double integral form with Q being the upper limit of integration of the cumulative normal distribution in (A.4),

$$A = e^{R\tau} \int_{\ln(F/H)}^{\infty} \int_{-\infty}^{Q} n_1(Z) n_1 \left(\frac{a - (R + \frac{1}{2}\sigma_H^2)\tau}{\sigma_H \sqrt{\tau}} \right) \, dZ \, da. \qquad (A.5)$$

Rewrite Q as $aX + B$. Use the change of variables $Y = -X$ and $U = aY + Z$ and evaluate the integrals in (A.5). Premultiplying A by $e^{-R\tau}$ yields the first term in (11). Following the same procedure for the two other terms defined earlier yields eq. (11).

Appendix 2 This appendix gives the partial derivatives of the price of the call option on the minimum of two risky assets with respect to H, F, and R,

$$\partial c/\partial H = N_2(\alpha_1, \alpha_2, \varrho_c) + N_1 \left(\frac{\alpha_1 - \varrho_c \alpha_2}{\sqrt{1 - \varrho_c^2}} \right) e^{-\frac{1}{2}\alpha_2^2} \frac{1}{k^{\frac{1}{2}}}$$

$$- \left(\frac{V}{H} \right) N_1 \left(\frac{\beta_1 - \varrho_C \beta_2}{\sqrt{1 - \varrho_C^2}} \right) e^{-\frac{1}{2}\beta_2^2} \frac{1}{k^{\frac{1}{2}}}, \qquad (A.6)$$

$$\partial C/\partial F = -e^{-R\tau} N_2(\gamma_1, \gamma_2, \varrho_{VH}) < 0, \qquad (A.7)$$

$$\partial C/\partial R = \tau e^{-R\tau} N_2(\gamma_1, \gamma_2, \varrho_{VH}) > 0. \qquad (A.8)$$

Appendix 3 Eq. (20) can be rewritten as

$$\frac{\partial C}{\partial \varrho_{VH}} = FN_1 \left(\frac{\alpha_1 - \varrho_c \alpha_2}{\sqrt{1 - \varrho_c^2}} \right) e^{\frac{1}{2}\alpha_2^2} e^{-\frac{1}{2}\alpha_1^2} e^{-\frac{1}{2}\gamma_1^2} \frac{1}{\sqrt{2\pi}} \left[\frac{\sigma_V \sigma_H \sqrt{\pi}}{\sigma} + \frac{\sigma_V \sigma_H \alpha_2}{\sigma^2} \right]$$

$$+ FN_1 \left(\frac{\beta_1 - \varrho_C \beta_2}{\sqrt{1 - \varrho_C^2}} \right) e^{-\frac{1}{2}\beta_2^2} e^{-\frac{1}{2}\beta_1^2} e^{-\frac{1}{2}\gamma_2^2} \frac{1}{\sqrt{2\pi}} \left[\frac{\sigma_V \sigma_H \sqrt{\tau}}{\sigma} + \frac{\sigma_V \sigma_H \beta_2}{\sigma^2} \right]$$

$$(A.9)$$

Note now that

$$\alpha_2 = (\gamma_2 \sigma_V - \gamma_1 \sigma_H \sqrt{\tau} + (\varrho_{VH} \sigma_V/\sigma_H - 1)\sigma_H^2 \tau)/\sqrt{\tau}\sigma$$

$$= (\ln(V/H) - \tfrac{1}{2}\sigma_V^2 \tau - \tfrac{1}{2}\sigma_H^2 \tau + \varrho_{VH} \sigma_V \sigma_H \tau)/\sqrt{\tau}\sigma$$

$$= \ln(V/H)/\sqrt{\tau}\sigma - \tfrac{1}{2}\sigma\sqrt{\tau}.$$

Similarly,

$$\beta_2 = \ln(H/V)/\sqrt{\tau}\sigma - \tfrac{1}{2}\sigma\sqrt{\tau}.$$

This implies that

$$\beta_2^2 = \alpha_2^2 - 2\ln(V/H).$$

It can also be shown that

$$(\alpha_1 - \varrho_c\alpha_2)/\sqrt{1 - \varrho_c^2} = (\beta_1 - \varrho_c\beta_2)/\sqrt{1 - \varrho_C^2}.$$

By substituting these results in (A.9), it follows that

$$\frac{\partial C}{\partial \varrho_{VH}} = VN_1\left(\frac{\beta_1 - \varrho_C\beta_2}{\sqrt{1 - \varrho_C^2}}\right)\frac{e^{-\frac{1}{2}\beta_2^2}}{\sqrt{2\pi}}\left[\frac{2\sigma_V\sigma_H\sqrt{\tau}}{\sigma} + \frac{\sigma_V\sigma_H(\beta_2 + \alpha_2)}{\sigma^2}\right]$$

$$= VN_1\left(\frac{\beta_1 - \varrho_C\beta_2}{\sqrt{1 - \varrho_C^2}}\right)\frac{e^{-\frac{1}{2}\beta_2^2}}{\sqrt{2\pi}}\cdot\frac{\sigma_V\sigma_H\sqrt{\tau}}{\sigma} > 0.$$

Note that to obtain (A.9), it is necessary to use a result on partial moments of normally distributed variables which can be found in Winkler et al. (1972).

References

Abramowitz, M. and I. Stegum, 1970, Handbook of mathematical functions, NBS applied mathematical series 55, 9th printing, Nov. (National Bureau of Standards, Washington, DC).

Black, F. and M. Scholes, 1973, The pricing of options and corporate liabilities, *Journal of Political Economy* 81, 637-659.

Cox, J.C., J.E. Ingersoll and S.A. Ross, 1978, A theory of the term structure of interest rates, Research paper no. 468 (Graduate School of Business, Stanford University, Stanford, CA).

Cox, J.C. and S.A. Ross, 1976, The valuation of options for alternative stochastic processes, *Journal of Financial Economics* 3, 145-166.

Cummins, J.M., 1977, Incentive contracting for national defense: A problem in optimal risk sharing, *Bell Journal of Economics* 8, no. 1, 168-185.

Dothan, U. and J. Williams, 1980, Term-risk structures and the valuation of projects, *Journal of Financial and Quantitative Economics* 15, no. 4, 875-906.

Feiger, G. and B. Jacquillat, 1979, Currency option bonds, puts and calls on spot exchange and the hedging of contingent claims, *Journal of Finance* 34, 1129-1139.

Feiger, G. and B. Jacquillat, 1981, International finance (Allyn & Bacon, Boston, MA).

Fischer, S., 1978, Call option pricing when the exercise price is uncertain, *Journal of Finance* 33, 169-176.

Frenkel, J.A. and R.M. Levich, 1977, Transaction costs and interest arbitrate: Tranquil versus turbulent periods, *Journal of Political Economy* 85, no. 6, 1209-1226.

Geske, R., 1979, The valuation of compound options, *Journal of Financial Economics* 7, 63-82.

Harrison, J.M. and D.M. Kreps, 1979, Martingales and arbitrage in multiperiod securities markets, *Journal of Economic Theory* 20, 381-408.

Ingersoll, J.E., 1982, The pricing of commodity-linked bonds: Discussion, *Journal of Finance*, forthcoming.

Johnson, H., 1981, The pricing of complex options, Unpublished manuscript.

Margrabe, W., 1978, The value of an option to exchange one asset for another, *Journal of Finance* 33, 177-186.

Merton, R.C., 1971, Optimum consumption and portfolio rules in a continuous-time model, *Journal of Economic Theory* 3, 373-413.

Merton, R.C., 1973, The theory of rational option pricing, *Bell Journal of Economics and Management Science* 4, 141-183.

Merton, R.C., 1974, On the pricing of corporate debt: The risk structure of interest rates, *Journal of Finance* 29, 442-470.

Miller, M. and M. Scholes, 1980, Executive compensation, taxes and incentives, Working paper no. 42 (Graduate School of Business, University of Chicago, Chicago IL).

Myers, S., 1977, Determinants of corporate borrowing, *Journal of Financial Economics* 5, 147-175.

Officer, L.H. and T.O. Willet, 1980, The covered arbitrage schedule: A critical survey of recent developments, *Journal of Money, Credit and Banking* 2, 247-257.

Rodriguez, R.M. and E.E. Carter, 1979, International financial management (Prentice-Hall, Englewood Cliffs, NJ).

Schwartz, E., 1982, The pricing of commodity-linked bonds, *Journal of Finance*, forthcoming.

Scott, J.H., 1977, Bankruptcy, secured debt and optimal capital structure, *Journal of Finance* 32, 1-19.

Smith, C.W., 1976, Option pricing: A review, *Journal of Financial Economics* 3, 3-51.

Smith, C.W. and J.B. Warner, 1979, Bankruptcy, secured debt, and optimal capital structure: Comment, *Journal of Finance* 34, 247-251.

Smith, C.W. and R.L. Watts, 1981, Incentive and tax effects of U.S. executive compensation plans, Unpublished manuscript.

Stulz, R.M., 1981, A model of international asset pricing, *Journal of Financial Economics* 9, 383-407.

Winkler, R.L., G.N. Roodman and R.R. Britney, 1972, The determination of partial moments, *Management Science* 19, 290-297.

4

Options on the Maximum or the Minimum of Several Assets

Herb Johnson*

Abstract

Using an intuitive approach that also provides new intuition concerning the Black and Scholes equation, this paper extends the results of Johnson and Stulz to the pricing of options on the minimum or the maximum of several risky assets.

I. Introduction

By laborious calculation, Johnson [9] and Stulz [15] independently derived prices for options on the maximum and the minimum of two assets. This paper presents a simple, intuitive way, using the Cox and Ross [3] approach and a trick based on a device used by Margrabe [10], to write down the solution for the general case of an option on several assets. The result could be useful for pricing, among other things, currency option bonds, portfolio insurance, and the quality option in commodities contracts (see [6]).

In the next section, we first illustrate the procedure for the Black and Scholes equation, thereby obtaining some new intuition about this equation, and then develop the equations for calls on the maximum and the minimum. Section III is a summary.

II. The Pricing of a Call on the Maximum or the Minimum

First consider the Black and Scholes [1] equation. We can write the solution as

$$c = SN(d_1) - Xe^{-rT}N(d_2),$$

$$\text{where } d_2 = \frac{\log S/X + \left(r - \frac{1}{2}\sigma^2 \right)T}{\sigma\sqrt{T}},$$

*Graduate School of Administration, University of California, Davis, Davis, CA 95616. The author wishes to acknowledge useful comments from R. Castanias, P. Boyle, W. Margrabe, W. Bailey, J. Ingersoll, C. Smith, R. Stulz, and an anonymous *JFQA* referee.

Herb Johnson, "Options on the Maximum or the Minimum of Several Assets." Reprinted with permission from the *Journal of Financial and Quantitative Analysis*, Vol. 22, No. 3, September 1987.

$$d_1 = d_2 + \sigma\sqrt{T},$$

$N(x)$ is the standard cumulative normal, and c, S, X, r, σ^2, and T are the call price, stock price, exercise price, risk-free rate, variance of the rate of return on the stock, and time to expiration, respectively. Now, using the Cox and Ross approach, $N(d_2)$ can be interpreted as the probability (in a risk-neutral world) that the call will be exercised, i.e., the probability that S^*, the stock price at expiration, will be greater than X given that the stock price is S today. In the Cox and Ross approach, we ordinarily come up with $N(d_1)$ by taking the expectation of S^* for $S^* > X$, changing variables, completing the square, etc., until the desired form is obtained. However, if we use a trick based on a device first introduced in Margrabe [10], the $N(d_1)$ term can be written down immediately. A call option can be thought of as an option to exchange cash for a common stock. Thus, it is like Margrabe's option to exchange one asset for another. Hence, it can be valued by a change in numeraire, just as in Margrabe's case. In our case, we use the stock price as numeraire. (Note that Garman and Hawkins [5] used this same approach with regard to currency options.) The call price measured in units of the stock price looks like a European put on a risky asset with current price $x \equiv Xe^{-rT}/S$, with unit exercise price, and a zero interest rate,

$$\frac{c}{S} = 1 \cdot N(-d_2') - xN(-d_1'),$$

where $d_2' = \dfrac{\log x - \dfrac{1}{2}\sigma^2 T}{\sigma\sqrt{T}}$

and $d_1' = d_2' + \sigma\sqrt{T}$.

In this world, the stock price measured in units of itself is just the risk-free asset, with a zero return. By Ito's lemma,

$$\frac{dx}{x} = (r - \mu + \sigma^2)dt - \sigma dz,$$

where $t = -T$ is calendar time. Thus, the variance of the rate of return on x is just σ^2. In the Cox and Ross approach, we replace the drift term, $r - \mu + \sigma^2$, by the risk-free rate, which, in this case, is zero. Thus, $N(d_1) \equiv N(-d_2')$ is just the risk-neutral probability that this put will be exercised. Not only do we have this intuitive interpretation of $N(d_1)$, but, had we not known this factor, we could have written it down without going through any laborious calculations. While Smith [14] has noted that Boness [2] had a probability interpretation for $N(d_1)$, Boness evidently still had to do all the computations to find $N(d_1)$. These computations become extremely laborious when there are many possible exercise dates or many underlying assets. It should be noted that Merton ([11], [12]) also recognized the usefulness of the fact that an option price is generally linearly homogeneous in the stock price and the exercise price. We next apply our procedure to value calls on the maximum and the minimum.

We make the usual perfect market and European option assumptions. Consider n assets with current prices $S_1, S_2, \ldots, S_n$. We assume that each asset price follows geometric Brownian motion and that there are no dividends.

Consider a call on the maximum of the n assets with exercise price X and time to maturity T. Then, by the Cox and Ross [3] approach, we know one term in the expression for the price, c_{max}, of this call must be the negative of the discounted exercise price multiplied by the probability (in a risk-neutral world) that at least one of the asset prices will be greater than X. Hence, one term is

$$-Xe^{-rT} \left[1 - \text{Prob} \left(S_1^*, S_2^*, \ldots, S_n^* < X \right) \right],$$

where asterisks denote values at maturity. This probability expression is simply

$$1 - N_n \left(-d_2 \left(S_1, X, \sigma_1^2 \right), -d_2 \left(S_2, X, \sigma_2^2 \right), \ldots, -d_2 \left(S_n, X, \sigma_n^2 \right), \varrho_{12}, \varrho_{13}, \ldots \right),$$

$$\text{where, in general, } d_2 \left(s, x, \sigma^2 \right) = \frac{\log \frac{s}{x} + \left(r - \frac{1}{2} \sigma^2 \right) T}{\sigma \sqrt{T}},$$

N_i is the i-variate standard cumulative normal, σ_i^2 is the variance of the rate of return on the ith asset, and ϱ_{ij} is the correlation coefficient for the returns on the ith and jth assets.

We still need to identify the positive terms in the expression for c_{max}. We identify each of these terms, one by one, using a change of numeraire. Using the ith asset as numeraire means that we measure c_{max} in units of S_i, the ith asset price, i.e., divide by S_i. Then the call on the maximum in units of S_i is transformed into a complex security that consists of (1) a European put with unit exercise price, where the put is exercised by surrendering a risky asset, the current price of which is $x_i \equiv Xe^{-rT}/S_i$, provided

$$S_i^* = \max_{j=1,n} S_j^*,$$

(2) an option to exchange the risky asset for S_2, provided

$$S_2^* = \max_{j=1,n} S_j^*, \ldots,$$

and (n) an option to exchange the risky asset for S_n, provided

$$S_n^* = \max_{j=1,n} S_j^*.$$

In this transformed world, the interest rate is zero. The point of making this transformation is that we can immediately identify the positive term in the put as the risk-neutral joint probability that $x_i^* < 1$, $S_1^*/S_i^* < 1$, $\ldots$, $S_n^*/S_i^* < 1$. Thus, this term, which, when multiplied by S_i, is the ith term in the expression for c_{max}, can be written as

$$N_n\left(-d_2'\left(x_i, 1, \sigma_i^2\right), -d_2'\left(S_1, S_i, \sigma_{1i}^2\right), \ldots, -d_2'\left(S_n, S_i, \sigma_{ni}^2\right), \varrho_{i1i}, \varrho_{i2i}, \ldots\right),$$

or, equivalently, as

$$N_n\left(d_1\left(S_i, X, \sigma_i^2\right), d_1'\left(S_i, S_1, \sigma_{1i}^2\right), \ldots, d_n'\left(S_i, S_n, \sigma_{ni}^2\right), \varrho_{i1i}, \varrho_{i2i}, \ldots\right),$$

where primes indicate that the interest rate is set to zero, where, in general,

$$\sigma_{ij}^2 = \sigma_i^2 - 2\varrho_{ij}\,\sigma_i\,\sigma_j + \sigma_j^2,$$

and where the correlation coefficients are to be determined. Thus, we can identify each of the positive terms in the expression for c_{max} as the ith asset price multiplied by a probability term defined in terms of various d_1s. We therefore have

$$
\begin{aligned}
c_{max} = \; & S_1 N_n\left(d_1\left(S_1, X, \sigma_1^2\right), d_1'\left(S_1, S_2, \sigma_{12}^2\right), \ldots, \right. \\
& \qquad \left. d_1'\left(S_1, S_n, \sigma_{1n}^2\right), \varrho_{112}, \varrho_{113}, \ldots\right) \\
& + S_2 N_n\left(d_1\left(S_2, X, \sigma_1^2\right), d_1'\left(S_2, S_1, \sigma_{12}^2\right), \ldots, \right. \\
& \qquad \left. d_1'\left(S_2, S_n, \sigma_{2n}^2\right), \varrho_{212}, \varrho_{223}, \ldots\right) \\
& + \ldots \\
& + S_n N_n\left(d_1\left(S_n, X, \sigma_n^2\right), d_1'\left(S_n, S_1, \sigma_{1n}^2\right), \ldots, \right. \\
& \qquad \left. d_1'\left(S_n, S_{n-1}, \sigma_{n-1n}^2\right), \varrho_{n1n}, \varrho_{n2n}, \ldots\right) \\
& - Xe^{-rT}\left(1 - N_n\left(-d_2\left(S_1, X, \sigma_1^2\right), -d_2\left(S_2, X, \sigma_2^2\right), \ldots, \right.\right. \\
& \qquad \left.\left. -d_2\left(S_n, X, \sigma_n^2\right), \varrho_{12}, \varrho_{13}, \ldots\right)\right),
\end{aligned}
$$

(1)

where

$$d_1'\left(S_i, S_j, \sigma_{ij}^2\right) = \frac{\log \dfrac{S_i}{S_j} + \dfrac{1}{2}\sigma_{ij}^2\,T}{\sigma_{ij}\sqrt{T}},$$

(2)

and where the triple indexed correlation coefficients are found as follows. We have

$$
\begin{aligned}
\mathrm{Cov}\left(\log S_i^*, \log \frac{S_i^*}{S_j^*}\right) &= \mathrm{Var}\left(\log S_i^*\right) - \mathrm{Cov}\left(\log S_i^*, \log S_j^*\right) \\
&= \sigma_i^2 - \varrho_{ij}\sigma_i\sigma_j.
\end{aligned}
$$

(3)

But the left-hand side can also be defined as $\sigma_i\,\sigma_{ij}\,\varrho_{iij}$. Thus,

$$\varrho_{iij} = \frac{\sigma_i - \varrho_{ij}\,\sigma_j}{\sigma_{ij}}.$$

(4)

Similarly, $\quad \text{Cov}\left(\log \dfrac{S_i^*}{S_k^*}, \log \dfrac{S_i^*}{S_j^*}\right) = \sigma_i^2 - \varrho_{ij}\,\sigma_i\sigma_j - \varrho_{ik}\sigma_i\sigma_k + \varrho_{jk}\sigma_j\sigma_k,$

so that $\quad \varrho_{ijk} = \dfrac{\sigma_i^2 - \varrho_{ij}\sigma_i\sigma_j - \varrho_{ik}\sigma_i\sigma_k + \varrho_{jk}\sigma_j\sigma_k}{\sigma_{ij}\sigma_{ik}}.$ (5)

Tilley and Latainer [16] state an equation resembling (1). However, they leave the factors multiplying $S_1, \ldots, S_n$, and Xe^{-rT} undefined.

For $n = 2$, the expression simplifies to

$$c_{max} = S_1 N_2\big(d_1\big(S_1, X, \sigma_1^2\big), d_1'\big(S_1, S_2, \sigma_{12}^2\big), \varrho_{112}\big) \qquad (6)$$
$$+ S_2 N_2\big(d_1\big(S_2, X, \sigma_2^2\big), d_1'\big(S_2, S_1, \sigma_{12}^2\big), \varrho_{212}\big)$$
$$- Xe^{-rT}\big(1 - N_2\big(-d_2\big(S_1, X, \sigma_1^2\big), -d_2\big(S_2, X, \sigma_2^2\big), \varrho_{12}\big)\big),$$

which is consistent with the equations in Johnson [9] and Stulz [15], correcting for the typographical error in equation (11) of Stulz ($\sigma^2\sqrt{\tau}$ should be $\sigma^2\tau$).

Similarly, for the option on the minimum we have

$$c_{min} = S_1 N_n\big(d_1\big(S_1, X, \sigma_1^2\big), -d_1'\big(S_1, S_2, \sigma_{12}^2\big), \ldots, \qquad (7)$$
$$-d_1'\big(S_1, S_n, \sigma_{1n}^2\big), -\varrho_{112}, -\varrho_{113}, \ldots, \varrho_{123}, \ldots\big)$$
$$+ S_2 N_n\big(d_1\big(S_2, X, \sigma_2^2\big), -d_1'\big(S_2, S_1, \sigma_{12}^2\big), \ldots,$$
$$-d_1'\big(S_2, S_n, \sigma_{2n}^2\big), -\varrho_{212}, -\varrho_{223}, \ldots, \varrho_{213}, \ldots\big)$$
$$+ \ldots$$
$$+ S_n N_n\big(d_1\big(S_n, X, \sigma_n^2\big), -d_1'\big(S_n, S_1, \sigma_{1n}^2\big), \ldots,$$
$$-d_1'\big(S_n, S_{n-1}, \sigma_{n-1n}^2\big), -\varrho_{n1n}, \varrho_{n2n}, \ldots, \varrho_{n12}, \ldots\big)$$
$$- Xe^{-rT} N_n\big(d_2\big(S_1, X, \sigma_1^2\big), d_2\big(S_2, X, \sigma_2^2\big), \ldots,$$
$$d_2\big(S_n, X, \sigma_n^2\big), \varrho_{12}, \varrho_{13}, \ldots\big),$$

which for $n = 2$ reduces to

$$c_{min} = S_1 N_2\big(d_1\big(S_1, X, \sigma_1^2\big), -d_1'\big(S_1, S_2, \sigma_{12}^2\big), -\varrho_{112}\big) \qquad (8)$$
$$+ S_2 N_2\big(d_1\big(S_2, X, \sigma_2^2\big), -d_1'\big(S_2, S_1, \sigma_{12}^2\big), -\varrho_{212}\big)$$
$$- Xe^{-rT} N_2\big(d_2\big(S_1, X, \sigma_1^2\big), d_2\big(S_2, X, \sigma_2^2\big), \varrho_{12}\big),$$

which agrees with the corrected version of equation (11) of Stulz.

Note that there is linear homogeneity in that

$$c_{max} = S_1 \frac{\partial c_{max}}{\partial S_1} + \ldots S_n \frac{\partial c_{max}}{\partial S_n} + X \frac{\partial c_{max}}{\partial X} \tag{9}$$

and similarly for c_{min}. Also note that while c_{min} decreases as more assets are added, c_{max} increases and can have a very large value. Consider, for example, the case $S_1 = S_2 = \ldots = S_n = X$ and T very large. Then the d_1 terms for c_{max} are very large while Xe^{-rT} is very small. Thus, c_{max} approaches $S_1 + S_2 + \ldots + S_n$. If one had a thousand-year call on the maximum of all the stocks on the New York Stock Exchange, this would mean obtaining the best performing stock for an exercise price that is negligible in present value, and, provided no pair of stocks is perfectly positively correlated, the value of owning all the others together would very likely be small compared to the value of that best performing stock. In fact, for $n = 2$, $S_1 = S_2 = X = 40$, $r = 0.1$, $\sigma_1 = \sigma_2 = 0.3$, $\varrho = 0.5$, and $T = 1, 10$, and 100 years, we obtain $c_{max} = 9.96, 40.54$, and 74.65, respectively. Finally, note that the $n = 2$ identity, proved in Stulz [15] and Johnson [9],

$$c_{max} + c_{min} = c(S_1, X) + c(S_2, X), \tag{10}$$

where $c(S_i, X)$ is an ordinary call on S_i with exercise price X, can be extended to the general case by introducing calls on the second best, third best, etc.

Puts can be handled in the same way. See Geske [7], Geske and Johnson [8], and Schervish [13] for numerical methods for evaluating the multivariate normals. See Dothan and Williams [4] for a different application of complex options.

III. Summary

This paper develops equations for the prices of calls on the maximum and the minimum of several risky assets. The equations reduce to the results of Stulz [15] and Johnson [9] when there are only two assets. The technique used in this paper not only provides more intuition about the Black and Scholes equation, but can also be used to derive other results, such as those in Geske and Johnson [8], in a simple way.

References

1 Black, F., and M. Scholes. "The Pricing of Options and Corporate Liabilities." *Journal of Political Economy,* 81 (May/June 1973), 637-659.

2 Boness, A. J. "Elements of a Theory of Stock-Option Value." *Journal of Political Economy,* 72 (April 1964), 163-175.

3 Cox, J. C., and S. A. Ross. "The Valuation of Options for Alternative Stochastic Processes." *Journal of Financial Economics,* 3 (March 1976), 145-166.

4 Dothan, M. U., and J. Williams. "Education as an Option." *Journal of Business,* 54 (Jan. 1981), 117-139.

5 Garman, M., and G. Hawkins. "Another Look at Put-Call Parity." Unpubl. paper presented at the American Finance Association meetings (Dec. 1984).

6 Gay, G. D., and S. Manaster. "The Quality Option Implicit in Futures Contracts." *Journal of Financial Economics,* 13 (Sept. 1984), 353-370.

7 Geske, R. "The Valuation of Corporate Liabilities as Compound Options." *Journal of Financial and Quantitative Analysis,* 12 (Nov. 1977), 541-552.

8 Geske, R., and H. Johnson. "The American Put Option Valued Analytically." *Journal of Finance,* 39 (Dec. 1984), 1511-1524.

9 Johnson, H. "The Pricing of Complex Options." Unpubl. manuscript (Aug. 1981).

10 Margrabe, W. "The Value of an Option to Exchange One Asset for Another." *Journal of Finance,* 33 (March 1978), 177-186.

11 Merton, R. "A Rational Theory of Option Pricing." *Bell Journal of Economics and Management Science,* 4 (Spring 1973), 141-183.

12 ———. "On the Pricing of Corporate Debt: The Risk Structure of Interest Rates." *Journal of Finance,* 29 (May 1974), 449-470.

13 Schervish, M. "Algorithm AS195: Multivariate Normal Probabilities with Error Bound." *Applied Statistics,* 34 (Jan. 1985), 103-104.

14 Smith, C. "Option Pricing; A Review." *Journal of Financial Economics,* 3 (Jan./March 1976), 3-51.

15 Stulz, R. "Options on the Minimum or the Maximum of Two Risky Assets: Analysis and Applications." *Journal of Financial Economics,* 10 (July 1982), 161-185.

16 Tilley, J. A., and G. D. Latainer. "A Synthetic Option Framework for Asset Allocation." *Financial Analysts Journal,* 41 (May/June 1985), 32-43.

Section 3
Asset Options

The first exchange-traded asset options were stock options. In April 1973, the Chicago Board Options Exchange (CBOE) began trading in call options on 16 New York Stock Exchange (NYSE) stocks. For nearly 10 years, stock options remained the only asset options traded in the U.S., and then, in the early 1980s, stock index options, bond options, and foreign currency options were introduced.

This section contains three articles on physical commodity or asset options. The Black-Scholes framework is sufficiently general to permit valuation of any options where it is reasonable to assume that the underlying commodity has a constant, continuous cost-of-carry rate. In general, this is a good working approximation.[1] There are a few instances, however, where the Black-Scholes framework needs to be modified to account for particular properties of the underlying asset.

Options on dividend-paying stocks are one example. If the stock pays a known discrete dividend during the option's life, the Black-Scholes pricing model does not apply. For American-style calls, however, the option pricing problem remains tractable. The Roll [1977] and Whaley [1981] articles show how the Black-Scholes framework can be modified to deal with known, discrete cash flows on the underlying asset.

Stock index option valuation is little different from stock option valuation. The only distinction is that the stock index portfolio pays multiple discrete dividends during the option's life, while a stock option generally has no more than two. With multiple discrete dividends paid during the option's life, American-style index options such as the S&P 100 index options are most efficiently valued using a modified binomial method.[2] A description of such a method is contained in Harvey and Whaley [1992b].

The valuation of interest rate options can be another problem area. With interest rate options, it is sometimes unreasonable to

[1] Stoll and Whaley [1986] summarize the cases in which a constant carry rate assumption is reasonable.

[2] While it is possible to value American-style calls analytically using a compound option approach, the evaluation of the higher-order integrals winds up being too costly from a computational standpoint.

assume that the underlying instrument, say a T-bill, has a lognormal price distribution at the option's expiration date, as is assumed in the Black-Scholes framework.[3] For this reason, researchers assume that interest rates follow a particular stochastic process, and they price the bonds and then the options within some sort of lattice framework. Agreement on an appropriate interest rate process is not without controversy, as a review of the literature will show. Readers interested in learning about the pricing of interest rate derivatives might want to begin their study with Black, Derman, and Toy [1990] and/or Hull and White [1990].

Another case where the Black-Scholes mechanics may be inappropriate for commodity options is where the underlying commodity is a foreign currency. In foreign currency option valuation, the underlying source of uncertainty is the volatility of the spot exchange rate. Unfortunately, the Merton [1973] model, which is commonly used to price foreign currency options, assumes that the interest rates in both the domestic and foreign markets are constant. But, the same economic factors that cause the exchange rate to be volatile should cause interest rates to be volatile. Grabbe [1983] develops foreign currency option pricing formulas where interest rates are stochastic.

[3] A lognormal price distribution permits the asset price to rise without limit. T-bills have their prices bounded at their par value.

References and Bibliography

General Options
Stoll, H.R., and R.E. Whaley, 1986, "New Option Instruments: Arbitrageable Linkages and Valuation," *Advances in Futures and Options Research* 1, 25-62.

Stock Options
Black, F., and M.S. Scholes, 1973, "The Pricing of Options and Corporate Liabilities," *Journal of Political Economy* 81 (May/June), 637-59.

Merton, R.C., 1973, "The Theory of Rational Option Pricing," *Bell Journal of Economics and Management Science* 4, 141-83.

Roll, R. 1977, "An Analytic Valuation Formula for Unprotected American Call Options on Stocks with Known Dividends," *Journal of Financial Economics* 5 (November), 251-58.

Whaley, R.E., 1981, "On the Valuation of American Call Options on Stocks with Known Dividends," *Journal of Financial Economics* 9 (June), 207-11.

———, 1982, "Valuation of American Call Options on Dividend-Paying Stocks: Empirical Tests," *Journal of Financial Economics* 10, 29-58.

Stock Index Options
Chance, D.M., 1986, "Empirical Tests of the Pricing of Index Call Options," *Advances in Futures and Options Research* 1, 141-66.

Day, T.E., and C.M. Lewis, 1988, "The Behavior of the Volatility Implicit in the Prices of Stock Index Options," *Journal of Financial Economics* 22, 103-22.

———, 1992, "Stock Market Volatility and the Information Content of Stock Index Options," *Journal of Econometrics* (forthcoming).

Evnine, J., and A. Rudd, 1985, "Index Options: The Early Evidence," *Journal of Finance* 40, 743-56.

Fleming, J., 1991, "An Examination of the Informational Content and Forecast Efficiency of S&P 100 Implied Volatilities," Working paper, Fuqua School of Business, Duke University.

Franks, J.R., and E.S. Schwartz, 1988, "The Stochastic Behavior of Market Variance Implied in the Prices of Index Options: Evidence on Leverage, Volume and Other Effects," Working paper, University of California at Los Angeles.

Harvey, C.R., and R.E. Whaley, 1991, "S&P 100 Index Option Volatility," *Journal of Finance* 46 (September), 1551-61.

———, 1992a, "Dividends and S&P 100 Index Option Valuation," *Journal of Futures Markets* (April).

———, 1992b, "Market Volatility Prediction and the Efficiency of the S&P 100 Index Option Market," *Journal of Financial Economics.*

Interest Rate Options
Black, F., E. Derman, and W. Toy, 1990, "A One-Factor Model of Interest Rates and Its Application to Treasury Bond Options," *Financial Analysts Journal* (January/February), 33-39.

Courtadon, G., 1982, "The Pricing of Options on Default-Free Bonds," *Journal of Financial and Quantitative Analysis* 17, 75-100.

Ho, T.S.Y., and S.B. Lee, 1986, "Term Structure Movements and the Pricing of Interest Rate Claims," *Journal of Finance* 41, 1011-29.

Hull, J., and A. White, 1990, "Pricing Interest-Rate-Derivative Securities," *Review of Financial Studies* 3, 573-92.

Jamshidian, F., 1989, "An Exact Bond Option Formula," *Journal of Finance* 44, 205-9.

Foreign Currency Options

Adams, P.D., and S.B. Wyatt, 1987, "On the Pricing of European and American Foreign Currency Call Options," *Journal of International Money and Finance* 6 (September), 315-38.

Biger, N., and J. Hull, 1983, "The Valuation of Currency Options," *Financial Management* 12 (Spring), 24-28.

Bodurtha, J.N., and G.R. Courtadon, 1987a, *The Pricing of Foreign Currency Options,* Monograph Series in Finance and Economics, 1987-4/5, New York University, 90 pages.

———, 1987b, "Tests of an American Option Pricing Model on the Foreign Currency Options Market," *Journal of Financial and Quantitative Analysis* 22 (June), 153-68.

Feiger, G., and B. Jacquillat, 1979, "Current Option Bonds, Puts and Calls on Spot Exchange and Hedging of Contingent Foreign Earnings," *Journal of Finance* 34 (December), 1129-43.

Giddy, I.H., 1983, "Foreign Exchange Options," *Journal of Futures Markets* 3 (Summer), 143-46.

Garman, M.B., and S.W. Kohlhagen, 1983, "Foreign Currency Option Values," *Journal of International Money and Finance* 2 (December), 231-37.

Grabbe, J.O., 1983, "The Pricing of Call and Put Options on Foreign Exchange," *Journal of International Money and Finance* 2 (December), 239-53.

Melino, A., and S.M. Turnbull, 1990, "Pricing Foreign Currency Options with Stochastic Volatility," *Journal of Econometrics* 45 (July-August), 239-65.

Rumsey, J., 1991, "Pricing Cross-Currency Options," *Journal of Futures Markets* (February), 89-93.

Tucker, A.L., 1985, "Empirical Tests of the Efficiency of the Currency Option Market," *Journal of Financial Research* 8 (Winter), 275-85.

1

An Analytic Valuation Formula for Unprotected American Call Options on Stocks with Known Dividends

Richard Roll*

Sometimes it pays to exercise an American-type call option prematurely, just prior to a cash emission by the underlying security. Such an option can be expressed as a combination of three European-type options whose valuation formulae are known.

The unprotected American call written against a dividend-paying stock is the predominant actively-traded option. On the C.B.O.E., call options have no contracted 'protection' against the stock price decline that occurs when a dividend is paid. Thus, there is an important deficiency in option pricing theory in terms of its empirical applicability. All known valuation formulae assume an absence of dividends [Black-Scholes (1973)], or a continuous dividend generating process [Merton (1973), Geske (1975)], or else require numerical solution [Schwartz (1977)]. Furthermore, the original Black-Scholes formula is known to give biased predictions of market prices [see Black (1975, p. 64)]; and the bias is widely believed to be related at least partly to the dividend problem.

This note amends the theory by presenting a simple revised formula that could apply to many empirical situations and that can be extended to more complex situations with ease.

Richard Roll, Graduate School of Management, University of California, Los Angeles, CA 90024, U.S.A.

*Many useful comments and suggestions by Charles Davidson, Robert Geske, David Mayers and Stephen Ross are gratefully acknowledged.

Received April 1977, revised version received September 1977

The notation is the standard proposed by Smith (1976):

$c(S, T, X)$, the market value of a European call option,

$C(S, T, X)$, the market value of an American call option,

S, the current stock price, net of escrowed dividend (S_τ is the stock price after τ periods),

T, the time until expiration,

X, the exercise price,

r, the riskless (and constant) rate of interest, continuously compounded,

σ^2, the variance rate of the return on S.

Assuming that the stock pays no dividend and that its price follows a log-normal diffusion process, Black and Scholes used an arbitrage argument in a no-tax world to obtain their well-known analytic formula for c (which depends only on S, T, X, σ^2, and r). Other work has relaxed the diffusion process assumption [Cox and Ross (1976), Merton (1976), and Rubinstein (1977)], the constant riskless rate assumption [Merton (1973)], and the tax assumption [Ingersoll (1976, pp. 109-112)]. Smith (1976) gives a lucid review of some of this work.

When the stock pays no dividends, Merton has shown that the American and European call options have equal value because the American option will never be exercised before maturity. When dividends are paid, however, the American call can be worth more than the European because there is a non-zero probability of early exercise.

Let the stock's dividend history be described by the following additional assumptions:

D, a dividend of known size, will be paid to each shareholder with certainty.

t is the known time until the ex-dividend instant ($t < T$). At t, the stock has just gone ex-dividend.

α is the known decline in the stock price at the ex-dividend instant as a proportion of the dividend.

No other dividend will be paid before T has elapsed.

If the dividend is certain, the total market value of the stock *cum* dividend cannot follow a lognormal process; for there would then be some chance that the dividend could not be paid. This difficulty is easily and sensibly resolved by defining the 'stock price', S, as the total market price, P, less the discounted escrowed dividend; i.e., for any
$\tau < t$, $S_\tau = P_\tau - \alpha D e^{-r(t - \tau)}$ and for $\tau \geq t$, $S_\tau = P_\tau$. Note that the variance rate σ^2 applies to the process described by S.

At the instant before the stock goes ex-dividend, the American option holder observes that his option would be worth $c(S_t, T - t, X)$ an instant later if he allows it to remain unexercised. (Just after the ex-dividend date, the American and European options have equal value since no additional dividends will be paid before expiration.) If he exercises just before t, however, he will receive $S_t + \alpha D - X$. But we know from the Black-Scholes formula that c is bounded from below and is asymptotic to the lower bound for increasing stock price; i.e.,

$$\lim_{S \to \infty} c(S, T - t, X) = S_t - Xe^{-r(T - t)}.$$

Thus, if $\alpha D > X[1 - e^{-r(T - t)}]$, there exists some finite ex-dividend stock price above which the American option will be exercised just before t. Early exercise is more likely the larger the dividend, the higher the stock price relative to the exercise price (the more 'deeply-in-the-money' the option), and the shorter the time period between expiration and dividend payment dates.[1] Generally speaking whether or not an American call option will be exercised just an instant before the stock goes ex-dividend depends on the value of a European option just an instant after. Fig. 1 illustrates this with the well known chart of option price versus stock price at time t.

An example of these circumstances occurred in October 1976 when General Motors declared a three-dollar dividend to be paid to stockholders of record on November 4. The in-the-money option maturing in January ($X = \$60$, $T = 2$ months) was quoted for sale at near $P - X$ for a week before the ex-dividend date. On the ex-dividend day, the option closed at $S - X + 75¢$. This seemed to imply an option price decline of $16\frac{1}{2}\%$ in one day (accompanying the decline in P of about three dollars). The option price sequence was rational only if all of the outstanding options were exercised on November 3, new options having been written with the same exercise price and maturity date the next day. Only prices of newly-written options could have been quoted then. Notice that such large 'price declines' are easily forecastable but that they do not represent extraordinary profit opportunities for option writers.

[1] For an alternative proof of the early exercise of an American call, see Smith (1976, pp. 13-14).

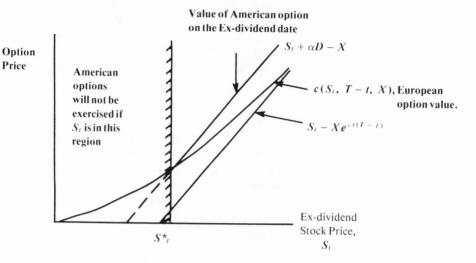

Figure 1. American option value at the ex-dividend time.

Value of American option
on the Ex-dividend date

Option
Price

American
options
will not be
exercised if
S_t is in this
region

$S_t + \alpha D - X$

$c(S_t,\ T - t,\ X)$, European
option value.

$S_t - X e^{-r(T - t)}$

S^*_t

Ex-dividend
Stock Price,
S_t

Anytime *before* the ex-dividend date, the American option should reflect the probability that it will be exercised early. In fact, there is one very simple circumstance in which the unprotected option valuation formula can be given directly. The option may be so deeply in the money that the probability is nil that it won't be exercised early. Formally:

> ***Proposition I.*** As Prob($c_t < S_t + \alpha D - X$) → 1, then an unprotected American option approaches the Black-Scholes valuation but with the ex-dividend date used in place of the option's contracted expiration date.[2]

The argument is rather obvious: Since the option is almost sure to be exercised an instant before t, t becomes its effective maturity. No dividend is paid before t so the Black-Scholes European formula applies, but over an interval shorter than the maturity stated on the option contract. Usually the probability will not be one, no matter how deeply-in-the-money an option may be.[3] In many practical situations, however, the probability may be so close to one that Proposition I gives a valuation whose error is within the bounds of transaction costs. Notice that this valuation formula would apply even with an uncertain dividend, provided that the dividend were known to be 'large' relative to $c - S + X$.

When Proposition I does not apply, similar reasoning can yield more general (but more complicated) results. We know the ex-dividend stock price above which the original American option will be exercised. It is the solution S^*_t to

---

[2]This valuation was suggested first by Black (1975, pp. 41, 61) as the lower bound on the value of an unprotected American call.
[3]Except for option contracts with unusually small exercise prices or for liquidating dividends.

$$c(S_t^*, T - t, X) = S_t^* + \alpha D - X. \qquad (1)$$

This is the critical ingredient in the more general result. Note that S_t^* is different for each option whose contractual features are different.

Since the stock price S_t^* that separates the exercise and non-exercise regions on the ex-dividend date is known in advance,[4] a combination of hypothetical options can be constructed which match perfectly the contingencies faced by the original American option holder. Formally:

> ***Proposition II.*** The value of an unprotected American call option with exercise price X, whose stock makes a single, certain dividend payment D after t periods and before the option's contracted expiration (which occurs after T periods) is the sum of the values of:
>
> (a) a European call option on the stock with an exercise price of X and maturity T,
>
> (b) plus a European call option on the stock with exercise price $S_t^* + \alpha D$ and maturity $t - \epsilon (\epsilon > 0, \epsilon \simeq 0)$.
>
> (c) minus a European call option on the option described under (a) with maturity of $t - \epsilon$ and exercise price of $S_t^* + \alpha D - X$.

At the instant after the ex-dividend date, the cash receipts and net position are as follows.

For $S_t > S_t^*$,		For $S_t < S_t^*$,	
Cash receipts are		Portfolio positions are	
From (a)	0	From (a)	Open
(b)	$S_t + \alpha D - S_t^* - \alpha D$	(b)	Expired
(c)	$S_t^* + \alpha D - X$	(c)	Expired
Total	$S_t + \alpha D - X$ in cash		Option on S until T with exercise price X

If the ex-dividend stock price is above S_t^*, options (b) and (c) are exercised. This provides a net cash flow of $S_t + \alpha D - X$ and leaves the investor with no open options [option (a) being taken by the exercise of (c)]. If the ex-dividend price is below S_t^*, however, options (b) and (c) are allowed to expire unexercised and (a) remains alive. No cash is transferred at the ex-dividend date in this case.

---

[4]Provided, of course, that the variance rate of the stock's return and the riskless rate of interest are known and constant. Schwartz (1977) mentioned this point and used the value of S^* in a numerical solution algorithm.

In order to calculate the value of the American option, we merely need to value the sum of its three components. Component (b) is no problem since the Black-Scholes formula applies directly. As for component (a), the Black-Scholes formula also applies because the stock price drop on the ex-dividend date is known in advance.[5]

Component (c) presents the most difficult valuation problem. Fortunately, the recent work of Geske (1976) provides a solution as his compound option formula can be applied directly. The details are given in the appendix and examples of the resulting formula are plotted in fig. 2.

Caveats and generalizations

The present modification to the Black-Scholes formula does not explain all the empirical facts. For example, the modified American call value curve always lies below the original Black-Scholes curve, as fig. 2 shows, and this makes the Black-Scholes bias worse for deep out-of-the-money options. Geske (1976) is able to explain the upward price bias of out-of-the-money options by noting that the stock of a levered firm is itself an option on the firm's assets. Perhaps a combination of these two formulations would explain better the prices of unprotected American calls on dividend-paying, levered firms. Then again, there are other candidates for explanatory variables such as transaction costs, non-lognormal processes ruling the stock price, and uncertainty in dividends. In this last regard, the stock price decline (α) on the ex-dividend date might be important. This decline is related to the capital gains/ordinary tax differential on personal income and to the 85 percent exclusion from corporate taxes of dividends. Conceivably, if the present modified formula were accurate, it could be used to estimate α for the next ex-dividend date, once the dividend is announced, and the marginal shareholder tax rate could thereby be deduced. (However, the slack in prices caused by trading costs would work against the accuracy of such an estimate.)

The basic solution can easily be generalized to cases where more than one future known cash payment will be made within the option's term. Two or more *known* successive dividends are rare for common stocks; but the generalization might apply to call options on corporate bonds or to prepayment options on standard mortgages (since the periodic cash payments are known throughout the lives of these contracts). To sketch the generalization, imagine a stock that has promised N successive known dividends. Between the ($N - 1$)st and the Nth dividends, the American option on the stock would be valued by the formula in this paper. Before the ($N - 1$)st dividend, a three part portfolio of options could again be constructed such that the contingencies were perfectly matched. This portfolio would consist of:

---

[5] As demonstrated by Rubinstein (1977, pp. 419-420), the value of a *European* option can also be obtained under the more general condition that the dividend *yield* is a non-stochastic function of time.

Figure 2.   Unprotected American call options with known dividends.

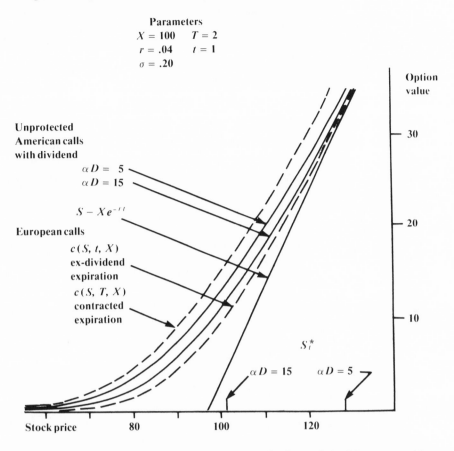

Parameters
$X = 100$ $T = 2$
$r = .04$ $t = 1$
$\sigma = .20$

Option value

Unprotected American calls with dividend
$\alpha D = 5$
$\alpha D = 15$

$S - Xe^{-rt}$

European calls
$c(S, t, X)$ ex-dividend expiration
$c(S, T, X)$ contracted expiration

S_t^*

$\alpha D = 15$ $\alpha D = 5$

30

20

10

Stock price   80   100   120

(a) a modified American option, valued by the formula in this paper, with the same parameters (X, T, plus the date and size of the Nth dividend),

(b) plus a European call on the stock with an exercise price of $S^{**} + \alpha D$ and maturity $t_{N-1} - \epsilon$ [where S^{**} is the stock price above which the American option would be exercised at t_{N-1}, the date of the $(N-1)$st dividend],

(c) minus a European option on the option in (a) with maturity $t_{N-1} - \epsilon$ and exercise price of $S^{**} + \alpha D - X$.

Of course, the resulting formulae would be more complex because there would now be an option (c) of an option of an option. For N payments, the final formulae would include an N-fold option of options. Conceptually, however, the generalization is straightforward. The only difficulty in obtaining the exact analytic formula seems to be the tedious algebra.

Appendix

According to Proposition II, the value of an unprotected American call option facing a known dividend payment is equal to the sum of three separate hypothetical options. This appendix presents details of the individual valuation expressions and gives the aggregate value.

Define the function q by

$$q(s, \tau, x) \equiv [\ln(s/x) + (r + \sigma^2/2)\tau]/\sigma\sqrt{\tau}.$$

Define $N(q)$ as the univariate standard normal probability distribution function (i.e., Prob $(y \leq q)$ where y is unit normal), and define $N(q, p)$ as the bivariate standard normal p.d.f. with correlation coefficient $+ \sqrt{(t/T)}$.

Define S_t^* as the solution to

$$S_t^* N[q(S_t^*, T - t, X)] - Xe^{-r(T-t)} N[q(S_t^*, T - t, X)$$

$$- \sigma\sqrt{(T - t)}] - S_t^* - \alpha D + X = 0.$$

The values of components (a) and (b) in Proposition II are then given by the Black-Scholes formulae,

$$c_a = SN[q(S, T, X)] - N[q(S, T, X) - \sigma\sqrt{T}]e^{-rT}X,$$

and

$$c_b = SN[q(S, t, S_t^* + \alpha D)] - (S_t^* + \alpha D)N[q(S, t, S_t^* + \alpha D)$$

$$- \sigma\sqrt{t}]e^{-rt},$$

and the value of component (c) is given by the Geske Formula

$$c_c = SN[q(S, t, S_t^*), q(S, T, X)] - XN[q(S, t, S_t^*)$$

$$- \sigma\sqrt{t}, q(S, T, X) - \sigma\sqrt{T}]e^{-rT} - (S_t^* + \alpha D - X)$$

$$N[q(S, t, S_t^*) - \sigma\sqrt{t}]e^{-rt}.$$

The unprotected American call option would then have the value

$$c_a + c_b - c_c.$$

References

Black, F., 1975, Fact and fantasy in the use of options, *Financial Analysts Journal* 31, 36-41, 61-72.

Black, F. and M. Scholes, 1973, The pricing of options and corporate liabilities, *Journal of Political Economy* 81, 637-654.

Cox, J. C. and S. Ross, 1976, The valuation of options for alternative stochastic processes, *Journal of Financial Economics* 3, 145-166.

Geske, R., 1975, The pricing of options with stochastic dividend yield, Working Paper (University of California, Berkeley, CA).

Geske, R., 1976, The valuation of compound options, Working Paper (University of California, Berkeley, CA).

Ingersoll, J. E., Jr., 1976, A theoretical and empirical investigation of the dual purpose funds, *Journal of Financial Economics* 3, 83-123.

Merton, R. C., 1976, Option pricing when underlaying stock returns are discontinuous, *Journal of Financial Economics* 3, 125-144.

Merton, R. C., 1973, The theory of rational option pricing, *Bell Journal of Economics and Management Science* 4, 141-183.

Rubinstein, M., 1977, The valuation of uncertain income streams and the pricing of options, *Bell Journal of Economics and Management Science* 7, 407-425.

Schwartz, E. S., 1977, The valuation of warrants: Implementing a new approach, *Journal of Financial Economics* 4, 79-93.

Smith, C. W., Jr., 1976, Option pricing: A review, *Journal of Financial Economics* 3, 3-51.

2

On the Valuation of American Call Options on Stocks with Known Dividends

Robert E. Whaley*

Both the Roll and the Geske equations for the valuation of the American call option on a stock with known dividends are incorrectly specified. This note presents the corrected valuation formula, explains the misspecifications and provides a numerical example.

In two recent articles of this *Journal,* Roll (1977) and Geske (1979b) present valuation formulae for an unprotected American call option on a stock with known dividends. While both authors demonstrate a great deal of ingenuity in their approaches to finding the solution to what was deemed to be an unmanageable pricing problem, their valuation equations are not correctly specified. This note presents the corrected valuation formula, compares it to the Roll and Geske models, and explains how their misspecification errors arise. To assist those who may attempt to implement this option pricing relationship, a numerical example is provided.

The assumptions underlying the valuation of the American call are:

(a) All individuals can borrow or lend without restriction at the instantaneous riskless rate of interest, r, and that rate is constant through the life of the option, T.
(b) At the ex-dividend instant, t ($t < T$), the stock pays a dividend of D which induces a stock price decline of αD.

Vanderbilt University, Nashville, TN 37203, USA

*Comments by Richard Roll are gratefully acknowledged.

Received August 1980, final version received October 1980

(c) The stock price net of the escrowed dividend, S ($S_\tau = P_\tau - \alpha D e^{-r(t-\tau)}$ for $\tau < t$ and $S_\tau = P_\tau$ for $t \leq \tau \leq T$, where P is the stock price *cum* dividend), is described by the stochastic differential equation

$$dS/S = \mu\, dt + \sigma\, dz,$$

where μ is the instantaneous expected rate of return on the common stock, σ is the instantaneous standard deviation of stock price return (assumed to be constant over the life of the option), and dz is a standard unit normally distributed variable.

Additionally, an assumption of perfect capital markets is invoked.

Under the assumptions listed above there exists some finite ex-dividend stock price S_t^* above which the option will be exercised early.[1] It is found by applying a numerical search procedure to

$$c(S_t^*, T - t, X) = S_t^* + \alpha D - X,$$

where X is the exercise price of the option and $c(\,\cdot\,)$ is the market value of a European call, as provided by Black and Scholes (1973). If, just prior to the ex-dividend instant, $S_t > S_t^*$, the American option holder will exercise realizing cash proceeds of $S_t + \alpha D - X$. If, on the other hand, $S_t \leq S_t^*$, the owner will choose to hold his position open until expiration since the option is worth more unexercised.

Once the value of S_t^* is established, the Roll (1977) and Ross (1978) valuation by duplication technique can be applied to solve the option pricing problem. For example, consider the following portfolio of options:

(a) a long position of one European call option with exercise price X and maturity T;
(b) a long position of one European call option with exercise price S_t^* and maturity $t - \epsilon$ ($\epsilon > 0, \epsilon \simeq 0$); and
(c) a short position in one European call option on the option described by (a) with exercise price $S_t^* + \alpha D - X$ and maturity $t - \epsilon$.

Since the income contingencies of this portfolio are identical to those posed by the American call option, the absence of costless arbitrage opportunities in a perfect capital market ensures that the market value of the American call is equal to the market value of the portfolio. Applying the Black-Scholes (1973) option pricing formula to options (a) and (b) of the portfolio and the Geske (1979a) compound option pricing formula to (c), substituting

---

[1] S_t^* is infinite, and early exercise is not possible, when $\alpha D \leq X(1 - e^{-rt})$. See Roll (1977, p. 252).

the identity $N_2(a, -b; -\varrho) = N_1(a) - N_2(a, b; \varrho)$,[2] and gathering terms on S, X and αD, the value of an American call option on a stock with a *single* known dividend paid during the life of the option is

$$C(S, T, X) = S[N_1(b_1) + N_2(a_1, -b_1; -\sqrt{t/T})]$$

$$- Xe^{-rT}[N_1(b_2)e^{r(T-t)} + N_2(a_2, -b_2; -\sqrt{t/T})]$$

$$+ \alpha De^{-rt}N_1(b_2), \tag{1}$$

where

$$a_1 = \frac{\ln(S/X) + (r + 0.5\sigma^2)T}{\sigma\sqrt{T}}, \qquad a_2 = a_1 - \sigma\sqrt{T},$$

$$b_1 = \frac{\ln(S/S_t^*) + (r + 0.5\sigma^2)t}{\sigma\sqrt{t}}, \qquad b_2 = b_1 - \sigma\sqrt{t},$$

$N_1(a)$ is the univariate cumulative normal density function with upper integral limit a and $N_2(a, b; \varrho)$ is the bivariate cumulative normal density function with upper integral limits a and b and correlation coefficient ϱ.

It should be noted that there is nothing unique about the set of options used to price the American call. Other portfolios, some, in fact, with fewer options, will work equally as well. Roll's (1977, p. 254) portfolio, however, will not. He expresses the value of the American call as the sum of the values of the following three options:

(a) c_a, a European call option with exercise price X and maturity T;
(b) c_b, a European call option with exercise price $S_t^* + \alpha D$ and maturity $t - \epsilon$; minus
(c) c_c, a European call option on the option described under (a) with exercise price $S_t^* + \alpha D - X$ and maturity $t - \epsilon$.

Algebraically,

$$C_{RLL} = c_a + c_b - c_c, \tag{2}$$

where

$$c_a = SN_1(a_1) - Xe^{-rT}N_1(a_2), \tag{2a}$$

$$c_b = SN_1(d_1) - (S_t^* + \alpha D)e^{-rt}N_1(d_2), \tag{2b}$$

---

[2] For an excellent discussion about the nature of the bivariate normal integral, see Johnson and Kotz (1972, pp. 93-100).

$$c_c = SN_2(a_1, b_1; \sqrt{t/T}) - Xe^{-rT}N_2(a_2, b_2; \sqrt{t/T})$$

$$- (S_t^* + \alpha D - X)e^{-rt}N_1(b_2), \tag{2c}$$

$$d_1 = \frac{\ln[S/(S_t^* + \alpha D)] + (r + 0.5\sigma^2)t}{\sigma\sqrt{t}} \quad \text{and } d_2 = d_1 - \sigma\sqrt{t}.$$

The misspecification in the value of C_{RLL} is contained within the second option (b): its exercise price should be S_t^* instead of $S_t^* + \alpha D$ unless it is P, the stock price *cum* dividend, that follows the log-normal diffusion process. This option should have cash proceeds of $S_t + \alpha D - S_t^* - \alpha D$ at the ex-dividend instant if the option is exercised just prior to ex-dividend. An option whose value is described by $c(P, t, S_t^* + \alpha D)$ has such proceeds. At t, the option holder receives

$$P_t - S_t^* - \alpha D \quad \text{if} \quad P_t > S_t^* + \alpha D,$$

and

$$0 \quad \text{if} \quad P_t \leq S_t^* + \alpha D.$$

Since $S_t \simeq P_t - \alpha D$ at $t - \epsilon$, these conditions can be alternatively expressed as

$$S_t - S_t^* \quad \text{if} \quad S_t > S_t^*,$$

and

$$0 \quad \text{if} \quad S_t \leq S_t^*.$$

The appropriate valuation equation for this latter set of conditions is

$$c_b = SN_1(b_1) - S_t^* e^{-rt}N_1(b_2). \tag{2b$'$}$$

Replacing c_b as it is described by eq. (2b) with c_b from (2b$'$), substituting the aforementioned identity, and gathering terms on S, X, and αD, the corrected Roll model simplifies to eq. (1).

By solving the option pricing problem directly, Geske (1979) values the American call as

$$C_{GES} = S[N_1(b_1) + N_2(a_1, c_1; \sqrt{t/T})]$$

$$- Xe^{-rT}[N_1(b_2)e^{r(T-t)} + N_2(a_2, c_2; \sqrt{t/T})]$$
$$+ \alpha De^{-rt}N_1(b_2), \tag{3}$$

where

$$c_1 = \frac{\ln(S_t^*/S) - (r + 0.5\sigma^2)t}{\sigma\sqrt{t}} \quad \text{and} \quad c_2 = c_1 + \sigma\sqrt{t}.$$

The problem with this specification is that the correlation coefficient should read $-\sqrt{t/T}$ rather than $\sqrt{t/T}$. When the correct value is substituted, eq. (3) is equivalent to (1) since the values of c_1 and c_2 are simply $-b_1$ and $-b_2$, respectively.

To assist those implementing this option pricing model, consider the following illustration. All computations are performed on an American call option with the parameters $X = 100$, $t = 1$, $T = 2$, $r = 0.04$, $\sigma = 0.20$ and $\alpha D = 5$.

The Black (1975, p. 41) dividend approximation technique values, $c(S, T, X)$, are included to facilitate comparison. Note that the values of $C(S, T, X)$ are not (and, in fact, cannot be) below the Black approximation values. Direct application of the pricing equations (2) and (3), however, does not ensure this result.

Table 1. Hypothetical American call option values[a]

Stock price cum dividend P	Stock price ex dividend S	Indifference price S_t^*	American call option value $C(S, T, X)$	Black approximation $c(S, T, X)$
80.0	75.196	123.582	3.212	3.208
85.0	80.196	123.582	4.818	4.808
90.0	85.196	123.582	6.839	6.820
95.0	90.196	123.582	9.276	9.239
100.0	95.196	123.582	12.111	12.048
105.0	100.196	123.582	15.316	15.215
110.0	105.196	123.582	18.851	18.703
115.0	110.196	123.582	22.676	22.470
120.0	115.196	123.582	26.748	26.476

[a] The American call option contract in the above illustration is assumed to have an exercise price of 100 and a time to expiration of 2 periods. The underlying common stock has a rate of return standard deviation of 0.2 and a known stock price decline of 5 at the end of 1 period. The riskless rate of return is 4 percent.

In summary, both the Roll and the Geske equations for the valuation of the American call option on a stock with known dividends are incorrectly specified. This note presents the corrected valuation formula, explains the misspecifications and provides a numerical example.

References

Black, F., 1975, Fact and fantasy in the use of options, *Financial Analysts Journal* 31, 36-41, 61-72.

Black, F. and M. Scholes, 1973, The pricing of options and corporate liabilities, *Journal of Political Economy* 81, 637-659.

Geske, R., 1979a, The valuation of compound options, *Journal of Financial Economics* 7, 63-81.

Geske, R., 1979b, A note on an analytical valuation formula for unprotected American call options on stocks with known dividends, *Journal of Financial Economics* 7, 375-380.

Johnson, N. L. and S. Kotz, 1972, Distributions in statistics: Continuous multivariate distributions (Wiley, New York).

Roll, R., 1977, An analytical valuation formula for unprotected American call options on stocks with known dividends, *Journal of Financial Economics* 5, 251-258.

Ross, S., 1978, A simple approach to the valuation of risky streams, *Journal of Business* 51, 453-475.

3

The Pricing of Call and Put Options on Foreign Exchange

J. Orlin Grabbe*

This paper derives pricing equations for European puts and calls on foreign exchange. The call and put pricing formulas are unlike the Black-Scholes equations for stock options in that there are two relevant interest rates, interest rates are stochastic, and boundary constraints differ. In addition, it is shown that both American call and put options have values larger than their European counterparts.

This paper develops pricing relationships for European and American call and put options on foreign currency. Foreign exchange (FX) options have features that distinguish them from options on common stock. Consequently, commonly used models for pricing stock options, such as the popular Black-Scholes model, are inadequate for FX options.

Some previous studies have also looked at foreign currency option pricing. Feiger and Jacquillat (1979) attempt to obtain foreign currency option prices by first pricing a currency option bond. They are not able, however, to obtain simple, closed-form solutions by this procedure. Stulz (1982) looks also at currency option bond pricing, but his paper is primarily concerned with the question of default risk on part of a contract, and it is not easy to grasp the fundamentals of foreign currency option pricing in the context of his more general investigation. Black (1976) examines commodity options, and although his results have some relevance if interest rates are non-

The Wharton School, University of Pennsylvania, Philadelphia, PA 19104, USA

*I am grateful to Robert Geske and René Stulz for noting an error in a previous draft, and to Robert Geske and Wayne Ferson for additional comments. The Rodney L. White Center for Financial Research provided partial research support.

J. Orlin Grabbe, "The Pricing of Call and Put Options on Foreign Exchange." Reprinted with permission from *Journal of International Money and Finance* (1983), 2, 239-53.

stochastic, they are not suitably general when the primary focus is foreign currency options.

An *American call option* is a security issued by an individual which gives its owner the right to purchase a given amount of an asset at a stated price (the exercise or striking price) on or before a stated date (the expiration or maturity date). For example, a call option on the British pound might give one the right to purchase £12,500 at 1.70$/£ on or before the second Saturday in December 1983. A *European call option* is the same as the American call, except that it may be exercised only on the expiration date. In the previous example, only on the second Saturday in December 1983. An *American put option* is a security issued by an individual which gives its owner the right to sell a given amount of an asset at a stated price on or before a stated date. For example, a put option on the yen might give one the right to sell ¥6,250,000 at 0.004$/¥ on or before 13 June. A *European put option* is the same as the American put, except that it may be exercised only on the expiration date. In the preceding example, only on 13 June.

Foreign currency options arise in international finance in three principal contexts. The first is organized trading on an exchange. A number of exchanges have trading in at least one foreign currency option, but presently the FX option market at the Philadelphia Stock Exchange (PHLX) is the broadest. Over the period December 1982-February 1983 the PHLX began trading American call and put options on five foreign currencies—the West German mark, the British pound, the Swiss franc, the Canadian dollar, and the Japanese yen. The exercise price of each option is stated as the US dollar price of a unit of foreign exchange, and the number of foreign currency units is one-half the contract size of the corresponding currency futures contract traded on the International Money Market of the Chicago Mercantile Exchange. Option contract sizes are £12,500; DM62,500; Swiss Franc 62,500; ¥6,250,000; and C$50,000. The expiration dates of the options are set to correspond to the March, June, September, December delivery dates on futures. Futures contracts expire on the second business day prior to the third Wednesday of each of these months, and option contracts expire on the second Saturday of each of these months. For each currency, options are opened with terms to maturity of 3, 6, and 9 months, corresponding to the March, June, September, December cycle. Exercise price intervals are $0.05 for the £; $0.02 for the DM, Swiss Franc, C$; and $0.0002 for the ¥. (If, for example, the spot price of the £ is 1.82$/£ when June pounds open for trading, exercise prices are set at 1.80$/£ and 1.85$/£. If the £ then drops to $1.80, a new series with exercise prices of 1.75 $/£ is opened.)

A second type of FX option market is the bank market by which large money-center banks write FX options directly to their corporate customers. This market is largely invisible because banks are currently reluctant to make public any data regarding their activities in this sphere. Finally, one may note the frequent appearance of foreign currency option features on bond contracts in the international bond markets. For example, take the case of a Japanese company which issues $1000 bonds at par in the Eurobond market. The coupon rate is 12% payable annually in US dollars, and the bonds mature in May 1990. At maturity the bonds may be redeemed, at the owner's discretion, for dollars or for yen at an exchange rate of 0.005$/yen. What value would one place on such a bond? Clearly the bond owner will opt for repayment of principal in yen if the spot price of yen is greater than 0.005$/yen in May 1990. (For example, if the spot rate is 0.006$/yen, she would redeem her bond for 1000/0.005 = 200,000 yen and then sell the yen for (200,000)(0.006) = $1200.) Thus the value of this Eurobond can be viewed as the sum of the value of an ordinary $1000 bond with a 12% coupon, plus the value of a European call option on 200,000 yen, with an exercise price of 0.005$/yen, and with an expiration date in May 1990. Thus, provided we can value European options on foreign currency, we can place a value on this Japanese currency-option bond.

The organization of this paper is as follows. Section I sets out notation and assumptions. Section II derives some inequalities and equivalences for puts and calls on foreign exchange. In Section III, some strong distributional assumptions are imposed, and exact pricing equations for European options derived. Section IV looks at American FX options. Section V briefly considers the use of the equations for hedging and speculation, and Section VI concludes the paper.

I. Notation and Assumptions

Throughout this paper it will be assumed that contracts are default-free. In addition we will assume the absence of transaction costs, taxes, exchange controls, or similar factors. Trading takes place in continuous time. Finally, there exist discount bonds at which each currency may be borrowed or lent. The interest parity theorem is assumed for some results.

The symbols used will follow Smith's (1976) notation, except for some minor variations that are tailored to the foreign exchange market. The notation is:

$S(t)$ — the spot domestic currency price of a unit of foreign exchange at time t.

$F(t, T)$ — the forward domestic currency price of a unit of foreign exchange, for a contract made at time t and which matures at time $t + T$.

T — the time until expiration.

$C(t)$ — the domestic currency price at time t of an American call option written on one unit of foreign exchange.

$C^*(t)$ — the foreign currency price at time t of an American call option written on one unit of domestic currency.

$c(t)$ — the domestic currency price at time t of a European call option written on one unit of foreign exchange.

$c^*(t)$ — the foreign currency price at time t of a European call option written on one unit of domestic currency.

$P(t)$ — the domestic currency price at time t of an American put option written on one unit of foreign currency.

$P^*(t)$ — the foreign currency price at time t of an American put option written on one unit of domestic currency.

$p(t)$ — the domestic currency price at time t of a European put option written on one unit of foreign currency.

$p^*(t)$ — the foreign currency price at time t of a European put option written on one unit of domestic currency.

$B(t, T)$ — the domestic currency price of a pure discount bond which pays one unit of domestic currency at time $t + T$.

$B^*(t, T)$ — the foreign currency price of a pure discount bond which pays one unit of foreign exchange at time $t + T$.

X — the domestic currency exercise price of an option on foreign currency.

X^* — the foreign currency exercise price of an option on domestic currency.

II. Some Basic Relationships

Consider the following two portfolio strategies undertaken at time t when the spot exchange rate is $S(t)$:

II.A

Strategy A: 1. Purchase for $c(S(t), X, t, T)$ a European call option, with an exercise price of X and which expires in T units of time, on one unit of foreign exchange.
2. Purchase X domestic currency discount bonds, which mature in T units of time, at the current price $B(t, T)$.
Total Domestic Currency Investment: $c + XB$.

Strategy B: 1. Purchase one foreign discount bond, which matures in T units of time, at a domestic currency price of $S(t)B^*(t, T)$.

At time $t + T$, the spot exchange rate $S(t + T)$ will either be less than X, or greater than or equal to X. The bonds will have values, in their respective currencies, of $B(t + T, 0) = 1$, $B^*(t + T, 0) = 1$. The call option will have a value $c(S(t + T), X, T, 0) = \max(0, S(t + T) - X)$. Therefore:

	Value of Strategy A	Value of Strategy B
$S(t + T) < X$	X	$S(t + T)$
$S(t + T) \geq X$	$S(t + T)$	$S(t + T)$

In either case, the payoff to strategy A will always be as good or better than strategy B. Hence the cost of A must, in economic equilibrium, be at least as great as that of B. Thus $c + XB \geq SB^*$ or $c \geq SB^* - XB$. Since an American call must be at least as valuable as its European counterpart (because it has all the same features plus the additional one that it can be exercised at any time), we get

$$C(S(t), X, t, T) \geq c(S(t), X, t, T) \geq S(t)B^*(t, T) - XB(t, T) \quad (1)$$

For example, if one-year Eurodollar deposits have an interest rate of 11.11% ($B(t, 1) = 1/1.1111 = 0.9$), one-year Euro-Swiss franc deposits have an interest rate of 5.26% ($B^*(t, 1) = 1/1.0526 = 0.95$), and the spot dollar price of Swiss francs is $S(t) = 0.55$ \$/Swiss fr., then a 12-month American option on one Swiss franc with an exercise price of $X = \$0.50$ will have a value

$$C(0.55, 0.50, t, 1) \geq c(0.55, 0.50, t, 1)$$
$$\geq (0.55)(0.95) - (0.50)(0.9) = \$0.0725$$

Since an American option can be exercised at any time, and must have a value at least as large as its immediate exercise value, we get the stronger inequality

$$C(S(t), X, t, T) \geq \max(0, S(t) - X, S(t)B^*(t, T) - XB(t, T))$$

(2)

II.B

Using the notation of Section I, we may write the Interest Parity Theorem as

$$F(t, T) = S(t)\ \frac{B^*(t, T)}{B(t, T)}$$

(3)

Substituting for $S(t)B^*(t, T)$ in equation (1), we obtain the relation

$$C(S(t), X, t, T) \geq c(S(t), X, t, T) \geq B(t, T)[F(t, T) - X]$$

(4)

The call option on one unit of foreign exchange must have a value at least as great as the discounted difference between the forward exchange rate and the exercise price. This assumes that interest parity holds. (Hence, in practical application $B(t, T)$ and $B^*(t, T)$ should be thought of as Eurocurrency securities, rather than as treasury bills.) The intuition is clear if we consider the case $F > X$. An owner of a European call can sell foreign currency forward for $F(t, T)$ even though the purchase price will be X. Thus such an option has a value at least as large as this difference, $F - X$, once it is discounted to the present.

II.C

Here we derive a relationship between the prices of European calls and European puts. Consider the following two portfolio strategies:

Strategy A: 1. Buy, at a domestic currency price of $p(S(t), X, t, T)$, a put option on one unit of foreign currency, with exercise price X.

Strategy B: 1. Issue a foreign-currency-denominated discount bond at $B^*(t, T)$ and sell the foreign currency for $S(t)B^*(t, T)$.
2. Buy X domestic discount bonds at a price of $B(t)$ each, for a total domestic currency amount of $XB(t)$.
3. Buy, at a domestic currency price of $c(S(t), X, t, T)$, a European call option on one unit of foreign currency, with an exercise price of X. Total domestic currency investment: $c - SB^* + XB$.

203

At time $t + T$ the spot exchange rate $S(t+T)$ will be such that either $S(t + T) < X$ or $S(t + T) \geq X$. In each case, since $p(S(t + T), X, T, 0) = \max(0, X - S(t + T))$, the strategies will have the payoffs:

	Value of Strategy A	Value of Strategy B
$S(t + T) < X$	$X - S(t + T)$	$X - S(t + T)$
$S(t + T) \geq X$	0	0

Since each strategy gives the same payoff, each must cost the same in equilibrium. Hence

$$p(S(t), X, t, T) = c(S(t), X, t, T) - S(t)B^*(t, T) + XB(t, T) \quad (5)$$

Thus the price of a European put is totally determined by the price of the corresponding European call, the spot exchange rate, and the prices of discount bonds denominated in the two currencies. Equation (5) is the put-to-call conversion equation for European FX options.

II.D   Using the Interest Parity Theorem, equation (3), and substituting into equation (5), we obtain

$$p(S(t), X, t, T) = c(S(t), X, t, T) + B(t, T)[X - F(t, T)] \quad (6)$$

The price of a European put differs from the price of the corresponding call by a factor which represents the discounted difference between the exercise price and the forward exchange rate.

II.E   A call option on a foreign currency, written at an exercise price in terms of the domestic currency, is a put option on the domestic currency, written at an exercise price in terms of the foreign currency. For example, take the PHLX call option on 62,500 DM and suppose that the exercise price is 0.40\$/DM. This option gives one the right to buy 62,500 DM for $(62,500)(0.40) = \$25,000$. But at the same time it gives the right to sell \$25,000 for DM62,500. Thus it is a put option on \$25,000 with an exercise price of $1/0.40 = 2.5$ DM/\$. This is a simple consequence of the fact an exchange rate has two sides. Hence, whether viewed as a call or a put, a contract must have the same domestic currency value.

For American option contracts, this observation implies[1]

$$C(S(t), X, t, T) = S(t)XP^*(1/S(t), 1/X, t, T) \quad (7)$$

---

[1] By contrast to the example, equations (7) and (8) are not purely identities, since use is also made of the fact that the option is first degree homogeneous in the price of the underlying asset and the exercise price:

$$C(NS(t), NX, t, T) = NC(S(t), X, t, T), \text{ for } N > 0$$

(For example, if C is the value of an American call on 1 DM with an exercise price $X = \$0.40$, then the same contract is a put option on $0.40 with an exercise price of 1 DM. Hence it has the value of $40/100$ of $P^*(1/S(t), 2.5, t, T)$, where P^* is the DM value of a put option on $1 with an exercise price of 2.5 DM. But the dollar value of $0.40P^* = XP^*$ is just SXP^*, which must be equal to C.)

For domestic-currency-valued puts on foreign exchange, we have

$$P(S(t), X, t, T) = S(t) X C^*(1/S(t), 1/X, t, T) \qquad (8)$$

Analogous equations hold for European options. Notice that equations (7) and (8) imply that if we obtain a pricing equation for American call options on foreign exchange, then we immediately get a pricing equation for American put options. We can take either currency as the 'domestic' currency, and then using (7) or (8) translate the call equation for the 'domestic' currency into a put equation on the second currency.[2]

III. Pricing Equations for European Call and Put Options

Here we derive exact pricing equations for European calls and puts. The initial relationships apply to both American and European FX options. Once through the preliminaries, we will give the European solutions, and defer to the following section continued discussion of American options.

Equation (1) suggests that the value of an American call C (or European call c) will be a function of $S(t)B^*(t, T), B(t, T), X, T$. The first assumption, then, is that C has the general functional form $C = C(S(t)B^*(t, T), B(t, T), X, T)$. Such a function would be subject to the boundary conditions

$$C(S(t + T), 1, X, 0) = \max(0, S(t + T) - X) \qquad (9)$$

$$C(0, B(t, T), X, T) = 0 \qquad (10)$$

$$C(S(t)B^*(t, T), B(t, T), X, T) \geq \max(0, S(t) - X) \qquad (11)$$

The first boundary condition is the terminal value of the call option, which has to be the greater of zero or the exercise value. The second boundary

---

and similarly for the put option. Since two call options on 1 DM, each with an exercise price of N, give me the same privileges as a single option on 2 DM with an exercise price of $2N$, first degree homogeneity ought to hold for rationally-priced foreign exchange options just as it does for stock options. See Merton (1973), Theorem 6, p. 147, and Theorem 9, p. 149, for discussion of the stock option case.

[2] The same is true with stock options, since a call on a share of stock with an exercise price in terms of money is a put option on money with an exercise price in terms of stock. The symmetry breaks down, however, in that money (a bond) bears interest while the stock does not. Thus while the American call option on money gives us an American put option on stock, we are brought no closer to our goal if we do not have a pricing formula for the American call on money.

condition says that when the value of spot exchange is zero, the option to buy it has a zero value. The third boundary condition says the value of an American call can never be less than its immediate exercise value. (This third boundary condition does not necessarily apply in the case of a European call option.)

The second assumption has to do with the dynamics of S, B^*, and B. Let dx, dy, dz denote standardized Wiener processes with unit instantaneous variances and correlation matrix

$$\begin{bmatrix} 1 & \varrho_{SB^*} & \varrho_{SB} \\ \varrho_{SB^*} & 1 & \varrho_{B^*B} \\ \varrho_{SB} & \varrho_{B^*B} & 1 \end{bmatrix} dt$$

where $\varrho_{ij} = \varrho_{ij}(t, T)$ may be a known function of time (t) and the term to maturity of the bond (T). Then S, B^*, B are assumed to follow the diffusion processes

$$\frac{dS}{S} = \mu_S(t) \, dt + \sigma_S(t) \, dx$$

$$\frac{dB^*}{B^*} = \mu_{B^*}(t, T) \, dt + \sigma_{B^*}(t, T) \, dy$$

$$\frac{dB}{B} = \mu_B(t, T) \, dt + \sigma_B(t, T) \, dz$$

On the basis of these assumptions we can define new variables dG, dw, as

$$\frac{dG}{G} = \frac{d(SB^*)}{SB^*} = (\mu_S + \mu_{B^*} + \varrho_{SB^*} \sigma_S \sigma_{B^*}) \, dt + \sigma_S \, dx + \sigma_{B^*} \, dy$$

$$\equiv \mu_G(t, T) \, dt + \sigma_G(t, T) \, dw$$

and write the correlation matrix of dw, dz as

$$\begin{bmatrix} 1 & \varrho_{GB} \\ \varrho_{GB} & 1 \end{bmatrix} dt$$

where $\varrho_{GB} = \varrho_{GB}(t, T)$.

We know from equation (1) that the derived call option value must satisfy the condition $C(t) \geq S(t)B^*(t, T) - XB(t, T)$. But that does not ensure that the boundary constraint in (11) will not be violated, since $S(t)B^*(t, T) - XB(t, T) < S - X$ for sufficiently large S. Thus we have to take explicit account of (11) in deriving the American pricing equation.

It is plausible to assume that the call option dynamics will be different away from the boundary than on the boundary. Thus we first consider the case that either $C(t) > S - X > 0$, or $C(t) > 0 > S - X$. We will assume that in this region, where the constraint (11) is not binding, that $C(t)$ is everywhere twice continuously differentiable. In order to derive the call option pricing equation for this case, we form a zero-wealth portfolio, the return to which is non-stochastic, or riskless. In economic equilibrium, the return to such a portfolio must be zero.

Now applying Ito's lemma to the function $C(SB^*, B, X, T) = C(G, B, X, T)$, we get the option dynamics, for $C > S - X > 0$ or $C > 0 > S - X$,

$$dC = \frac{\partial C}{\partial G}\ dG + \frac{\partial C}{\partial B}\ dB + \frac{\partial C}{\partial T}\ dT$$

$$- \frac{1}{2} \left(\frac{\partial^2 C}{\partial G^2}\ G^2 \sigma^2{}_G + 2\ \frac{\partial^2 C}{\partial G \partial B}\ GB\ \varrho_{GB}\ \sigma_G\ \sigma_B + \frac{\partial^2 C}{\partial B^2}\ B^2 \sigma^2{}_B \right) dT$$

$$= \frac{\partial C}{\partial G}\ dG + \frac{\partial C}{\partial B}\ dB + \frac{\partial C}{\partial T}\ dT - \frac{1}{2}\phi\, dT$$

where ϕ represents the elements involving second derivatives, and the relation $dt = -\,dT$ has been used.

Let V be a portfolio composed of one option, b units of G, and e units of B:

$$V = C + bG + eB$$

The dynamics of this portfolio are

$$dV = dC + b\,dG + e\,dB$$

Choose b, e such that $b = -\ \frac{\partial C}{\partial G}$, $e = -\ \frac{\partial C}{\partial B}$.

Then

$$dV = \left(\frac{\partial C}{\partial T} - \frac{1}{2}\phi \right) dT$$

If the portfolio V uses no wealth, then in equilibrium it should yield a zero return. That is, if

$$V = C - \frac{\partial C}{\partial G}\ G - \frac{\partial C}{\partial B}\ B = 0 \tag{12}$$

then $dV = 0$, which in turn implies that

$$\frac{\partial C}{\partial T} = \frac{1}{2}\phi \tag{13}$$

For the American call option, we look for a function $C(G, B, X, T)$ that solves equations (12) and (13), and is also subject to the boundary conditions (9) − (11). For the European call option, $c(G, B, X, T)$, condition (11) may be omitted.

It may be verified by direct substitution that a solution to the European call is

$$c(t) = S(t)B^*(t, T)N(d_1) - XB(t, T)N(d_2) \tag{14}$$

where $N(d)$ is the standard normal distribution

$$N(d) = \int_{-\infty}^{d} \frac{1}{\sqrt{2\pi}} \exp(-x^2/2)\, dx$$

and

$$d_1 = \frac{\ln(SB^*/XB) + \frac{\sigma^2}{2} T}{\sigma\sqrt{T}}$$

$$d_2 = \frac{\ln(SB^*/XB) - \frac{\sigma^2}{2} T}{\sigma\sqrt{T}}$$

$$\sigma^2 = \int_{0}^{T} \frac{1}{T} [\sigma_G^2(t + T - u, u) + \sigma_B^2(t + T - u, u)$$

$$- 2\varrho_{GB}(t + T - u, u)\sigma_G(t + T - u, u) \cdot \sigma_B(t + T - u, u)]\, du$$

The equation for pricing European calls on foreign exchange, (14), differs from the Black-Scholes formula for pricing European options on common stock in three respects. First, there are two interest rates, not one. These interest rates are represented in the current prices of discount bonds $B(t, T)$, $B^*(t, T)$. In the Black-Scholes model, money (a bond) yields interest, but not stock. Hence interest at the domestic rate is foregone if a call option is purchased, and there is no possibility of receiving interest if the option is exercised. For an option on foreign exchange, however, the situation is different. One acquires foreign exchange if the option is exercised, and one may then receive interest at the foreign interest rate. Hence both the foreign and domestic interest rates form part of the expected return on an FX call. Second, the Black-Scholes model assumes a constant interest rate, and hence explicitly excludes covariation between movements in stock prices and interest rate movements. While this may be a reasonable simplification for the stock market, it is not appropriate for the foreign exchange market, where interest rate movements induce co-movements in spot and forward exchange rates. [3] Third, the asymmetry between interest payments on money (positive interest) and stock (zero interest, ignoring dividends) means that an American call option on stock is always worth more alive than dead, so that it will not be exercised prematurely. Thus American call options on stock have the same price as their European counterparts. American calls on foreign currency, however, have values strictly greater than European calls. This is shown in the following section.

The European call option formula may be rewritten, using the Interest Parity relation $S(t)B^*(t, T) = F(t, T)B(t, T)$, as

$$c(t) = B(t, T)[F(t, T)N(d_1) - XN(d_2)] \tag{15}$$

where

$$d_1 = \frac{\ln(F/X) + \dfrac{\sigma^2}{2} T}{\sigma\sqrt{T}}$$

$$d_2 = \frac{\ln(F/X) - \dfrac{\sigma^2}{2} T}{\sigma\sqrt{T}}$$

and

$$\sigma^2 = \int_0^\tau \frac{1}{T} \sigma_F^2(t + T - u, u)\,du,$$

where $\sigma_F^2(t, T)$ is the instantaneous variance of $dF(t, T)/F$. (Note that σ^2 here is exactly the same variable as in equation (14), as may be verified by applying Ito's lemma to the interest parity relation (3).)

What is remarkable about equation (15) is the disappearance of the price of spot exchange, which is the underlying asset on which the option is written. This results because, given the current price of domestic currency discount bonds B, all of the relevant information concerning both the spot exchange rate and the foreign currency discount bond price that is necessary for option pricing is already reflected in the forward rate. (That the forward and spot rates are not independent follows, of course, from the Interest Parity Theorem.)

---

[3] The FX call equation here is closer to Merton's (1973) stochastic interest rate version of the Black-Scholes model. The FX model, however, is complicated by the presence of two correlated interest rates. If both interest rates were constant, so that B and B^* could be rewritten as $B = e^{-rT}$, $B^* = e^{-r^*T}$, then equation (14) becomes identical to the solution for the value of a call option on a stock with a constant proportional dividend rate. See Merton (1973), p. 171, footnote 62, for the latter solution.

Using the put to call conversion equation (5), we get that the value of the European put on 1 unit of foreign currency is

$$p(t) = XB(t, T)N(d_1^*) - S(t)B^*(t, T)N(d_2^*)$$ (16)

where (referring to equation (14)) $d_1^* = -d_2$ and $d_2^* = -d_1$.

Equation (16) may be rewritten in terms of the forward rate as

$$p(t) = B(t, T)[XN(d_1^*) - FN(d_2^*)]$$ (17)

where (referring now to equation (15)) $d_1^* = -d_2$ and $d_2^* = -d_1$.

Table 1 shows values, in US cents, for a European call option on one British pound when the spot rate is 1.60 \$/£. Values are given for $\sigma = 0.10, 0.20$; $T = 3, 6, 9$ months; and $X = \$1.55, \$1.60, \$1.65$. B and B^*, with maturities of 3, 6, 9 months, are members of the set $\{(0.97\,0.94\,0.91), (0.98\,0.96\,0.94), (0.99\,0.98\,0.97)\}$. The values for B, B^* imply the term structures of interest rates are upward sloping in all cases.

Diagonal cells in the table illustrate that a lower level of interest rates yields higher option values when the term structure is the same in both countries. Cells below the diagonal show option values are an increasing function of the positive difference of domestic over foreign interest rates. Cells above the diagonal not only demonstrate that option prices are a decreasing function of the positive difference of foreign over domestic interest rates, but that the option can have an ambiguous time derivative. For $\sigma = 0.10$, $X = \$1.55$, $B = (0.99\,0.98\,0.97)$, $B^* = (0.97\,0.94\,0.91)$, for example, the value of the option decreases from 4.03 cents for a three-month term to maturity to 3.08 cents for a nine-month term to maturity.

These relations can be seen more exactly from an inspection of partial derivatives in equation (14). The option price is decreasing with respect to domestic bond prices,

$$\frac{\partial c}{\partial B} = -XN(d_2) < 0$$ (18)

increasing with respect to foreign bond prices,

$$\frac{\partial c}{\partial B^*} = SN(d_1) > 0$$ (19)

increasing with respect to the domestic currency value of a foreign bond $(G = SB^*)$,

$$\frac{\partial c}{\partial G} = N(d_1) > 0$$ (20)

Table 1. European call values*

σ = 0.10

	Months			Months			Months		
	3	**6**	**9**	**3**	**6**	**9**	**3**	**6**	**9**
B	0.97	0.94	0.91	0.98	0.96	0.94	0.99	0.98	0.97
B^*	0.97	0.94	0.91	0.97	0.94	0.91	0.97	0.94	0.91
1.55	6.07	6.94	7.55	4.99	5.07	4.98	4.03	3.55	3.08
1.60	3.10	4.24	5.03	2.38	2.88	3.07	1.78	1.86	1.74
1.65	1.30	2.36	3.15	0.92	1.47	1.77	0.63	0.88	0.92
B	0.97	0.94	0.91	0.98	0.96	0.94	0.99	0.98	0.97
B^*	0.98	0.96	0.94	0.98	0.96	0.94	0.98	0.96	0.94
1.55	7.31	9.29	11.03	6.13	7.09	7.80	5.05	5.21	5.22
1.60	3.98	6.08	7.87	3.13	4.33	5.19	2.41	2.96	3.22
1.65	1.80	3.64	5.32	1.31	2.41	3.26	0.93	1.52	1.86
B	0.97	0.94	0.91	0.98	0.96	0.94	0.99	0.98	0.97
B^*	0.99	0.98	0.97	0.99	0.98	0.97	0.99	0.98	0.97
1.55	8.64	11.93	15.02	7.37	9.44	11.27	6.19	7.23	8.05
1.60	4.98	8.26	11.34	4.01	6.16	8.02	3.16	4.42	5.36
1.65	2.42	5.30	8.18	1.81	3.69	5.41	1.32	2.46	3.36

σ = 0.20

	Months			Months			Months		
B	0.97	0.94	0.91	0.98	0.96	0.94	0.99	0.98	0.97
B^*	0.97	0.94	0.91	0.97	0.94	0.91	0.97	0.94	0.91
1.55	8.82	10.90	12.33	7.91	9.26	10.00	7.07	7.79	8.01
1.60	6.19	8.48	10.05	5.45	7.06	7.99	4.78	5.83	6.27
1.65	4.16	6.46	8.09	3.59	5.28	6.31	3.09	4.27	4.85
B	0.97	0.94	0.91	0.98	0.96	0.94	0.99	0.98	0.97
B^*	0.98	0.96	0.94	0.98	0.96	0.94	0.98	0.96	0.94
1.55	9.88	12.97	15.41	8.91	11.14	12.74	8.00	9.49	10.40
1.60	7.05	10.26	12.79	6.25	8.66	10.38	5.52	7.24	8.32
1.65	4.82	7.97	10.50	4.20	6.60	8.36	3.64	5.42	6.57
B	0.97	0.94	0.91	0.98	0.96	0.94	0.99	0.98	0.97
B^*	0.99	0.98	0.97	0.99	0.98	0.97	0.99	0.98	0.97
1.55	11.00	15.20	18.81	9.97	13.20	15.81	9.00	11.37	13.14
1.60	7.98	12.23	15.87	7.12	10.44	13.12	6.32	8.84	10.71
1.65	5.56	9.67	13.25	4.87	8.11	10.76	4.24	6.74	8.62

*Entries in the table are prices, in US cents, of a European call option on one British pound, with the designated standard deviation rate (σ), strike price ($1.55, $1.60, $1.65), time to maturity (3, 6, 9 months), and domestic (B) and foreign (B^*) bond prices, when the spot rate is $1.60 per pound.

decreasing with respect to exercise price,

$$\frac{\partial c}{\partial X} = -BN(d_2) < 0 \tag{21}$$

and increasing with respect to the spot or forward rate (where $F = SB^*/B$),

$$\frac{\partial c}{\partial S} = B^*N(d_1) > 0 \tag{22}$$

$$\frac{\partial c}{\partial F} = BN(d_1) > 0 \tag{23}$$

The partial derivative with respect to term to maturity has to be interpreted with care:

$$\frac{\partial c}{\partial T} = \frac{SB^*N'(d_1)}{2\sigma\sqrt{T}}[\sigma^2{}_G - 2\varrho_{GB}\sigma_G\sigma_B + \sigma_B^2] > 0 \tag{24}$$

The fact that $\partial c/\partial T > 0$ does not mean the option price c strictly increases with term to maturity. On the contrary, by the relation $\partial c/\partial T = \frac{1}{2}\phi$ of equation (13), the incremental change in the option value, dc, is independent of this partial derivative. We have

$$dc = \frac{\partial c}{\partial G} dG + \frac{\partial c}{\partial B} dB + \frac{\partial c}{\partial T} dT - \frac{1}{2}\phi dT \tag{25}$$

$$= N(d_1) dG - XN(d_2) dB$$

so that in fact d$c > 0$ if d$G > X(N(d_2))/(N(d_1))$ dB. If incremental foreign interest is too great (dG too large for a fixed S) relative to incremental domestic interest (relative to dB), then the European option price will decrease with an increment in term to maturity (recalling that d$T = -$dt).

Finally, defining σ as $\sigma \equiv [\sigma^2 T]^{\frac{1}{2}}/\sqrt{T}$, we have

$$\frac{\partial c}{\partial \sigma} = \sqrt{T}SB^*N'(d_1) > 0 \tag{26}$$

The option price is an increasing function of the average instantaneous standard deviation rate of the forward rate, where the time average is taken over the interval $(t, t + T)$ for forward contracts maturing at time $t + T$.

The above partial derivatives were derived from equation (14). An additional result is obtained if we take the partial derivative with respect to the domestic bond price in equation (15):

$$\left.\frac{\partial c}{\partial B}\right|_{F=\bar{F}} = \frac{c}{B} > 0 \tag{27}$$

In equation (18) the spot rate was held constant, while in equation (27) the forward rate is held constant. The derivative in equation (27) is positive because if the domestic bond price rises (the domestic interest rate falls) with the forward rate held constant, then from the interest parity relation we know that the domestic currency price of a foreign bond ($G = SB^*$) rises, which increases the option value by equation (20).

IV. American Options

If $c(t)$ is the price of a European FX call expiring at $t + T$, then the price $C(t)$ of an American call expiring at $t + T$ satisfies the inequality

$$C(t) \geq \max[S(t) - X, c(t)]$$

A pricing equation for the European call $c(t)$ was derived in the previous section. The American price will be strictly greater than this European price only if the additional constraint (11) is binding. That is,

$$C(t) > c(t) \text{ iff } \Prob_{\tau \in (t, t+T)} [S(\tau) - X > c(\tau)] > 0$$

But it is clear that $S(\tau) - X > c(\tau)$ for sufficiently large S. To see this, note that as $S \to \infty$, $c(\tau) = SB^*N(d_1) - XBN(d_2) \to SB^* - XB$. But $S - X > SB^* - XB$ for $S > X(1 - B)/(1 - B^*)$. Thus we know that $C(t) > c(t)$.

Now an exercised option always has a value of $S - X$. Thus, if an American option is rationally exercised prematurely when the exchange rate is S_e, we must have the relation

$$C(S_e(t), t) = S_e(t) - X \tag{28}$$

But we know there is a positive probability of premature exercise, because if an American option were always exercised only at expiration it would be indistinguishable from, and hence priced the same as, a European option. But $C(t) > c(t)$, so it follows that an $S_e(t)$ always exists such that for $S(t) > S_e(t)$ the call will be worth more exercised than held. The American call therefore satisfies (12) and (13) for $0 \leq S \leq S_e$, and has as additional boundary conditions (28) and (9) − (10).

Using equation (7), we see that an American put will be exercised prior to expiration for a sufficiently low value of S (relative to X), namely for $S < S_e'(t)$, where $S_e'(t)$ satisfies the relation

$$P(S_e', t) = X - S_e'(t)$$

At present, a simple solution for $C(t)$ (or $P(t)$) is not known. However, approximate solutions may be found numerically by following procedures similar to those used to calculate American put prices for stock options. Geske and Johnson (1982) compare the efficiency of three approaches to the latter problem—namely numerical integration, a binomial approximation, and a type of polynomial approximation to an infinite series solution. The reader is referred to their paper for discussion and references.

V. Use of the Pricing Formulas for Hedging or Speculation

There are a wide variety of hedging relationships and speculative strategies that may be based on the option pricing formulas derived in Section III. For the purpose of illustration, we will look at one hedging example and one speculative strategy.

V. A. Hedging the Domestic Currency Value of a Discount Foreign Bond

We will only consider the case of a long position in a foreign-currency discount bond, since the case of borrowing is symmetrical. The domestic-currency value of the foreign-currency bond is $G = S(t) B^*(t, T)$. Then for a European call option c, the hedge is that previously described in equation (12). Equation (12) may be rewritten as

$$G + \left[\frac{\partial c}{\partial B} \Big/ \frac{\partial c}{\partial G} \right] B - \left[1 \Big/ \frac{\partial c}{\partial G} \right] c = 0$$

Thus for each domestic-currency unit of the foreign-currency bond held long, the hedge is effected by buying $[(\partial c/\partial B) / (\partial c/\partial G)]$ units of the domestic currency bond and writing $[1/(\partial c/\partial G)]$ call options. Such a hedge would yield a change in wealth of zero, if the hedge were continually adjusted to reflect any change in the state variables.

A similar hedge may be formed with the European put option p. First, verify that

$$p - \frac{\partial p}{\partial G} G - \frac{\partial p}{\partial B} B = 0$$

Then for each domestic-currency unit of the foreign-currency bond held long, the hedge is brought about through the purchase of $[(\partial p/\partial B)/(\partial p/\partial G)]$ units of the domestic currency bond and writing $[1/(\partial p/\partial G)]$ put options.

V. B. The Mutual Consistency of Option Prices

The option pricing formulas depend on six variables, five of which are observable. The variance rate involved in each formula must be estimated from past data in order to obtain a dollar figure for the price of the option. But it is not necessary to know the variance rate in order to price options relative to each other.

To price options relative to a given option, say a call option with exercise price X_1 and time to expiration T_1, take the five observable variables and the current market price c_1 of the given option, and solve the call option equation backwards to obtain the implied variance rate σ_1^2. Then, assuming that σ_i^2 is the correct variance rate for the currency in question, use σ_i^2 with the five observable variables to price all other call options with a different exercise price or, if the variance rate is assumed constant, with a different term to maturity, and also to price all put options on the same currency. The prices obtained may be lower than or greater than the market prices of the other options. If, for example, a three-month option is used to calculate σ_i^2, and using σ_i^2 to price the corresponding six-month option yields a theoretical value larger than the market price of the six-month option, then we can say that six-month options are 'underpriced' relative to three-month options, or that three-month options are 'overpriced' relative to six-month options. The strategy, then, would be to buy six-month options and to write or sell three-month options. (The existence of transactions costs allows, of course, a certain amount of non-profitable inconsistency in implied variance rates.) The profitability of such a strategy would depend on the relation between the assumptions employed in the derivation of the pricing formula and the actual variables that determine market prices, as well as whether the variance rate is really constant.

VI. Conclusion   This paper has explored a set of inequality-equality constraints on rational pricing of foreign currency options, and has developed exact pricing equations for European puts and calls when interest rates are stochastic. The assumption that relevant variables follow diffusion processes allows us to set up a riskless hedge that uses no wealth, and which therefore must have a zero return in equilibrium. The construction of this hedge yields a partial differential equation whose solution is the European call option value. The put option equations are obtained immediately from the call equations through a put-to-call conversion equation that holds for FX options. Finally, it was shown that for sufficiently high values (low values) of the spot rate relative to the exercise price, American calls (puts) will be exercised prior to maturity. Hence (for positive interest rates) American FX options have values strictly greater than European FX options.

References

Black, F., 'The Pricing of Commodity Contracts', *J. Fin. Econ.*, January 1976, 3: 167-179.

Black, F. and M. Scholes, 'The Pricing of Options and Corporate Liabilities', *J. Pol. Econ.*, May 1973, 81: 637-659.

Feiger, G. and B. Jacquillat, 'Currency Option Bonds, Puts and Calls on Spot Exchange and the Hedging of Contingent Claims', *J. Finance,* December 1979, 34: 1129-1139.

Geske, R. and H.E. Johnson, 'The American Put Valued Analytically', Working Paper 17-82. UCLA Graduate School of Management, August 1982.

Merton, R.C., 'Theory of Rational Option Pricing', *Bell J. of Econ. Management Sci.,* Spring 1973, 4: 141-183.

Smith, C.W., 'Option Pricing: a Review', *J. Fin. Econ.*, January 1976, 3: 3-51.

Stulz, R., 'Options on the Minimum or Maximum of Two Risky Assets', *J. Fin. Econ.,* July 1982, 10: 161-185.

Section 4
Futures Options

The first futures option markets appeared in late 1982. At that time, the CBOT launched the Treasury bond futures option contract and the CME launched the Eurodollar futures option contract. In 1983, futures options on stock indexes were introduced, and foreign currency futures option contracts were introduced in 1984. Futures option contracts require the delivery of the underlying futures. Upon the exercise of a call option on a futures, for example, the option holder receives a long futures position at the exercise price of the option. At the end of the trading day when the futures position is marked-to-market, the option holder can withdraw the difference between the futures price and the exercise price of the option.

This section contains three articles on futures option valuation. The first is Black's [1976] development of a pricing formula for European-style options on forward contracts. This follows straightforwardly from the Black-Scholes model, when it is recognized that the cost of carrying a forward contract equals zero (the Black-Scholes model implicitly assumes that the cost-of-carry rate is the riskless rate of interest). The contribution of the Cox, Ingersoll, and Ross [1982] article to futures option valuation is that it shows the equivalence of forward and futures prices under the Black-Scholes assumptions. This means that the Black model applies to European-style futures options as well as forward options. Finally, since all exchange-traded futures options in the U.S. are American-style, an article by Whaley [1986a] that provides an approximation method for pricing American-style futures options is included.

Much of the published research on futures options has been empirical. Bailey [1987], for example, investigates gold futures option prices, Ogden and Tucker [1987] examine currency futures option prices, and Whaley [1986a] examines S&P 500 futures option prices. An interesting and innovative type of empirical study is by Gay, Kolb, and Yung [1989]. Rather than performing the standard tests of a model's option pricing performance, they examine the ability of the option pricing model to predict early exercise behavior of market participants. More specifically, they compare actual T-bond futures prices to the critical futures prices implied in the Whaley [1986a] quadratic approximation to deduce whether the T-bond futures option holder should optimally exercise early. Their evidence indicates that the frequency with which T-bond futures option holders do *not* exercise when it is rational to do so is quite high.

References and Bibliography

Asay, M.R., 1983, "A Note on the Design of Commodity Option Contracts," *Journal of Futures Markets* 2, (Spring), 1-8.

Bailey, W.B., 1987, "An Empirical Investigation of the Markets for Comex Gold Futures Options," *Journal of Finance* 42 (December), 1187-94.

Ball, C., and W.N. Torous, 1986, "Futures Options and the Volatility of Futures Prices," *Journal of Finance* 41 (September), 857-70.

Black, F., 1976, "The Pricing of Commodity Contracts," *Journal of Financial Economics* 3, 167-79.

Brenner, M., G. Courtadon, and M. Subrahmanyam, 1985, "Options on the Spot and Options on Futures," *Journal of Finance* 40 (December), 1303-17.

Cox, J.C., F.E. Ingersoll, and S.A. Ross, 1982, "The Relation Between Forward and Futures Prices," *Journal of Financial Economics* 9, 321-46.

Gay, G., R.W. Kolb, and K. Yung, 1989, "Trader Rationality in the Exercise of Futures Options," *Journal of Financial Economics* 23 (August), 339-61.

Hoag, J.W., 1983, "The Valuation of Commodity Options," in *Option Pricing,* ed. Menachem Brenner, 183-221, Lexington, MA: D.C. Heath.

Ogden, J.P., and A. Tucker, 1987, "Empirical Tests of the Efficiency of the Currency Futures Options Market," *Journal of Futures Markets* 7 (December), 695-703.

Ramaswamy, K., and S.M. Sundaresan, 1985, "The Valuation of Options on Futures Contracts," *Journal of Finance* 40 (December), 1319-40.

Whaley, R.E., 1986a, "Valuation of American Futures Options: Theory and Empirical Tests," *Journal of Finance* 41 (March), 127-50.

——, 1986b, "On Valuing American Futures Options," *Financial Analysts Journal* 42 (May/June), 49-59.

Wolf, A., 1982, "Fundamentals of Commodity Options on Futures," *Journal of Futures Markets* 2, 391-408.

1

The Pricing of Commodity Contracts*

Fischer Black

The contract price on a forward contract stays fixed for the life of the contract, while a futures contract is rewritten every day. The value of a futures contract is zero at the start of each day. The expected change in the futures price satisfies a formula like the capital asset pricing model. If changes in the futures price are independent of the return on the market, the futures price is the expected spot price. The futures market is not unique in its ability to shift risk, since corporations can do that too. The futures market is unique in the guidance it provides for producers, distributors, and users of commodities. Using assumptions like those used in deriving the original option formula, we find formulas for the values of forward contracts and commodity options in terms of the futures price and other variables.

1. Introduction

The market for contracts related to commodities is not widely understood. Futures contracts and forward contracts are often thought to be identical, and many people don't know about the existence of commodity options. One of the aims of this paper is to clarify the meaning of each of these contracts.[1]

The spot price of a commodity is the price at which it can be bought or sold for immediate delivery. We will write p for the spot price, or $p(t)$ for the spot price at time t.

Sloan School of Management, M.I.T., Cambridge, Mass. 02139, U.S.A.

*I am grateful for comments on earlier drafts by Michael Jensen, Myron Scholes, Edward Thorp, and Joseph Williams. This work was supported in part by the Center for Research in Security Prices (sponsored by Merrill Lynch, Pierce, Fenner & Smith Inc.) at the Graduate School of Business, University of Chicago.

[1] For an introduction to commodity markets, see Chicago Board of Trade (1973).

Received July 1975, revised version received July 1975

The spot price of an agricultural commodity tends to have a seasonal pattern: it is high just before a harvest, and low just after a harvest. The spot price of a commodity such as gold, however, fluctuates more randomly.

Predictable patterns in the movement of the spot price do not generally imply profit opportunities. The spot price can rise steadily at any rate lower than the storage cost for the commodity (including interest) without giving rise to a profit opportunity for those with empty storage facilities. The spot price can fall during a harvest period without giving rise to a profit opportunity for growers, so long as it is costly to accelerate the harvest.

The futures price of a commodity is the price at which one can agree to buy or sell it at a given time in the future without putting up any money now. We will write x for the futures price, or $x(t, t^*)$ for the futures price at time t for a transaction that will occur at time t^*.

For example, suppose that it is possible today to enter into a contract to buy gold six months from now at $160 an ounce, without either party to the contract being compensated by the other. Both parties may put up collateral to guarantee their ability to fulfill the contract, but if the futures price remains at $160 an ounce for the next six months, the collateral will not be touched. If the contract is left unchanged for six months, then the gold and the money will change hands at that time. In this situation, we say that the six month futures price of gold is $160 an ounce.

The futures price is very much like the odds on a sports bet. If the odds on a particular baseball game between Boston and Chicago are 2:1 in favor of Boston, and if we ignore the bookie's profit, then a person who bets on Chicago wins $2 or loses $1. No money changes hands until after the game. The odds adjust to balance the demand for bets on Chicago and the demand for bets on Boston. At 2:1, balance occurs if twice as many bets are placed on Boston as on Chicago.

Similarly, the futures price adjusts to balance demand to buy the commodity in the future with demand to sell the commodity in the future. Whenever a contract is opened, there is someone on each side. The person who agrees to buy is long the commodity, and the person who agrees to sell is short. This means that when we add up all positions in contracts of this kind, and count short positions as negative, we always come out with zero. The total long interest in commodity contracts of any type must equal the total short interest.

When the two times that specify a futures price are equal, the futures price must equal the spot price,

$$x(t, t) \equiv p(t). \tag{1}$$

Expression (1) holds for all times t. For example, it says that the May futures price will be equal to the May spot price in May, and the September futures price will be equal to the September spot price in September.

Now let us define the three kinds of commodity contracts: forward contracts, futures contracts, and option contracts. Roughly speaking, a forward contract is a contract to buy or sell at a price that stays fixed for the life of the contract; a futures contract is settled every day and rewritten at the new futures price; and an option contract can be exercised by the holder when it matures, if it has not been closed out earlier.

We will write v for the value of a forward contract, u for the value of a futures contract, and w for the value of an option contract. Each of these values will depend on the current futures price $x(t, t^*)$ with the same transaction time t^* as the contract, and on the current time t, as well as on other variables. So we will write $v(x, t)$, $u(x, t)$, and $w(x, t)$. The value of the short side of any contract will be just the negative of the value of the long side. So we will treat v, u, and w as the values of a forward contract to buy, a long futures contract, and an option to buy.

The value of a forward contract depends also on the price c at which the commodity will be bought, and the time t^* at which the transaction will take place. We will sometimes write $v(x, t, c, t^*)$ for the value of a long forward contract. From the discussion above, we know that the futures price is that price at which a forward contract has a current value of zero. We can write this condition as

$$v(x, t, x, t^*) \equiv 0. \tag{2}$$

In effect, eq. (2) says that the value of a forward contract when it is initiated is always zero. When it is initiated, the contract price c is always equal to the current futures price $x(t, t^*)$.

Increasing the futures price increases the value of a long forward contract, and decreasing the futures price decreases the value of the contract. Thus we have

$$v(x, t, c, t^*) > 0, \quad x > c, \tag{3}$$

$$v(x, t, c, t^*) < 0, \quad x < c.$$

The value of a forward contract may be either positive or negative.

When the time comes for the transaction to take place, the value of the forward contract will be equal to the spot price minus the contract price. But by eq. (1), the futures price $x(t, t^*)$ will be equal to the spot price at that time. Thus the value of the forward contract will be the futures price minus the spot price,

$$v(x, t^*, c, t^*) = x - c. \tag{4}$$

Later we will use eq. (4) as the main boundary condition for a differential equation describing the value of a forward contract.

The difference between a futures contract and a forward contract is that the futures contract is rewritten every day with a new contract price equal to the corresponding futures price. A futures contract is like a series of forward contracts. Each day, yesterday's contract is settled, and today's contract is written with a contract price equal to the futures price with the same maturity as the futures contract.

Eq. (2) shows that the value of a forward contract with a contract price equal to the futures price is zero. Thus the value of a futures contract is reset to zero every day. If the investor has made money, he will be given his gains immediately. If he has lost money, he will have to pay his losses immediately. Thus we have

$$u(x, t) \equiv 0. \tag{5}$$

Technically, eq. (5) applies only to the end of the day, after the futures contract has been rewritten. During the day, the futures contract may have a positive or negative value, and its value will be equal to the value of the corresponding forward contract.

Note that the futures price and the value of a futures contract are not at all the same thing. The futures price refers to a transaction at times t^* and is never zero. The value of a futures contract refers to time t and is always zero (at the end of the day).

In the organized U.S. futures markets, both parties to a futures contract must post collateral with a broker. This helps to ensure that the losing party each day will have funds available to pay the winning party. The amount of collateral required varies from broker to broker.

The form in which the collateral can be posted also varies from broker to broker. Most brokers allow the collateral to take the form of Treasury Bills or marginable securities if the amount exceeds a certain minimum. The brokers encourage cash collateral, however, because they earn the interest on customers' cash balances.

The value of a futures customer's account with a broker is entirely the value of his collateral (at the end of the day). The value of his futures contracts is zero. The value of the collateral posted to ensure performance of a futures contract is not the value of the contract.

As futures contracts are settled each day, the value of each customer's collateral is adjusted. When the futures price goes up, those with long positions have money added to their collateral, and those with short positions have money taken away from their collateral. If a customer at any time has more collateral than his broker requires, he may withdraw the excess. If he has less than his broker requires, he will have to put up additional collateral immediately.

Commodity options have a bad image in the U.S., because they were recently used to defraud investors of many millions of dollars. There are no organized commodity options markets in this country. In the U.K., however, commodity options have a long and relatively respectable history.

A commodity option is an option to buy a fixed quantity of a specified commodity at a fixed time in the future and at a specified price. It differs from a security option in that it can't be exercised before the fixed future date. Thus it is a 'European option' rather than an 'American option'.

A commodity option differs from a forward contract because the holder of the option can choose whether or not he wants to buy the commodity at the specified price. With a forward contract, he has no choice: he must buy it, even if the spot price at the time of the transaction is lower than the price he pays.

At maturity, the value of a commodity option is the spot price minus the contract price, if that is positive, or zero. Writing c^* for the exercise price of the option, and noting that the futures price equals the spot price at maturity, we have

$$w(x, t^*) = x - c^*, \quad x \geq c^*, \tag{6}$$

$$= 0, \quad x < c^*.$$

Expression (6) looks like the expression for the value of a security option at maturity as a function of the security price.

2. The behavior of the futures price

Changes in the futures price for a given commodity at a given maturity give rise to gains and losses for investors with long or short positions in the corresponding futures contracts. An investor with a position in the futures market is bearing risk even though the value of his position at the end of each day is zero. His position may also have a positive or negative expected dollar return, even though his investment in the position is zero.

Since his investment is zero, it is not possible to talk about the percentage or fractional return on the investor's position in the futures market. Both his risk and his expected return must be defined in dollar terms.

In deriving the expressions for the behavior of the futures price, we will assume that taxes are zero. However, tax factors will generally affect the behavior of the futures price. There are two peculiarities in the tax laws that make them important.

First, the IRS assumes that a gain or loss on a futures contract is realized only when the contract is closed out. The IRS does not recognize, for tax purposes, the fact that a futures contract is effectively settled and rewritten every day. This makes possible strategies for deferring the taxation of capital gains. For example, the investor can open a number of different contracts, both long and short. The contracts that develop losses are closed out early, and are replaced with different contracts so that the long and short positions stay balanced. The contracts that develop gains are allowed to run unrealized into the next tax year. In the next year, the process can be repeated. Whether this process is likely to be profitable depends on the special factors affecting each investor, including the size of the transaction costs he pays.

Second, the IRS treats a gain or loss on a long futures position that is closed out more than six months after it is opened as a long-term capital gain or loss, while it treats a gain or loss on a short futures position as a short-term capital gain or loss no matter how long the position is left open. Thus if the investor opens both long and short contracts, and if he realizes losses on the short contracts and gains on the long contracts, he can convert short-term gains (from other transactions) into long-term gains. Again, whether this makes sense for a particular investor will depend on his transaction costs and other factors.

However, we will assume that both taxes and transaction costs are zero. We will further assume that the capital asset pricing model applies at each instant of time.[2] This means that investors will be compensated only for bearing risk that cannot be diversified away. If the risk in a futures contract is independent of the risk of changes in value of all assets taken together, then investors will not have to be paid for taking that risk. In effect, they don't have to take the risk because they can diversify it away.

The usual capital asset pricing formula is

$$E(\tilde{R}_i) - R = \beta_i [E(\tilde{R}_m) - R]. \tag{7}$$

In this expression, $\tilde{R}_i$ is the return on asset i, expressed as a fraction of its initial value; R is the return on short-term interest-bearing securities; and $\tilde{R}_m$ is the return on the market portfolio of all assets taken together. The coefficient β_i is a measure of the extent to which the risk of asset i cannot be diversified away. It is defined by

$$\beta_i = \text{cov}(\tilde{R}_i, \tilde{R}_m)/\text{var}(\tilde{R}_m). \tag{8}$$

[2]For an introduction to the capital asset pricing model, see Jensen (1972). The behavior of futures prices in a model of capital market equilibrium was first discussed by Dusak (1973).

The market portfolio referred to above includes corporate securities, personal assets such as real estate, and assets held by non-corporate businesses. To the extent that stocks of commodities are held by corporations, they are implicitly included in the market portfolio. To the extent that they are held by individuals and non-corporate businesses, they are explicitly included in the market portfolio. This market portfolio cannot be observed, of course. It is a theoretical construct.

Commodity contracts, however, are not included in the market portfolio. Commodity contracts are pure bets, in that there is a short position for every long position. So when we are taking all assets together, futures contracts, forward contracts, and commodity options all net out to zero.

Eq. (7) cannot be applied directly to a futures contract, because the initial value of the contract is zero. So we will rewrite the equation so that it applies to dollar returns rather than percentage returns.

Let us assume that asset i has no dividends or other distributions over the period. Then its fractional return is its end-of-period price minus its start-of-period price, divided by its start-of-period price. Writing P_{io} for the start-of-period price of asset i, writing $\tilde{P}_{i1}$ for its end-of-period price, and substituting from eq. (8), we can rewrite eq. (7) as

$$E\{(\tilde{P}_{i1} - P_{io})/P_{io}\} - R = [\text{cov}\{(\tilde{P}_{i1} - P_{io})/P_{io}, \tilde{R}_m\}/\text{var}(\tilde{R}_m)]$$

$$\times [E(\tilde{R}_m) - R]. \tag{9}$$

Multiplying through by P_{io}, we get an expression for the expected dollar return on an asset,

$$E(\tilde{P}_{i1} - P_{io}) - RP_{io} = [\text{cov}(\tilde{P}_{i1} - P_{io}, \tilde{R}_m)/\text{var}(\tilde{R}_m)]$$

$$[E(\tilde{R}_m) - R]. \tag{10}$$

The start-of-period value of a futures contract is zero, so we set P_{io} equal to zero. The end-of-period value of a futures contract, before the contract is rewritten and its value set to zero, is the change in the futures price over the period. In practice, commodity exchanges set daily limits which constrain the reported change in the futures price and the daily gains and losses of traders. We will assume that these limits do not exist. So we set $\tilde{P}_{i1}$ equal to $\Delta\tilde{P}$, the change in the futures price over the period,

$$E(\Delta\tilde{P}) = [\text{cov}(\Delta\tilde{P}, \tilde{R}_m)/\text{var}(\tilde{R}_m)][E(\tilde{R}_m) - R]. \tag{11}$$

In effect, we have applied expression (10) to a futures contract, and have come up with expression (11), which refers to the change in the futures price. For the rest of this section, we can forget about futures contracts and work only with the futures price.

Writing β^* for the first factor on the right-hand side of eq. (11), we have

$$E(\Delta \tilde{P}) = \beta^*[E(\tilde{R}_m) - R].\qquad(12)$$

Expression (12) says that the expected change in the futures price is proportional to the 'dollar beta' of the futures price. If the covariance of the change in the futures price with the return on the market portfolio is zero, then the expected change in the futures price will be zero,[3]

$$E(\Delta \tilde{P}) = 0, \text{ when } \text{cov}(\Delta \tilde{P}, \tilde{R}_m) = 0.\qquad(13)$$

Expressions (12) and (13) say that the expected change in the futures price can be positive, zero, or negative. It would be very surprising if the β^* of a futures price were exactly zero, but it may be approximately zero for many commodities. For these commodities, neither those with long futures positions nor those with short futures positions have significantly positive expected dollar returns.

3. Futures prices and spot prices

When eq. (13) holds at all points in time, the expected change in the futures price will always be zero. This means that the expected futures price at any time t' in the future, where t' is between the current time t and the transaction time t^*, will be equal to the current futures price. The mean of the distribution of possible futures prices at time t' will be the current futures price.[4]

But the futures price at time t^* is the spot price at time t^*, from expression (1). So the mean of the distribution of possible spot prices at time t^* will be the current futures price, when eq. (13) always holds.

Even when (13) doesn't hold, we may still be able to use eq. (12) to estimate the mean of the distribution of possible spot prices at time t^*. To use (12), though, we need to know β^* at each point in time between t and t^*, and we need to know $E(\tilde{R}_m) - R$.

A farmer may not want to know the mean of the distribution of possible spot prices at time t^*. He may be interested in the discounted value of the distribution of possible spot prices. In fact, it seems plausible that he can make his investment decisions as if β^* were zero, even if it is not zero. He can assume that the β^* is zero, and that the futures price is the expected spot price.

To see why this is so, note that he can hedge his investments by taking a short position in the futures market. By taking the right position in the futures

---

[3] In the data she analyzed on wheat, corn, and soybean futures, Dusak (1973) found covariances that were close to zero.

[4] The question of the relation between the futures price and the expected spot price is discussed under somewhat different assumptions by Cootner (1960a, 1960b) and Telser (1960).

market, he can make the β of his overall position zero. Assuming that the farmer is not concerned about risk that can be diversified away, he should make the same investment decisions whether or not he actually takes offsetting positions in the futures market.

In fact, futures prices provide a wealth of valuable information for those who produce, store, and use commodities. Looking at futures prices for various transaction months, participants in this market can decide on the best times to plant, harvest, buy for storage, sell from storage, or process the commodity. A change in a futures price at time t is related to changes in the anticipated distribution of spot prices at time t^*. It is not directly related to changes in the spot price at time t. In practice, however, changes in spot prices and changes in futures prices will often be highly correlated.

Both spot prices and futures prices are affected by general shifts in the cost of producing the commodity, and by general shifts in the demand for the commodity. These are probably the most important factors affecting commodity prices. But an event like the arrival of a prime producing season for the commodity will cause the spot price to fall, without having any predictable effect on the futures price.

Changes in commodity prices are also affected by such factors as the interest rate, the cost of storing the commodity, and the β of the commodity itself.[5] These factors may affect both the spot price and the futures price, but in different ways.

Commodity holdings are assets that form part of investors' portfolios, either directly or indirectly. The returns on such assets must be defined to include such things as the saving to a user of commodities from not running out in the middle of a production run, or the benefit to anyone storing the commodity of having stocks on hand when there is an unusual surge in demand. The returns on commodity holdings must be defined net of all storage costs, including deterioration, theft, and insurance premiums. When the returns on commodity holdings are defined in this way, they should obey the capital asset pricing model, as expressed by eq. (7), like any other asset. If the β of the commodity is zero, as given in eq. (7), then we would expect the β^* of a futures contract to be approximately zero too, as given in eq. (12). And vice versa.

The notion that commodity holdings are priced like other assets means that investors who own commodities are able to diversify away that part of the risk that can be diversified away. One way this can happen is through futures markets: those who own commodities can take short positions, and those who hold diversified portfolios of assets can include long positions in commodity contracts.

[5]Some of the factors affecting changes in the spot price are discussed by Brennan (1958) and Telser (1958).

But there are other ways that the risk in commodity holdings can be largely diversified away. The most common way for risk to be spread is through a corporation. The risk of a corporation's business or assets is passed on to the holders of the corporation's liabilities, especially its stockholders. The stockholders have, or could have, well diversified portfolios of which this stock is only a small part.

Thus if stocks of a commodity are held by a corporation, there will normally be no need for the risk to be spread through the futures market. (There are special cases, however, such as where the corporation has lots of debt outstanding and the lenders insist that the commodity risk be hedged through the futures market.) There are corporations at every stage in a commodity's life cycle: production, distribution, and processing. Even agricultural commodities are generally produced by corporations these days, though the stock may be closely held. Any of these corporate entities can take title to the stocks of commodities, no matter where they are located, and thus spread the risk to those who are in the best position to bear it. For example, canners of tomatoes often buy a farmer's crop before the vines are planted. They may even supply the vines.

This means that a futures market does not have a unique role in the allocation of risk. Corporations in the commodity business play the same role. Which kind of market is best for this role depends on the specifics of such things as transaction costs and taxes in each individual case. It seems clear that corporations do a better job for most commodities, because organized futures markets don't even exist for most commodities. Where they do exist, most of the risk is still transferred through corporations rather than through futures markets.

Thus there is no reason to believe that the existence of a futures market has any predictable effect on the path of the spot price over time. It is primarily the storage of a commodity that reduces fluctuations in its price over time. Storage will occur whether or not there is any way of transferring risk. If there were no way to transfer risk, the price of a seasonal commodity might be somewhat higher before the prime production periods than it is now. But since there are good ways to transfer risk without using the futures market, even this benefit of futures markets is minimal.

I believe that futures markets exist because in some situations they provide an inexpensive way to transfer risk, and because many people both in the business and out like to gamble on commodity prices. Neither of these counts as a major benefit to society. The big benefit from futures markets is the side effect: the fact that participants in the futures markets can make production, storage, and processing decisions by looking at the pattern of futures prices, even if they don't take positions in that market.

This, of course, assumes that futures markets are efficient. It assumes that futures prices incorporate all available information about the future spot price of a commodity. It assumes that investors act quickly on any information they receive, so that the price reacts quickly to the arrival of the information. So quickly that individual traders find it very difficult to make money consistently by trading on information.

4. The pricing of forward contracts and commodity options

We have already discussed the pricing of futures contracts and the behavior of futures prices. In order to derive formulas for the other kinds of commodity contracts, we must make a few more assumptions.

First, let us assume that the fractional change in the futures price over any interval is distributed log-normally, with a known variance rate s^2. The derivations would go through with little change if we assumed that the variance rate is a known function of the time between t and t^*, but we will assume that the variance rate is constant.

Second, let us assume that all of the parameters of the capital asset pricing model, including the expected return on the market, the variance of the return on the market, and the short-term interest rate, are constant through time.

Third, let us continue to assume that taxes and transaction costs are zero.

Under these assumptions, it makes sense to write the value of a commodity contract only as a function of the corresponding futures price and time. If we did not assume the parameters of the capital asset pricing model were constant, then the value of a commodity contract might also depend on those parameters. Implicitly, of course, the value of the contract still depends on the transaction price and the transaction time.

Now let us use the same procedure that led to the formula for an option on a security.[6] We can create a riskless hedge by taking a long position in the option and a short position in the futures contract with the same transaction date. Since the value of a futures contract is always zero, the equity in this position is just the value of the option.

The size of the short position in the futures contract that makes the combined position riskless is the derivative of $w(x, t)$ with respect to x, which we will write w_1. Thus the change in the value of the hedged position over the time interval Δt is

$$\Delta w - w_1 \Delta x. \tag{14}$$

Expanding Δw, and noting that the return on the hedge must be at the instantaneous riskless rate r, we have the differential equation[7]

[6]The original option formula was derived by Black and Scholes (1973). Further results were obtained by Merton (1973).
[7]For the details of this expansion, see Black and Scholes (1973, p. 642 or p. 646).

$$w_2 = r w - \frac{1}{2} s^2 x^2 w_{11}. \tag{15}$$

Note that this is like the differential equation for an option on a security, but with one term missing. The term is missing because the value of a futures contract is zero, while the value of a security is positive.

The main boundary condition for this equation is expression (6).[8] Using standard methods to solve eqs. (15) and (6), we obtain the following formula for the value of a commodity option:

$$w(x, t) = e^{r(t - t^*)} [x N(d_1) - c^* N(d_2)], \tag{16}$$

$$d_1 = \left[\ln \frac{x}{c^*} + \frac{s^2}{2} (t^* - t) \right] \Big/ s\sqrt{(t^* - t)},$$

$$d_2 = \left[\ln \frac{x}{c^*} - \frac{s^2}{2} (t^* - t) \right] \Big/ s\sqrt{(t^* - t)}.$$

This formula can be obtained from the original option formula by substituting $x e^{r(t - t^*)}$ for x everywhere in the original formula.[9] It is the same as the value of an option on a security that pays a continuous dividend at a rate equal to the stock price times the interest rate, when the option can only be exercised at maturity.[10] Again, this happens because the investment in a futures contract is zero, so an interest rate factor drops out of the formula.

Eq. (16) applies to a 'European' commodity option, that can only be exercised at maturity. If the commodity option can be exercised before maturity, the problem of finding its value becomes much more complex.[11] Among other things, its value will depend on the spot price and on futures prices with various transaction dates before the option expires.

Eq. (16) also assumes that taxes are zero. But if commodity options are taxed like security options, then there will be substantial tax benefits for high tax bracket investors who write commodity options.[12] These benefits

[8] Another boundary condition and a regulatory condition are needed to make the solution to (15) and (6) unique. The boundary condition is $w(0, t) = 0$. The need for these additional conditions was not noted in Black and Scholes (1973).

[9] Thorp (1973) obtains the same formula for a similar problem, related to the value of a security option when an investor who sells the underlying stock short does not receive interest on the proceeds of the short sale.

[10] Merton (1973) discusses the valuation of options on dividend-paying securities. The formula he obtains (f. 62) should be eq. (16), but he forgets to substitute $x e^{r(t - t^*)}$ for x in d_1 and d_2.

[11] See Merton (1973) for a discussion of some of the complexities in finding a value for an option that can be exercised early.

[12] For a discussion of tax factors in the pricing of options, see Black (1975).

may be passed on in part or in full to buyers of commodity options in the form of lower prices. So taxes may reduce the values of commodity options.

Compared with the formula for a commodity option, the formula for the value of a forward contract is very simple. The differential equation it must satisfy is the same. Substituting $v(x, t)$ for $w(x, t)$ in eq. (15), we have

$$v_2 = rv - \frac{1}{2} s^2 x^2 v_{11}. \tag{17}$$

The main boundary condition is eq. (4), which we can rewrite as

$$v(x, t^*) = x - c. \tag{18}$$

The solution to (17) and (18) plus the implicit boundary conditions is

$$v(x, t) = (x - c)e^{r(t - t^*)}. \tag{19}$$

Expression (19) says that the value of a forward contract is the difference between the futures price and the forward contract price, discounted to the present at the short-term interest rate. It is independent of any measure of risk. It does not depend on the variance rate of the fractional change in the futures price or on the covariance rate between the change in the futures price and the return on the market.

References

Black, F., 1975, Fact and fantasy in the use of options, *Financial Analysts Journal* 31, July/Aug.

Black, F. and M. Scholes, 1973, The pricing of options and corporate liabilities, *Journal of Political Economy* 81, May/June, 637-654.

Brennan, M. J., 1958, The supply of storage, *American Economic Review* 48, March, 50-72.

Chicago Board of Trade, 1973, Commodity trading manual (Board of Trade of the City of Chicago, Chicago, Ill.).

Cootner, P. H., 1960a, Returns to speculators: Telser versus Keynes, *Journal of Political Economy* 68, Aug., 396-404.

Cootner, P. H., 1960b, Rejoinder, *Journal of Political Economy* 68, Aug., 415-418.

Dusak, K., 1973, Futures trading and investor returns: An investigation of commodity market risk premiums, *Journal of Political Economy* 81, Nov./Dec., 1387-1406.

Jensen, M. C., 1972, Capital markets: Theory and evidence, *Bell Journal of Economics and Management Science* 3, Autumn, 357-398.

Merton, R. C., 1973, The theory of rational option pricing, *Bell Journal of Economics and Management Science* 4, Spring, 141-183.

Telser, L., 1958, Futures trading and the storage of cotton and wheat, *Journal of Political Economy* 66, June, 233-255.

Telser, L., 1960, Returns to speculators: Telser versus Keynes, Reply, *Journal of Political Economy* 67, Aug., 404-415.

Thorp, E., 1973, Extensions of the Black-Scholes options model, *Bulletin of the International Statistical Institute,* Proceedings of the 39th Session, 522-529.

2

The Relation Between Forward Prices and Futures Prices *

John C. Cox
Jonathan E. Ingersoll, Jr.
Stephen A. Ross

This paper consolidates the results of some recent work on the relation between forward prices and futures prices. It develops a number of propositions characterizing the two prices. These propositions contain several testable implications about the difference between forward and futures prices. Many of the propositions show that equilibrium forward and futures prices are equal to the values of particular assets, even though they are not in themselves asset prices. The paper then illustrates these results in the context of two valuation models and discusses the effects of taxes and other institutional factors.

1. Introduction   Forward markets and futures markets have long played an important role in economic affairs. In spite of the attention that they have collectively received, virtually no consideration has been given to the differences between the two types of markets. Indeed, most of the academic literature has treated them as if they were synonymous. Similarly, most practitioners

John C. Cox, Stanford University, Stanford, CA 94305, USA

Jonathan E. Ingersoll, Jr., University of Chicago, Chicago, IL 60637, USA

Stephen A. Ross, Yale University, New Haven, CT 06520, USA

*This paper is a substantial expansion of part of the 1977 version of Cox, Ingersoll and Ross (1978). We are grateful to our many colleagues who provided helpful comments and suggestions on that paper. Special thanks go to Fischer Black, Douglas Breeden, Robert Merton, Merton Miller, George Oldfield, and the referee, John Long. This research was supported by the Center for the Study of Futures Markets at Columbia University and by the National Science Foundation under Grants Nos. SOC 77-18087 and SOC 77-22301.

Received October 1980, final version received June 1981

John C. Cox, Jonathan E. Ingersoll, Jr., and Stephen A. Ross, ''The Relation Between Forward Prices and Futures Prices.'' Reprinted with permission from the *Journal of Financial Economics*, Vol. 9, 1982, pp. 321-46.

have viewed the differences as irrelevant administrative details and acted as if the two served exactly the same economic functions. Given the similarity of the two markets, such conclusions are quite understandable, but they are nevertheless incorrect. Forward markets and futures markets differ in fundamental ways.

An individual who takes a long position in a forward contract agrees to buy a designated good or asset on a specified future date, the maturity date, for the forward price prevailing at the time the contract is initiated. On the maturity date, then, the forward price must equal the spot price of the underlying good or asset. No money changes hands initially or during the lifetime of the contract, only on the maturity date. The equilibrium forward price must thus continually change over time in a way such that newly created forward contracts will always have a zero value when they are initiated.

A futures contract is similar in many ways, but there is an important difference. An individual who takes a long position in a futures contract nominally agrees to buy a designated good or asset on the maturity date for the futures price prevailing at the time the contract is initiated. Hence, the futures price must also equal the spot price on the maturity date. Again, no money changes hands initially. Subsequently, however, as the futures price changes, the party in whose favor the price change occurred must immediately be paid the full amount of the change by the losing party. As a result, the payment required on the maturity date to buy the underlying good or asset is simply its spot price at that time. The difference between that amount and the initial futures price has been paid (or received) in installments throughout the life of the contract. Like the forward price, the equilibrium futures price must also continually change over time. It must do so in such a way that the remaining stream of future payments described above always has a value of zero.

The difference in the payment schedules is clearly explained in a seminal article by Black (1976). While Black's discussion is completely correct, it is unfortunately presented in the context of a constant interest rate. As it turns out, this obscures a basic economic difference between the two types of markets. With a constant interest rate, the two are essentially equivalent and forward prices are equal to futures prices, but in general this is not true.

Several studies in addition to ours have independently noted the critical role of stochastic interest rates. To our knowledge, the first to do so was Margrabe (1976). Working in a continuous-time framework, Margrabe shows that if forward and futures prices are equal there will be an arbitrage opportunity unless a certain special condition is satisfied; constant interest rates are sufficient but not necessary for this condition to be met. Merton (1979) uses a discrete-time arbitrage argument to derive a way to sign the difference between forward and futures prices. Although Merton considers only forward and futures contracts on Treasury bills, his approach is such that this involves no loss of generality. Jarrow and Oldfield (1981) provide a perspicuous discussion of the contractual differences and use an arbitrage argument to show the importance of stochastic interest rates. They also show the connection between forward contracts and options. Richard and Sundaresan (1981) derive a continuous-time equilibrium model and use it to analyze forward and futures contracts. Sundaresan (1980) employs the Richard and Sundaresan model to develop and test a number of explicit formulas for forward and futures prices. French (1981) examines a discrete-time utility-based model of forward and futures pricing and undertakes several empirical tests of his results.

One purpose of our paper is to consolidate some of the results of these studies. In so doing, we hope to help clarify the relation between forward prices and futures prices. Section 2 develops a number of propositions characterizing the two prices. These propositions contain several testable implications about the difference between forward and futures prices. Many of the propositions show that equilibrium forward and futures prices are equal to the values of particular assets. This allows one to apply any framework for valuing assets to the determination of forward and futures prices, even though they are not in themselves asset prices. Section 3 illustrates some of these results in a simple two-period framework with a complete set of state prices. Section 4 then uses the propositions developed in section 2 to examine forward and futures prices in the context of a continuous-time valuation model. This model gives a basis for obtaining explicit formulas for equilibrium forward and futures prices and hence provides further opportunities for empirical testing. In section 5, we conclude the paper with some comments and conjectures about the effects of taxes and other institutional factors.

2. Some fundamental propositions about forward prices and futures prices

For the most part, our results in this section are based on arbitrage arguments and thus are quite general. They are consequences of what is sometimes called the law of one price: investment strategies which have the same payoffs must have the same current value. To concentrate on the basic issues, we assume perfect frictionless markets. Hence, we shall ignore both taxes and transactions costs until section 5.

We shall use the following notation:

s = maturity date of the forward and futures contracts,
$V(s)$ = price at time s of the good or asset on which the contracts are written,
$P(t)$ = price at time t of a default-free discount bond paying one dollar at time s,
$G(t)$ = forward price at time t,
$H(t)$ = futures price at time t,
R_t = one plus the spot interest rate prevailing from time t to time $t + 1$.

Our first two propositions express forward prices and futures prices in terms of assets making particular payments on the maturity date:

Proposition 1.   *The forward price G(t) is the value at time t of a contract which will pay at time s the amount*

$$V(s)/P(t). \tag{1}$$

Proof.   Consider the following strategy: take a long position in $1/P(t)$ forward contracts and place the amount $G(t)$ in bonds maturing at time s. The current investment required is $G(t)$. There are no interim payoffs, and the payoff at time s is

$$\frac{1}{P(t)}[G(s) - G(t)] + \frac{G(t)}{P(t)} = \frac{V(s)}{P(t)} . \blacksquare \tag{2}$$

Proposition 2.   *The futures price (H)t is the value at time t of a contract which will pay at time s the amount*

$$V(s) \prod_{k=t}^{s-1} R_k . \tag{3}$$

Proof.   Consider the following strategy: at time t, take the amount $H(t)$ and continually reinvest it and the accumulated interest in one-period bonds until time s. At each time $j, j = t, t + 1, \ldots, s - 1$, take a long position in $\prod_{k=t}^{j} R_k$ futures contracts. Liquidate each contract after one period and continually reinvest the (possibly negative) proceeds and accumulated interest in one-period bonds until time s. The current investment required for this strategy is $H(t)$. The payoff at time s is

$$H(t) \prod_{k=t}^{s-1} R_k + \sum_{j=t}^{s-1} \left(\prod_{k=t}^{j} R_k \right) [H(j + 1) - H(j)] \left(\prod_{k=j+1}^{s-1} R_k \right)$$

$$= H(s) \prod_{k=t}^{s-1} R_k = V(s) \prod_{k=t}^{s-1} R_k . \blacksquare \tag{4}$$

Propositions 1 and 2 show that the distinction between forward prices and futures prices is very much like the distinction between 'going long' and 'rolling over shorts' in the bond market. Each price is equal to the value of a claim which will pay a particular number of units of the underlying good or asset on the maturity date. For the forward price, this number is the total return which will be earned on an investment in a discount bond maturing at time s. For the futures price, it is the total return which will be earned from a policy of continual reinvestment in one-period bonds. This characterization draws attention to an important difference between futures prices and forward prices: futures prices will depend on the correlation of spot prices and interest rates, while forward prices will not.

Jarrow and Oldfield (1981) show that forward and futures contracts can be used to create a portfolio which will give a sure return on the maturity date if interest rates are constant, but not if they are random. Propositions 1 and 2, taken together, give essentially the same conclusion. Proposition 2 is identical to a result derived by Richard and Sundaresan (1981) using their equilibrium model and by French (1981) using a discrete-time arbitrage approach. Our next three propositions follow immediately from Propositions 1 and 2.

Proposition 3 [Black (1976)]. *If interest rates are non-stochastic, then $G(t) = H(t)$.*

Proof. If interest rates are non-stochastic, then

$$\frac{1}{P(t)} = \prod_{k=t}^{s-1} R_k . \quad \blacksquare$$ (5)

If there is only one period remaining before the maturity date, $1/P(t)$ will always equal R_t. Consequently, there will be no difference between forward and futures contracts in any one-period model or in any two-period model where all goods are consumed in the final period.

Proposition 4. *If $V(s)$ is non-stochastic, then $G(t) = H(t) = V(s)$.*

Proof. If $V(s)$ is non-stochastic, then a current investment of the amount $V(s)$ in bonds maturing at time s produces a payoff at that time of $V(s)/P(t)$, so $G(t) = V(s)$. Similarly, a current investment of $V(s)$ in a strategy of rolling over one-period bonds gives a payoff at time s of $V(s)\prod_{k=t}^{s-1} R_k$, so $H(t) = V(s)$. $\blacksquare$

Proposition 5. *Let $h_i(t)$ be the futures prices and $g_i(t)$ be the forward price at time t of a good i whose spot price at time s is $v_i(s)$. If*

$$V(s) = \sum_i a_i \, v_i(s) \ \ for \ some \ constants \ a_i,$$

then

$$H(t) = \sum_i a_i \, h_i(t) \ \ and \ \ G(t) = \sum_i a_i \, g_i(t).$$

Proof. This follows immediately from the linearity in $V(s)$ of the right-hand side of (1) and (3). $\blacksquare$

This result states that the futures price of a portfolio is equal to a corresponding portfolio of futures prices and the same is true for forward prices. If the payoffs were not linear, then this conclusion would not hold; for example, it is well known that an option on a portfolio is not the same as a portfolio of options. While Proposition 5 is quite obvious, it is nevertheless very useful. One example is provided by the forward and futures prices of non-callable government bonds. These bonds can be thought of as portfolios of discount bonds. Consequently, any method for finding the futures price of a discount bond will also give the futures prices for all coupon bonds.

Our next proposition expresses the difference between forward prices and futures prices in terms of the relation between futures prices and bond prices. It is very similar to a result of Merton (1979). Loosely stated, it says that if futures prices and bond prices are positively correlated, then the futures price is less than the forward price; if they are negatively correlated, then the futures price is greater than the forward price. In this and the following propositions, we shall occasionally refer to a continuous-time, continuous-state economy. By this, we mean an economy in which trading takes place continuously and in which all variables relevant to the equilibrium follow diffusion processes.

Proposition 6. $G(t) - H(t)$ *is the value at time t of a payment of*

$$-\sum_{j=t}^{s-1} [H(j+1) - H(j)] \left[\frac{P(j)}{P(j+1)} - 1 \right] \Big/ P(t), \tag{6}$$

to be received at time s. For a continuous-time, continuous-state economy, this sum becomes

$$\int_{t}^{s} H(u) [\text{cov } H(u), P(u)] \, du/P(t), \tag{7}$$

where [cov $H(u)$, $P(u)$] *stands for the local covariance of the percentage changes in H with the percentage changes in P. Hence,* [cov $H(u)$, $P(u)$] > 0 *for all u implies* $G(t) > H(t)$ *and* [cov $H(u)$, $P(u)$] < 0 *for all u implies* $G(t) < H(t)$.

Proof. Consider the following strategy, which requires no investment. Take a short position in a forward contract at time t. In each period $j, j = t, \ldots, s - 1$, take a long position in $P(j)$ futures contracts, liquidate them after one period, and place the (possibly negative) proceeds in bonds with maturity date s. At time s, the payoff to this strategy is

$$G(t) - G(s) + \sum_{j=t}^{s-1} P(j)[H(j+1) - H(j)] \left(\frac{1}{P(j+1)} \right)$$

$$= G(t) - G(s) + \sum_{j=t}^{s-1} [H(j+1) - H(j)]$$

$$+ \sum_{j=t}^{s-1} [H(j+1) - H(j)] \left[\frac{P(j)}{P(j+1)} - 1 \right]$$

$$= H(s) - G(s) + G(t) - H(t)$$

$$+ \sum_{j=t}^{s-1} [H(j+1) - H(j)] \left[\frac{P(j)}{P(j+1)} - 1 \right]. \tag{8}$$

Since this strategy requires no investment, the current values of this payoff must be zero. Now note that $G(s) = H(s)$ and that the current value of a certain payment of $G(t) - H(t)$ at time s is $P(t)[G(t) - H(t)]$. Consequently, $G(t) - H(t)$ is the current value of a payment at time s of

$$- \sum_{j=t}^{s-1} [H(j+1) - H(j)] \left[\frac{P(j)}{P(j+1)} - 1 \right] \Big/ P(t).$$

Hence, in a continuous-time, continuous-state economy, if the local covariance of the percentage changes in H and P will always have one sign from t to s, then $G(t) - H(t)$ has the same sign. ∎

Like Proposition 2, the following proposition equates the futures price, which is not itself the value of an asset, with another quantity which is the value of an asset. This allows us to apply any equilibrium framework for valuing assets to the determination of equilibrium futures prices. Proposition 8 establishes an analogous result for forward prices.

Proposition 7. $H(t)$ *is the value at time* t *of a contract which gives a payment of* $V(s)$ *at time* s *and a flow from time* t *to time* s *of the prevailing spot rate times the prevailing futures price. That is,* $H(t)$ *is the value at time* t *of a contract which pays* $V(s)$ *at time* s *and* $(R_u - 1)H(u)$ *at each time* $u + 1$ *for* $u = t, t+1, \ldots, s - 1$.

Proof. Consider strategy A: continually reinvest the payouts received from this security and the accumulated interest in one-period bonds. At time s, the proceeds will be

$$\sum_{j=t}^{s-1} (R_j - 1)H(j) \prod_{k=j+1}^{s-1} R_k + V(s). \tag{9}$$

But since $V(s) = H(s)$, this can be rewritten as

$$H(t) \prod_{k=t}^{s-1} R_k + \sum_{j=t}^{s-1} [H(j+1) - H(j)] \prod_{k=j+1}^{s-1} R_k. \tag{10}$$

Now consider strategy B: invest $H(t)$ in a one-period bond at time t and then continually reinvest the proceeds in one-period bonds. Take a long position in one futures contract and continually reinvest the (possibly negative) proceeds received at the end of each period in one-period bonds. At time s, the proceeds of strategy B will be

$$H(t) \prod_{k=t}^{s-1} R_k + \sum_{j=t}^{s-1} [H(j+1) - H(j)] \prod_{k=j+1}^{s-1} R_k. \tag{11}$$

This is the same as the proceeds of strategy A. Since the current value of B is $H(t)$, the current value of A must also be $H(t)$. ∎

Proposition 8. $G(t)$ *is the value at time t of a contract which pays* $V(s)$ *at time s and the flow*

$$(R_u - 1)G(u) + [G(u+1) - G(u)] \left[\frac{P(u+1)}{P(u)} - 1 \right], \tag{12}$$

at each time $u + 1$ *for* $u = t, \ldots, s - 1$.

Proof. Let strategy A be the following: continually reinvest the payouts received from this security and the accumulated interest in one-period bonds. At time s the proceeds will be

$$\sum_{j=t}^{s-1} (R_j - 1)G(j) \prod_{k=j+1}^{s-1} R_k$$

$$+ \sum_{j=t}^{s-1} [G(j+1) - G(j)] \left[\frac{P(j+1)}{P(j)} - 1 \right] \prod_{k=j+1}^{s-1} R_k + V(s). \tag{13}$$

Since $G(s) = V(s)$, this can be rewritten as

$$G(t) \prod_{k=t}^{s-1} R_k + \sum_{j=t}^{s-1} [G(j+1) - G(j)] \prod_{k=j+1}^{s-1} R_k$$

$$+ \sum_{j=t}^{s-1} [G(j+1) - G(j) \left[\frac{P(j+1)}{P(j)} - 1\right] \prod_{k=j+1}^{s-1} R_k \qquad (14)$$

$$= G(t) \prod_{k=t}^{s-1} R_k + \sum_{j=t}^{s-1} [G(j+1) - G(j)] \left[\frac{P(j+1)}{P(j)}\right] \prod_{k=j+1}^{s-1} R_k.$$

Now consider strategy B: invest $G(t)$ in a one-period bond at time t and then continually reinvest the proceeds in one-period bonds. At each time j, $j = t, \ldots, s - 1$, take a long position in $1/P(j)$ forward contracts. Close out each contract after one period, thereby locking in the amount $G(j + 1) - G(j)$ to be received at time s. Obtain the present value of this amount, $P(j + 1)[G(j + 1) - G(j)]$, and invest it in one-period bonds. Continually reinvest the proceeds in one-period bonds thereafter. At time s, the proceeds of strategy B will be

$$G(t) \prod_{k=t}^{s-1} R_k + \sum_{j=t}^{s-1} [G(j+1) - G(j)] \left[\frac{P(j+1)}{P(j)}\right] \prod_{k=j+1}^{s-1} R_k. \qquad (15)$$

This is identical to the proceeds of strategy A. Since the current value of B is $G(t)$, the current value of A must also be $G(t)$. ∎

Propositions 7 and 8 are useful not only in their own right, but also for obtaining Proposition 9. This proposition shows for forward prices a result analogous to Proposition 6 for futures prices. It expresses the difference between forward prices and futures prices in terms of the relation between forward prices and bond prices.

Proposition 9. $G(t) - H(t)$ *is the value at time t of a payment of*

$$\left(\prod_{k=t}^{s-1} R_k\right) \left[\sum_{j=t}^{s-1} [G(j+1) - G(j)] \left[\frac{P(j+1)}{P(j)} - 1\right]\right], \qquad (16)$$

to be received at time s. For a continuous-time, continuous-state economy, the above expression becomes

$$\left[\exp\left(\int_t^s \log R(u) \, du\right)\right] \int_t^s G(u) [\text{cov } G(u), P(u)] \, du. \qquad (17)$$

Hence, [cov $G(u)$, $P(u)$] > 0 *for all u implies* $G(t) > H(t)$ *and* [cov $G(u)$, $P(u)$] < 0 *for all u implies* $G(t) < H(t)$.

Proof. Propositions 7 and 8 imply that $H(t) - G(t)$ is the current value of a contract which pays

$$(R_u - 1)[H(u) - G(u)] - [G(u+1) - G(u)]\left[\frac{P(u+1)}{P(u)} - 1\right],$$
(18)

at each time $u + 1$ for $u = t, \ldots, s - 1$. Consider the following strategy.

Over each period j, take a long position in $\Pi_{k=t}^{j} R_k$ of these contracts. Do this with no net investment in the following way. If the current value of the contract is positive, borrow the amount and use the first component of the payout, which will be positive, to repay the borrowing; if the current value is negative, lend the amount and use the proceeds of the lending to make restitution for the first component of the payout, which will be negative. After doing this, the remaining proceeds at time $j + 1$ from the position taken at time j will be

$$\left[[H(j+1) - G(j+1)] - [H(j) - G(j)]\right.$$
$$\left. - [G(j+1) - G(j)]\left[\frac{P(j+1)}{P(j)} - 1\right]\right]\prod_{k=t}^{j} R_k.$$
(19)

Invest this amount in one period bonds at time $j + 1$ and then continually reinvest it and the accumulated interest in one-period bonds. At time s the total proceeds from all positions taken from t to s will be

$$\left[\sum_{j=t}^{s-1}[H(j+1) - G(j+1)] - [H(j) - G(j)]\right.$$
$$\left. - \sum_{j=1}^{s-1}[G(j+1) - G(j)]\left[\frac{P(j+1)}{P(j)} - 1\right]\right]\prod_{k=t}^{s-1} R_k.$$
(20)

Note that since $G(s) = H(s)$, then

$$\sum_{j=t}^{s-1}[[H(j+1) - G(j+1)] - [H(j) - G(j)]] = G(t) - H(t).$$
(21)

Since the entire position requires no net investment, its current value must be zero. The current value of the amount $[G(t) - H(t)] \prod_{k=t}^{s-1} R_k$ received at time s is $G(t) - H(t)$. Consequently, $G(t) - H(t)$ is the current value of a payment at time s of

$$\left(\prod_{k=t}^{s-1} R_k \right) \left[\sum_{j=t}^{s-1} [G(j+1) - G(j)] \left[\frac{P(j+1)}{P(j)} - 1 \right] \right]. \qquad (22)$$

Hence, for a continuous-time, continuous-state economy, if [cov $G(u)$, $P(u)$] always has one sign, then $G(t) - H(t)$ has the same sign. ∎

Note that Propositions 6 and 9 show the relation between forward and futures prices when both forward and futures markets exist simultaneously. If we find, for example, that $G(t) > H(t)$, this does not imply that replacing a forward market with a futures market will result in a lower price. Such a change could conceivably affect the equilibrium valuation of all assets and lead instead to a higher price. At the present time, simultaneous forward and futures markets are available for certain U.S. Treasury and Government National Mortgage Association securities, some foreign currencies, and a number of commodities. However, the forward contracts are typically traded with standardized times to maturity rather than standardized maturity dates. In these cases, corresponding forward and futures contracts exist simultaneously only on the days for which a standardized time to maturity in the forward market coincides with a standardized maturity date in the futures market.

Up to this point, nothing we have said has depended on the existence of a spot market or on the characteristics of the underlying good or asset. Indeed, this good or asset need not even exist at the current time. This could be the case, for example, with a perishable commodity before the next crop is harvested. However, if there is a spot market, or an options market, then we can express our results in terms of spot prices and option prices.

If $V(s)$ is the price at time s of a currently traded good or asset, then

$$G(t) = O(t)/P(t), \qquad (23)$$

where $O(t)$ is the current value of a European call option with maturity date s and exercise price zero. [The strategy of buying $1/P(t)$ options gives a payoff at time s of $V(s)/P(t)$.] In that case

$$[G(j+1) - G(j)] \left[\frac{P(j+1)}{P(j)} - 1 \right] \tag{24}$$

$$= \frac{O(j)}{P(j)} \left[\frac{O(j+1)}{O(j)} - 1 \right] \left[\frac{P(j+1)}{P(j)} - 1 \right] - \frac{O(j+1)}{P(j+1)} \left[\frac{P(j+1)}{P(j)} - 1 \right]^2 ,$$

and for continuous-time, continuous-state economies this becomes

$$G[\operatorname{cov} G, P] = (O/P)[\operatorname{cov} O, P - \operatorname{var} P]. \tag{25}$$

If the asset makes no payouts between t and s, then $O(t) = V(t)$. This immediately leads to a result which was obtained in a different way by Margrabe (1976):

(i) $\operatorname{cov} V, P > \operatorname{var} P$ implies $G(t) > H(t),$

(ii) $\operatorname{cov} V, P < \operatorname{var} P$ implies $G(t) < H(t).$ $\tag{26}$

For Treasury bills, V is itself a discount bond maturing at some time after s. We would thus expect V and P to be highly correlated and var $V >$ var P. Hence, we would expect cov $V, P >$ var P and $G(t) > H(t)$. For an asset which is a hedge against bond price fluctuations (i.e., is negatively correlated with bond prices), we would have cov $V, P <$ var P and $G(t) < H(t)$.

With the existence of a spot market, we can also obtain another result somewhat similar to Proposition 6, but involving payouts depending on the spot price rather than the futures price. This gives an additional way to determine the futures price. It also allows us to express the relation between futures prices and spot prices in terms of the relation between the interest rate and the spot rental rate on the good or asset. By the spot rental rate at time u, we mean the fraction of the beginning-of-period spot price which would have to be paid at the end of the period to obtain the full use of the good or asset during the period, including the right to receive any payouts such as dividends.

Proposition 10.   Let Y_u be the spot rental rate at time u. Then $H(t) - V(t)$ is equal to the value of a contract which gives a payment of

$$[(R_u - 1 - Y_u)V(u)] \prod_{k=t}^{u-1} R_k , \tag{27}$$

at each time $u + 1$ for $u = t, t + 1, \ldots, s - 1$. Consequently, if the spot interest rate is always greater (less) than the spot rental rate, then the futures price is greater (less) than the spot price.

Proof. Let $Z(t)$ be the value at time t of the contract described. Consider the following strategy. At time t, take a long position in one contract and buy one unit of the good or asset in the spot market for $V(t)$. Finance the spot purchase by rolling over one-period loans. The total investment required is thus $Z(t)$. At each time j, for $j = t + 1, \ldots, s - 1$, use the payment received from the contract and the proceeds from spot rental over the previous period to increase the number of units of the spot good or asset held from $\prod_{k=t}^{j-1} R_k$ to $\prod_{k=t}^{j} R_k$. The total volume of the position at time s is

$$
V(s) \prod_{k=t}^{s-1} R_k - V(t) \prod_{k=t}^{s-1} R_k. \tag{28}
$$

Using Proposition 2, the current value of this amount is $H(t) - V(t)$. Consequently, $Z(t) = H(t) - V(t)$. If all of the payments given by the contract are positive (negative), then its current value must be positive (negative), so $H(t) > V(t) H(t) < V(t))$. ∎

Our final proposition relates our results to the continuous-time capital asset pricing model (CAPM). It is stated in terms of the CAPM in consumption form as derived by Breeden (1979), but the same conclusions hold for the original multi-factor model of Merton (1973).

Proposition 11. *Futures prices will satisfy the capital asset pricing model for arbitrary $V(s)$, but forward prices will do so only if interest rates are nonstochastic.*

Proof. Consider the dollar return from holding over one period a long position in $1/P(t)$ forward contracts and the amount $G(t)$ in one-period bonds. The dollar return is

$$
\frac{1}{P(t)} [P(t + 1) [G(t + 1) - G(t)]] + R_t G(t). \tag{29}
$$

Denote the expected value of the dollar return as μG. The CAPM in consumption form says that

$$
\mu G - R_t G = \beta_{c, K} \left(\frac{\mu_M M - R_t M}{\beta_{c, M}} \right), \tag{30}
$$

where

$$
\beta_{c, K} = \mathrm{cov} \left(\frac{P(t + 1)}{P(t)} [G(t + 1) - G(t)], C(t + 1) - C(t) \right) \Big/ \sigma_C^2,
$$

$C(t)$ is aggregate consumption at time t, $M(t)$ is the value of the market portfolio at time t, and K is the portfolio described above. Consequently, we can write

$$E\left(\frac{P(t+1)}{P(t)}[G(t+1)-G(t)]\right)$$

$$= \text{cov}\left(\frac{P(t+1)}{P(t)}[G(t+1)-G(t)], C(t+1)-C(t)\right)$$

$$\times \left(\frac{\mu_M M - R_t M}{\sigma_C^2 \beta_{C,M}}\right), \tag{31}$$

where E indicates expectation. Also, we have

$$\frac{P(t+1)}{P(t)}[G(t+1)-G(t)]$$

$$= [G(t+1)-G(t)] + \left(\frac{P(t+1)}{P(t)}-1\right)[G(t+1)-G(t)]. \tag{32}$$

Thus, in the limit for continuous-time, continuous-state economies,

$$\text{cov}\left(\frac{P(t+1)}{P(t)}[G(t+1)-G(t)], C(t+1)-C(t)\right)$$

$$= \text{cov}[G(t+1)-G(t), C(t+1)-C(t)], \tag{33}$$

so forward prices can satisfy the CAPM only if

$$E\left(\left(\frac{P(t+1)}{P(t)}-1\right)[G(t+1)-G(t)]\right)\bigg/[(t+1)-t] \to 0 \tag{34}$$

in the limit, which will be true for arbitrary V only if interest rates are nonstochastic.

Consequently, any attempt to apply the CAPM to a series of forward prices will be misdirected. However, a slight modification of this line of reasoning shows that changes in futures prices, when combined with a portfolio as described above, will satisfy the CAPM in consumption form, as is discussed in Breeden (1980). ∎

This concludes our series of propositions relating forward prices and futures prices. Although we hope that our list contains the most important propositions, it is not meant to be exhaustive; we have not found a general way to characterize all possible relations between the two prices.

In the remainder of this section, we discuss how some of the features of forward and futures contracts could be combined. Forward contracts provide an easy way for an individual to lock in at time t the amount he will have to pay at time s for one unit of the underlying good or asset. By taking a long position in a forward contract, the individual can arrange today to buy the good on the maturity date for a price of $G(t)$. An important implication of our results is that futures contracts cannot in general provide exactly the same service. An exact hedging strategy using only (a finite number of) futures contracts may not be possible, and even if possible, it would typically require more information than is needed when employing forward contracts.

It may appear that this is a necessary consequence of the resettlement feature of futures contracts. This would be unfortunate, since resettlement may provide certain advantages. With forward contracts significant implicit or explicit collateral may be necessary; with futures contracts the requirements would be much smaller. Futures markets thus to a large extent separate the actual transactions in the good from the issues of collateralization and financing, while forward markets do not. However, it is easy to specify a contract which will meet the dual requirements of providing a simple exact hedging procedure and requiring only minimal collateral. This is in fact exactly what would be accomplished with a forward contract which had to be settled and rewritten continually.

To make this more precise, we introduce a quasi-futures contract, which is exactly the same as a regular futures contract, except that at the end of each period the person in whose favor the price change occurred is paid not the full amount of the change, but instead the present value that this full amount would have if it were paid on the maturity date. If we denote the quasi-futures price at time t as $Q(t)$, then an individual having a long position in such a contract receives at each time $j + 1$, for $j = t, \ldots, s - 1$, the amount $P(j + 1)[Q(j + 1) - Q(j)]$. If the individual invests the (possibly negative) proceeds received at each time $j + 1$ in bonds maturing at time s, then the value of his position at time s will be

$$\sum_{j=t}^{s-1} P(j+1)[Q(j+1) - Q(j)] \left(\frac{1}{P(j+1)} \right) = V(s) - Q(t). \quad (35)$$

This strategy allows the individual to arrange today to buy the good on the maturity date for a designated price $Q(t)$. Since the strategy requires no net investment, it is equivalent to a forward contract, and hence $Q(t) = G(t)$.

3. A two-period example

In this section, we give a simple example in which forward and futures prices can be found directly and use it to illustrate some of our propositions. In the next section, we shall reverse this procedure and use the propositions to determine forward and futures prices in a more complex setting.

For our first example, we consider a two-period model with a complete system of state prices. We shall supplement our earlier notation in the following way:

p_i = price at time t of a claim which will pay one dollar at time $t + 1$ if the economy is in state i at time $t + 1$,

p_{ij} = price at time $t + 1$ of a claim which will pay one dollar at time $t + 2$ if the economy is in state i at time $t + 1$ and state j at time $t + 2$,

V_{ij} = price of the underlying good or asset at time $t + 2$ if the economy is in state i at time $t + 1$ and state j at time $t + 2$,

H_i = futures price at time $t + 1$ if the economy is in state i at time $t + 1$.

As before, $G(t)$ and $H(t)$ stand for the current forward price and futures price, respectively.

At time $t + 2$, the value of a forward contract written at time t will be

$$V_{ij} - G(t),\tag{36}$$

and the current value of this amount is

$$\sum_{i,j} p_i p_{ij}[V_{ij} - G(t)].\tag{37}$$

Since no money changes hands initially, both parties will be willing to enter into the contract only if its current value is zero. Consequently,

$$G(t) = \sum_{i,j} p_i p_{ij} V_{ij} \bigg/ \sum_{i,j} p_i p_{ij}.\tag{38}$$

The current value of a bond paying one dollar at time $t + 2$ is $\sum_{i,j} p_i p_{ij}$, so this verifies that $G(t)$ can be found as shown in Proposition 1.

Now we turn to determining the current futures price. Note that at time $t + 1$ the futures contract is the same as a forward contract, so

$$H_i = \sum_{j} p_{ij} V_{ij} \bigg/ \sum_{j} p_{ij}.\tag{39}$$

At time t, the holder of a futures contract knows that he will receive at time $t + 1$ the amount

$$H_i - H(t),\tag{40}$$

the current value of which is

$$\sum_i p_i[H_i - H(t)]. \tag{41}$$

Again, since no money changes hands when the contract is initiated, this current value must be zero, so

$$H(t) = \sum_i p_i H_i \bigg/ \sum_i p_i$$

$$= \sum_i p_i \left[\sum_j p_{ij} V_{ij} \bigg/ \sum_j p_{ij} \right] \bigg/ \sum_i p_i$$

$$= \sum_{i,j} p_i p_{ij} \left(1 \bigg/ \sum_i p_i \right) \left(1 \bigg/ \sum_j p_{ij} \right) V_{ij}. \tag{42}$$

Since $R_t = 1/\sum_i p_i$ and $R_{t+1} = 1/\sum_i p_{ij}$, this result illustrates Proposition 2. The current futures price is the same as the value of a claim which will pay at time $t + 2$ the amount V_{ij} times the total return from rolling over one-period bonds.

If interest rates are non-stochastic, then $\sum_j p_{ij}$ is the same for all i, and $\sum_{i,j} p_i p_{ij} = (\sum_i p_i)(\sum_j p_{ij})$. Hence, it is apparent by inspection that $G(t) = H(t)$. Similarly, if V_{ij} is a constant, then it is obvious that $G(t) = H(t)$.

4. Futures prices and forward prices in continuous-time, continuous-state economies

Propositions 2, 7 and 10 show how to construct assets whose current value must be equal to the current futures price. Propositions 1 and 8 do the same for forward prices. These results enable us to apply any intertemporal valuation model to the determination of forward and futures prices.

For our second example, we shall use a valuation framework which has become standard in finance. It has been shown by various arguments that in a continuous-time, continuous-state economy the value of any contingent claim F will satisfy the fundamental partial differential equation

$$\tfrac{1}{2} \sum_{i,j} (\text{cov}\, X_i, X_j) F_{x_i x_j} + \sum_i (\mu_i - \phi_i) F_{x_i} + F_t - r(X, t)F$$

$$+ \delta(X, t) = 0, \tag{43}$$

where subscripts on F indicate partial derivatives and X is a vector containing all variables necessary to describe the current state of the economy. The remaining symbols are as follows: μ_i is the local mean of changes in X_i, $\text{cov}\, X_i, X_j$ is the local covariance of the changes in X_i with the changes in X_j, $r(X, t)$ is the spot interest rate, $\delta(X, t)$ is the continuous payment flow (if any) received by the claim, and ϕ_i is the factor risk premium associated with X_i.

A number of studies have derived equations similar to (43) based on arbitrage arguments. For example, see Brennan and Schwartz (1979), Garman (1977), and Richard (1978). In these models, the factor risk premiums and the processes driving the state variables are determined exogenously or remain unspecified.

A somewhat different approach leading to the same type of equation is taken in Cox, Ingersoll and Ross (1978). In that paper, an intertemporal equilibrium model is developed in which all economic variables, including the interest rate and the factor risk premiums, are endogenously determined and explicitly identified in terms of individual preferences and production possibilities. Richard and Sundaresan (1981) extend this model to include multiple goods and use it to examine forward and futures contracts. In that setting, Sundaresan (1980) develops several explicit formulas for forward and futures prices. Most of our results in this section are special cases of their results.

Proposition 7 states that the futures price is equal to the value of an asset which receives a continual payout flow of $(R_u - 1)H(u)$ and the amount $V(s)$ at time s. In the present application, this would correspond to $\delta(X, t) = r(X, t)H(X, t)$ and $H(X, s) = V(X, s)$. The futures price must thus satisfy the partial differential equation

$$\frac{1}{2} \sum_{i, j} (\operatorname{cov} X_i, X_j) H_{x_i x_j} + \sum_i (\mu_i - \phi_i) H_{x_i} + H_t = 0, \tag{44}$$

with terminal condition $H(X, s) = V(X, s)$.

Two results from Cox, Ingersoll and Ross (1978) will be useful in characterizing futures prices. Lemma 4 of that paper shows that with $\delta = 0$ the solution of (43) for a claim paying $\theta(X(s))$ at time s can be written as

$$\hat{E} \left[\theta(X(s)) \left[\exp \left(- \int_t^s r(X(u)) \, du \right) \right] \right], \tag{45}$$

where $\hat{E}$ indicates expectation taken with respect to a risk-adjusted process for the state variables. The risk adjustment is accomplished by reducing the local mean of each underlying variable by the corresponding factor risk premium. Proposition 2 states that the futures price is the same as the current value of an asset which will receive a single payment of $\theta(X(s)) = V(X(s)) [\exp(\int_t^s r(X(u)) \, du)]$ at time s. Consequently, we can write the futures price as the risk-adjusted expected spot price at time s,

$$H(X, t) = \hat{E}[V(X(s))]. \tag{46}$$

An immediate application of theorem 4 of Cox, Ingersoll and Ross (1978) shows that the futures price can be written in yet another way as

$$H(X, t) = E\left[V(X(s))\left[\exp\left(\int_t^s r(X(u))\,du \right) \right]\left(\frac{J_w(s)}{J_w(t)} \right) \right], \quad (47)$$

where E indicates expectation with respect to the actual process (with no risk-adjustment) for the state variables and $J_w(\,\cdot\,)$ is the marginal utility of wealth of the representative individual. Given proposition 2, this is an intuitively sensible result. Since H is the value of a security which will pay $V(X(s))\exp[\int_t^s r(X(u))\,du)]$ at time s, (47) simply says that the value of this security is the expectation of its marginal-utility-weighted payoffs.

Forward prices can be obtained in a very straightforward way. From Proposition 1, $G(X, t)$ will equal $(1/P(t))$ times the solution to (43) with $\delta = 0$ and $F(X, s) = V(X, s)$. Similarly, we can write

$$G(X, t) = \hat{E}\left[V(X(s))\left[\exp\left(-\int_t^s r(X(u))\,du \right) \right] \right]\Big/ P(t)$$

$$= E\left[V(X(s))\left(\frac{J_w(s)}{J_w(t)} \right) \right]\Big/ P(t). \quad (48)$$

As we have noted, an important historical role of forward and futures markets has been to provide a mechanism by which individuals can lock in today the price which they will have to pay for a good or asset on a future date. The simple strategy of taking a long position in one forward contract will accomplish exactly that, but the corresponding strategy of taking a long position in one futures contract will not. However, this does not rule out the possibility of achieving the same outcome by using futures contracts in a more complicated strategy. In the present context, with say n state variables, the results of Black (1976) indicate that we should be able to find a controlled hedging portfolio, along the lines of Merton (1977), containing n futures contracts and borrowing or lending at the spot interest rate r which will require no subsequent investment and will duplicate the payoff to a forward contract on the maturity date.

To pursue this without unnecessary complications, we shall consider the case of $n = 1$; generalization to an arbitrary number of state variables is straightforward. Let π be the value of the hedging portfolio, and let α be the number of futures contracts held in this portfolio. Further, let $D(t)$ be the value at time t of a forward contract written at time q; if q is the current time t, then $D(t) = 0$. Consider the following strategy. At time t, make an investment of $D(t)$ in the hedging portfolio. Place this amount in spot lending (rolling over shorts). At each time τ, take a long position in $D_x(\tau)/H_x(\tau)$ futures contracts, using (41) and (42) to find D and H in terms of X and t. Invest all money received from the futures position in spot lending and finance all money due by spot borrowing. If it is always possible to trade at equilibrium futures prices and interest rates, then this hedging portfolio will have the same value as the forward contract on the maturity date. To see this, consider the following argument. Let $w(t)$ be the Wiener process driving the state variable, and let LH denote the differential generator of H, $LH \equiv \frac{1}{2}\sigma^2(X)H_{xx} + \mu_x H_x + H_t$, where $\sigma^2(X)$ is the local variance of the changes in X. From Itô's formula, the value of the hedging portfolio will follow the stochastic differential equation

$$d\pi(t) = r(X, t)\pi(t)dt + \alpha(X, t)dH(t). \tag{49}$$

Hence, the value of the portfolio at time s is

$$\pi(s) = \left[\exp\left(\int_t^s r(u)\,du\right)\right]$$

$$\times \left[\pi(t) + \int_t^s \left[\exp\left(-\int_t^z r(u)\,du\right)\right]\alpha(z)LH(z)\,dz\right.$$

$$\left. + \int_t^s \left[\exp\left(-\int_t^z r(u)\,du\right)\right]\alpha(z)H_x(z)\sigma(z)\,dw(z)\right]. \tag{50}$$

Now note that (43) implies that $LD = \phi_x D_x + rD$ and (44) implies that $LH = \phi_x H_x$, so $LH = (LD - rD)/(D_x/H_x)$. Substituting this expression for LH into (50) and letting $\alpha = D_x/H_x$ gives

$$\pi(s) = \exp\left(\int_t^s r(u)\,du\right)$$

$$\times \left[\pi(t)\int_t^s \left[\exp\left(-\int_t^z r(u)\,du\right)\right](LD(z) - r(z)D(z))\,dz\right.$$

$$\left. + \int_t^s \left[\exp\left(-\int_t^z r(u)\,du\right)\right]D_x(z)\sigma(z)\,dw(z)\right]$$

$$= D(s) + \left[\exp\left(\int_t^s r(u)\,du\right)\right][\pi(t) - D(t)]. \tag{51}$$

Since $\pi(t) = D(t)$, then $\pi(s) = D(s)$, so the hedging portfolio will have the same value as a forward contract on the maturity date. The particular nature of the payoff received by a forward contract played no role in the argument, so there is no problem in specifying a more general payoff. Similarly, with multiple state variables, both traded assets and futures contracts can be included in the hedging portfolio. However, readers should be aware that our discussion has not gone into certain technical difficulties connected with continuous trading [see Harrison and Kreps (1979)].

An important advantage of the framework used in this example is that it can easily be specialized to produce testable explicit formulas. An illustration of this is its application to the term structure of interest rates. For instance, under the additional assumptions of logarithmic utility and a technology which leads to a spot interest rate following the stochastic differential equation

$$dr = \varkappa(\mu - r)dt + \sigma\sqrt{r}\,dw, \tag{52}$$

it is shown in Cox, Ingersoll and Ross (1978) that the prices of discount bonds will satisfy the partial differential equation

$$\tfrac{1}{2}\sigma^2 r P_{rr} + [\varkappa\mu - (\varkappa + \lambda)r]P_r + P_t - rP = 0, \tag{53}$$

where $\varkappa$, μ and σ are the parameters of the interest rate process and λr is the local covariance of changes in the interest rate with percentage changes in aggregate wealth (the market portfolio).

Now consider the forward and futures prices for contracts with maturity date s on a discount bond paying one dollar at time T, with $T > s$. Straightforward application of the methods discussed earlier shows that

$$G(t) = \left(\frac{A(T-t)}{A(s-t)}\right)\exp[-r(B(T-t) - B(s-t))], \tag{54}$$

and

$$H(t) = A(T-s)\left[\frac{\eta}{B(T-s) + \eta}\right]^{2\varkappa\mu/\sigma^2}$$

$$\times \exp\left[-r\left(\frac{\eta B(T-s)e^{-(\varkappa+\lambda)(s-t)}}{B(T-s) + \eta}\right)\right], \tag{55}$$

where

$$A(T-t) = \left[\frac{2\gamma e^{[(\varkappa+\lambda+\gamma)(T-t)]/2}}{(\gamma + \varkappa + \lambda)(e^{\gamma(T-t)} - 1) + 2\gamma}\right]^{2\varkappa\mu/\sigma^2},$$

$$B(T-t) = \frac{2(e^{\gamma(T-t)} - 1)}{(\gamma + \varkappa + \lambda)(e^{\gamma(T-t)} - 1) + 2\gamma},$$

$$\gamma = [(\varkappa + \lambda)^2 + 2\sigma^2]^{\frac{1}{2}}, \qquad \eta = \frac{2(\varkappa + \lambda)}{\sigma^2(1 - e^{-(\varkappa+\lambda)(s-t)})}.$$

Note that since $A(0) = 1$ and $B(0) = 0$, $G(s) = H(s)$, as of course it must. For all $t < s$, $G(t) > H(t)$, confirming the observation made about Treasury bill futures in the discussion following Proposition 9. It is apparent by inspection that forward and futures prices are decreasing convex functions of the interest rate, as is also true of bill prices in this model. However, unlike the bill prices, the forward prices and futures prices can be increasing functions of the time to maturity for sufficiently high interest rates.

This approach can be generalized in a number of ways. For example, the simple mean-reverting drift for the interest rate in (52) can be replaced with exponentially weighted extrapolative and regressive components, as in the De Leeuw-Malkiel term structure hypotheses [see Cox, Ingersoll and Ross (1981)]. Although the resulting forward and futures prices are more complicated than (54) and (55), they still retain the simple exponential form. Furthermore, Proposition 5 shows that our results for discount bonds can be immediately applied to coupon bonds.

Formulas such as (54) and (55) make predictions about simultaneous prices in different markets, and hence offer interesting opportunities for empirical testing. However, the empirical magnitude of the effect introduced by the continual resettlement feature of futures contracts remains an open question. Capozza and Cornell (1979) analyzed futures prices and implicit forward prices in the Treasury bill market and found that, except for very short maturities, forward prices exceeded futures prices and that the difference increased with time to maturity. Rendleman and Carabini (1979) independently reached a similar but less definitive conclusion. These findings are generally consistent with the qualitative predictions of (26). However, Rendleman and Carabini have examined (54) and (55) for a range of parameter values and have concluded that the implied differences do not fully explain the observed differences between forward prices and futures prices in the Treasury bill market. This may indicate that one of the generalizations mentioned above will be more appropriate. Another possible explanation for the observed discrepancies lies in various tax effects which we have thus far ignored but shall consider in the next section.

5. The effects of taxes and other institutional factors

We shall postpone a complete discussion of taxes until another occasion, but some informal comments and conjectures may still be worthwhile. The simplest way to introduce taxes into the setting of section 4 is as follows. Taxes are collected continuously at constant rates which are the same for all individuals. Capital gains are taxed as they accrue, rather than when realized, with full loss offsets. The dollar receipts from futures price changes are taxed as capital gains.

In such a world, investors will be concerned with their after-tax returns and will value contingent claims accordingly. For any given claim F, let the tax rate for capital gains be c and the tax rate for payouts and interest income be d. It can then be shown that the fundamental valuation equation becomes

$$\frac{1}{2} \sum_{i,j} (\text{cov}\, X_i, X_j) F_{x_i x_j} + \sum_i (\mu_i - \phi_i) F_{x_i}$$

$$+ F_t - \left(\frac{1-d}{1-c}\right) \text{r}(X, t) F + \left(\frac{1-d}{1-c}\right) \delta(X, t) = 0. \qquad (56)$$

Since the last two terms will not apply for a futures price, taxes of this type will have no direct effect upon its value. Of course, there will be indirect effects, since taxes will in general affect the factor risk premiums and the current values and stochastic processes of all endogenously determined state variables. However, if we are considering the comparative effect of a change only in the tax rate applicable to futures markets, then these general equilibrium effects would presumably be negligible or non-existent, and the futures prices would remain unchanged. Notice, too, that for Treasury bills $\delta = 0$ and $c = d$, since their price changes are taxed at the rate for ordinary income. Hence, their valuation equation would remain the same as well.

The actual tax law is of course more complex than this, particularly with regard to Treasury bill futures. It currently appears that a gain on a long position in a Treasury bill futures contract will be taxed as a long-term or short-term capital gain, depending on whether the holding period is longer or shorter than six months. On the other hand, if the position shows a loss, by taking delivery and selling the Treasury bills, the basis can be taken to be the original futures price and the loss will be considered as an ordinary loss. If the taxes are collected on the maturity date and all individuals are taxed at the same rate, then a modification of the above analysis can be used to find the futures price. With this type of tax, the terminal condition will depend on the initial value, so a recursive procedure is necessary. The problem is first solved with an arbitrary parameter replacing the initial value in the terminal condition. This parameter is then varied until the initial value and the parameter value are equal. As one would expect, other things equal, this tax option results in a higher futures price.

We have not gone through this analysis explicitly only because we are not convinced of its relevance. Additional considerations may bring us full circle. Although we cannot provide a formal model which includes both differential taxes and transactions costs, it seems likely to us that the agents with transactions costs low enough to be able to conduct arbitrage operations are likely to be professionals who are taxed at the same rate for all trading income and who consequently derive no benefit from the special tax option. The actions of arbitrageurs would thus tend to keep futures prices near the levels we have predicted; simultaneously, individuals who cannot conduct arbitrage operations could nevertheless obtain tax advantages at these prices. Cornell (1980) has persuasively advanced this point of view and has provided some interesting empirical support. If the actions of arbitrageurs did not effectively determine the Treasury bill futures price, then one would expect a discontinuous change in the price (though not in the after-tax returns to the marginal investor) when a contract changes from long-term to short-term tax treatment, but Cornell found no evidence of this.

Some additional institutional factors may have an effect on the futures price in particular markets. In the basic futures contract we described, the seller of the contract can on the maturity date close out his position either by taking an offsetting long position or by delivering the specified amount of the underlying good or asset. In many markets, the seller has somewhat more flexibility than this. He may have one or more of three additional alternatives which we will refer to as a quality option, a quantity option, and a timing option.

The quality option allows the seller some discretion in the good which can be delivered. For example, several different types of a particular grain may all be acceptable. If the spot price of one of the types would always be less than the others, then this is the one the seller would choose, and the contract would in effect become an ordinary futures on that type. The situation is only slightly more complicated when the price ordering is not always the same. In that case, all of our results would hold, or would require only minor modification, when $V(s)$ is replaced by the minimum of the spot prices of the acceptable goods on the maturity date.

The quantity option allows the seller some choice in the amount of the good which is to be delivered. In this case, the futures price is quoted on a per unit basis, so the choice concerns only the scale of the contract. In perfect, competitive markets, as we have assumed, the quantity option will be a matter of indifference and will have no effect on the futures price.

The timing option gives the seller some flexibility in the delivery date of the good. In this case, delivery can be made at any time during a designated period beginning on the maturity date. Typically, the designated period is one month or less. Since delivery can be postponed, the futures price will not necessarily be equal to the spot price on the maturity date. Clearly, the futures price cannot be greater than the spot price during the designated period. If it were, then it would be possible to make an arbitrage profit by simultaneously selling a futures contract, purchasing the good in the spot market, and making delivery. Consequently, we must append to any valuation framework the arbitrage condition $H(\tau) \leq V(\tau)$ for all τ such that $s \leq \tau \leq s'$ and $H(s') = V(s')$, where s' is the end of the designated period. Readers familiar with option pricing theory will note the similarity to the arbitrage condition for an American option. We can now use Proposition 10 to give a sufficient condition for the effective delivery date to be s or s'. According to this proposition, if the spot rental rate is always greater than the spot interest rate, then the futures price with maturity date s' is always less than the spot price. Consequently, the arbitrage condition will always be satisfied and the futures price can be determined as if the maturity date were s'. On the other hand, if the rental rate is always less than the interest rate, then the arbitrage condition cannot be satisfied for any maturity date later than s and all deliveries would be made at that time. In this case, the futures price can thus be determined as if the maturity date were s.

References

Black, Fischer, 1976, The pricing of commodity contracts, *Journal of Financial Economics* 3, 167-179.

Brennan, Michael J. and Eduardo S. Schwartz, 1979, A continuous time approach to the pricing of bonds, *Journal of Banking and Finance* 3, 133-155.

Breeden, Douglas T., 1979, An intertemporal asset pricing model with stochastic consumption and investment opportunities, *Journal of Financial Economics* 7, 265-296.

Breeden, Douglas T., 1980, Consumption risk in futures markets, *Journal of Finance* 35, 503-520.

Capozza, Dennis R. and Bradford Cornell, 1979, Treasury bill pricing in the spot and futures markets, *Review of Economics and Statistics* 61, 513-520.

Cornell, Bradford, 1980, Taxes and the pricing of Treasury bill futures contracts, Unpublished working paper (Graduate School of Management, University of California, Los Angeles, CA).

Cox, John C., Jonathan E. Ingersoll, Jr. and Stephen A. Ross, 1978, A theory of the term structure of interest rates, Research paper no. 468 (Graduate School of Business, Stanford University, Stanford, CA).

Cox, John C., Jonathan E. Ingersoll, Jr. and Stephen A. Ross, 1981, A reexamination of traditional hypotheses about the term structure of interest rates, *Journal of Finance* 36, 796-800.

French, Kenneth R., 1981, The pricing of futures contracts, Unpublished working paper (Graduate School of Management, University of Rochester, Rochester, NY).

Garman, Mark B., 1977, A general theory of asset valuation under diffusion processes, Working paper no. 50, Research Program in Finance (Institute of Business and Economic Research, University of California, Berkeley, CA).

Harrison, J. Michael and David M. Kreps, 1979, Martingales and arbitrage in multiperiod securities markets. *Journal of Economic Theory* 20, 381-408.

Jarrow, Robert A. and George S. Oldfield, 1981, Forward contracts and futures contracts, *Journal of Financial Economics,* this issue.

Margrabe, William, 1976, A theory of forward and futures prices, Unpublished working paper (The Wharton School, University of Pennsylvania, Philadelphia, PA).

Merton, Robert C., 1973, An intertemporal capital asset pricing model, *Econometrica* 41, 867-887.

Merton, Robert C., 1977, On the pricing of contingent claims and the Modigliani-Miller theorem, *Journal of Financial Economics* 5, 241-249.

Merton, Robert C., 1979, Unpublished class notes (Sloan School of Management, Massachusetts Institute of Technology, Cambridge, MA).

Rendleman, Richard J., Jr. and Christopher E. Carabini, 1979, The efficiency of the Treasury bill futures market, *Journal of Finance* 34, 895-914.

Richard, Scott F., 1978, An arbitrage model of the term structure of interest rates, *Journal of Financial Economics* 6, 33-57.

Richard, Scott F. and M. Sundaresan, 1981, A continuous time equilibrium model of forward prices and future prices in a multigood economy, *Journal of Financial Economics,* this issue.

Sundaresan, M., 1980, A study of commodity futures prices, Unpublished doctoral dissertation (Graduate School of Industrial Administration, Carnegie-Mellon University, Pittsburgh, PA).

3

Valuation of American Futures Options: Theory and Empirical Tests

Robert E. Whaley*

Abstract

This paper reviews the theory of futures option pricing and tests the valuation principles on transaction prices from the S&P 500 equity futures option market. The American futures option valuation equations are shown to generate mispricing errors which are systematically related to the degree the option is in-the-money and to the option's time to expiration. The models are also shown to generate abnormal risk-adjusted rates of return after transaction costs. The joint hypothesis that the American futures option pricing models are correctly specified and that the S&P 500 futures option market is efficient is refuted, at least for the sample period January 28, 1983 through December 30, 1983.

Futures option contracts now trade on every major futures exchange and on a wide variety of underlying futures contracts. The Chicago Mercantile Exchange, the Chicago Board of Trade, the New York Futures Exchange, and the Commodity Exchange now collectively have more than twenty options written on futures contracts, where the underlying spot commodities are financial assets such as stock portfolios, bonds, notes and Eurodollars, foreign currencies such as West German marks, Swiss francs and British pounds, precious metals such as gold and silver, livestock commodities such as cattle and hogs, and agricultural commodities such as corn and soybeans. Moreover, new contract applications are before the Commodity Futures Trading Commission and should be actively trading in the near future.

*Associate Professor of Finance, University of Alberta and Visiting Associate Professor of Finance, University of Chicago. This research was supported by the Finance Research Foundation of Canada. Comments and suggestions by Fred D. Arditti, Warren Bailey, Giovanni Barone-Adesi, Bruce Cooil, Theodore E. Day, Thomas S. Y. Ho, Hans R. Stoll, and a referee and an Associate Editor of this *Journal* are gratefully acknowledged.

Robert E. Whaley, ''Valuation of American Futures Options: Theory and Empirical Tests.'' Reprinted with permission from *The Journal of Finance,* Vol. XLI, No. 1, March 1986.

With the markets for these new contingent claims becoming increasingly active, it is appropriate that the fundamentals of futures option valuation be reviewed and tested. Black [5] provides a framework for the analysis of commodity futures options. Although his work is explicitly directed at pricing European options on forward contracts, it applies to European futures contracts as well if the riskless rate of interest is constant during the futures option life.[1] The options currently trading, however, are American options, and only recently has theoretical work begun to focus on the American futures option pricing problem.[2]

The purpose of this paper is to review the theory underlying American futures option valuation and to test it on transaction prices from the S&P 500 equity futures option market. In the first section of the paper, the theory of futures option pricing is reviewed. The partial differential equation of Black ([5]) is presented, and the boundary conditions of the American and European futures option pricing problems are shown to imply different valuation equations. For the American futures options, efficient analytic approximations of the values of the call and put are presented, and the magnitude of the early exercise premium is simulated.

In the second section of the paper, the American futures option valuation principles are tested on S&P 500 futures option contract data for the period January 28, 1983 through December 30, 1983. Included are an examination of the systematic biases in the mispricing errors of the option pricing models, a test of the stationarity of the volatility of the futures price change relatives, and a test of the joint hypothesis that the American futures option models are correctly specified and that the S&P market is efficient. The paper concludes with a summary of the major results of the study.

I. Theory of Futures Option Valuation

An option on a futures contract is like an option on a common stock in the sense that it provides its holder with the right to buy or sell the underlying security at the exercise price of the option. Unlike a stock option, however, a cash exchange in the amount of the exercise price does not occur when the futures option is exercised. Upon exercise, a futures option holder merely acquires a long or short futures position with a futures price equal to the exercise price of the option. When the futures contract is marked-to-market at the close of the day's trading, the option holder is free to withdraw in cash an amount equal to the futures price less the exercise price in the case of a call and the exercise price less the futures price in the case of a put. Thus, exercising a futures option is like receiving in cash the exercisable value of the option.

---

[1] Cox, Ingersoll, and Ross [11, p. 324] demonstrate that the price of a futures contract is equal to the price of a forward contract when interest rates are nonstochastic.

[2] Following Black's [5] seminal article, Moriarity, Phillips, and Tosini [18], Asay [1], Wolf [24], and others discussed the European futures option pricing problem. Other than the studies by Whaley [22] and Stoll and Whaley [21], the theoretical work on American futures options is unpublished and includes studies by Ramaswamy and Sundaresan [19] and Brenner, Courtadon, and Subrahmanyam [9].

A. Assumptions and Notation   Black [5] provides the groundwork for futures option valuation. Although his work is directed at pricing a European call option, it is general in the sense that the partial differential equation describing the dynamics of the call option price through time applies to put options as well as call options and to American options as well as European options. The assumptions necessary to develop Black's partial differential equation are as follows:

(A1)   There are no transaction costs in the option, futures, and bond markets. These include direct costs such as commissions and implicit costs such as the bid-ask spread and penalties on short sales.

(A2)   Markets are free of costless arbitrage opportunities. If two assets or portfolios of assets have identical terminal values, they have the same price, and/or, if an asset or portfolio of assets has a future value which is certain to be positive, the initial value (cost) of the asset or portfolio is certain to be negative (positive).

(A3)   The short-term riskless rate of interest is constant through time.

(A4)   The instantaneous futures price change relative is described by the stochastic differential equation,

$$dF/F = \mu\, dt + \sigma\, dz,$$

where μ is the expected instantaneous price change relative of the futures contract, σ is the instantaneous standard deviation, and z is a Wiener process.

Assumptions (A1) and (A2) are fairly innocuous. Transaction costs are trivial for those making the market in the various financial assets, and available empirical evidence suggests investors behave rationally. Assumption (A3) may appear contradictory, since some futures options are written on long-term debt instrument futures contracts[3] where the driving force behind the volatility of the futures price change relatives is interest rate uncertainty. The two interest rates are, to some degree, separable, however. Assumption (A3) describes the behavior of the short-term interest rate on, say, Treasury bills, while the volatility of T-bond futures prices, for example, is related to the volatility of the long-term U.S. Treasury bond forward rate.[4] Assumption (A4) describes the dynamics of

[3]The Chicago Board of Trade, for example, lists options on U.S. T-bond and T-note futures contracts.
[4]A priori, the assumption of constant short-term interest rate is untenable for all option pricing models. A constant short-term rate implies a constant, flat term structure, with interest rate uncertainty having no bearing on the volatility of the underlying asset prices. Such is hardly the case. The validity of such option pricing models, however, need not be evaluated on the basis of their assumptions and can be judged on the merits of their predictions.

the futures price movements through time. It is important to note that no assumption about the relationship between the futures price and the price of the underlying spot commodity has been invoked.[5] The valuation results presented in this section, therefore, apply to any futures option contract, independent of the nature of the underlying spot commodity.

For expositional purposes, the following notation is adopted in this study to describe futures options and their related parameters:

F = current futures price
F_T = random futures price at expiration
$C(F, T; X)[c(F, T; X)]$ = American [European] call option price
$P(F, T; X)[p(F, T; X)]$ = American [European] put option price
$\epsilon_C(F, T; X)[\epsilon_p(F, T; X)]$ = early exercise premium of American call [put] option
r = riskless rate of interest
T = time to expiration of futures options
X = exercise price of futures options.

---

[5]Note that Assumption (A4) defines the dynamics of the futures price movements with no reference to the relationship between the futures price and the price of the underlying spot commodity. Whether such an assumption is more appropriate for the futures price dynamics or the underlying spot commodity dynamics is an open empirical question.

Assumption (A4) is consistent with the assumption that the underlying spot price, S, follows the stochastic differential equation.

$$dS/S = \alpha\, dt + \sigma\, dz,$$

where α is the expected relative spot price change, and σ is the instantaneous standard deviation if there is (a) a constant, continuous riskless rate of interest, r, and (b) a constant, continuous proportional rate of receipt (payment), d, for holding the underlying spot commodity. To show this result, apply Ito's lemma to the cost-of-carry relationship, $S_t = F_t\, e^{-(r-d)(T-t)}$, where F_t is defined in (A4). The expected futures price change relative, μ, is equal to the expected spot price change relative less the difference between the riskless rate of interest and the continuous rate of receipt, $\alpha - (r - d)$, and the standard deviation, σ, is the same for both the underlying spot commodity and futures price changes.

The interpretation of d depends on the nature of the underlying spot commodity. For example, in the foreign currency futures market, d represents the foreign interest rate earned on the investment in the foreign currency. For agricultural commodity futures, d is less than zero and represents the rate of cost for holding the spot commodity (i.e., storage costs, insurance costs, etc.), and for stock index futures, d represents the continuous proportional dividend yield on the underlying stock portfolio.

A continuous proportional dividend yield assumption may not be appropriate for a stock index since dividend payments are discrete and have a tendency to cluster according to the day of the week and the month of the year. With uncertain discrete dividend payments during the futures' life, the cost-of-carry relationship between the prices of the stock index and stock index futures is unclear, however, as long as (A4) holds for the futures price dynamics, the option pricing relationships contained in the paper will hold.

B. Solution to
Futures Option
Pricing Problem

Under the above-stated assumptions, Black demonstrates that, if a riskless hedge can be formed between the futures option and its underlying futures contract, the partial differential equation governing the movements of the futures option price (V) through time is

$$\tfrac{1}{2}\sigma^2 F^2 V_{FF} - rV + V_t = 0. \tag{1}$$

This equation applies to American call ($C = V$) and put ($P = V$) options, as well as European call ($c = V$) and put ($p = V$) options. What distinguishes the four valuation problems is the set of boundary conditions applied to each problem.

C. European
Futures Options

The boundary condition necessary to develop an analytic formula for the European call option is that the terminal call price is equal to the maximum value of 0 or the in-the-money amount of the option, that is, max $(0, F_T - X)$. Black shows that, when this terminal boundary condition is applied to Equation (1) where $c = V$, the value of a European call option on a futures contract is

$$c(F, T; X) = e^{-rT}[FN(d_1) - XN(d_2)], \tag{2}$$

Figure 1. European and American Call Option Prices As a Function of the Underlying Futures Contract Price

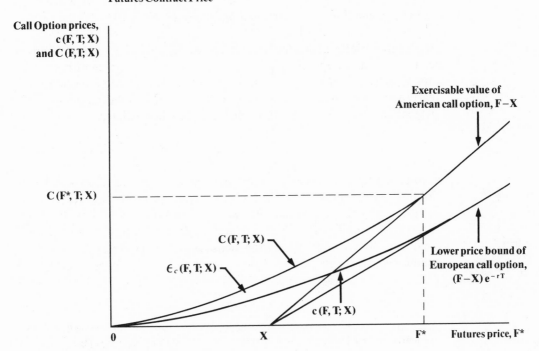

where $d_1 = [\ln(F/X) + 0.5\sigma^2 T]/\sigma\sqrt{T}$, and $d_2 = d_1 - \sigma\sqrt{T}$, and where $N(\ )$ is the cumulative univariate normal distribution. When the lower boundary condition for the European put, $\max(0, X - F_T)$, is applied to the partial differential Equation (1), the analytic solution is

$$p(F, T; X) = e^{-rT}[XN(-d_2) - FN(-d_1)], \tag{3}$$

where all notation is as it was defined above.

D. American Futures Options

The European call formula (2) provides a convenient way of demonstrating that the American call option may be exercised early. As the futures price becomes extremely large relative to the exercise of the option, the values of $N(d_1)$ and $N(d_2)$ approach one, and the European call value approaches $(F - X)e^{-rT}$. But, the American option may be exercised immediately for $F - X$, which is higher than the European option value. Thus, the American call option may be worth more "dead" than "alive"[6] and will command a higher price than the European call option.

Figure 1 illustrates the value of the American call option's early exercise privilege. In the figure, F^* represents the critical current futures price level where the American call option holder is indifferent about exercising his option immediately or continuing to hold it. Below F^*, the value of the early exercise premium, $\epsilon_C(F, T; X)$, is equal to the difference between the American and European call functions, $C(F, T; X) - c(F, T; X)$. Above F^*, $\epsilon_C(F, T; X)$ is equal to $(F - X) - c(F, T; X)$. Note that as the futures price becomes large relative to the exercise price, the European call option value approaches $(F - X)e^{-rT}$, and the early exercise premium approaches $(F - X)(1 - e^{-rT})$. In other words, the maximum value the early exercise premium may attain is the present value of the interest income which can be earned if the call option is exercised immediately.

Unlike the European option case, there are no known analytic solutions to the partial differential Equation (1), subject to the American call option on a futures contract boundary condition, $C(F, t; X) \geq \max(0, F_t - X)$ for all $0 \leq t \leq T$, and, subject to the American put option on a futures contract boundary condition, $P(F, t; X) \geq \max(0, X - F_t)$ for all $0 \leq t \leq T$. Usually, the valuation of American futures options has resorted to finite difference approximation methods.[7] Ramaswamy and Sundaresan [19] and Brenner, Courtadon, and Subrahmanyam [9], for

[6]Merton (17) demonstrates that, because the exercisable value of an American call option on a nondividend-paying stock, $S - X$, is always below the lower price bound of the corresponding European option, $S - Xe^{-rT}$, the American call option is always worth more alive than dead, and, therefore, will not be exercised early.

[7]The first applications of finite difference methods to option pricing problems were by Schwartz [20] who valued warrants written on dividend-paying stocks and by Brennan and Schwartz [7] who priced American put options on nondividend-paying stocks. These techniques are reviewed in Brennan and Schwartz [8] and Geske and Shastri [15].

example, use such techniques. Unfortunately, finite difference methods are computationally expensive because they involve enumerating every possible path the futures option price could travel during its remaining time to expiration.

Whaley [23] adapts the Geske-Johnson [13] compound option analytic approximation method to price American futures options. In addition to being computationally less expensive than numerical methods, the compound option approach offers the advantages of being intuitively appealing and easily amenable to comparative statics analysis. Unfortunately, even though the compound option approach is about twenty times faster than numerical methods, it is still not inexpensive because it requires the evaluation of cumulative bivariate and cumulative trivariate normal density functions.

The analytic approximation of American futures option values used in this study is that derived by Barone-Adesi and Whaley [3]. The method is based on MacMillan's [16] quadratic approximation of the American put option on a stock valuation problem and is considerably faster than either the finite difference or the compound option approximation methods.

The quadratic approximation of the American call option on a futures contract, as provided in Barone-Adesi and Whaley [3], is

$$C(F, T; X) = c(F, T; X) + A_2(F/F^*)^{q_2}, \quad \text{where } F < F^*, \quad \text{and}$$

$$C(F, T; X) = F - X, \qquad\qquad \text{where } F \geq F^*, \qquad (4)$$

and where $A_2 = (F^*/q_2)\{1 - e^{-rT}N[d_1(F^*)]\}$, $d_1(F^*) = [\ln(F^*/X) + 0.5\sigma^2 T]/\sigma\sqrt{T}$, $q_2 = (1 + \sqrt{1 + 4k})/2$, and $k = 2r/[\sigma^2(1 - e^{-rT})]$. F^* is the critical futures price above which the American futures option should be exercised immediately (see Figure 1) and is determined iteratively by solving

$$F^* - X = c(F^*, T; X) + \{1 - e^{-rT}N[d_1(F^*)]\}F^*/q_2. \qquad (4a)$$

Although the valuation equation may appear ominous, its intuition is simple. For a current futures price below the critical stock price, F^*, the American call value is equal to the European value plus the early exercise premium, as approximated by the term, $A_2(F/F^*)^{q_2}$. Above F^*, the worth of the American call is its exercisable proceeds.

The only parameter to the American option formula (4) which requires computational sophistication beyond that required for the European formula (2) is the determination of the critical futures price F^*. To this end, Barone-Adesi and Whaley [3] provide an algorithm for solving (4a) in five iterations or less.

The quadratic approximation of the American put option on a futures contract is

$$P(F, T; X) = p(F, T; X) + A_1 (F/F^{**})^{q_1}, \quad \text{where } F > F^{**}, \text{ and}$$
$$P(F, T; X) = X - F, \quad\quad\quad\quad\quad\quad \text{where } F \leq F^{**}, \quad (5)$$

and where $A_1 = -(F^{**}/q_1)\{1 - e^{-rT}N[-d_1(F^{**})]\}$, $q_1 = (1 - \sqrt{1 + 4k})/2$, and where all other notation is as it was defined for the American call, F^{**} is the critical futures price below which the American futures option should be exercised immediately and is determined iteratively by solving

$$X - F^{**} = p(F^{**}, T; X) - \{1 - e^{-rT}N[-d_1(F^{**})]\} F^{**}/q_1. \quad (5a)$$

E. Simulation of Early Exercise Premium Values

To demonstrate plausible magnitudes of the early exercise premium on American futures options, the European and American models prices were computed for a range of option pricing parameters. The results are reported in Table I. It is interesting to note that out-of-the-money futures options have negligible early exercise premiums. For example, when the futures price (F) is 90, the riskless rate of interest (r) is 8 percent, and the standard deviation of the futures price relatives (σ) is 0.15, an out-of-the-money call option with an exercise price (X) of 100 and a time to expiration (T) of 0.5 years has an early exercise premium of 0.0106, only slightly more than 1 percent of the American option price. Even at-the-money options have small early exercise premiums which account for only a small percentage of the option price. Only when the option is considerably in-the-money does the early exercise premium account for a significant proportion of the price of the option.

In summary, the theory of futures option valuation suggests that the early exercise privilege of American futures options contributes meaningfully to the futures option value. The simulation results, based on option pricing parameters that are typical for S&P 500 futures option contracts, suggest that this is true, but only for in-the-money options.

II. Empirical Tests

In this section, the performance of the American futures option pricing models is analyzed using transaction information for S&P 500 equity futures options. After the description of the data in the first subsection, the implied standard deviation methodology is discussed. Volatility estimates are made using nonlinear regression of observed futures option prices on model prices. The third subsection presents an examination of the systematic patterns in the models prediction errors. This analysis is motivated by the evidence reported in the stock option pricing tests. In the fourth subsection, the hypothesis that the standard deviation of futures price change relatives is the same across call and put options is tested. The final subsection presents the results of a joint test of the hypothesis that the American futures option pricing models are correctly specified and that the S&P 500 futures option market is efficient.

Table I. Theoretical European and American Futures Option Values: Exercise Price $(X) = 100$

Futures Option Parameters[a]	Futures Price (F)	Call Options			Put Options		
		European $c(F, T; X)$[b]	American $C(F, T; X)$[c]	Early Exercise Premium $\epsilon_C(F, T; X)$	European $p(F, T; X)$[b]	American $P(F, T; X)$[c]	Early Exercise Premium $\epsilon_p(F, T; X)$
$r = 0.08$	80	0.0027	0.0029	0.0002	19.6067	20.0000	0.3933
$\sigma = 0.15$	90	0.2529	0.2547	0.0018	10.0549	10.1506	0.0957
$T = 0.25$	100	2.9321	2.9458	0.0137	2.9321	2.9458	0.0137
	110	10.1752	10.2627	0.0875	0.3732	0.3756	0.0024
	120	19.6239	20.0000	0.3761	0.0199	0.0204	0.0005
$r = 0.12$	80	0.0027	0.0030	0.0003	19.4116	20.0000	0.5884
$\sigma = 0.15$	90	0.2504	0.2533	0.0029	9.9549	10.1153	0.1605
$T = 0.25$	100	2.9029	2.9257	0.0228	2.9029	2.9257	0.0228
	110	10.0740	10.2205	0.1465	0.3695	0.3734	0.0039
	120	19.4286	20.0000	0.5714	0.0197	0.0205	0.0008
$r = 0.08$	80	0.3956	0.3986	0.0030	19.9996	20.2032	0.2036
$\sigma = 0.30$	90	1.9817	1.9913	0.0096	11.7837	11.8543	0.0707
$T = 0.25$	100	5.8604	5.8878	0.0274	5.8604	5.8878	0.0274
	110	12.2527	12.3237	0.0710	2.4507	2.4624	0.0116
	120	20.4776	20.6470	0.1694	0.8737	0.8790	0.0053
$r = 0.08$	80	0.0583	0.0603	0.0020	19.2740	20.0000	0.7260
$\sigma = 0.15$	90	0.8150	0.8256	0.0106	10.4229	10.6044	0.1815
$T = 0.50$	100	4.0637	4.1099	0.0463	4.0637	4.1099	0.0463
	110	10.6831	10.8584	0.1753	1.0752	1.0887	0.0134
	120	19.4105	20.0018	0.5913	0.1947	0.1991	0.0043

[a] The notation used in this column is as follows: r = riskless rate of interest; σ = standard deviation of the futures price change relative; and T = time to expiration.
[b] The European futures option values are computed using the Black [5] pricing equation.
[c] The American futures option values are computed using the Barone-Adesi and Whaley [3] analytic approximations.

Table II. Summary of S&P 500 Futures Option Transactions during the Period January 28, 1983 through December 30, 1983

Futures Price/ Exercise Price (F/X)	No. of Transactions			Time to Expiration (in weeks) (T)	No. of Transactions		
	Call	Put	Both		Call	Put	Both
$F/X < 0.90$	11	2	13	$T < 2$	2,307	2,234	4,541
$0.90 \leq F/X < 0.92$	77	9	86	$2 \leq T < 4$	2,375	2,190	4,565
$0.92 \leq F/X < 0.94$	339	42	381	$4 \leq T < 6$	2,567	2,211	4,778
$0.94 \leq F/X < 0.96$	1,014	191	1,205	$6 \leq T < 8$	2,480	2,064	4,544
$0.96 \leq F/X < 0.98$	2,281	773	3,054	$8 \leq T < 10$	1,708	1,623	3,331
$0.98 \leq F/X < 1.00$	4,091	2,615	6,706	$10 \leq T < 12$	1,479	1,371	2,850
$1.00 \leq F/X < 1.02$	4,260	4,252	8,512	$12 \leq T < 14$	1,255	1,164	2,419
$1.02 \leq F/X < 1.04$	1,783	2,559	4,342	$14 \leq T < 16$	337	445	782
$1.04 \leq F/X < 1.06$	830	1,524	2,354	$16 \leq T < 18$	222	173	395
$1.06 \leq F/X < 1.08$	241	875	1,116	$18 \leq T < 20$	175	90	265
$1.08 \leq F/X < 1.10$	78	453	531	$20 \leq T$	158	108	266
$1.10 \leq F/X$	58	378	436				
All	15,063	13,673	28,736	All	15,063	13,673	28,736

A. Data
The data used in this study consist of transaction information for the S&P 500 equity futures and futures option contracts traded on the Chicago Mercantile Exchange (CME) from the first day of trading of the S&P futures options, January 28, 1983, through the last business day of the year, December 30, 1983. The data were provided by the CME and are referred to as "Quote Capture" information. Essentially, the data set contains the time and the price of every transaction in which the price changed from the previously recorded transaction. Bid and ask prices are also recorded if the bid price exceeds or the ask price is below the price at the last transaction. The volume of each transaction and the number of transactions at a particular price are not recorded.

Two exclusionary criteria were applied to the Quote Capture information. First, bid and ask price quotes were eliminated because they do not represent prices at which there were both a buyer and seller available to transact. Both sides of the market transaction were necessary within the market efficiency test design. Second, futures options with times to expiration in excess of 26 weeks were excluded. The trading activity in these options and their underlying futures contracts was too sparse to warrant consideration with the market efficiency test. What remained was a sample of 28,736 transactions, 26,613 in the nearest contract month, and 7,123 in the second nearest contract month.

The futures option pricing models require the futures price at the instant at which the option is traded. To represent the contemporaneous futures price, the futures price at the trade most closely preceding the futures option trade is used. Because the S&P 500 futures market was so active during the investigation period, the average time between the futures and the subsequent futures option transactions was only 21 seconds.

Table II offers a summary of the characteristics of the transactions contained in the 232-day sample period. Of the 28,736 transactions, 15,063 were call option transactions and 13,763 were puts. The at-the-money options appear to have been the most active, with 55 percent of the call option trades and 50 percent of the put option trades being at futures prices ±2 percent of the exercise price. Out-of-the-money options were more active than in-the-money options: 25 percent of total trades to 20 percent of total trades for calls and 42 percent to 8 percent for puts, respectively. Over 64 percent of the transactions were on options with maturities of less than 8 weeks, verifying that most of the trading activity was in the nearest contract month.

The yield on the U.S. Treasury bill maturing on the contract month expiration day[8] was used to proxy for the riskless rate on interest. The yields

---

[8]S&P 500 futures option contracts expired the third Thursday of the contract month until the June 1984 contract. Beginning with the June 1984 contract, the third Friday of the month is the expiration day.

Table III. Summary of Average Mispricing Errors of American Futures Option Pricing Models by the Option's Moneyness (F/X) and by the Option's Time to Expiration in Weeks (T) for S&P 500 Futures Option Transactions during the Period January 28, 1983 through December 30, 1983

	$C - C(F, T; X)$				$P - P(F, T; X)$			
	$T < 6$	$6 \leq T < 12$	$T \geq 12$	All T	$T < 6$	$6 \leq T < 12$	$T \geq 12$	All T
$F/X < 0.98$	-0.0630^a	-0.1372	-0.0872	-0.1028	-0.1064	-0.0914	-0.1056	-0.1014
	(1,221)	(1,760)	(741)	(3,722)	(593)	(335)	(89)	(1,017)
$0.98 \leq F/X < 1.02$	-0.1228	-0.0775	0.0073	-0.0924	-0.0816	-0.0196	0.1336	-0.0406
	(4,452)	(2,858)	(951)	(8,351)	(3,999)	(2,193)	(675)	(6,867)
$F/X \geq 1.02$	0.0577	0.1175	0.0702	0.0806	0.1286	0.1906	30.3060	0.1929
	(1,486)	(1,049)	(455)	(2,990)	(2,043)	(2,530)	(1,216)	(5,789)
All F/X	-0.0757	-0.0599	-0.0120	-0.0606	-0.0191	0.0808	0.2287	0.0537
	(7,249)	(5,667)	(2,147)	(15,063)	(6,635)	(5,058)	(1,980)	(13,673)

^{a} The average deviation of the observed option price from the model price for the 1,221 call option transaction prices with in-the-moneyness (F/X) less than 0.98 and time to expiration (T) less than 6 weeks is -0.0630.

were computed daily on the basis of the average of the T-bill's bid and ask discounts reported in the *Wall Street Journal*.

B. Implied Standard Deviation Methodology

The American futures option pricing models have five parameters: $F, X, T, r,$ and σ. Of these, four are known or are easily estimated. The exercise price, X, and the time to expiration, T, are terms of the futures option contract, and the futures price, F, and the riskless rate of interest, r, are easily accessible market values. The troublesome parameter to estimate is the standard deviation of the futures price change relatives.

The methodology used to estimate the standard deviation of the futures price change relative is described in Whaley [22, pp. 39-40]. Observed futures option prices, V_j, were regressed on their respective model prices, $V_j(\sigma)$, that is

$$V_j = V_j(\sigma) + \epsilon_j. \tag{6}$$

where ϵ_j is a random disturbance term,[9] each day during the sample period. All transaction prices for the day were used in each regression. The number of transactions used to estimate σ in a given day ranged from 30 to 300, with the average number being 124. The estimates of σ ranged from 0.1009 to 0.2176, with the average being approximately 0.1555.

The time series of standard deviation estimates indicates that the volatility of S&P 500 futures price relatives declined during 1983. During the first 116 trading days of the sample period, the average estimate of σ using the American model was 0.1711, while, during the last 116 days of the period, it

[9] The relationship between observed and model prices is not exact and is affected by: (a) model misspecification; (b) nonsimultaneity of futures and futures option price quotations; and (c) the bid-ask spread in the futures and futures option markets. If the residuals in the nonlinear regression (6) are independent and normally distributed, the resulting value of σ is the maximum likelihood estimate.

was 0.1399. It is interesting to note that, during the same two subperiods, the S&P 500 Index rose by 15.07 percent and −0.65 percent, respectively.[10]

C. Tests for Systematic Biases

One way in which the performance of an option pricing model may be evaluated is by examining its mispricing errors for systematic tendencies. Whaley [22] demonstrates that, when the early exercise premium of the American call option on a dividend-paying stock is accounted for in the valuation model, the exercise price and time to expiration biases which had been documented for the European model disappear. Geske and Roll [14] later verify this result and also attempt to explain the variance bias. Here, the variance bias is not of concern since there is only one underlying commodity. The ability of the American futures option models to eliminate the first two biases, however, should be examined.

The tests for systematic biases in the futures option pricing models involved clustering and then averaging the price deviations by the degree the option is in-the-money of the option and by the option's time to expiration. Table III contains a summary of the results for the 15,063 call option and the 13,673 put option transactions in the sample.

Both a "moneyness" bias and a "maturity" bias appear for the call option transaction prices of the sample. The moneyness bias is just the opposite of that reported for stock options.[11] The further the call option is in-the-money, the lower is the model price relative to the observed price (i.e., out-of-the-money calls are overpriced by the model and the in-the-money calls are underpriced). This is true for the American models when all maturities are clustered together and when the intermediate-term and long-term options are considered separately. For the short-term options, the greatest mispricing occurs for the at-the-money calls, which appear dramatically underpriced relative to the model [e.g., for the American call option pricing model, the average value of $C - C(F, T; X)$ is −0.1228].

The maturity bias for the calls is also just the opposite of that reported for call options on stocks. Here, the model prices are higher than the observed prices for short-term options and are lower than observed for long-term options. The relationship is not consistent across the moneyness groupings, however. For out-of-the-money calls, the mispricing is greatest for the intermediate term options with the model considerably overstating observed values [e.g., the average $C - C(F, T; X)$ is −0.1372], and, for in-the-money options, the mispricing is still greatest for the intermediate term options, but with the models understating observed values [e.g., the average $C - C(F, T; X)$ is 0.1175]. Overall, however, the maturity bias does not appear to be as serious as the moneyness bias for the sample of call option transaction prices.

[10]This evidence is consistent with the notion that the variance rate depends on the price of the underlying asset.

[11]See, e.g., Black [4] or Whaley [22].

The average price deviations for the put options appear to have a more orderly pattern, with the relationships between average price deviation and the moneyness and maturity of the options monotonic. Like the call option results, the maturity bias takes the form of short-term options being underpriced relative to the model and long-term options being overpriced. Unlike the call option results, however, the maturity bias is almost as serious as the moneyness bias, and the moneyness bias takes the form of out-of-the-money options being overpriced relative to the model and in-the-money options underpriced. (Recall the put option is in-the-money where $F/X < 1$.) A possible explanation of this latter result is that floor traders engage in conversion/reversal arbitrage using the European put-call parity relationship,[12]

$$c(F, T; X) - p(F, T; X) = (F - X)e^{-rT}. \tag{7}$$

If the put-call parity relationship (7) is actively arbitraged, overpricing of in-the-money call options should result in overpricing of out-of-the-money put options, and underpricing of out-of-the-money call options should result in underpricing of in-the-money put options, or vice versa.

One final note about the results in Table III is worthwhile. During the period examined, put options were overpriced on average while call options were underpriced. Obviously, this result is sensitive to the volatility estimate used to price the option, but, nonetheless, the difference between the average mispricing errors of the put and call option formulas would be approximately the same even if a different estimate of σ were used. This peculiarity indicates that the market's assessment of the volatility of the relative futures price changes may be greater for puts than for calls and provides the motivation for the tests in the next subsection.

D. Stationarity of Volatility Estimates Across Options

To test the hypothesis that the standard deviation of future price change relatives is the same in the pricing of call and put options on the S&P 500 futures contracts, the ratio,

$$R = [SSE_C(\sigma_C) + SSE_p(\sigma_p)]/SSE(\sigma), \tag{8}$$

was computed each day during the sample period. In (8), $SSE_C(\sigma_C)$ is the sum of squared errors realized by estimating the nonlinear regression (6) using only the call option transaction prices during the day, and $SSE_p(\sigma_p)$ is

<hr>

[12] The European put-call parity relationship can be found in a variety of papers, including Black [5], Moriarity, Phillips, and Tosini [18], Asay [1], and Wolf [24]. In all of these studies, the futures contract underlying the option contract is treated like a forward, but no problems arise because the European option can be exercised only at expiration.

For American futures options, the assumption of equivalence between forward and futures contract positions can lead to erroneous statements about futures option pricing. Some of these results are outlined in Ramaswamy and Sundaresan [19]. Stoll and Whaley [21] derive the put-call parity relationship for American futures options.

the sum of squared errors realized by estimating the nonlinear regression (6) using only the call option transaction prices during the day, and $SSE_p(\sigma_p)$ is the sum of squared errors using both the call and put option prices. $SSE(\sigma)$ is the sum of squared errors using both the call and put option prices. If the residuals of the regressions are independent and normally distributed, Gallant [12] shows that the test statistic,

$$F = (n - 2)(1 - R), \tag{9}$$

is approximately distributed, $F_{1,\,n-2}$.[13] The results of these tests are reported in Table IV.

The test results indicate that the null hypothesis that the volatility estimates are equal for calls and puts is rejected in 75 percent of the cases for the American model. The standard deviation of futures price relatives implied by call option prices is lower, on average, than that implied by put option prices. The cause of this anomaly is difficult to determine. One possible explanation is that the stochastic process governing the futures price movements is ill-defined, so the option pricing models are misspecified. Another is that perhaps two separate clienteles trade in call options and in put options. But, this latter explanation fails to account for the floor traders who could costlessly benefit from such a clientele arrangement.

Regardless of the explanation, the anomaly may be only transitory. The only fact established so far is that the futures option pricing models do not adequately explain the observed structure of option prices. It may well be the case that the market is mispricing S&P 500 futures options and that abnormal risk-adjusted rates of return may be earned by trading on the basis of the models' prices.

Table IV.   Frequency Distribution of Non-Rejection/Rejection of the Null Hypothesis that the Standard Deviations Implied by Option Prices Are Equal for Call-and-Put Options Using S&P 500 Futures Option Transaction Prices during the Period January 28, 1983 through December 30, 1983

Hypothesis[a,b]	Frequency
H_0: The standard deviation of the futures price relatives for call options is equal to the standard deviation for put options.	59
H_A: The standard deviation of the futures price relatives for call options is *not* equal to the standard deviation for put options.	173
Total	232

[a]The probability level used in the evaluation of the test statistics is 5 percent.
[b]The test statistic for the hypothesis test is $F = (n - 2)(1 - R)$, where n is the number of option transactions and $R = [SSE_C(\sigma_C) + SSE_p(\sigma_p)] / SSE(\sigma)$. Assuming the residuals are independent and normally distributed, the ratio F is approximately distributed as $F_{1,\,n-2}$.

[13] Barone-Adesi [2] uses a similar maximum likelihood test to compare the structural forms of competing option pricing models.

E. Market Efficiency Test

The systematic biases reported in Table III and the σ-anomaly reported in Table IV may result because the futures option pricing models are misspecified or because the S&P 500 futures option market is inefficient or both. One way of attempting to isolate the two effects is to test whether abnormal rates of return after transaction costs may be earned by trading futures options on the basis of the models' prices. If abnormal returns after transaction costs can be earned, it is likely to be the case that the market is inefficient. The price deviations, systematic or not, signal profit opportunities. If abnormal profits cannot be earned, there are no grounds for rejecting the null hypothesis that the model is correctly specified and that the S&P 500 futures option market is efficient.

The market efficiency test design involved hedging mispriced futures options against the underlying futures contract. Each day options were priced using the American futures option pricing models and the standard deviations estimated from *all* of the previous day's transaction prices.[14] Because no estimate of σ was available for the transactions of the first day of the sample period, January 28, 1983, the first day's transactions were eliminated, and only 231 days and 28,493 options remained in the sample.

Each of the 28,493 option transactions was examined to see whether the option was undervalued or overvalued relative to the futures option pricing models. The hedge formed at that instant in time[15] depended on the nature of the transaction price:

Nature of transaction price	Futures option position	Futures position
Undervalued call	Long 1 contract	Short $\delta C/\delta F$ contracts
Overvalued call	Short 1 contract	Long $\delta C/\delta F$ contracts
Undervalued put	Long 1 contract	Long $-\delta P/\delta F$ contracts
Overvalued put	Short 1 contract	Short $-\delta P/\delta F$ contracts

where the partial derivatives of the call and put option prices were computed using valuation Equations (4) and (5).

Two types of hedge portfolios were considered in the analysis. The first was a "buy-and-hold" hedge portfolio. Each hedge was formed according to the weights described above and was held until the futures option/futures

---

[14] Because both call and put option transaction prices are used in the daily regression to estimate the σ, the estimate is, in essence, an average of the estimates implied by call and puts separately.

[15] The hedge portfolio strategy assumed that the hedge is formed at the prices which signalled the profit opportunity. This was done for two reasons. First, floor traders have the opportunity to transact at these prices. If a sell order at a price below the model price enters the pit, the floor trader can buy the options and then hedge his position within seconds using the futures. Second, the transaction price for retail customers may be handled by simply adding the bid-ask spread to the price which triggered a buy and subtracting the bid-ask spread from the price which triggered a sell.

expiration or until the end of the sample period, whichever came first. At such time, the futures option/futures positions were closed, and the hedge profit was computed. The second was the "rebalanced" hedge portfolio. Here, the initial hedge composition was the same as the buy-and-hold strategy, but at the end of each day, the futures position was altered to account for the change in the futures option's hedge ratio. The difference between the profits of these two hedge portfolio strategies was, therefore, the net gain or loss on the intermediate futures position adjustments within the rebalanced portfolio.[16]

Note that the hedge portfolios are assumed to be held until the option's expiration. This is unlike the empirical procedures used in the stock option market efficiency tests which assume that an option position is opened at one price and then closed at the next available price. If the option pricing models have systematic mispricing tendencies, an option which is undervalued on one day is likely to be undervalued on the next. By holding the option position open until expiration, at which time the observed and model prices converge to the same value, there is some assurance that the prospective option mispricing profits are being captured.

In Table V, the average cost, profit, and rate of return of the hedge portfolios formed on the basis of the American futures option prices are presented. When no minimum size restriction was placed on the absolute price deviation, 28,493 hedge portfolios were formed. On an average, the number of futures contracts in each hedge at formation was 0.442 (1.442 less one futures option contract). The average investment cost of each hedge was − $46.75 (−0.0935 × $500),[17] indicating that, on an average, money was collected when the hedge portfolios were formed.

[16] To illustrate the mechanics of the buy-and-hold and rebalanced hedge portfolio strategies, consider the following example. A call option with an exercise price of $100 and with two days to expiration is priced at $1, where its theoretical price is $1.50 and its hedge ratio is 0.8. The current futures price is $100. Because the call is underpriced relative to the model, it is purchased, and 0.8 futures contracts are sold. The net investment of both the buy-and-hold and rebalanced hedge portfolios is, therefore, $1 (i.e., one option contract times $1 per contract).

By the end of the day before expiration, the futures price rises to say, $102. At the new futures price, the model price is $3.00 and the hedge ratio is 0.9. Since the hedge ratio has changed, 0.1 more futures contracts must be sold in order to maintain the riskless hedge of the rebalanced portfolio. The additional futures contracts are assumed to be bought or sold at the day's closing price, in this case $102.

Now, suppose that on the following day, the futures expires at $106, and the futures option at $6.00 (i.e., the futures price $106 less the exercise price $100). The buy-and-hold hedge portfolio profit would be computed as the option position profit, $6 − 1 = $5, plus the futures position profit, − 0.8 × ($106 − 100) = − $4.80, or $0.20 in total. The rebalanced hedge portfolio profit is computed as the $0.20 buy-and-hold profit plus the net gain (loss) on the intermediate futures position change, − 0.1 × ($106 − 102) = − $0.40, or − $0.20 in total.

[17] The value for the S&P 500 futures and futures options are index values. The dollar worth of the contract is obtained by multiplying the index value by $500.

Table V. Average Cost, Profit, and Rate of Return of Hedge Portfolios by Size of Absolute Price Deviation from the American Futures Option Pricing Models for S&P 500 Futures Option Transaction Prices during the Period January 31, 1983 through December 30, 1983

Minimum absolute price deviation $\|\Delta\|$	No. of observations	Average investment[a]	Average no. of contracts[b]	Buy-and-Hold portfolio profit[c]	Rebalanced portfolio profit[d]	Break-Even transaction cost rate[e]	Rebalanced portfolio excess rate of return[f]	Rebalanced portfolio excess return after transaction costs[g]	Relative systematic risk[h]
All $\|\Delta\|$	28,493	-0.0935	1.442	0.1760 (15.39)[i]	0.1557 (30.64)	0.1152	0.0905 (35.77)	0.0696 (27.78)	0.1193 (2.11)
$\|\Delta\| \geq 0.05$	22,850	-0.1035	1.441	0.2054 (15.83)	0.1854 (31.41)	0.1372	0.1026 (38.48)	0.0850 (32.21)	0.0745 (1.27)
$\|\Delta\| \geq 0.10$	17,596	-0.1160	1.437	0.2444 (16.24)	0.2181 (30.70)	0.1615	0.1164 (39.91)	0.1006 (34.81)	0.0375 (0.59)
$\|\Delta\| \geq 0.15$	13,116	-0.1370	1.430	0.2507 (14.07)	0.2424 (27.53)	0.1802	0.1247 (37.69)	0.1099 (33.48)	0.0924 (1.30)
$\|\Delta\| \geq 0.20$	9,521	-0.1200	1.425	0.2607 (12.18)	0.2696 (23.82)	0.2006	0.1309 (33.64)	0.1168 (30.20)	0.1632 (1.98)

[a] The cost of the hedge portfolio is equal to the option price if the option is purchased and minus the option price if the option is sold. The futures position involves no net investment.

[b] The average absolute number of option and futures contracts in the hedge.

[c] The buy-and-hold portfolio profit assumes the hedge is formed and held until the expiration of the contracts or the end of the sample period.

[d] The rebalanced portfolio profit is equal to the buy-and-hold profit plus (less) the net gains (losses) from the futures position adjustments made during the option's life.

[e] The break-even transaction cost per contract sufficient to eliminate the rebalanced portfolio profit.

[f] The rate of return of the rebalanced hedge portfolio less the riskless rate of interest.

[g] The excess rate of return of the rebalanced hedge portfolio after a $10 per contract transaction cost.

[h] The relative systematic risk is estimated by regressing the excess rate of return of the hedge on the relative futures price changes over the same period.

[i] The values in parentheses are t-ratios for the null hypothesis that the parameter is equal to 0.

The average profit for the buy-and-hold hedge portfolio was $88 (0.1760 × $500), and the average rebalanced hedged portfolio profit was $77.85. The daily rebalancing of the futures position lowered overall hedge profits. On the other hand, the standard deviation of the buy-and-hold profit was 1.9302 compared with 0.8574 for the rebalanced portfolio profits.[18] The daily rebalancing of the futures position decreased the volatility of the hedge profits portfolio by more than 55 percent.

Immediately to the right of the rebalanced portfolio profit column is a column with break-even transaction cost rates. These numbers represent the average of the transaction cost rate per contract sufficient to eliminate rebalanced portfolio profit. In other words, if the transaction cost rate was less than $57.60 (0.1152 × $500) per contract, the average portfolio profit was greater than zero. Note that the transaction costs were assumed to be paid only on the contracts bought or sold when the portfolio was formed. The overall net effect of the incremental transaction costs on the intermediate daily rebalancing of the futures position of the hedge portfolios was assumed to be equal to zero.[19]

The rebalanced portfolio excess rate of return column contains the average rate of return and the net of any interest carrying charge. If the option in the hedge portfolio was purchased, the excess rate of return of the hedge was equal to the rate of return on the hedge less the riskless rate of interest. If the option was sold, interest was assumed to be earned on the proceeds from the sale, so the excess rate of return on the hedge was equal to the rate of return on the hedge plus the riskless rate of interest. The excess rate of return for the rebalanced portfolio using all of the transactions was 9.05 percent and is significantly greater than zero.

Before proceeding with a description of the remaining two columns, it is worthwhile to point out three facts about the excess rates of return for the rebalanced hedge portfolio. First, the excess return did not fall very much if the proceeds from the futures option sales were assumed to earn no interest. In this case, the average excess rate of return was 8.41 percent, with a t-ratio of 33.49. Second, the excess rate of return for the American model was only slightly higher than it was for the European model. For the latter model, the average return was 8.91 percent, with a t-ratio of 35.03. This evidence is consistent with the simulation results in the last section. Finally, the use of Student t-ratios to evaluate the significance of the excess rates of return is appropriate since the return distributions were symmetric and only slightly leptokurtic.

[18] The standard deviations are not reported, but they can be inferred from the reported numbers of observations and the t-ratios.
[19] To account for the transaction costs of the daily readjustment of the futures position within each portfolio separately would dramatically overstate the role of transaction costs within the hedge portfolio because, at the end of the day, some hedges will require that futures contracts be purchased and some that futures be sold. The net overall daily adjustment in the futures position would likely be near zero, so no intermediate transaction costs were imposed.

The column labelled excess rate of return after transaction costs incorporated a $10 per contract transaction cost assumption. Such a fee is probably appropriate for a floor trader.[20] The average excess rate of return after transaction costs was 6.96 percent, again significantly greater than zero.

The final column contains estimated slope coefficients from the regression of rebalanced portfolio excess rates of return on the futures price change relatives over the corresponding period. In essence, this regression is intended to evaluate the effectiveness of the portfolio rebalancing at maintaining a riskless hedge. For the entire sample of hedge portfolio, the relative systematic risk is significantly positive at the 5 percent level, however its magnitude, 0.1193, is very small.

Table V also contains the hedge portfolio profit characteristics when minimum absolute option price deviation of 0.05, 0.10, 0.15, and 0.20 were imposed. Naturally, the higher was the demanded absolute price deviation, the fewer were the option transactions to qualify as hedge portfolio candidates. In the case where the minimum absolute deviation was set equal to 0.10, for example, only 17,596 hedges were formed.

With all of the price deviation strategies reported in Table V, the average excess rates of return are significantly greater than zero. For floor traders, demanding a minimum price deviation of 0.05 is reasonable since they face only the cost of clearing their transactions, which is considerably less than $25 per contract. When such a minimum price deviation was imposed, the average hedge portfolio excess rate of return was 10.26 percent before clearing costs and 8.50 percent after a $10 per contract clearing cost was applied to both the futures option and futures transactions. Retail customers, however, not only face the commission rates imposed by their broker, but also the bid-ask spread imposed by the market maker. Assuming a commission rate of $50 per contract and a bid-ask spread of $50 per

[20] Actually, the assumed $10 per contract overstates the transaction costs a floor trader might face. The only transaction cost paid by floor traders is a clearing fee, which is on order of $1.50 per contract. The $10 per contract assumption, therefore, presents a conservative view of the floor trader's hedge portfolio profits after transaction costs.

Two other institutional considerations are worthy of note. The transaction cost rates in this market are quoted on a "round-turn" basis. That is, a $50 per contract commission charge covers the cost of entering the market at the time of purchase or sale and the cost of closing the position at a subsequent date. For futures contract positions, the broker charges all of the commission when the position is closed, and, for futures option positions, half the commission is charged when the position is opened and half when it is closed.

Since commission rates are negotiated between each customer and his or her broker, it is difficult to assess what are representative commission charges for the various futures/futures option customers. Large institutional customers such as mutual funds typically pay commissions at a rate of $20 to $30 per contract and are allowed to post margin requirement in the form of interest-bearing T-bills. Smaller customers likely pay commissions of $50 or more, and are also allowed to the T-bill margin-posting privilege. Some brokers quote lower rates for small customers, but demand margin money in the form of cash.

option contract, demanding a minimum price deviation of 0.20 is reasonable. However, in this case, the average break-even transaction cost rate was 0.2006, so the retail customer would have earned about $0.30 per hedge after transaction costs.

In the previous section, systematic mispricing errors related to the moneyness of the option were documented. For this reason, the option transactions were categorized by the type of option and by the degree to which the option is in-the-money. The results are reported in Table VI. Most of the abnormal profits associated with the trading strategy appear to be concentrated in out-of-the-money put options. The average excess rate of return after the floor trader's clearing costs was 16.88 percent. In comparison, none of the other option categories had an average return greater than 3 percent after clearing costs.

One plausible explanation for this result is that more than 72 percent out-of-the-money put options were overpriced (see Table III) and thus sold within the trading strategy. Over the period January 31, 1983 through December 30, 1983, the S&P 500 Index rose from 145.30 to 164.93, indicating that writing out-of-the-money puts would have been profitable indeed. But, the put options sold within the hedge strategy were balanced against short positions in the futures, so what was gained on the put transactions should have been lost on the futures transactions. Moreover, the estimated systematic risk for the hedge portfolios in this category was significantly negative, indicating that, if anything, not enough put options were sold to immunize the portfolio against movements in the underlying futures price. The overall upward market movement in the equity market during the examination period must, therefore, be discounted as a potential explanation of the market inefficiency.

Although the results of Table VI indicate that floor traders could profit by writing out-of-the-money puts, it is doubtful whether retail customers could profit by such a strategy. As was noted in Table II, at-the-money options enjoyed the greatest volume of activity and, therefore, probably experienced the lowest bid-ask spread. Out-of-the-money S&P 500 futures options have less liquidity, and it is not uncommon to find the bid-ask spread as high as 0.15 or 0.20. Assuming a commission rate of $50 per contract and a bid-ask spread of $50 per contract takes the average profit from $159.70 per hedge to an average gain after transaction costs of $45.40.

Overall, the results reported in Tables V and VI provide evidence that the joint hypothesis that the American futures option valuation models are correctly specified and that the S&P 500 futures option market is efficient is refuted for the period January 31, 1983 through December 30, 1983, at least from the standpoint of floor traders who stood ready to transact based on model prices. From a retail customer's standpoint, however, it is doubtful whether abnormal profits after transaction costs could have been earned.

Table VI.   Average Cost, Profit, and Rate of Return of Hedge Portfolios by the Moneyness of the Option for the S&P 500 Futures Option Transaction Prices during the Period January 31, 1983 through December 30, 1983

Futures option category	No. of observations	Average investment[a]	Average no. of contracts[b]	Buy-and-Hold portfolio profit[c]	Rebalanced portfolio profit[d]	Break-Even transaction cost rate[e]	Rebalanced portfolio excess rate of return[f]	Rebalanced portfolio excess return after transaction costs[g]	Relative systematic risk[h]
Calls	7,736	−1.0521	1.339	−0.0077	0.0204	0.0160	0.0432	0.0159	0.7339
F/X < 1				(−0.34)[i]	(2.34)		(7.00)	(2.60)	(5.25)
Calls	7,150	0.5963	1.670	0.1052	0.1284	0.0763	0.0295	0.0206	0.4858
F/X ≥ 1				(4.60)	(16.81)		(12.58)	(8.84)	(9.02)
Puts	3,620	−1.9300	1.646	0.0975	0.0497	0.0273	0.0186	0.0074	0.4150
F/X < 1				(2.98)	(1.95)		(3.99)	(1.61)	(3.66)
Puts	9,987	0.8208	1.286	0.3979	0.3194	0.2518	0.1968	0.1688	−0.7379
F/X ≥ 1				(21.53)	(37.46)		(42.10)	(36.42)	(−7.56)

[a] The cost of the hedge portfolio is equal to the option price if the option is purchased and minus the option price if the option is sold. The futures position involves no net investment.

[b] The average absolute number of option and futures contracts in the hedge.

[c] The buy-and-hold portfolio profit assumes the hedge is formed and held until the expiration of the contracts or the end of the sample period.

[d] The rebalanced portfolio profit is equal to the buy-and-hold profit plus (less) the net gains (losses) from the futures position adjustments made during the option's life.

[e] The break-even transaction cost per contract sufficient to eliminate the rebalanced portfolio profit.

[f] The rate of return of the rebalanced hedge portfolio less the riskless rate of interest.

[g] The excess rate of return of the rebalanced hedge portfolio after a $10 per contract transaction cost.

[h] The relative systematic risk is estimated by regressing the excess rate of return of the hedge on the relative futures price changes over the same period.

[i] The value in parentheses are t-ratios for the null hypothesis that the parameter is equal to 0.

Table VII. Average Cost, Profit, and Rate of Return of Hedge Portfolios by Subperiod for S&P 500 Futures Option Transaction Prices during the Period January 31, 1983 through December 30, 1983

Subperiod	No. of observations	Average investment[a]	Average no. of contracts[b]	Buy-and-Hold portfolio profit[c]	Rebalanced portfolio profit[d]	Break-Even transaction cost rate[e]	Rebalanced portfolio excess rate of return[f]	Rebalanced portfolio excess return after transaction costs[g]	Relative systematic risk[h]
1/31/83- 4/21/83	9,846	−0.0509	1.454	−0.1758 (−8.73)[i]	0.0308 (7.01)	0.0271	0.0047 (1.56)	−0.1024 (−4.13)	0.8848 (15.40)
4/22/83- 7/14/83	8,237	−0.1623	1.450	0.5118 (22.84)	0.3884 (55.08)	0.2682	0.2067 (50.06)	0.1876 (39.82)	0.8641 (5.66)
7/15/83- 10/6/83	6,001	−0.1902	1.423	0.2323 (8.86)	0.0953 (7.25)	0.0780	0.0737 (10.97)	0.0515 (7.72)	−0.2587 (−0.90)
10/7/83- 12/30/83	4,409	0.0710	1.430	0.2588 (14.55)	0.0968 (4.49)	0.0740	0.0879 (12.48)	0.0567 (8.14)	−1.769 (−4.52)

[a] The cost of the hedge portfolio is equal to the option price if the option is purchased and minus the option price if the option is sold. The futures position involves no net investment.

[b] The average absolute number of option and futures contracts in the hedge.

[c] The buy-and-hold portfolio profit assumes the hedge is formed and held until the expiration of the contracts or the end of the sample period.

[d] The rebalanced portfolio profit is equal to the buy-and-hold profit plus (less) the net gains (losses) from the futures position adjustments made during the option's life.

[e] The break-even transactions cost per contract sufficient to eliminate the rebalanced portfolio profit.

[f] The rate of return of the rebalanced hedge portfolio less the riskless rate of interest.

[g] The excess rate of return of the rebalanced hedge portfolio after a $10 per contract transaction cost.

[h] The relative systematic risk is estimated by regressing the excess rate of return of the hedge on the relative futures price changes over the same period. The values in parentheses are t-ratios for the null hypothesis that the parameter is equal to 0.

In Table VII, the option transactions in four separate subperiods are considered. In the first subperiod, the average excess rate of return on the hedge portfolio was 0.47 percent, insignificantly different from zero. In the remaining three subperiods, the excess rate of return was significantly greater than zero, with the return highest in the second subperiod and second highest in the final subperiod. In other words, there does not appear to be any indication that the market became more efficient during 1983. Whether floor traders can continue to earn abnormal rates of return after clearing costs by buying undervalued and selling overvalued S&P 500 futures options must await further empirical investigation.

III. Summary and Conclusions

The purpose of this paper is to review the theory underlying American futures option valuation and to test the theory in one of the recently developed futures option markets. The theoretical work begins by focusing on the partial differential equation of Black [5] and by discussing how the boundary conditions to the equation imply different structural forms to the pricing equations. Although no analytic solutions to the American futures option pricing problems are provided, efficient analytic approximations are presented. Simulations of futures option prices using the European and American models and plausible option pricing parameters show that the early exercise premium of the American futures option has a significant impact on pricing if the option is in-the-money.

The empirical work focuses on transaction prices for S&P 500 equity futures options during the first 232 trading days of the market's existence, the period from January 28, 1983 through December 30, 1983. The major empirical results are as follows:

1. A moneyness bias and a maturity bias appear for the American futures option pricing models. For calls, the moneyness bias is the opposite of that reported for stock options — out-of-the-money options are underpriced relative to the model and in-the-money options are overpriced. For puts, just the reverse is true — out-of-the-money puts are overpriced relative to the model and in-the-money puts are underpriced. The maturity bias is the same for both the calls and the puts — short time-to-expiration options are underpriced relative to the model and long time-to-expiration are overpriced, but the bias appears more serious for put options than for call options.
2. The standard deviation implied by call option transaction prices is lower, on average, than that implied by put option prices.
3. A riskless hedging strategy using the American futures option pricing models (as well as the European futures option pricing models) generates abnormal risk-adjusted rates of return after the transaction costs paid by floor traders or large institutional customers. If a retail customer was to try to capture the profits implied by the futures option mispricing, however, transaction costs will likely eliminate the hedge portfolio profit opportunities.

References

1. M. R. Asay. "A Note on the Design of Commodity Contracts." *Journal of Futures Markets* 2 (Spring 1982), 1-7.

2. G. Barone-Adesi. "Maximum Likelihood Tests of Option Pricing Models." *Advances in Futures and Option Research* 1, forthcoming, 1985.

3. _____ and R. E. Whaley. "Efficient Analytic Approximation of American Option Values." Working Paper No. 15, Institute for Financial Research, University of Alberta, 1985.

4. F. Black. "Fact and Fantasy in the Use of Options." *Financial Analysts Journal* 31 (July/August 1975), 36-41, 61-72.

5. _____. "The Pricing of Commodity Contracts." *Journal of Financial Economics* 3 (January-March 1976), 167-79.

6. _____ and M. Scholes. "The Pricing of Options and Corporate Liabilities." *Journal of Political Economy* 81 (May-June 1973), 637-59.

7. M. J. Brennan and E. S. Schwartz. "The Valuation of American Put Options." *Journal of Finance* 32 (May 1977), 449-62.

8. _____. "Finite Difference Methods and Jump Processes Arising in the Pricing of Contingent Claims: A Synthesis." *Journal of Financial and Quantitative Analysis* 13 (September 1978), 461-74.

9. M. Brenner, G. R. Courtadon, and M. Subrahmanyam. "Option on Stock Indices and Stock Index Futures." Working Paper, New York University, 1984.

10. G. Courtadon. "The Pricing of Options on Default-Free Bonds." *Journal of Financial and Quantitative Analysis* 17 (March 1982), 75-100.

11. J. C. Cox, J. E. Ingersoll, and S. A. Ross. "The Relation Between Forward and Futures Prices." *Journal of Financial Economics* 9 (December 1981), 321-46.

12. R. Gallant. "Nonlinear Regression." *American Statistician* 29 (May 1975), 73-81.

13. R. Geske and H. E. Johnson. "The American Put Valued Analytically." *Journal of Finance* 39 (December 1984), 1511-24.

14. R. Geske and R. Roll. "Isolating the Observed Biases in American Call Option Pricing: An Alternative Estimator." Working Paper, Graduate School of Management, UCLA, 1984.

15. R. Geske and K. Shastri. "Valuation by Approximation: A Comparison of Alternative Valuation Techniques." *Journal of Financial and Quantitative Analysis* 20 (March 1985), 45-71.

16. L. W. MacMillan. "Analytic Approximation for the American Put Option." *Advances in Futures and Options Research* 1, forthcoming, 1985.

17. R. C. Merton. "The Theory of Rational Option Pricing." *Bell Journal of Economics and Management Science* 4 (Spring 1973), 141-83.

18. E. Moriarity, S. Phillips, and P. Tosini. "A Comparison of Options and Futures in the Management of Portfolio Risk." *Financial Analysts Journal* 37 (January-February 1981), 61-67.

19. K. Ramaswamy and S. M. Sundaresan. "The Valuation of Options on Futures Contracts." Working Paper, Graduate School of Business, Columbia University, 1984.

20. E. S. Schwartz. "The Valuation of Warrants: Implementing a New Approach." *Journal of Financial Economics* 4 (January 1977), 79-93.

21. H. R. Stoll and R. E. Whaley. "The New Options: Arbitrageable Linkages and Valuation." *Advances in Futures and Options Research* 1, forthcoming, 1985.

22. R. E. Whaley. "Valuation of American Call Options on Dividend-Paying Stocks: Empirical Tests." *Journal of Financial Economics* 10 (March 1982), 29-57.

23. _____. "On Valuing American Futures Options." *Financial Analysts Journal* (forthcoming) and Working Paper No. 4, Institute for Financial Research, University of Alberta, 1984.

24. A. Wolf. "Fundamentals of Commodity Options on Futures." *Journal of Futures Markets* 2 (1982), 391-408.

Approximation Techniques

Within the Black-Scholes framework, certain types of option pricing problems do not have closed-form solutions. This means that it is either impossible to derive an analytical valuation equation to price the option or, alternatively, that an analytical valuation equation has yet to be found. In fact, most American-style options fall into this category.[1]

This section provides four separate types of approximation methods that have appeared in the finance literature. The first approach to have appeared is the finite difference method. The earliest applications were by Schwartz [1977] for the valuation of warrants, and by Brennan and Schwartz [1977] for American-style put options on common stocks. The Brennan and Schwartz [1978] article reprinted here is more generally focused and is a synthesis of finite difference methods and jump processes that are used in the pricing of option contracts.

The finite difference method involves replacing the Black-Scholes assumption that a commodity price moves smoothly and continuously through time during the option's life, with an assumption that the commodity price can move up by a discrete amount, down by the same amount, or stay at the same level over each of a number of discrete time intervals during the option's life. (The size of the commodity price increment and the length of the time step are user-set amounts—the larger the amounts, the more imprecise the approximation method becomes.) Under this arrangement, all possible paths that the commodity price may take between now and the expiration day of the option may be enumerated. The procedure then starts at the end of the option's life and works backward. At the end of the option's life, the value of the option is known for each possible level of commodity price since the option is simply worth its intrinsic value. At one step back in time from expiration, the option's worth at each commodity price level is computed by taking the present value of its expected worth in one period. The expected worth is computed by summing the products of the probabilities of up, down, and across commodity price

---

[1] The exceptions to this rule, along with an intuitive discussion about why analytical solutions are not possible, are contained in Stoll and Whaley [1992, Ch. 10].

moves and the option values conditional upon each of the three possible future commodity price levels, respectively. Before proceeding back another time step, it is necessary to see if any of the computed option values is below its early-exercise proceeds at the respective commodity price levels. If the exercise proceeds are greater than the computed option value, the computed value is replaced with the early-exercise proceeds. If they are not, the value is left undisturbed. If this step is not performed, the procedure will produce the value of a European put option. The approach is then repeated for all time steps during the option's life until the current option price is computed.

The second approach, the binomial method, was developed by Cox, Ross, and Rubinstein [1979] and Rendleman and Bartter [1979]. It is similar in spirit to the finite-difference method. In fact, the only real distinction is that the binomial method permits only two commodity price moves—up or down—by a constant proportion of the commodity price (rather than a constant amount). The Cox, Ross, and Rubinstein article is reprinted here, and the Rendleman and Bartter reference is listed in the bibliography. The Geske and Shastri [1985] article, also listed in the bibliography, provides an analysis of the strengths and weaknesses of the finite-difference and binomial methods.

Geske and Johnson [1984] use a compound option pricing approach to value American-style options. The approach is intuitively appealing. Conceptually, an American-style option is a compound option with an infinite number of early exercise opportunities. From a computational standpoint, valuing such an option is impossible, however, we can extrapolate the value of such an option by using a sequence of "pseudo-American" option prices that allow zero, one, two, and perhaps more early exercise opportunities at discrete, equally spaced intervals during the

option's life. The benefit that this offers is that pricing each of these options can be done analytically. However, with each new option added to the price sequence, the evaluation of a higher and higher-order multivariate normal integral is required. With no early exercise opportunities, only a univariate function is required. With one early exercise opportunity, a bivariate; with two opportunities, a trivariate; and so on. The more of these options used in the series, the greater is the precision in approximating the limiting value of the sequence where an infinite number of early exercise opportunities are allowed. The cost is that higher-order multivariate integral evaluations is very time-consuming computationally. The Geske-Johnson article is reprinted here.

Finally, Barone-Adesi and Whaley [1987] present a quadratic approximation. Their approach, based on the work of MacMillan [1986], separates the value of an American-style option into two components: the European-style option value and an early exercise premium. Since we have an analytical equation for pricing the European option, they focus on approximating the value of the early exercise premium. The quadratic approximation that they provide is fast and accurate, particularly for short-term options.

The bibliography contains many other articles of approximation techniques. Some are extensions or refinements of the techniques discussed. Others offer still different approximation methods, which include numerical integration (see Parkinson [1977]) and Monte Carlo methods (see Boyle [1977]). Yet others address more complex option valuation problems with more than one source of underlying uncertainty (see Boyle [1988]). The reader interested in understanding the workings of American-style option valuation approximations will find many of these articles useful.

References and Bibliography

Barone-Adesi, G., and R.E. Whaley, 1987, "Efficient Analytical Approximation of American Option Values," *Journal of Finance* 42, 301-20.

Boyle, P.P., 1977, "Options: A Monte Carlo Approach," *Journal of Financial Economics* 4(3), 323-38.

———, 1986, "Option-Valuation Using a Three-Jump Process," *International Options Journal* 3, 7-12.

———, 1988, "A Lattice Framework for Option Pricing with Two State Variables," *Journal of Financial and Quantitative Analysis* 23, 1-12.

———, and Y.K. Tse, 1990, "An Algorithm for Computing Values on the Maximum or Minimum of Several Assets," *Journal of Financial and Quantitative Analysis* 25, 215-30.

Boyle, P.P., J. Evnine, and S. Gibbs, 1989, "Numerical Evaluation of Multivariate Contingent Claims," *Review of Financial Studies* 2, 241-50.

Breen, R., 1990, "Binomial Option Pricing and the Conditions for Early Exercise: An Example Using Foreign Exchange Options," *Economic and Social Review* 21, 151-61.

———, 1991, "The Accelerated Binomial Option Pricing Model," *Journal of Financial and Quantitative Analysis* 26, 153-64.

Brennan, M.J., and E.S. Schwartz, 1977, "The Valuation of American Put Options," *Journal of Finance* 32, 449-62.

———, 1978, "Finite Difference Methods and Jump Processes Arising in the Pricing of Contingent Claims: A Synthesis," *Journal of Financial and Quantitative Analysis* 13, 461-74.

Cox, J.C., S.A. Ross, and M. Rubinstein, 1979, "Option Pricing: A Simplified Approach," *Journal of Financial Economics* 7, 229-63.

Courtadon, G., 1982, "A More Accurate Finite Difference Approximation for the Valuation of Options," *Journal of Financial and Quantitative Analysis* 17, 697-703.

Geske, R., and H.E. Johnson, 1984, "The American Put Option Valued Analytically," *Journal of Finance* 34, 1511-24.

Geske, R., and K. Shastri, 1985, "Valuation of Approximation: A Comparison of Alternative Approaches," *Journal of Financial and Quantitative Analysis* 20, 45-72.

Hsia, C.C., 1983, "On Binomial Option Pricing," *Journal of Financial Research* 6, 41-46.

Hull, J.C., and A. White, 1988. "The Use of Control-Variate Technique in Option-Pricing," *Journal of Financial and Quantitative Analysis* 23, 237-51.

Hull, J., and A. White, 1990, "Valuing Derivative Securities Using the Explicit Finite Difference Method," *Journal of Financial and Quantitative Analysis* 25, 87-100.

Johnson, H.E., 1983, "An Analytic Approximation to the American Put Price," *Journal of Financial and Quantitative Analysis* 18, 141-48.

Parkinson, M., 1977, "Option-Pricing: The American Put," *Journal of Business*, 50, 21-36.

MacMillan, L.W., 1986, "Analytic Approximation for the American Put Option," *Advances in Futures and Options Research* 1, 119-39.

Nelson, D.B., and K. Ramaswamy, 1990, "Simple Binomial Processes as Diffusion Approximations in Financial Models," *Review of Financial Studies* 3, 393-430.

Omberg, E., 1987, "A Note on the Convergence of Binomial Pricing and Compound-Option Models," *Journal of Finance* 42, 463-69.

Rendleman, R.J., and B.J. Bartter, 1979, "Two-State Option Pricing," *Journal of Finance* 34, 1093-1110.

Schwartz, E.S., 1977, "The Valuation of Warrants: Implementing a New Approach," *Journal of Financial Economics* 4(January), 79-93.

Stapleton, R.C., and M.G. Subrahmanyam, 1984, "The Valuation of Options When Asset Returns Are Generated by a Binomial Process," *Journal of Finance* 39, 1525-39.

1

Finite Difference Methods and Jump Processes Arising in the Pricing of Contingent Claims: A Synthesis

Michael J. Brennan and Eduardo S. Schwartz*

Since the seminal article by Black and Scholes on the pricing of corporate liabilities, the importance in finance of contingent claims has become widely recognized. The key to the valuation of such claims has been found to lie in the solution to certain partial differential equations. The best known of these was derived by Black and Scholes, in their original article, from the assumption that the value of the asset underlying the contingent claim follows a geometric Brownian motion.

Depending on the nature of the boundary conditions which must be satisfied by the value of the contingent claim, the Black-Scholes partial differential equation and its extensions may or may not have an analytic solution. Analytic solutions have been derived under certain conditions for the values of a call option (Black and Scholes [1], Merton [11]), of a risky corporate discount bond (Merton [12]), of European put options (Black and Scholes [1], Merton [11]), of the capital shares of dual funds (Ingersoll [8]), and of convertible bonds (Ingersoll [9]). In many realistic situations, however, analytic solutions do not exist, and the analyst must resort to other methods. These include the finite difference approximation to the differential equation employed extensively by Brennan and Schwartz [3, 4, 5], numerical integration used by Parkinson [13], and Monte Carlo methods advocated by Boyle [2].

*Both, University of British Columbia. The authors gratefully acknowledge financial support from The S.S. Huebner Foundation, The Wharton School, University of Pennsylvania. They also thank Phelim Boyle for helpful comments.

Michael J. Brennan and Eduardo S. Schwartz, "Finite Difference Methods and Jump Processes Arising in the Pricing of Contingent Claims: A Synthesis." Reprinted with permission from *Journal of Financial and Quantitative Analysis*, 13, 1978.

Complementing the above work, Cox and Ross [6, 7] have analyzed the pricing of contingent claims when the value of the underlying asset follows a jump process rather than a diffusion process, and have shown that in the limit the jump process approaches a pure diffusion process. The major purpose of this paper is to demonstrate that approximation of the Black-Scholes partial differential equation by use of the finite difference method is equivalent to approximating the diffusion process by a jump process and that therefore the finite difference approximation is a type of numerical integration. In particular, we establish that the simpler explicit finite difference approximation is equivalent to approximating the diffusion process by one of the jump processes described by Cox and Ross, while the implicit finite difference approximation amounts to approximating the diffusion process by a more general type of jump process. As a preliminary to this, we show that certain simplifications of the numerical procedure are made possible by taking a log transform of the Black-Scholes equation. In the subsequent sections we discuss the explicit and implicit finite difference approximations, respectively.

I. The Log Transform of the Black-Scholes Equation

The basic Black-Scholes equation is

$$1/2\sigma^2 S^2 H_{ss} + rS H_s + H_t - rH = 0 \tag{1}$$

where S is the value of the underlying asset, t is time, $H(S, t)$ is the value of the contingent claim, r is the riskless rate of interest, σ^2 is the instantaneous variance rate of the return on the underlying asset, and subscripts denote partial differentiation.

To obtain the log transform of (1) we define

$$Y \equiv \ln S \tag{2}$$

$$W(y,t) \equiv H(S,t) \tag{3}$$

so that

$$H_s = W_y e^{-y} \tag{4}$$

$$H_{ss} = (W_{yy} - W_y)e^{-2y} \tag{5}$$

$$H_t = W_t. \tag{6}$$

Then, making the appropriate substitutions in (1), we obtain the transformed equation:

$$\frac{1}{2}\sigma^2 W_{yy} + (r - \frac{1}{2}\sigma^2) W_y + W_t - rW = 0. \tag{7}$$

Notice that (7) unlike (1) is a partial differential equation with constant coefficients. This simplifies the numerical analysis, and, as we shall see below, makes it possible to employ an explicit finite difference approximation to (7), whereas the explicit finite difference approximation to (1) is in general unstable.

II. The Explicit Finite Difference Approximation

To obtain a finite difference approximation to (7), we replace the partial derivatives by finite differences, and to this end define

$$W(y, t) = W(ih, jk) = W_{i,j}$$

where h and k are the discrete increments in the value of the underlying asset and the time dimension, respectively. For the explicit approximation, the partial derivatives are approximated by

$$W_y = (W_{i+1,j+1} - W_{i-1,j+1})/2h$$

$$W_{yy} = (W_{i+1,j+1} - 2W_{i,j+1} + W_{i-1,j+1})/h^2$$

$$W_t = (W_{i,j+1} - W_{i,j})/k$$

so that the corresponding difference equation is

$$W_{i,j}(1 + rk) = aW_{i-1,j+1} + bW_{i,j+1} + cW_{i+1,j+1} \tag{8}$$

$$i = 1, \ldots, (n-1)$$
$$j = 1, \ldots, m$$

where

$$a = [\frac{1}{2}(\sigma/h)^2 - \frac{1}{2}(r - \frac{1}{2}\sigma^2)/h]k,$$

$$b = [1 - (\sigma/h)^2 k], \text{ and}$$

$$c = [\frac{1}{2}(\sigma/h)^2 + \frac{1}{2}(r - 1/2\sigma^2)/h]k.$$

For any given value of j, (8) allows us to solve for $W_{i,j}$ ($i = 1, \ldots, n-1$) in terms of $W_{i,j+1}$. The extreme values of $W_{i,j}$, $W_{o,j}$, and $W_{n,j}$, must be given by the boundary conditions to the problem.[1] Then, given the values of $W_{i,j}$ corresponding to the maturity of the contingent claim, we may solve (8) recursively for all values of $W_{i,j}$.

Notice that the coefficients of (8) are independent of i and that $a + b + c = 1$. For the stability of the explicit solution, it is necessary that the coefficients of (8) be nonnegative (McCracken and Dorn [10]). While appropriate choice of h and k may guarantee this for (8), the corresponding

---

[1]Note that we are implicitly assuming that the lower boundary condition is of the form $W(0, t) = Z_t$. More generally the boundary condition may be $W(i_j h, t) = Z_t$; this will simply change the range of i in (8) without changing anything essential.

coefficients of the explicit approximation to (1) depend on i, and will be negative for sufficiently large values of i, so that this explicit finite difference approximation may not be applied to the untransformed equation (1).

For the nonnegativity condition to be satisfied, it is necessary that h and k be chosen so that

$$h \leq \sigma^2 / \left| \left(r - \frac{1}{2}\sigma^2 \right) \right|$$

and   (9)

$$k \leq \sigma^2 / \left(r - \frac{1}{2}\sigma^2 \right)^2 .$$

If the conditions (9) are satisfied, the coefficients of the *RHS* of (8) may be interpreted as probabilities since they are nonnegative. Writing p^- for a, p for b and p^+ for c, (8) becomes

$$W_{i,j} = \frac{1}{(1+rk)}\, p^- W_{i-1,j+1} + p W_{i,j+1} + p^+ W_{i+1,j+1} \qquad (10)$$

Thus the value of the contingent claim at time instant j may be regarded as given by its expected value at $(j + 1)$ discounted at the riskless rate, r. The expected value of the claim at the next instant is obtained by assuming that y, the logarithm of the stock price follows the jump process

$$\mathrm{d}y = \begin{cases} h & p^+ \\ 0 & p \\ -h & p^- \end{cases} \qquad (11)$$

which is formally identical to a jump process discussed by Cox and Ross [6, equation (8)], where $\mu = 0$. The local mean and variance of (11) are

$$E[\mathrm{d}y] = h[p^+ - p^-] \qquad (12)$$

$$= \left(r - \frac{1}{2}\sigma^2 \right) k .$$

$$V[\mathrm{d}y] = h^2 [p^+ + p^-] - (E[\mathrm{d}y])^2 \qquad (13)$$

$$= \sigma^2 k - \left(r - \frac{1}{2}\sigma^2 \right)^2 k^2 .$$

Thus the diffusion limit of (11) is

$$\mathrm{d}y = (r - 1/2\,\sigma^2)\,\mathrm{d}t + \sigma\,\mathrm{d}z \qquad (14)$$

where dz is a Gauss-Wiener process with $E[dz^2] = 0, E[dz^2] = dt$; this implies that the diffusion limit of dS is

$$\frac{dS}{S} = r\,dt + \sigma\,dz. \tag{15}$$

Now as Cox and Ross [6] have pointed out, if a riskless arbitrage portfolio can be established between the contingent claim and the underlying asset, the resulting valuation equation is preference free. Therefore we may value the contingent claim under any convenient assumption about preferences, in particular under the assumption of risk neutrality, which implies that the diffusion process for the underlying asset is (15) and that the value of the contingent claim is obtained by discounting its expected future value at the riskless rate of interest as is done in (10).

We have established therefore that the explicit finite difference approximation to the Black-Scholes differential equation is equivalent to making the permissible assumption of risk-neutrality and approximating the diffusion process (15) by the jump process (11). Notice however that the variance of the approximating jump process given by (13) is a downward biased estimate of the variance of the approximated diffusion process (14). The bias is equal to the square of the expected jump, $(r - \frac{1}{2}\sigma^2)k$. Using the stability condition (9), the upper bound on this bias is σ^4.

The recursive valuation equation (10) may be regarded as a type of numerical integration where the probabilities are taken, not from the normal density function, but from a jump process, (11), approximating the Gauss-Wiener process (14). This approach is almost identical to the numerical integration procedure employed by Parkinson [13], who also approximated the normal distribution by a related but different three-point distribution.

III. The Implicit Finite Difference Approximation

The implicit finite difference approximation to (7) is obtained by approximating the partial derivatives by the finite differences

$$W_{yy} = (W_{i+1,j} - 2W_{i,j} + W_{i-1,j})/h^2 \tag{16}$$

$$W_y = (W_{i+1,j} - W_{i-1,j})/2h \tag{17}$$

$$W_t = (W_{i,j+1} - W_{i,j})/k \tag{18}$$

so that the differential equation is written in finite difference form as:

$$a\,W_{i-1,j} + b\,W_{i,j} + c\,W_{i+1,j} = (1 - rk)\,W_{i,j+1} \tag{19}$$

$$i = 1, \ldots n$$
$$j = 1, \ldots m$$

where

$$a = [-\frac{1}{2}(\sigma/h)^2 + \frac{1}{2}(r - \frac{1}{2}\sigma^2)/h]k \qquad (20)$$

$$b = 1 + (\sigma/h)^2 k \qquad (21)$$

$$c = [-\frac{1}{2}(\sigma/h)^2 - \frac{1}{2}(r - \frac{1}{2}\sigma^2)/h]k \qquad (22)$$

For any value of j, (19) constitutes a system of n equations in the $(n + 2)$ unknowns $W_{i,j}$ $(i = 0, 1, \ldots, n + 1)$. To complete the system, it is necessary to introduce two boundary conditions. Assume that these are given by knowing $W_{0,j}$ and $W_{n+1,j}$:

$$W_{0,j} = \alpha_j \qquad (23)$$

$$W_{n+1,j} = \beta_j \qquad (24)$$

Then we may eliminate $W_{0,j}$ and $W_{n+1,j}$ from the first and last equations of (19) to obtain:

$$bW_{1,j} + cW_{2,j} \qquad\qquad = (1-rk)W_{1,j+1} - a\alpha_j = f_1$$
$$-- \circ \circ \circ --$$
$$aW_{i-1,j} + bW_{i,j} + cW_{i+1,j} = (1-rk)W_{i,j+1} \qquad = f_i \qquad (25)$$
$$-- \circ \circ \circ --$$
$$aW_{n-1,j} + bW_{n,j} = (1-rk)W_{n,j+1} - c\beta_j = f_n$$

This system of equations may be written in matrix form as

$$\underline{\underline{A}}\, \underline{W} = \mathbf{f}. \qquad (26)$$

And by recursive solution of (26), knowing the values of $W_{i,j}$ at maturity, we generate the whole set of $W_{i,j}$ values. Note that since $\underline{\underline{A}}$ is independent of j, the matrix must be inverted only once, so that each time step simply involves the multiplication of a vector by this matrix inverse. This is admittedly a more complex calculation than was required for the explicit solution: on the other hand, the implicit solution procedure is potentially more accurate.

Our objective is to demonstrate that the elements of this matrix inverse may be viewed as discounted probabilities, and that therefore the implicit solution procedure generates successively earlier values of $W_{i,j}$ by discounting the expected value at the end of the next time increment assuming risk neutral preferences.

The simple form of the matrix, $\underline{\underline{A}}$, suggests the use of Gaussian elimination to solve the equation system. We proceed by multiplying the second equation of (25) by (b/a) and subtracting from it the first equation to obtain a transformed second equation from which $W_{1,j}$ has been eliminated: we proceed in this way, multiplying each equation by (b/a) and subtracting from it its transformed predecessor, obtaining the transformed system of equations:

$$b_1^* W_{1,j} + c_1^* W_{2,j} \qquad\qquad\qquad = f_1^*$$
$$b_2^* W_{2,j} + c_2^* W_{3,j} \qquad\qquad\qquad = f_2^*$$
$$- - \circ \circ \circ - -$$
$$b_{n-1}^* W_{n-1,j} + c_{n-1}^* W_{n,j} = f_{n-1}^*$$
$$b_n^* W_{n,j} = f_n^* \qquad (27)$$

In the first equation

$$b_1^* = b, \ c_1^* = c, \ f_1^* = f_1$$

and in general

$$b_i^* = (b/a)\, b_{i-1}^* - c_{i-1}^* \qquad\qquad\qquad (28)$$

$$c_i^* = (c/a)\, b_{i-1}^* \qquad\qquad\qquad (29)$$

$$f_i^* = (f_i/a)\, b_{i-1}^* - f_{i-1}^*. \qquad\qquad\qquad (30)$$

Substituting for c_{i-1}^* in (28) from (29), we obtain the difference equation for b_i^*:

$$b_i^* = (b/a)\, b_{i-1}^* - (c/a)\, b_{i-2}^*. \qquad\qquad\qquad (31)$$

The solution to this difference equation, given the initial conditions $b_1^* = b$, $c_1^* = c$ is:

$$b_i^* = (a^2/\sqrt{b^2 - 4ac})(\lambda_1^{i+1} - \lambda_2^{i+1}) \qquad\qquad\qquad (32)$$

where

$$\lambda_1 = (b + \sqrt{b^2 - 4ac})/2a \qquad\qquad\qquad (33)$$

$$\lambda_2 = (b - \sqrt{b^2 - 4ac})/2a. \qquad\qquad\qquad (34)$$

Then, substituting for b_{i-1}^* from (32) in (29), c_i^* may be written as:

$$c_i^* = (ac/\sqrt{b^2 - 4ac})(\lambda_1^i - \lambda_2^i). \qquad\qquad\qquad (35)$$

The expression f_i^* is obtained by substituting for b_i^* in (30) and solving recursively for $f_2^*, f_3^* \ldots$ This yields

$$f_i^* = (a/\sqrt{b^2 - 4ac}) \sum_{j=1} L_j f_j (-1)^{(i-j)} \tag{36}$$

where

$$L_j = \lambda_1^j - \lambda_2^j .$$

The matrix inversion is completed by solving the system of equations (27) starting with the last equation. Define $Z_i = \sum_{j=1}^{i} L_j f_j (-1)^{(i-j)}$.

Then

$$W_{n,j} = f_n^* / b_n^* = Z_n / a L_n$$

$$W_{n-1,j} = \frac{Z_{n-1}}{aL_n} - \frac{c}{a^2} \frac{L_{n-1}Z_n}{L_n L_{n+1}}$$

$$-- \circ \circ \circ --$$

$$W_{n-q'j} = \frac{L_{n-q}}{a} \left[\frac{Z_{n-q}}{L_{n-q}L_{n-q+1}} - \frac{c}{a} \frac{Z_{n-q+1}}{L_{n-q+1}L_{n-q+2}} \right. \tag{37}$$

$$\left. + \frac{c^2}{a^2} \frac{Z_{n-q+2}}{L_{n-q+2}L_{n-q+3}} + \dots - \right.$$

$$\left. + (\frac{-c}{a})^q \frac{Z_n}{L_n L_{n+1}} \right]$$

$$-- \circ \circ \circ -- .$$

Set $(n - q) = i$ and collect coefficients of $W_{i,j+1}$ in (37), recalling that $f_j = (1 - rk) W_{i,j+1}$. Denoting the coefficient of $W_{i,j+1}$ by $(1 - rk) p_i$, we have:

$$p_i = \frac{L_i^2}{a} \Sigma_{j=i}^n (c/a)^{j-i} (1/L_j L_{j+1}) \tag{38}$$

$$p_{i-q} = (-1)^q \frac{L_i L_{i-q}}{a} \Sigma_{j=i}^n (c/a)^{j-i} (1/L_j L_{j+1}) \tag{39}$$

$$p_{i+q} = (-1)^q \frac{L_i L_{i+q}}{a} \Sigma_{j=i+q}^n (c/a)^{j-(i+q)} (1/L_j L_{j+1}) . \tag{40}$$

The values of p_{i+q} ($q = 1-i, \dots, -1, 0, +1, \dots n-i$) are the elements of the ith row of $\underline{A}^{-1}$. We shall now show that as the boundaries become indefinitely remote p_{i+q} may be interpreted as the probability that the logarithm of the stock price will jump by qh. As the lower boundary becomes remote $i \to \infty$, while $(n - i) \to \infty$ as the upper boundary becomes remote.

First note that

$$\frac{L_i}{L_{i+q}} = \frac{\lambda_1^i - \lambda_2^i}{\lambda_1^{i+q} - \lambda_2^{i+q}} = \frac{1}{\lambda_1^q} \frac{1 - (\lambda_2/\lambda_1)^i}{1 - (\lambda_2/\lambda_1)^{i+q}} \tag{41}$$

and that since $|\lambda_2/\lambda_1| < 1$

$$\lim_{i \to \infty} \frac{L_i}{L_{i+q}} = \frac{1}{\lambda_1^q}. \tag{42}$$

Hence as $(n-i), i \to \infty$,[2]

$$\lim_{\substack{i \to \infty \\ n-i \to \infty}} p_i = p_o^* = \frac{1}{a} \left[\frac{1}{\lambda_1} + \frac{c}{a} \frac{1}{\lambda_1^3} + \frac{c^2}{a^2} \frac{1}{\lambda_1^5} \cdots \right] \tag{43}$$

$$= \lambda_1/(a\lambda_1^2 - c)$$

and from (38) and (39)

$$\lim_{\substack{i \to \infty \\ n-i \to \infty}} p_{i-q} = p_{-q}^* = (-\frac{1}{\lambda_1})^q p_i^*, \text{ for } q = 1, \ldots, \infty \tag{44}$$

$$\lim_{i \to \infty} p_{i+q} = p_q^* = (\frac{-c}{a\lambda_1})^q p_i^*, \text{ for } q = 1, \ldots, \infty. \tag{45}$$

Consider the sum of the $p_q^* (q = {}^{-\infty}, \ldots, {}^{+\infty}), S$:

$$S = p_o^* \left[(1 - \frac{c}{a\lambda_1} + (\frac{c}{a\lambda_1})^2 - (\frac{c}{a\lambda_1})^3 \ldots) - \frac{1}{\lambda_1}(1 - \frac{1}{\lambda_1} + (\frac{1}{\lambda_1})^2 \ldots) \right]$$

$$= p_o^* \left[\frac{a\lambda_1}{a\lambda_1+c} - \frac{1}{1-\lambda_1} \right] = p_o^* \left[\frac{a\lambda_1^2 - c}{(1+\lambda_1)(a\lambda_1+c)} \right] \tag{46}$$

and, substituting for p_o^* from (43)

$$S = \frac{\lambda_1}{(1+\lambda_1)(a\lambda_1+c)}. \tag{47}$$

But since λ_1 is a root of the auxiliary equation of (31) and $b = 1 - (a + c)$, $(1 + \lambda_1)(a\lambda_1 + c) = \lambda_1$ so that $S = 1$. Thus the sum of the weights $p_q^* (q = -\infty, \ldots, +\infty)$ equals 1.

---

[2] Since λ_1 and λ_2 are the roots of the auxiliary equation of the difference equation (31), $\lambda_1 \lambda_2 = c/a$. Therefore, $|c/a\lambda_1^2| = |\lambda_2/\lambda_1| < 1$.

Moreover each element p_q^* is nonnegative so long as[3]

$$h^2 \leq \sigma^4 / (r - \frac{1}{2}\sigma^2)^2. \tag{48}$$

Thus since the p_q^* are nonnegative and sum to unity, they may be interpreted as probabilities and we have

$$W_{i,j} = (1-rk) \sum_{q=-\infty}^{\infty} p_q^* \; W_{i+q,j+1} \tag{49}$$

$$\simeq \frac{1}{1+rk} \sum_{q=-\infty}^{\infty} p_q^* \; W_{i+q,j+1}.$$

Again, the value of the contingent claim at time instant j may be regarded as given by the expected value of its value at $(j + 1)$ discounted at the riskless rate, r. In this case the expected value of the claim at the next instant is obtained by assuming that y, the logarithm of the stock price, follows the generalized jump process

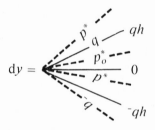

The local mean and variance of this process are shown in the Appendix to be given by

$$E[dy] = (r - \frac{1}{2}\sigma^2)k \tag{50}$$

$$V[dy] = \sigma^2 k + (r - \frac{1}{2}\sigma^2)^2 k^2. \tag{51}$$

Taking the diffusion limit as $k \to 0$, y again follows the stochastic differential equation (14) which again implies that the stochastic process for S is (15). Notice that for finite k the variance of the jump process approximation to the diffusion process is biased upwards by the square of the expected size of the jump. This suggests that the accuracy of the implicit method could be improved by adjusting the variance used in (19) by subtracting from the true variance the square of the expected change in the logarithm of the underlying asset value obtained under the assumption of risk neutrality.

---

[3]For a proof see Appendix.

Thus the implicit finite difference approximation to the log transform of the Black-Scholes differential equation (7) is also equivalent to approximating the diffusion process by a jump process. In this case the jump process is a generalized one which allows for the possibility that the stock price will jump to an infinity of possible future values rather than just three. It would appear that this "more realistic" approximation would result in more accurate determination of the value of the contingent claim, but this conjecture must wait upon detailed numerical analysis.

IV. Summary

In this paper we have established that the coefficients of the difference equation approximation to the Black-Scholes partial differential equation correspond to the probabilities of a jump process approximation to the underlying diffusion process. The simpler explicit finite difference approximation corresponds to a three-point jump process of the type discussed by Cox and Ross [6], while the more complex implicit finite difference approximation corresponds to a generalized jump process to an infinity of possible points.

Appendix

1. Condition for nonnegativity of weights in implicit solution.
(43) can also be written as

$$p_o^* = (b + \sqrt{b^2 - 4ac})/(b^2 - 4ac + b\sqrt{b^2 - 4ac})$$

but from (21) $b > 0$, and from (20), (21) and (22) $b^2 - 4ac > 0$. Therefore $p_o^* > 0$.

Then from (44) $p_{-q}^* > 0$, if $f\lambda_1 < 0$ which from (33) requires that $a < 0$. Then from (45), $p_q^* > 0$, also if $fc/a > 0$, so that c must also be negative. From (20) and (22), c and a are negative if and only if (48) is satisfied.

2. Mean and variance of the generalized Jump Process.

$$E(\mathrm{d}y) = h\left[\sum_{q=1}^{\infty} q\, p_q^* - \sum_{q=1}^{\infty} q\, p_{-q}^*\right].$$

Substituting for p_q^* and p_{-q}^* from (44) and (45),

$$E(\mathrm{d}y) = h\left[-\frac{c}{a\lambda_1}(1 - 2\frac{c}{a\lambda_1} + 3(\frac{c}{a\lambda_1})^2 - \ldots)\right.$$

$$\left. + \frac{1}{\lambda_1}(1 - \frac{2}{\lambda_1} + \frac{3}{\lambda_1^2} - \ldots)\right] p_i^*.$$

Summing and using (43),

$$E(dy) = h\left[-\frac{ac\lambda_1}{(a\lambda_1+c)}2 + \frac{\lambda_1}{(1+\lambda_1)}2\right]\frac{\lambda_1}{a\lambda_1^2-c}$$

$$E(dy) = (a-c)h = (r - \frac{1}{2}\sigma^2)k.$$

Q.E.D

$$V(dy) = \sum_{q=0}^{\infty} p_{-q}^*(-qh-(a-c)h)^2 + \sum_{q=1}^{\infty} p_q^*(qh-(a-c)h)^2$$

$$= h^2\left[\sum_{q=0}^{\infty} q^2\, p_{-q}^* + \sum_{q=1}^{\infty} q^2\, p_q^* -(a-c)^2\right].$$

Summing the series and substituting for p_o^* as above we obtain :

$$V(dy) = h^2\left[\{\frac{\lambda_1(1-\lambda_1)}{(1+\lambda_1)^3} - \frac{ac\lambda_1(a\lambda_1-c)}{(a\lambda_1+c)^3}\}\frac{\lambda_1}{a\lambda_1^2-c} - (a-c)^2\right].$$

Simplifying yields:

$$V(dy) = -h^2[(a+c)b + 4ac]$$

and, substituting for a, b, and c, we obtain (51).

References

1 Black, F., and M. Scholes. "The Pricing of Options and Corporate Liabilities." *Journal of Political Economy,* Vol. 81 (1973), pp. 637-659.

2 Boyle, P. "Options: A Monte Carlo Approach." *Journal of Financial Economics* (1976).

3 Brennan, M., and E. Schwartz. "The Pricing of Equity-Linked Life Insurance Policies with an Asset Value Guarantee." *Journal of Financial Economics,* Vol. 3 (1976), pp. 195-214.

4 ——— . "Convertible Bonds: Valuation and Optimal Strategies for Call and Conversion." *Journal of Finance* (1976).

5 ——— . "The Valuation of American Put Options." *Journal of Finance* (1976).

6 Cox, J. C., and S. A. Ross. "The Valuation of Options for Alternative Stochastic Processes." *Journal of Financial Economics,* Vol. 3 (1976), pp. 145-166.

7 ——— . "A Survey of Some New Results in Financial Option Pricing Theory." *Journal of Finance,* Vol. 31 (1976), pp. 383-402.

8 Ingersoll, J. "A Theoretical and Empirical Investigation of the Dual Purpose Funds: An Application of Contingent Claims Analysis." *Journal of Financial Economics,* Vol. 3 (1976), pp. 83-124.

9 ——— . "A Contingent Claims Valuation of Convertible Bonds." Unpublished Manuscript, University of Chicago (1976).

10 McCracken, D., and W. Dorn. "Numerical Methods and Fortran Programming." New York: John Wiley and Sons, Inc. (1969).

11 Merton, R. C. "Theory of Rational Option Pricing." *Bell Journal of Economics and Management Science,* Vol. 4 (1973), pp. 141-183.

12 ——— . "On the Pricing of Corporate Debt: The Risk Structure of Interest Rates." *Journal of Finance,* Vol. 29 (1974), pp. 449-470.

13 Parkinson, M. "Option Pricing: The American Put." *Journal of Business* (1976).

2

Option Pricing: A Simplified Approach*

John C. Cox
Stephen A. Ross
Mark Rubinstein

This paper presents a simple discrete-time model for valuing options. The fundamental economic principles of option pricing by arbitrage methods are particularly clear in this setting. Its development requires only elementary mathematics, yet it contains as a special limiting case the celebrated Black-Scholes model, which has previously been derived only by much more difficult methods. The basic model readily lends itself to generalization in many ways. Moreover, by its very construction, it gives rise to a simple and efficient numerical procedure for valuing options for which premature exercise may be optimal.

1. Introduction   An option is a security which gives its owner the right to trade in a fixed number of shares of a specified common stock at a fixed price at any time on or before a given date. The act of making this transaction is referred to as exercising the option. The fixed price is termed the striking price, and the given date, the expiration date. A call option gives the right to buy the shares; a put option gives the right to sell the shares.

John C. Cox, Massachusetts Institute of Technology, Cambridge, MA 02139, USA
Stanford University, Stanford, CA 94305, USA

Stephen A. Ross, Yale University, New Haven, CT 06520, USA

Mark Rubinstein, University of California, Berkeley, CA 94720, USA

*Our best thanks go to William Sharpe, who first suggested to us the advantages of the discrete-time approach to option pricing developed here. We are also grateful to our students over the past several years. Their favorable reactions to this way of presenting things encouraged us to write this article. We have received support from the National Science Foundation under Grants Nos. SOC-77-18087 and SOC-77-22301.

Received March 1979, revised version received July 1979

Options have been traded for centuries, but they remained relatively obscure financial instruments until the introduction of a listed options exchange in 1973. Since then, options trading has enjoyed an expansion unprecedented in American securities markets.

Option pricing theory has a long and illustrious history, but it also underwent a revolutionary change in 1973. At that time, Fischer Black and Myron Scholes presented the first completely satisfactory equilibrium option pricing model. In the same year, Robert Merton extended their model in several important ways. These path-breaking articles have formed the basis for many subsequent academic studies.

As these studies have shown, option pricing theory is relevant to almost every area of finance. For example, virtually all corporate securities can be interpreted as portfolios of puts and calls on the assets of the firm.[1] Indeed, the theory applies to a very general class of economic problems—the valuation of contracts where the outcome to each party depends on a quantifiable uncertain future event.

Unfortunately, the mathematical tools employed in the Black-Scholes and Merton articles are quite advanced and have tended to obscure the underlying economics. However, thanks to a suggestion by William Sharpe, it is possible to derive the same results using only elementary mathematics.[2]

In this article we will present a simple discrete-time option pricing formula. The fundamental economic principles of option valuation by arbitrage methods are particularly clear in this setting. Sections 2 and 3 illustrate and develop this model for a call option on a stock which pays no dividends. Section 4 shows exactly how the model can be used to lock in pure arbitrage profits if the market price of an option differs from the value given by the model. In section 5, we will show that our approach includes the Black-Scholes model as a special limiting case. By taking the limits in a different way, we will also obtain the Cox-Ross (1975) jump process model as another special case.

Other more general option pricing problems often seem immune to reduction to a simple formula. Instead, numerical procedures must be employed to value these more complex options. Michael Brennan and Eduardo Schwartz (1977) have provided many interesting results along these lines. However, their techniques are rather complicated and are not directly

---

[1]To take an elementary case, consider a firm with a single liability of a homogeneous class of pure discount bonds. The stockholders then have a 'call' on the assets of the firm which they can choose to exercise at the maturity date of the debt by paying its principal to the bondholders. In turn, the bonds can be interpreted as a portfolio containing a default-free loan with the same face value as the bonds and a short position in a put on the assets of the firm.

[2]Sharpe (1978) has partially developed this approach to option pricing in his excellent new book, *Investments*. Rendleman and Bartter (1978) have recently independently discovered a similar formulation of the option pricing problem.

related to the economic structure of the problem. Our formulation, by its very construction, leads to an alternative numerical procedure which is both simpler, and for many purposes, computationally more efficient.

Section 6 introduces these numerical procedures and extends the model to include puts and calls on stocks which pay dividends. Section 7 concludes the paper by showing how the model can be generalized in other important ways and discussing its essential role in valuation by arbitrage methods.

2. The basic idea   Suppose the current price of a stock is $S = \$50$, and at the end of a period of time, its price must be either $S* = \$25$ or $S* = \$100$. A call on the stock is available with a striking price of $K = \$50$, expiring at the end of the period.[3] It is also possible to borrow and lend at a 25% rate of interest. The one piece of information left unfurnished is the current value of the call, C. However, if riskless profitable arbitrage is not possible, we can deduce from the given information *alone* what the value of the call *must* be!

Consider forming the following levered hedge:

> (1) Write 3 calls at C each,
> (2) buy 2 shares at \$50 each, and
> (3) borrow \$40 at 25%, to be paid
>   back at the end of the period.

Table 1 gives the return from this hedge for each possible level of the stock price at expiration. Regardless of the outcome, the hedge exactly breaks even on the expiration date. Therefore, to prevent profitable riskless arbitrage, its current cost must be zero; that is,

$$3C - 100 + 40 = 0.$$

The current value of the call must then be $C = \$20$.

Table 1.   Arbitrage table illustrating the formation of a riskless hedge.

	Present date	Expiration date $S* = \$25$	$S* = \$100$
Write 3 calls	$3C$	-	-150
Buy 2 shares	-100	50	200
Borrow	40	-50	-50
Total		-	-

If the call were not priced at \$20, a sure profit would be possible. In particular, if $C = \$25$, the above hedge would yield a current cash inflow of

---

[3] To keep matters simple, assume for now that the stock will pay no cash dividends during the life of the call. We also ignore transaction costs, margin requirements and taxes.

$15 and would experience no further gain or loss in the future. On the other hand, if $C = \$15$, then the same thing could be accomplished by buying 3 calls, selling short 2 shares, and lending \$40.

Table 1 can be interpreted as demonstrating that *an appropriately levered position in stock will replicate the future returns of a call.* That is, if we buy shares and borrow against them in the right proportion, we can, in effect, duplicate a pure position in calls. In view of this, it should seem less surprising that all we needed to determine the *exact* value of the call was its *striking price, underlying stock price, range of movement in the underlying stock price, and the rate of interest.* What may seem more incredible is what we do not need to know: among other things, *we do not need to know the probability that the stock price will rise or fall.* Bulls and bears must agree on the value of the call, relative to its underlying stock price!

This example is very simple, but is shows several essential features of option pricing. And we will soon see that it is not as unrealistic as it seems.

3. The binomial option pricing formula

In this section, we will develop the framework illustrated in the example into a complete valuation method. We begin by assuming that the stock price follows a multiplicative binomial process over discrete periods. The rate of return on the stock over each period can have two possible values: $u - 1$ with probability q, or $d - 1$ with probability $1 - q$. Thus, if the current stock price is S, the stock price at the end of the period will be either uS or dS. We can represent this movement with the following diagram:

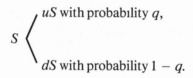

We also assume that the interest rate is constant. Individuals may borrow or lend as much as they wish at this rate. To focus on the basic issues, we will continue to assume that there are no taxes, transaction costs, or margin requirements. Hence, individuals are allowed to sell short any security and receive full use of the proceeds.[4]

Letting r denote one plus the riskless interest rate over one period, we require $u > r > d$. If these inequalities did not hold, there would be profitable riskless arbitrage opportunities involving only the stock and riskless borrowing and lending.[5]

To see how to value a call on this stock, we start with the simplest situation: the expiration date is just one period away. Let C be the current value of the

---

[4]Of course, restitution is required for payouts made to securities held short.
[5]We will ignore the uninteresting special case where q is zero or one and $u = d = r$.

call, C_u be its value at the end of the period if the stock price goes to uS, and C_d be its value at the end of the period if the stock price goes to dS. Since there is now only one period remaining in the life of the call, we know that the terms of its contract and a rational exercise policy imply that $C_u = \max[0, uS - K]$ and $C_d = \max[0, dS - K]$. Therefore,

$$C \begin{cases} C_u = \max[0, uS - K] \text{ with probability } q, \\ \\ C_d = \max[0, dS - K] \text{ with probability } 1 - q. \end{cases}$$

Suppose we form a portfolio containing Δ shares of stock and the dollar amount B in riskless bonds.[6] This will cost $\Delta S + B$. At the end of the period, the value of this portfolio will be

$$\Delta S + B \begin{cases} \Delta uS + rB \text{ with probability } q, \\ \\ \Delta dS + rB \text{ with probability } 1 - q. \end{cases}$$

Since we can select Δ and B in any way we wish, suppose we choose them to equate the end-of-period values of the portfolio and the call for each possible outcome. This requires that

$$\Delta uS + rB = C_u,$$

$$\Delta dS + rB = C_d.$$

Solving these equations, we find

$$\Delta = \frac{C_u - C_d}{(u - d)S}, \qquad B = \frac{uC_d - dC_u}{(u - d)r}. \tag{1}$$

With Δ and B chosen in this way, we will call this the hedging portfolio.

If there are to be no riskless arbitrage opportunities, the current value of the call, C, cannot be less than the current value of the hedging portfolio, $\Delta S + B$. If it were, we could make a riskless profit with no net investment by buying the call and selling the portfolio. It is tempting to say that it also cannot be worth more, since then we would have a riskless arbitrage opportunity by reversing our procedure and selling the call and buying the portfolio. But this overlooks the fact that the person who bought the call we sold has the right to exercise it immediately.

[6]Buying bonds is the same as lending; selling them is the same as borrowing.

Suppose that $\Delta S + B < S - K$. If we try to make an arbitrage profit by selling calls for more than $\Delta S + B$, but less than $S - K$, then we will soon find that we are the source of arbitrage profits rather than their recipient. Anyone could make an arbitrage profit by buying our calls and exercising them immediately.

We might hope that we will be spared this embarrassment because everyone will somehow find it advantageous to hold the calls for one more period as an investment rather than take a quick profit by exercising them immediately. But each person will reason in the following way. If I do not exercise now, I will receive the same payoff as a portfolio with ΔS in stock and B in bonds. If I do exercise now, I can take the proceeds, $S - K$, buy this same portfolio and some extra bonds as well, and have a higher payoff in every possible circumstance. Consequently, no one would be willing to hold the calls for one more period.

Summing up all of this, we conclude that if there are to be no riskless arbitrage opportunities, it must be true that

$$
\begin{aligned}
C &= \Delta S + B \\
&= \frac{C_u - C_d}{u - d} + \frac{uC_d - dC_u}{(u - d)r} \\
&= \left[\left(\frac{r - d}{u - d} \right) C_u + \left(\frac{u - r}{u - d} \right) C_d \right] \Big/ r,
\end{aligned}
$$

(2)

if this value is greater than $S - K$, and if not, $C = S - K$.[7]

Eq. (2) can be simplified by defining

$$
p \equiv \frac{r - d}{u - d} \text{ and } 1 - p \equiv \frac{u - r}{u - d},
$$

so that we can write

$$
C = [pC_u + (1 - p)C_d]/r.
$$

(3)

It is easy to see that in the present case, with no dividends, this will always be greater than $S - K$ as long as the interest rate is positive. To avoid spending time on the unimportant situations where the interest rate is less

[7]In some applications of the theory to other areas, it is useful to consider options which can be exercised only on the expiration date. These are usually termed European options. Those which can be exercised at any earlier time as well, such as we have been examining here, are then referred to as American options. Our discussion could be easily modified to include European calls. Since immediate exercise is then precluded, their values would always be given by (2), even if this is less than $S - K$.

than or equal to zero, we will now assume that r is always greater than one. Hence, (3) is the exact formula for the value of a call one period prior to expiration in terms of $S, K, u, d,$ and r.

To confirm this, note that if $uS \leq K$, then $S < K$ and $C = 0$, so $C > S - K$. Also if $dS \geq K$, then $C = S - (K/r) > S - K$. The remaining possibility is $uS > K > dS$. In this case, $C = p(uS - K)/r$. This is greater than $S - K$ if $(1 - p)dS > (p - r)K$, which is certainly true as long as $r > 1$.

This formula has a number of notable features. First, the probability q does not appear in the formula. This means, surprisingly, that even if different investors have different subjective probabilities about an upward or downward movement in the stock, they could still agree on the relationship of C to $S, u, d,$ and r.

Second, the value of the call does not depend on investors' attitudes toward risk. In constructing the formula, the only assumption we made about an individual's behavior was that he prefers more wealth to less wealth and therefore has an incentive to take advantage of profitable riskless arbitrage opportunities. We would obtain the same formula whether investors are risk-averse or risk-preferring.

Third, the only random variable on which the call value depends is the stock price itself. In particular, it does not depend on the random prices of other securities or portfolios, such as the market portfolio containing all securities in the economy. If another pricing formula involving other variables was submitted as giving equilibrium market prices, we could immediately show that it was incorrect by using our formula to make riskless arbitrage profits while trading at those prices.

It is easier to understand these features if it is remembered that the formula is only a relative pricing relationship giving C in terms of $S, u, d,$ and r. Investors' attitudes toward risk and the characteristics of other assets may indeed influence call values indirectly, through their effect on these variables, but they will not be separate determinants of call value.

Finally, observe that $p \equiv (r - d)/(u - d)$ is always greater than zero and less than one, so it has the properties of a probability. In fact, p is the value q would have in equilibrium if investors were risk-neutral. To see this, note that the expected rate of return on the stock would then be the riskless interest rate, so

$$q(uS) + (1 - q)(dS) = rS,$$

and

$$q = (r - d)/(u - d) = p.$$

Hence, the value of the call can be interpreted as the expectation of its discounted future value in a risk-neutral world. In light of our earlier observations, this is not surprising. Since the formula does not involve q or any measure of attitudes toward risk, then it must be the same for any set of preferences, including risk neutrality.

It is important to note that this does not imply that the equilibrium expected rate of return on the call is the riskless interest rate. Indeed, our argument has shown that, in equilibrium, holding the call over the period is exactly equivalent to holding the hedging portfolio. Consequently, the risk and expected rate of return of the call must be the same as that of the hedging portfolio. It can be shown that $\Delta \geq 0$ and $B \leq 0$, so the hedging portfolio is equivalent to a particular levered long position in the stock. In equilibrium, the same is true for the call. Of course, if the call is currently mispriced, its risk and expected return over the period will differ from that of the hedging portfolio.

Now we can consider the next simplest situation: a call with two periods remaining before its expiration date. In keeping with the binomial process, the stock can take on three possible values after two periods,

$$
S \left\{
\begin{array}{l}
uS \left\{
\begin{array}{l}
u^2 S, \\
\\
duS, \\
\end{array}
\right. \\
\\
dS \left\{
\begin{array}{l}
\\
d^2 S;
\end{array}
\right.
\end{array}
\right.
$$

similarly, for the call,

$$
C \left\{
\begin{array}{l}
C_u \left\{
\begin{array}{l}
C_{uu} = \max [0, u^2 S - K], \\
\\
C_{du} = \max [0, duS - K], \\
\end{array}
\right. \\
\\
C_d \left\{
\begin{array}{l}
\\
C_{dd} = \max [0, d^2 S - K].
\end{array}
\right.
\end{array}
\right.
$$

C_{uu} stands for the value of a call two periods from the current time if the stock price moves upward each period; C_{du} and C_{dd} have analogous definitions.

At the end of the current period there will be one period left in the life of the call and we will be faced with a problem identical to the one we just solved. Thus, from our previous analysis, we know that when there are two periods left,

$$C_u = [pC_{uu} + (1 - p)C_{ud}]/r,$$

and

$$C_d = [pC_{du} + (1 - p)C_{dd}]/r. \tag{4}$$

Again we can select a portfolio with ΔS in stock and B in bonds whose end-of-period value will be C_u if the stock price goes to uS and C_d if the stock price goes to dS. Indeed, the functional form of Δ and B remains unchanged. To get the new values of Δ and B, we simply use eq. (1) with the new values of C_u and C_d.

Can we now say, as before, that an opportunity for profitable riskless arbitrage will be available if the current price of the call is not equal to the new value of this portfolio or $S - K$, whichever is greater? Yes, but there is an important difference. With one period to go, we could plan to lock in a riskless profit by selling an overpriced call and using part of the proceeds to buy the hedging portfolio. At the end of the period, we knew that the market price of the call must be equal to the value of the portfolio, so the entire position could be safely liquidated at that point. But this was true only because the end of the period was the expiration date. Now we have no such guarantee. At the end of the current period, when there is still one period left, the market price of the call could still be in disequilibrium and be greater than the value of the hedging portfolio. If we closed out the position then, selling the portfolio and repurchasing the call, we could suffer a loss which would more than offset our original profit. However, we could always avoid this loss by maintaining the portfolio for one more period. The value of the portfolio at the end of the current period will always be exactly sufficient to purchase the portfolio we would want to hold over the last period. In effect, we would have to readjust the proportions in the hedging portfolio, but we would not have to put up any more money.

Consequently, we conclude that even with two periods to go, there is a strategy we could follow which would guarantee riskless profits with no net investment if the current market price of a call differs from the maximum of $\Delta S + B$ and $S - K$. Hence, the larger of these is the current value of the call.

Since Δ and B have the same functional form in each period, the current value of the call in terms of C_u and C_d will again be $C = [pC_u + (1 - p)C_d]/r$ if this is greater than $S - K$, and $C = S - K$ otherwise. By substituting from eq. (4) into the former expression, and noting that $C_{du} = C_{ud}$, we obtain

$$C = [p^2 C_{uu} + 2p(1-p)C_{ud} + (1-p)^2 C_{dd}]/r^2$$

$$= [p^2 \max[0, u^2 S - K] + 2p(1-p)\max[0, duS - K]$$

$$+ (1-p)^2 \max[0, d^2 S - K]]/r^2. \tag{5}$$

A little algebra shows that this is always greater than $S - K$ if, as assumed, r is always greater than one, so this expression gives the exact value of the call.[8]

All of the observations made about formula (3) also apply to formula (5), except that the number of periods remaining until expiration, n, now emerges clearly as an additional determinant of the call value. For formula (5), $n = 2$. That is, the full list of variables determining C is S, K, n, u, d, and r.

We now have a recursive procedure for finding the value of a call with any number of periods to go. By starting at the expiration date and working backwards, we can write down the general valuation formula for any n:

$$C = \left[\sum_{j=0}^{n} \left(\frac{n!}{j!(n-j)!} \right) p^j (1-p)^{n-j} \max[0, u^j d^{n-j} S - K] \right] \Big/ r^n. \tag{6}$$

This gives us the complete formula, but with a little additional effort we can express it in a more convenient way.

Let a stand for the minimum number of upward moves which the stock must make over the next n periods for the call to finish in-the-money. Thus a will be the smallest non-negative integer such that $u^a d^{n-a} S > K$. By taking the natural logarithm of both sides of this inequality, we could write a as the smallest non-negative integer greater than $\log(K/Sd^n)/\log(u/d)$.

For all $j < a$,

$$\max[0, u^j d^{n-j} S - K] = 0,$$

and for all $j \geq a$,

$$\max[0, u^j d^{n-j} S - K] = u^j d^{n-j} S - K.$$

---

[8]In the current situation, with no dividends, we can show by a simple direct argument that if there are no arbitrage opportunities, then the call value must always be greater than $S - K$ before the expiration date. Suppose that the call is selling for $S - K$. Then there would be an easy arbitrage strategy which would require no initial investment and would always have a positive return. All we would have to do is buy the call, short the stock, and invest K dollars in bonds. See Merton (1973). In the general case, with dividends, such an argument is no longer valid, and we must use the procedure of checking every period.

Therefore,

$$C = \left[\sum_{j=a}^{n} \left(\frac{n!}{j!(n-j)!} \right) p^j (1-p)^{n-j} [u^j d^{n-j} S - K] \right] \Big/ r^n.$$

Of course, if $a > n$, the call will finish out-of-the-money even if the stock moves upward every period, so its current value must be zero.

By breaking up C into two terms, we can write

$$C = S \left[\sum_{j=a}^{n} \left(\frac{n!}{j!(n-j)!} \right) p^j (1-p)^{n-j} \left(\frac{u^j d^{n-j}}{r^n} \right) \right]$$

$$- Kr^{-n} \left[\sum_{j=a}^{n} \left(\frac{n!}{j!(n-j)!} \right) p^j (1-p)^{n-j} \right].$$

Now, the latter bracketed expression is the complementary binomial distribution function $\phi[a; n, p]$. The first bracketed expression can also be interpreted as a complementary binomial distribution function $\phi[a; n, p']$, where

$$p' \equiv (u/r)p \text{ and } 1 - p' \equiv (d/r)(1-p).$$

p' is a probability, since $0 < p' < 1$. To see this, note that $p < (r/u)$ and

$$p^j (1-p)^{n-j} \left(\frac{u^j d^{n-j}}{r^n} \right) = \left[\frac{u}{r} p \right]^j \left[\frac{d}{r} (1-p) \right]^{n-j}$$

$$= p'^j (1-p')^{n-j}.$$

In summary:

Binomial Option Pricing Formula

$$C = S\phi[a; n, p'] - Kr^{-n}\phi[a; n, p],$$

where

$$p \equiv (r-d)/(u-d) \text{ and } p' \equiv (u/r)p,$$

$a \equiv$ the smallest non-negative integer greater than $\log(K/Sd^n), \log(u/d)$

If $a > n$, $C = 0$.

It is now clear that all of the comments we made about the one period valuation formula are valid for any number of periods. In particular, the value of a call should be the expectation, in a risk-neutral world, of the discounted value of the payoff it will receive. In fact, that is exactly what eq. (6) says. Why, then, should we waste time with the recursive procedure when we can write down the answer in one direct step? The reason is that while this one-step approach is always technically correct, it is really useful only if we know in advance the circumstances in which a rational individual would prefer to exercise the call before the expiration date. If we do not know this, we have no way to compute the required expectation. In the present example, a call on a stock paying no dividends, it happens that we can determine this information from other sources: the call should never be exercised before the expiration date. As we will see in section 6, with puts or with calls on stocks which pay dividends, we will not be so lucky. Finding the optimal exercise strategy will be an integral part of the valuation problem. The full recursive procedure will then be necessary.

For some readers, an alternative 'complete markets' interpretation of our binomial approach may be instructive. Suppose that π_u and π_d represent the state-contingent discount rates to states u and d, respectively. Therefore, π_u would be the current price of one dollar received at the end of the period, if and only if state u occurs. Each security—a riskless bond, the stock, and the option—must all have returns discounted to the present by π_u and π_d if no riskless arbitrage opportunities are available. Therefore,

$$1 = \pi_u r + \pi_d r,$$

$$S = \pi_u (uS) + \pi_d (dS),$$

$$C = \pi_u C_u + \pi_d C_d.$$

The first two equations, for the bond and the stock, imply

$$\pi_u = \left(\frac{r-d}{u-d} \right) \frac{1}{r} \text{ and } \pi_d = \left(\frac{u-r}{u-d} \right) \frac{1}{r}.$$

Substituting these equalities for the state-contingent prices in the last equation for the option yields eq. (3).

It is important to realize that we are not assuming that the riskless bond and the stock and the option are the only three securities in the economy, or that other securities must follow a binomial process. Rather, however these securities are priced in relation to others in equilibrium, among themselves they must conform to the above relationships.

From either the hedging or complete markets approaches, it should be clear that three-state or trinomial stock price movements will not lead to an option pricing formula based solely on arbitrage considerations. Suppose, for example, that over each period the stock price could move to uS or dS or remain the same at S. A choice of Δ and B which would equate the returns in two states could not in the third. That is, a riskless arbitrage position could not be taken. Under the complete markets interpretation, with three equations in now three unknown state-contingent prices, we would lack the redundant equation necessary to price one security in terms of the other two.

4. Riskless trading strategies

The following numerical example illustrates how we could use the formula if the current *market price M* ever diverged from its *formula value C*. If $M > C$, we would hedge, and if $M < C$, 'reverse hedge', to try and lock in a profit. Suppose the values of the underlying variables are

$$S = 80, \quad n = 3, \quad K = 80, \quad u = 1.5, \quad d = 0.5, \quad r = 1.1.$$

In this case, $p = (r - d)/(u - d) = 0.6$. The relevant values of the discount factor are

$$r^{-1} = 0.909, \quad r^{-2} = 0.826, \quad r^{-3} = 0.751.$$

The paths the stock price may follow and their corresponding probabilities (using probability p) are, when $n = 3$, with $S = 80$,

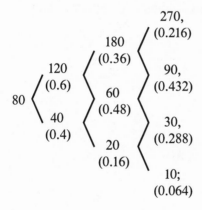

when $n = 2$, if $S = 120$,

180
(0.6)

270,
(0.36)

120

90,
(0.48)

60
(0.4)

30;
(0.16)

when $n = 2$, if $S = 40$,

$$40 \begin{cases} 60 \\ (0.6) \\ \\ 20 \\ (0.4) \end{cases} \begin{matrix} 90, \\ (0.36) \\ \\ 30, \\ (0.48) \\ \\ 10. \\ (0.16) \end{matrix}$$

Using the formula, the current value of the call would be

$$C = 0.751[0.064(0) + 0.288(0) + 0.432(90 - 80) + 0.216(270 - 80)]$$

$$= 34.065.$$

Recall that to form a riskless hedge, for each call we sell, we buy and subsequently keep adjusted a portfolio with ΔS in stock and B in bonds, where $\Delta = (C_u - C_d)/(u - d)S$. The following tree diagram gives the paths the call value may follow and the corresponding values of Δ:

$$34.065 \atop (0.719) \begin{cases} 60.463 \\ (0.848) \\ \\ 2.974 \\ (0.136) \end{cases} \begin{cases} 107.272 \\ (1.00) \\ \\ 5.454 \\ (0.167) \\ \\ 0 \\ (0.00) \end{cases} \begin{matrix} 190, \\ \\ 10, \\ \\ 0, \\ \\ 0. \end{matrix}$$

With this preliminary analysis, we are prepared to use the formula to take advantage of mispricing in the market. Suppose that when $n = 3$, the market price of the call is 36. Our formula tells us the call should be worth 34.065. The option is overpriced, so we could plan to sell it and assure ourselves of a profit equal to the mispricing differential. Here are the steps you could take for a typical path the stock might follow.

Step 1 ($n = 3$): Sell the call for 36. Take 34.065 of this and invest it in a portfolio containing $\Delta = 0.719$ shares of stock by borrowing $0.719(80) - 34.065 = 23.455$. Take the remainder, $36 - 34.065 = 1.935$, and put it in the bank.

Step 2 ($n = 2$): Suppose the stock goes to 120 so that the new Δ is 0.848. Buy $0.848 - 0.719 = 0.129$ more shares of stock at 120 per share for a total expenditure of 15.480. Borrow to pay the bill. With an interest rate of 0.1, you already owe $23.455(1.1) = 25.801$. Thus, your total current indebtedness is $25.801 + 15.480 = 41.281$.

Step 3 ($n = 1$): Suppose the stock price now goes to 60. The new Δ is 0.167. Sell $0.848 - 0.167 = 0.681$ shares at 60 per share, taking in $0.681(60) = 40.860$. Use this to pay back part of your borrowing. Since you now owe $41.281(1.1) = 45.409$, the repayment will reduce this to $45.409 - 40.860 = 4.549$.

Step 4d ($n = 0$): Suppose the stock price now goes to 30. The call you sold has expired worthless. You own 0.167 shares of stock selling at 30 per share, for a total value of $0.167(30) = 5$. Sell the stock and repay the $4.549(1.1) = 5$ that you now owe on the borrowing. Go back to the bank and withdraw your original deposit, which has now grown to $1.935(1.1)^3 = 2.575$.

Step 4u ($n = 0$): Suppose, instead, the stock price goes to 90. The call you sold is in the money at the expiration date. Buy back the call, or buy one share of stock and let it be exercised, incurring a loss of $90 - 80 = 10$ either way. Borrow to cover this, bringing your current indebtedness to $5 + 10 = 15$. You own 0.167 shares of stock selling at 90 per share, for a total value of $0.167(90) = 15$. Sell the stock and repay the borrowing. Go back to the bank and withdraw your original deposit, which has now grown to $1.935(1.1)^3 = 2.575$.

In summary, if we were correct in our original analysis about stock price movements (which did not involve the unenviable task of predicting whether the stock price would go up or down), and if we faithfully adjust our portfolio as prescribed by the formula, then we can be assured of walking away in the clear at the expiration date, while still keeping the original differential and the interest it has accumulated. It is true that closing out the position before the expiration date, which involves buying back the option at its then current market price, might produce a loss which would more than offset our profit, but this loss could always be avoided by waiting until the expiration date. Moreover, if the market price comes into line with the formula value before the expiration date, we can close out the position then with no loss and be rid of the concern of keeping the portfolio adjusted.

It still might seem that we are depending on the rational behavior by the person who bought the call we sold. If instead he behaves foolishly and exercises at the wrong time, could he make things worse for us as well as for himself? Fortunately, the answer is no. Mistakes on his part can only mean greater profits for us. Suppose that he exercises too soon. In that circumstance, the hedging portfolio will always be worth more than $S - K$, so we could close out the position then with an extra profit.

Suppose, instead, that he fails to exercise when it would be optimal to do so. Again there is no problem. Since exercise is now optimal, our hedging portfolio will be worth $S - K$.[9] If he had exercised, this would be exactly sufficient to meet the obligation and close out the position. Since he did not, the call will be held at least one more period, so we calculate the new values of C_u and C_d and revise our hedging portfolio accordingly. But now the amount required for the portfolio, $\Delta S + B$, is less than the amount we have available, $S - K$. We can withdraw these extra profits now and still maintain the hedging portfolio. The longer the holder of the call goes on making mistakes, the better off we will be.

Consequently, we can be confident that things will eventually work out right no matter what the other party does. The return on our total position, when evaluated at prevailing market prices at intermediate times, may be negative. But over a period ending no later than the expiration date, it will be positive.

In conducting the hedging operation, the essential thing was to maintain the proper proportional relationship: for each call we are short, we hold Δ shares of stock and the dollar amount B in bonds in the hedging portfolio. To emphasize this, we will refer to the number of shares held for each call as the hedge ratio. In our example, we kept the number of calls constant and made adjustments by buying or selling stock and bonds. As a result, our profit was independent of the market price of the call between the time we initiated the hedge and the expiration date. If things got worse before they got better, it did not matter to us.

Instead, we could have made the adjustments by keeping the number of shares of stock constant and buying or selling calls and bonds. However, this could be dangerous. Suppose that after initiating the position, we needed to increase the hedge ratio to maintain the proper proportions. This can be achieved in two ways:

(a) buy more stock, or
(b) buy back some of the calls.

If we adjust through the stock, there is no problem. If we insist on adjusting through the calls, not only is the hedge no longer riskless, but it could even end up losing money! This can happen if the call has become even more overpriced. We would then be closing out part of our position in calls at a loss. To remain hedged, the number of calls we would need to buy back depends on their value, not their price. Therefore, since we are uncertain about their price, we then become uncertain about the return from the hedge. Worse yet, if the call price gets high enough, the loss on the closed portion of our position could throw the hedge operation into an overall loss.

[9] If we were reverse hedging by buying an undervalued call and selling the hedging portfolio, then we would ourselves want to exercise at this point. Since we will receive $S - K$ from exercising, this will be exactly enough money to buy back the hedging portfolio.

To see how this could happen, let us rerun the hedging operation, where we adjust the hedge ratio by buying and selling calls.

Step 1 ($n = 3$): Same as before.

Step 2 ($n = 2$): Suppose the stock goes to 120, so that the new $\Delta = 0.848$. The call price has gotten further out of line and is now selling for 75. Since its value is 60.463, it is now overpriced by 14.537. With 0.719 shares, you must buy back $1 - 0.848 = 0.152$ calls to produce a hedge ratio of $0.848 = 0.719/0.848$. This costs $75(0.152) = 11.40$. Borrow to pay the bill. With the interest rate of 0.1, you already owe $23.455(1.1) = 25.801$. Thus, your total current indebtedness is $25.801 + 11.40 = 37.201$.

Step 3 ($n = 1$): Suppose the stock goes to 60 and the call is selling for 5.454. Since the call is now fairly valued, no further excess profits can be made by continuing to hold the position. Therefore, liquidate by selling your 0.719 shares for $0.719(60) = 43.14$ and close out the call position by buying back 0.848 calls for $0.848(5.454) = 4.625$. This nets $43.14 - 4.625 = 38.515$. Use this to pay back part of your borrowing. Since you now owe $37.20(1.1) = 40.921$, after repayment you owe 2.406. Go back to the bank and withdraw your original deposit, which has now grown to $1.935(1.1)^2 = 2.341$. Unfortunately, after using this to repay our remaining borrowing, you still owe 0.065.

Since we adjusted our position at Step 2 by buying overpriced calls, our profit is reduced. Indeed, since the calls were considerably overpriced, we actually lost money despite apparent profitability of the position at Step 1. We can draw the following adjustment rule from our experiment: *To adjust a hedged position, never buy an overpriced option or sell an underpriced option.* As a corollary, whenever we can adjust a hedged position by buying more of an underpriced option or selling more of an overpriced option, our profit will be enhanced if we do so. For example, at Step 3 in the original hedging illustration, had the call still been overpriced, it would have been better to adjust the position by selling more calls rather than selling stock. In summary, by choosing the right side of the position to adjust at intermediate dates, *at a minimum* we can be assured of earning the original differential and its accumulated interest, and we may earn considerably more.

5. Limiting cases   In reading the previous sections, there is a natural tendency to associate with each period some particular length of calendar time, perhaps a day. With this in mind, you may have had two objections. In the first place, prices a day from now may take on many more than just two possible values. Furthermore, the market is not open for trading only once a day, but, instead, trading takes place almost continuously.

These objections are certainly valid. Fortunately, our option pricing approach has the flexibility to meet them. Although it might have been natural to think of a period as one day, there was nothing that forced us to do so. We could have taken it to be a much shorter interval—say an hour—or even a minute. By doing so, we have met both objections simultaneously. Trading would take place far more frequently, and the stock price could take on hundreds of values by the end of the day.

However, if we do this, we have to make some other adjustments to keep the probability small that the stock price will change by a large amount over a minute. We do not want the stock to have the same percentage up and down moves for one minute as it did before for one day. But again there is no need for us to have to use the same values. We could, for example, think of the price as making only a very small percentage change over each minute.

To make this more precise, suppose that h represents the elapsed time between successive stock price changes. That is, if t is the fixed length of calendar time to expiration, and n is the number of periods of length h prior to expiration, then

$$h \equiv t/n.$$

As trading takes place more and more frequently, h gets closer and closer to zero. We must then adjust the interval-dependent variables r, u, and d in such a way that we obtain empirically realistic results as h becomes smaller, or, equivalently, as $n \to \infty$.

When we were thinking of the periods as having a fixed length, r represented both the interest rate over a fixed length of calendar time and the interest rate over one period. Now we need to make a distinction between these two meanings. We will let r continue to mean one plus the interest rate over a fixed length of calendar time. When we have occasion to refer to one plus the interest rate over a period (trading interval) of length h, we will use the symbol $\hat{r}$.

Clearly, the size of $\hat{r}$ depends on the number of subintervals, n, into which t is divided. Over the n periods until expiration, the total return is $\hat{r}^n$, where $n = t/h$. Now not only do we want $\hat{r}$ to depend on n, but we want it to depend on n in a particular way—so that as n changes the total return $\hat{r}^n$ over the fixed time t remains the same. This is because the interest rate obtainable over some fixed length of calendar time should have nothing to do with how we choose to think of the length of the time interval h.

If r (without the 'hat') denotes one plus the rate of interest over a *fixed* unit of calendar time, then over elapsed time t, r^t is the total return.[10]

---

[10]The scale of this unit (perhaps a day, or a year) is unimportant as long as r and t are expressed in the same scale.

Observe that this measure of total return does not depend on n. As we have argued, we want to choose the dependence of $\hat{r}$ on n, so that

$$\hat{r}^n = r^t,$$

for any choice of n. Therefore, $\hat{r} = r^{t/n}$. This last equation shows how $\hat{r}$ must depend on n for the total return over elapsed time t to be independent of n.

We also need to define u and d in terms of n. At this point, there are two significantly different paths we can take. Depending on the definitions we choose, as $n \to \infty$ (or, equivalently, as $h \to 0$), we can have either a continuous or a jump stochastic process. In the first situation, very small random changes in the stock price will be occurring in each very small time interval. The stock price will fluctuate incessantly, but its path can be drawn without lifting pen from paper. In contrast, in the second case, the stock price will usually move in a smooth deterministic way, but will occasionally experience sudden discontinuous changes. Both can be derived from our binomial process simply by choosing how u and d depend on n. We examine in detail only the continuous process which leads to the option pricing formula originally derived by Fischer Black and Myron Scholes. Subsequently, we indicate how to develop the jump process formula originally derived by John Cox and Stephen Ross.

Recall that we supposed that over each period the stock price would experience a one plus rate of return of u with probability q and d with probability $1 - q$. It will be easier and clearer to work, instead, with the natural logarithm of the one plus rate of return, $\log u$ or $\log d$. This gives the continuously compounded rate of return on the stock over each period. It is a random variable which, in each period, will be equal to $\log u$ with probability q and $\log d$ with probability $1 - q$.

Consider a typical sequence of five moves, say u, d, u, u, d. Then the final stock price will be $S^* = uduud\,S$; $S^*/S = u^3 d^2$, and $\log(S^*/S) = 3 \log u + 2 \log d$. More generally, over n periods,

$$\log(S^*/S) = j \log u + (n - j) \log d = j \log(u/d) + n \log d,$$

where j is the (random) number of upward moves occurring during the n periods to expiration. Therefore, the expected value of $\log(S^*/S)$ is

$$E[\log(S^*/S)] = \log(u/d) \cdot E(j) + n \log d,$$

and its variance is

$$\mathrm{var}[\log(S^*/S)] = [\log(u/d)]^2 \cdot \mathrm{var}(j).$$

Each of the n possible upward moves has probability q. Thus, $E(j) = nq$. Also, since the variance each period is $q(1 - q)^2 + (1 - q)(0 - q)^2 = q(1 - q)$, then var $(j) = nq(1 - q)$. Combining all of this, we have

$$E[\log(S*/S)] = [q\log(u/d) + \log d]n \equiv \hat{\mu}n,$$

$$\text{var}[\log(S*/S)] = q(1 - q)[\log(u/d)]^2 n \equiv \hat{\sigma}^2 n.$$

Let us go back to our discussion. We were considering dividing up our original longer time period (a day) into many shorter periods (a minute or even less). Our procedure calls for, over a fixed length of calendar time t, making n larger and larger. Now if we held everything else constant while we let n become large, we would be faced with the problem we talked about earlier. In fact, we would certainly not reach a reasonable conclusion if either $\hat{\mu}n$ or $\hat{\sigma}^2 n$ went to zero or infinity as n became large. Since t is a fixed length of time, in searching for a realistic result, we must make the appropriate adjustments in u, d, and q. In doing that, we would at least want the mean and variance of the continuously compounded rate of return of the assumed stock price movement to coincide with that of the actual stock price as $n \to \infty$. Suppose we label the actual empirical values of $\hat{\mu}n$ and $\hat{\sigma}^2 n$ as μt and $\sigma^2 t$, respectively. Then we would want to choose u, d, and q, so that

$$[q\log(u/d) + \log d]n \to \mu t$$
$$q(1 - q)[\log(u/d)]^2 n \to \sigma^2 t \qquad \text{as } n \to \infty.$$

A little algebra shows we can accomplish this by letting

$$u = e^{\sigma\sqrt{t/n}}, \quad d = e^{-\sigma\sqrt{t/n}}, \quad q = \tfrac{1}{2} + \tfrac{1}{2}(\mu/\sigma)\sqrt{t/n}.$$

In this case, for any n,

$$\hat{\mu}n = \mu t \quad \text{and} \quad \hat{\sigma}^2 n = [\sigma^2 - \mu^2(t/n)]t.$$

Clearly, as $n \to \infty$, $\hat{\sigma}^2 n \to \sigma^2 t$, while $\hat{\mu}n = \mu t$ for all values of n.

Alternatively, we could have chosen u, d, and q so that the mean and variance of the future stock price for the discrete binomial process approach the prespecified mean and variance of the actual stock price as $n \to \infty$. However, just as we would expect, the same values will accomplish this as well. Since this would not change our conclusions, and it is computationally more convenient to work with the continuously compounded rates of return, we will proceed in that way.

This satisfies our initial requirement that the limiting means and variances coincide, but we still need to verify that we are arriving at a sensible limiting probability distribution of the continuously compounded rate of return. The mean and variance only describe certain aspects of that distribution.

For our model, the random continuously compounded rate of return over a period of length t is the sum of n independent random variables, each of which can take the value $\log u$ with probability q and $\log d$ with probability $1 - q$. We wish to know about the distribution of this sum as n becomes large and $q, u,$ and d are chosen in the way described. We need to remember that as we change $n,$ we are not simply adding one more random variable to the previous sum, but instead are changing the probabilities and possible outcomes for every member of the sum. At this point, we can rely on a form of the central limit theorem which, when applied to our problem, says that, as $n \to \infty$, if

$$\frac{q|\log u - \hat{\mu}|^3 + (1 - q)|\log d - \hat{\mu}|^3}{\hat{\sigma}^3 \sqrt{n}} \to 0,$$

then

$$\text{Prob}\left[\left(\frac{\log(S^*/S) - \hat{\mu} n}{\hat{\sigma} \sqrt{n}}\right) \leqq z\right] \to N(z),$$

where $N(z)$ is the standard normal distribution function. Putting this into words, as the number of periods into which the fixed length of time to expiration is divided approaches infinity, the probability that the standardized continuously compounded rate of return of the stock through the expiration date is not greater than the number z approaches the probability under a standard normal distribution.

The initial condition says roughly that higher-order properties of the distribution, such as how it is skewed, become less and less important, relative to its standard deviation, as $n \to \infty$. We can verify that the condition is satisfied by making the appropriate substitutions and finding

$$\frac{q|\log u - \hat{\mu}|^3 + (1 - q)|\log d - \hat{\mu}|^3}{\hat{\sigma}^3 \sqrt{n}} = \frac{(1 - q)^2 + q^2}{\sqrt{nq(1 - q)}},$$

which goes to zero as $n \to \infty$ since $q = \frac{1}{2} + \frac{1}{2}(\mu/\sigma)\sqrt{t/n}$. Thus, the multiplicative binomial model for stock prices includes the lognormal distribution as a limiting case.

Black and Scholes began directly with continuous trading and the assumption of a lognormal distribution for stock prices. Their approach relied on some quite advanced mathematics. However, since our approach contains continuous trading and the lognormal distribution as a limiting case, the two resulting formulas should then coincide. We will see shortly that this is indeed true, and we will have the advantage of using a much simpler method. It is important to remember, however, that the economic arguments we used to link the option value and the stock price are exactly the same as those advanced by Black and Scholes (1973) and Merton (1973, 1977).

The formula derived by Black and Scholes, rewritten in terms of our notation, is

Black-Scholes Option Pricing Formula

$$C = SN(x) - Kr^{-t}N(x - \sigma\sqrt{t}),$$

where

$$x \equiv \frac{\log(S/Kr^{-t})}{\sigma\sqrt{t}} + \frac{1}{2}\sigma\sqrt{t}.$$

We now wish to confirm that our binomial formula converges to the Black-Scholes formula when t is divided into more and more subintervals, and $\hat{r}$, u, d, and q are chosen in the way we described—that is, in a way such that the multiplicative binomial probability distribution of stock prices goes to the lognormal distribution.

For easy reference, let us recall our binomial option pricing formula:

$$C = S\phi[a;n, p'] - K\hat{r}^{-n}\phi[a;n, p].$$

The similarities are readily apparent. $\hat{r}^{-n}$ is, of course, always equal to r^{-t}. Therefore, to show the two formulas converge, we need only show that as $n \to \infty$,

$$\phi[a;n, p'] \to N(x) \quad \text{and} \quad \phi[a;n, p] \to N(x - \sigma\sqrt{t}).$$

We will consider only $\phi[a;n, p]$, since the argument is exactly the same for $\phi[a;n, p']$.

The complementary binomial distribution function $\phi[a;n, p]$ is the probability that the sum of n random variables, each of which can take on the value 1 with probability p and 0 with probability $1 - p$, will be greater than or equal to a. We know that the random value of this sum, j, has mean np and standard deviation $\sqrt{np(1 - p)}$. Therefore,

$$1 - \phi[a;n, p] = \text{Prob}[j \leq a - 1]$$

$$= \text{Prob}\left[\frac{j - np}{\sqrt{np(1 - p)}} \leq \frac{a - 1 - np}{\sqrt{np(1 - p)}}\right].$$

Now we can make an analogy with our earlier discussion. If we consider a stock which in each period will move to uS with probability p and dS with probability $1 - p$, then $\log(S^*/S) = j \log(\mu d) + n \log d$. The mean and variance of the continuously compounded rate of return of this stock are

$$\hat{\mu}_p = p \log(u/d) + \log d \ \text{ and } \ \hat{\sigma}_p^2 = p(1 - p)[\log(u/d)]^2.$$

Using these equalities, we find that

$$\frac{j - np}{\sqrt{np(1 - p)}} = \frac{\log(S^*/S) - \hat{\mu}_p n}{\hat{\sigma}_p \sqrt{n}}.$$

Recall from the binomial formula that

$$a - 1 = \log(K/Sd^n)/\log(u/d) - \epsilon$$

$$= [\log(K/S) - n \log d]/\log(u/d) - \epsilon,$$

where ϵ is a number between zero and one. Using this and the definitions of $\hat{\mu}_p$ and $\hat{\sigma}_p^2$, with a little algebra, we have

$$\frac{a - 1 - np}{\sqrt{np(1 - p)}} = \frac{\log(K/S) - \hat{\mu}_p n - \epsilon \log(u/d)}{\hat{\sigma}_p \sqrt{n}}.$$

Putting these results together,

$$1 - \phi[a; n, p]$$

$$= \text{Prob} \left[\frac{\log(S^*/S) - \hat{\mu}_p n}{\hat{\sigma}_p \sqrt{n}} \leqq \frac{\log(K/S) - \hat{\mu}_p n - \epsilon \log(u/d)}{\hat{\sigma}_p \sqrt{n}} \right].$$

We are now in a position to apply the central limit theorem. First, we must check if the initial condition,

$$\frac{p|\log u - \hat{\mu}_p|^3 + (1 - p)|\log d - \hat{\mu}_p|^3}{\hat{\sigma}_p \sqrt{n}} = \frac{(1 - p)^2 + p^2}{\sqrt{np(1 - p)}} \to 0,$$

as $n \to \infty$, is satisfied. By first recalling that $p \equiv (\hat{r} - d)/(u - d)$, and then $\hat{r} = r^{t/n}$, $u = e^{\sigma\sqrt{t/n}}$, and $d = e^{-\sigma\sqrt{t/n}}$, it is possible to show that as $n \to \infty$,

$$p \to \frac{1}{2} + \frac{1}{2} \left(\frac{\log r - \frac{1}{2}\sigma^2}{\sigma} \right) \sqrt{\frac{t}{n}}.$$

As a result, the initial condition holds, and we are justified in applying the central limit theorem.

To do so, we need only evaluate $\hat{\mu}_p n$, $\hat{\sigma}_p^2 n$ and $\log(u/d)$ as $n \to \infty$.[11]
Examination of our discussion for parameterizing q shows that as $n \to \infty$,

$$\hat{\mu}_p n \to (\log r - \tfrac{1}{2}\sigma^2)t \text{ and } \hat{\sigma}_p \sqrt{n} \to \sigma\sqrt{t}.$$

Furthermore, $\log(u/d) \to 0$ as $n \to \infty$.

For this application of the central limit theorem, then, since

$$\frac{\log(K/S) - \hat{\mu}_p n - \epsilon \log(u/d)}{\hat{\sigma}_p \sqrt{n}} \to z = \frac{\log(K/S) - (\log r - \tfrac{1}{2}\sigma^2)t}{\sigma\sqrt{t}},$$

we have

$$1 - \phi[a; n, p] \to N(z) = N\left[\frac{\log(Kr^{-t}/S)}{\sigma\sqrt{t}} + \tfrac{1}{2}\sigma\sqrt{t}\right].$$

The final step in the argument is to use the symmetry property of the standard normal distribution that $1 - N(z) = N(-z)$. Therefore, as $n \to \infty$,

$$\phi[a; n, p] \to N(-z) = N\left[\frac{\log(S/Kr^{-t})}{\sigma\sqrt{t}} - \tfrac{1}{2}\sigma\sqrt{t}\right] = N(x - \sigma\sqrt{t}).$$

---

[11] A surprising feature of this evaluation is that although $p = q$ and thus $\hat{\mu}_p \neq \hat{\mu}$, and $\hat{\sigma}_p \neq \hat{\sigma}$, nonetheless $\hat{\sigma}_p \sqrt{n}$, and $\hat{\sigma}\sqrt{n}$, have the same limiting value as $n \to \infty$. By contrast, since $\mu \neq \log r - (\tfrac{1}{2}\sigma^2)$, $\hat{\mu}_p n$ and $\hat{\mu} n$ do not. This results from the way we needed to specify u and d to obtain convergence to a lognormal distribution. Rewriting this as $\sigma\sqrt{t} = (\log u)\sqrt{n}$, it is clear that the limiting value σ of the standard deviation does not depend on p or q, and hence must be the same for either. However, at any point before the limit, since

$$\hat{\sigma}^2 n = \left(\sigma^2 - \mu^2 \frac{t}{n}\right)t \text{ and } \hat{\sigma}_p^2 n = \left[\sigma^2 - (\log r - \tfrac{1}{2}\sigma^2)^2 \frac{t}{n}\right]t,$$

$\hat{\sigma}$ and $\hat{\sigma}_p$ will generally have different values.

The fact that $\hat{\mu}_p n \to (\log r - \tfrac{1}{2}\sigma^2)t$ can also be derived from the property of the lognormal distribution that

$$\log E[S^*/S] = \mu_p t + \tfrac{1}{2}\sigma^2 t,$$

where E and μ_p are measured with respect to probability p. Since $p = (\hat{r} - d)/(u - d)$, it follows that $\hat{r} = pu + (1 - p)d$. For independently distributed random variables, the expectation of a product equals the product of their expectations. Therefore,

$$E[S^*/S] = [pu + (1 - p)d]^n = \hat{r}^n = r^t.$$

Substituting r^t for $E[S^*/S]$ in the previous equation, we have

$$\mu_p = \log r - \tfrac{1}{2}\sigma^2.$$

Since a similar argument holds for $\phi[a; n, p']$, this completes our demonstration that the binomial option pricing formula contains the Black-Scholes formula as a limiting case.[12, 13]

As we have remarked, the seeds of both the Black-Scholes formula and a continuous-time jump process formula are both contained within the binomial formulation. At which end point we arrive depends on how we take limits. Suppose, in place of our former correspondence for u, d, and q, we instead set

$$u = u, \qquad d = e^{t(t/n)}, \qquad q = \lambda(t/n).$$

This correspondence captures the essence of a pure jump process in which each successive stock price is almost always close to the previous price ($S \to dS$), but occasionally, with low but continuing probability, significantly different ($S \to uS$). Observe that, as $n \to \infty$, the probability of a change by d becomes larger and larger, while the probability of a change by u approaches zero.

With these specifications, the initial condition of the central limit theorem we used is no longer satisfied, and it can be shown the stock price movements converge to a log-Poisson rather than a lognormal distribution as $n \to \infty$. Let us define

$$\psi[x; y] \equiv \sum_{i=x}^{\infty} \frac{e^{-y} y^i}{i!},$$

[12]The only difference is that, as $n \to \infty$, $p' \to \frac{1}{2} + \frac{1}{2}[(\log r + \frac{1}{2}\sigma^2)/\sigma]\sqrt{t/n}$.

Further, it can be shown that as $n \to \infty$, $\Delta \to N(x)$. Therefore, for the Black-Scholes model, $\Delta S = SN(x)$ and $B = -Kr^{-t}N(x - \sigma\sqrt{t})$.

[13]In our original development, we obtained the following equation (somewhat rewritten) relating the call prices in successive periods:

$$\left(\frac{\hat{r} - d}{u - d}\right) C_u + \left(\frac{u - \hat{r}}{u - d}\right) C_d - \hat{r} C = 0.$$

By their more difficult methods, Black and Scholes obtained directly a partial differential equation analogous to our discrete-time difference equation. Their equation is

$$\frac{1}{2} \sigma^2 S^2 \frac{\partial^2 C}{\partial S^2} - (\log r) S \frac{\partial C}{\partial S} - \frac{\partial C}{\partial t} - (\log r) C = 0.$$

The value of the call, C, was then derived by solving this equation subject to the boundary condition $C^* = \max[0, S^* - K]$.

Based on our previous analysis, we would now suspect that, as $n \to \infty$, our difference equation would approach the Black-Scholes partial differential equation. This can be confirmed by substituting our definitions of $\hat{r}, u, d$ in terms of n in the way described earlier, expanding C_u, C_1 in a Taylor series around $(e^{\sigma\sqrt{h}} S, t - h)$ and $(e^{-\sigma\sqrt{h}} S, t - h)$, respectively, and then expanding $e^{\sigma\sqrt{h}}, e^{-\sigma\sqrt{h}}$, and r^h in a Taylor series, substituting these in the equation and collecting terms. If we then divide by h and let $h \to 0$, all terms of higher order than h go to zero. This yields the Black-Scholes equation.

as the complementary Poisson distribution function. The limiting option pricing formula for the above specifications of u, d, and q is then

Jump Process Option Pricing Formula

$$C \equiv S\psi[x; y] - Kr^{-t}\psi[x; y/u],$$

where

$$y \equiv (\log r - \zeta)ut/(u-1),$$

and

$x \equiv$ the smallest non-negative integer greater than $(\log(K/S) - \zeta t)/\log u$.

A very similar formula holds if we let $u = e^{\zeta(t/n)}$, $d = d$, and $1 - q = \lambda(t/n)$.

6. Dividends and put pricing

So far we have been assuming that the stock pays no dividends. It is easy to do away with this restriction. We will illustrate this with a specific dividend policy: the stock maintains a constant yield, δ, on each ex-dividend date. Suppose there is one period remaining before expiration and the current stock price is S. If the end of the period is an ex-dividend date, then an individual who owned the stock during the period will receive at that time a dividend of either δuS or δdS. Hence, the stock price at the end of the period will be either $u(1 - \delta)^v S$ or $d(1 - \delta)^v S$, where $v = 1$ if the end of the period is an ex-dividend date and $v = 0$ otherwise. Both δ and v are assumed to be known with certainty.

When the call expires, its contract and a rational exercise policy imply that its value must be either

$$C_u = \max[0, u(1 - \delta)^v S - K],$$

or

$$C_d = \max[0, d(1 - \delta)^v S - K].$$

Therefore,

$$C \begin{cases} C_u = \max[0, u(1 - \delta)^v S - K], \\ \\ C_d = \max[0, d(1 - \delta)^v S - K]. \end{cases}$$

Now we can proceed exactly as before. Again we can select a portfolio of Δ shares of stock and the dollar amount B in bonds which will have the same end-of-period value as the call.[14] By retracing our previous steps, we can show that

$$C = [pC_u + (1 - p)C_d]/\hat{r},$$

if this is greater than $S - K$, and $C = S - K$ otherwise. Here, once again, $p = (\hat{r} - d)/(u - d)$ and $\Delta = (C_u - C_d)/(u - d)S$.

Thus far the only change is that $(1 - \delta)^v S$ has replaced S in the values for C_u and C_d. Now we come to the major difference: early exercise may be optimal. To see this, suppose that $v = 1$ and $d(1 - \delta)S > K$. Since $u > d$, then, also, $u(1 - \delta)S > K$. In this case, $C_u = u(1 - \delta)S - K$ and $C_d = d(1 - \delta)S - K$. Therefore, since $(u/\hat{r})p + (d/\hat{r})(1 - p) = 1$, $[pC_u + (1 - p)C_d]/\hat{r} = (1 - \delta)S - (K/\hat{r})$. For sufficiently high stock prices, this can obviously be less than $S - K$. Hence, there are definitely some circumstances in which no one would be willing to hold the call for one more period.

In fact, there will always be a critical stock price, $\hat{S}$, such that if $S > \hat{S}$, the call should be exercised immediately. $\hat{S}$ will be the stock price at which $[pC_u + (1 - p)C_d]/\hat{r} = S - K$.[15] That is, it is the lowest stock price at which the value of the hedging portfolio exactly equals $S - K$. This means $\hat{S}$ will, other things equal, be lower the higher the dividend yield, the lower the interest rate, and the lower the striking price.

We can extend the analysis to an arbitrary number of periods in the same way as before. There is only one additional difference, a minor modification in the hedging operation. Now the funds in the hedging portfolio will be increased by any dividends received, or decreased by the restitution required for dividends paid while the stock is held short.

Although the possibility of optimal exercise before the expiration date causes no conceptual difficulties, it does seem to prohibit a simple closed-form solution for the value of a call with many periods to go. However, our analysis suggests a sequential numerical procedure which will allow us to calculate the continuous-time value to any desired degree of accuracy.

Let C be the current value of a call with n periods remaining. Define

$$\bar{v}(n, i) \equiv \sum_{k=1}^{n-i} v_k,$$

so that $\bar{v}(n, i)$ is the number of ex-dividend dates occurring during the next $n - i$ periods. Let $C(n, i, j)$ be the value of the call $n - i$ periods from

---

[14]Remember that if we are long the portfolio we will receive the dividend at the end of the period; if we are short, we will have to make restitution for the dividend.
[15]Actually solving for $\hat{S}$ explicitly is straightforward but rather tedious, so we will omit it.

now, given that the current stock price S has changed to $u^j d^{n-i-j}(1-\delta)^{\bar{v}(n,i)} S$, where $j = 0, 1, 2, \ldots, n - i$.

With this notation, we are prepared to solve for the current value of the call by working backward in time from the expiration date. At expiration, $i = 0$, so that

$$C(n, 0, j) = \max[0, u^j d^{n-j}(1-\delta)^{\bar{v}(n,0)} S - K] \text{ for } j = 0, 1, \ldots, n.$$

One period before the expiration date, $i = 1$ so that

$$C(n, 1, j) = \max[u^j d^{n-1-j}(1-\delta)^{\bar{v}(n,1)} S - K,$$

$$[pC(n, 0, j+1) + (1-p)C(n, 0, j)]/\hat{r}]$$

$$\text{for } j = 0, 1, \ldots, n-1.$$

More generally, i periods before expiration

$$C(n, i, j) = \max[u^j d^{n-i-j}(1-\delta)^{\bar{v}(n,i)} S - K,$$

$$[pC(n, i-1, j+1) + (1-p)C(n, i-1, j)]/\hat{r}]$$

$$\text{for } j = 0, 1, \ldots, n-i.$$

Observe that each prior step provides the inputs needed to evaluate the right-hand arguments of each succeeding step. The number of calculations decreases as we move backward in time. Finally, with n periods before expiration, since $i = n$,

$$C = C(n, n, 0) = \max[S - K, [pC(n, n-1, 1)$$

$$+ (1-p)C(n, n-1, 0)]/\hat{r}],$$

and the hedge ratio is

$$\Delta = \frac{C(n, n-1, 1) - C(n, n-1, 0)}{(u-d)S}.$$

We could easily expand the analysis to include dividend policies in which the amount paid on any ex-dividend date depends on the stock price at that time in a more general way.[16] However, this will cause some minor complications. In our present example with a constant dividend yield, the possible stock prices $n - i$ periods from now are completely determined by the total number of upward moves (and ex-dividend dates) occurring during that interval. With other types of dividend policies, the enumeration will be

---

[16] We could also allow the amount to depend on previous stock prices.

more complicated, since then the terminal stock price will be affected by the timing of the upward moves as well as their total number. But the basic principle remains the same. We go to the expiration date and calculate the call value for all of the possible prices that the stock could have then. Using this information, we step back one period and calculate the call values for all possible stock prices at that time, and so forth.

We will now illustrate the use of the binomial numerical procedure in approximating continuous-time call values. In order to have an exact continuous-time formula to use for comparison, we will consider the case with no dividends. Suppose that we are given the inputs required for the Black-Scholes option pricing formula: S, K, t, σ, and r. To convert this information into the inputs d, u, and $\hat{r}$ required for the binomial numerical procedure, we use the relationships:

$$d = 1/u, \qquad u = e^{\sigma\sqrt{t/n}}, \qquad \hat{r} = r^{t/n}.$$

Table 2 gives us a feeling for how rapidly option values approximated by the binomial method approach the corresponding limiting Black-Scholes values given by $n = \infty$. At $n = 5$, the values differ by at most \$0.25, and at $n = 20$, they differ by at most \$0.07. Although not shown, at $n = 50$, the greatest difference is less than \$0.03, and at $n = 150$, the values are identical to the penny.

To derive a method for valuing puts, we again use the binomial formulation. Although it has been convenient to express the argument in terms of a particular security, a call, this is not essential in any way. The same basic analysis can be applied to puts.

Letting P denote the current price of a put, with one period remaining before expiration, we have

$$P \left\{ \begin{array}{l} P_u = \max\,[0, K - u(1 - \delta)^v S], \\[2em] P_d = \max\,[0, K - d(1 - \delta)^v S]. \end{array} \right.$$

Once again, we can choose a portfolio with ΔS in stock and B in bonds which will have the same end-of-period values as the put. By a series of steps which are formally equivalent to the ones we followed in section 3, we can show that

$$P = [pP_u + (1 - p)P_d]/\hat{r},$$

if this is greater than $K - S$, and $P = K - S$ otherwise. As before, $p = (\hat{r} - d)(u - d)$ and $\Delta = (P_u - P_d)/(u - d)S$. Note that for puts, since $P_u \leqq P_d$, then $\Delta \leqq 0$. This means that if we sell an overvalued put, the hedging portfolio which we buy will involve a short position in the stock.

σ	K	$n = 5$			$n = 20$			$n = \infty$		
		(1)	(2)	(3)	(1)	(2)	(3)	(1)	(2)	(3)
	35	5.14	5.77	6.45	5.15	5.77	6.39	5.15	5.76	6.40
0.2	40	1.05	2.26	3.12	0.99	2.14	2.97	1.00	2.17	3.00
	45	0.02	0.54	1.15	0.02	0.51	1.11	0.02	0.51	1.10
	35	5.21	6.30	7.15	5.22	6.26	7.19	5.22	6.25	7.17
0.3	40	1.53	3.21	4.36	1.44	3.04	4.14	1.46	3.07	4.19
	45	0.11	1.28	2.12	0.15	1.28	2.23	0.16	1.25	2.24
	35	5.40	6.87	7.92	5.39	6.91	8.05	5.39	6.89	8.09
0.4	40	2.01	4.16	5.61	1.90	3.93	5.31	1.92	3.98	5.37
	45	0.46	1.99	3.30	0.42	2.09	3.42	0.42	2.10	3.43

[a]The January options have one month to expiration, the Aprils, four months, and the Julys, seven months; r and σ are expressed in annual terms.

We might hope that with puts we will be spared the complications caused by optimal exercise before the expiration date. Unfortunately, this is not the case. In fact, the situation is even worse in this regard. Now there are always some possible circumstances in which no one would be willing to hold the put for one more period.

To see this, suppose $K > u(1 - \delta)^v S$. Since $u > d$, then, also, $K > d(1 - \delta)^v S$. In this case, $P_u = K - u(1 - \delta)^v S$ and $P_d = K - d(1 - \delta)^v S$. Therefore, since $(u/\hat{r})p + (d/\hat{r})(1 - p) = 1$,

$$[pP_u + (1 - p)P_d]/\hat{r} = (K/\hat{r}) - (1 - \delta)^v S.$$

If there are no dividends (that is, $v = 0$), then this is certainly less than $K - S$. Even with $v = 1$, it will be less for a sufficiently low stock price.

Thus, there will now be a critical stock price, $\hat{S}$, such that if $S < \hat{S}$, the put should be exercised immediately. By analogy with our discussion for the call, we can see that this is the stock price at which $[pP_u + (1 - p)P_d]/\hat{r} = K - S$. Other things equal, $\hat{S}$ will be higher the lower the dividend yield, the higher the interest rate, and the higher the striking price. Optimal early exercise thus becomes more likely if the put is deep-in-the-money and the interest rate is high. The effect of dividends yet to be paid diminishes the advantages of immediate exercise, since the put buyer will be reluctant to sacrifice the forced declines in the stock price on future ex-dividend dates.

This argument can be extended in the same way as before to value puts with any number of periods to go. However, the chance for optimal exercise before the expiration date once again seems to preclude the possibility of expressing this value in a simple form. But our analysis also indicates that, with slight modification, we can value puts with the same numerical techniques we use for calls. Reversing the difference between the stock price and the striking price at each stage is the only change.[17]

The diagram presented in table 3 shows the stock prices, put values, and values of Δ obtained in this way for the example given in section 4. The values used there were $S = 80$, $K = 80$, $n = 3$, $u = 1.5$, $d = 0.5$, and $\hat{r} = 1.1$. To include dividends as well, we assume that a cash dividend of five percent ($\delta = 0.05$) will be paid at the end of the last period before the expiration date. Thus, $(1 - \delta)^{\nu(n, \, 0)} = 0.95$, $(1 - \delta)^{\nu(n, \, 1)} = 0.95$, and $(1 - \delta)^{\nu(n, \, 2)} = 1.0$. Put values in italics indicate that immediate exercise is optimal.

Table 3.

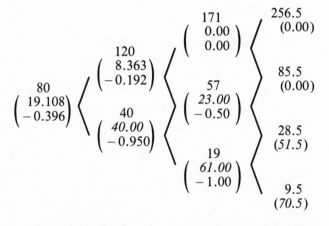

7. Conclusion

It should now be clear that whenever stock price movements conform to a discrete binomial process, or to a limiting form of such a process, options can be priced solely on the basis of arbitrage considerations. Indeed, we could have significantly complicated the simple binomial process while still retaining this property.

The probabilities of an upward or downward move did not enter into the valuation formula. Hence, we would obtain the same result if q depended on the current or past stock prices or on other random variables. In

[17]Michael Parkinson (1977) has suggested a similar numerical procedure based on a trinomial process, where the stock price can either increase, decrease, or remain unchanged. In fact, given the theoretical basis for the binomial numerical procedure provided, the numerical method can be generalized to permit $k + 1 \leqq n$ jumps to new stock prices in each period. We can consider exercise only every k periods, using the binomial formula to leap across intermediate periods. In effect, this means permitting $k + 1$ possible new stock prices before exercise is again considered. That is, instead of considering exercise n times, we would only consider it about n/k times. For fixed t and k, as $n \to \infty$, option values will approach their continuous-time values.

This alternative procedure is interesting, since it may enhance computer efficiency. At one extreme, for calls on stocks which do not pay dividends, setting $k + 1 = n$ gives the most efficient results. However, when the effect of potential early exercise is important and greater accuracy is required, the most efficient results are achieved by setting $k = 1$, as in our description above.

addition, u and d could have been deterministic functions of time. More significantly, the size of the percentage changes in the stock price over each period could have depended on the stock price at the beginning of each period or on previous stock prices.[18] However, if the size of the changes were to depend on any other random variable, not itself perfectly correlated with the stock price, then our argument will no longer hold. If any arbitrage result is then still possible, it will require the use of additional assets in the hedging portfolio.

We could also incorporate certain types of imperfections into the binomial option pricing approach, such as differential borrowing and lending rates and margin requirements. These can be shown to produce upper and lower bounds on option prices, outside of which riskless profitable arbitrage would be possible.

Since all existing preference-free option pricing results can be derived as limiting forms of a discrete two-state process, we might suspect that two-state stock price movements, with the qualifications mentioned above, must be in some sense necessary, as well as sufficient, to derive option pricing formulas based solely on arbitrage considerations. To price an option by arbitrage methods, there must exist a portfolio of other assets which exactly replicates in every state of nature the payoff received by an optimally exercised option. Our basic proposition is the following. Suppose, as we have, that markets are perfect, that changes in the interest rate are never random, and that changes in the stock price are always random. In a discrete time model, a necessary and sufficient condition for options of all maturities and striking prices to be priced by arbitrage using only the stock and bonds in the portfolio is that in each period,

(a) the stock price can change from its beginning-of-period value to only two ex-dividend values at the end of the period, and
(b) the dividends and the size of each of the two possible changes are presently known functions depending at most on: (i) current and past stock prices, (ii) current and past values of random variables whose changes in each period are perfectly correlated with the change in the stock price, and (iii) calendar time.

[18]Of course, different option pricing formulas would result from these more complex stochastic processes. See Cox and Ross (1976) and Geske (1979). Nonetheless, all option pricing formulas in these papers can be derived as limiting forms of a properly specified discrete two-state process.

The sufficiency of the condition can be established by a straightforward application of the methods we have presented. Its necessity is implied by the discussion at the end of section 3.[19],[20],[21]

This rounds out the principal conclusion of this paper: the simple two-state process is really the essential ingredient of option pricing by arbitrage methods. This is surprising, perhaps, given the mathematical complexities of some of the current models in this field. But it is reassuring to find such simple economic arguments at the heart of this powerful theory.

[19]Note that option values need not depend on the present stock price alone. In some cases, formal dependence on the entire series of past values of the stock price and other variables can be summarized in a small number of state variables.

[20]In some circumstances, it will be possible to value options by arbitrage when this condition does not hold by using additional assets in the hedging portfolio. The value of the option will then in general depend on the values of these other assets, although in certain cases only parameters describing their movement will be required.

[21]Merton's (1976) model, with both continuous and jump components, is a good example of a stock price process for which no exact option pricing formula is obtainable purely from arbitrage considerations. To obtain an exact formula, it is necessary to impose restrictions on the stochastic movements of other securities, as Merton did, or on investor preferences. For example, Rubinstein (1976) has been able to derive the Black-Scholes option pricing formula, under circumstances that do not admit arbitrage, by suitably restricting investor preferences. Additional problems arise when interest rates are stochastic, although Merton (1973) has shown that some arbitrage results may still be obtained.

References

Black, F. and M. Scholes, 1973, The pricing of options and corporate liabilities. *Journal of Political Economy* 3, 637-654.

Brennan, M. J. and E. S. Schwartz, 1977, The valuation of American put options, *Journal of Finance* 32, 449-462.

Cox, J. C. and S. A. Ross, 1975, The pricing of options for jump processes. Rodney L. White Center Working Paper no. 2-75 (University of Pennsylvania, Philadelphia, PA).

Cox, J. C. and S. A. Ross, 1976, The valuation of options for alternative stochastic processes, *Journal of Financial Economics* 3, 145-166.

Geske, R., 1979, The valuation of compound options, *Journal of Financial Economics* 7, 63-81.

Harrison, J. M. and D. M. Kreps, 1979, Martingales and arbitrage in multiperiod securities markets, *Journal of Economic Theory* 20, 381-408.

Merton, R. C., 1973, The theory of rational option pricing, *Bell Journal of Economics and Management Science* 4, 141-183.

Merton, R. C., 1976, Option pricing when underlying stock returns are discontinuous, *Journal of Financial Economics* 3, 125-144.

Merton, R. C., 1977, On the pricing of contingent claims and the Modigliani-Miller theorem, *Journal of Financial Economics* 5, 241-250.

Parkinson, M., 1977, Option pricing: The American put, *Journal of Business* 50, 21-36.

Rendleman, R. J. and B. J. Bartter, 1978. Two-state option pricing. Unpublished paper (Graduate School of Management, Northwestern University, Evanston, IL).

Rubinstein, M., 1976. The valuation of uncertain income streams and the pricing of options, *Bell Journal of Economics* 7, 407-425.

Sharpe, W. F., 1978, Investments (Prentice-Hall, Englewood Cliffs, NJ).

3

The American Put Option
Valued Analytically

Robert Geske and H.E. Johnson*

Abstract

An analytic solution to the American put problem is derived herein. The hedge ratio and
other derivatives of the solution are presented. The formula derived implies an exact
duplicating portfolio for the American put consisting of discount bonds and stock sold
short. The formula is extended to consider put options on stocks paying cash dividends. A
polynomial expression is developed for evaluating these formulae. Values and hedge ratios
for puts on both dividend and nondividend paying stocks are calculated, tabulated, and
compared with values derived by numerical integration and binomial approximation. As
with European options, evaluating an analytic formula is more efficient than
approximating the stock price process or the partial differential equation by binomial or
finite difference methods. Finally, applications of this American put solution are discussed.

Merton [16] showed that American put options are more difficult to value
than European puts because at every instant for American puts there is a
positive probability of premature exercise. Black and Scholes [1] derived a
formula for a European put when the stock price follows geometric
Brownian motion. For this same stock price distribution, Merton [16]
derived a formula for a perpetual American put. Brennan and Schwartz [2],
Cox and Rubinstein [4], and Parkinson [17] have developed numerical
solutions for the value of a finite-lived American put. However, numerical

* University of California-Los Angeles and Louisiana State University, respectively. This
paper was presented and benefitted from comments at the Western Finance Association in
Portland and the European Finance Association in Fontainbleau, France, and at seminars
at the University of Utah, Washington State University, and McGill University. The authors
are grateful for individual comments from Warren Bailey, Cliff Ball, Ed Blomeyer, Nai-fu
Chen, Ken French, Chi-Cheng Hsia, David Mayers, Richard Roll, Mark Rubinstein, and
Walt Torous, and the programming assistance of Ho Yang and B. F. Wexler.

Robert Geske and H.E. Johnson, "The American Put Option Valued Analytically."
Reprinted with permission from *The Journal of Finance,* Vol. XXXIX, No. 5, December
1984.

solutions are expensive and do not offer the intuition which the comparative statics of an analytic solution provide. An analytic approximation has been developed by Johnson [15], but it does not handle dividends or hedge ratios and there is no way to make this approximation arbitrarily accurate.

This paper presents an analytic formula which satisfies the partial differential equation and boundary conditions that characterize the American put valuation problem. Since at every instant there is a positive probability of premature exercise, this situation is equivalent to an infinite sequence of options on options, or compound options. Geske [8] originally showed how to value an option on an option. Using this solution technique, the American put formula is derived. The hedge ratio and all other derivatives of the formula with respect to its parameters are presented. Furthermore, it is easy to show that the formula satisfies the partial differential equation.

While formula evaluation is generally straightforward, this is not the case for most option formulae, and American options are more difficult than European. In order to evaluate our equation directly, it would be necessary to compute an infinite series of conditional exercise terms. Instead, we show that, since our formula is exact in the limit, arbitrary accuracy can be achieved by considering puts which can only be exercised at a few discrete dates and then using their prices to extrapolate to the price of a put which can be exercised at any date. This approach provides an efficient way to evaluate the American put formula and its derivatives.

Section I presents the analytic formula and its comparative statics, and extends the solution to the case of stocks paying cash dividends. Section II demonstrates that the formula can be evaluated to arbitrary accuracy by a polynomial expression similar to that used to evaluate the Black-Scholes European put and call option formulae. It is also shown that the hedge ratio and cash dividend adjustments can be similarly computed. Section II also notes that the same solution and evaluation techniques can be used to value other complex contracts, such as currency options, options on futures, coupon bonds, or warrants on dividend paying stocks. Section III summarizes the paper.

I. The Formulae

A. The Solution

Let S, σ^2, r, T, X, and P be the underlying stock price, the variance of the rate of return on the stock, the risk-free rate, the time to maturity of the put, the exercise price, and the American put price, respectively. Following Black and Scholes [1], we assume perfect markets, constant r and σ, no dividends, and geometric Brownian motion for the stock price. We set current time to zero.

The stochastic process for stock price changes is assumed to be:

$$\frac{dS}{S} = \mu\,dt + \sigma\,dz \tag{1}$$

where μ is the expected return on the stock and dz is the differential of a Gauss-Wiener process. Since the only parameters which are assumed variable are the stock price and time, and the stock price is stochastic, put price changes can be characterized using Itô's lemma. Then, by constructing a self-financing, risk-free hedge between the put, the stock, and a riskless security, the put's equilibrium price path can be described by the familiar Black-Scholes partial differential equation:

$$\frac{\partial P}{\partial t} = rP - rS \frac{\partial P}{\partial S} - \frac{1}{2} \sigma^2 S^2 \frac{\partial^2 P}{\partial S^2}. \tag{2}$$

Because the American put can be exercised at any instant and because the stock price boundary which triggers exercise is not constant, the problem is termed a free boundary problem.

The free boundary condition which the American put must satisfy at every instant is

$$P(S, T) \geq \max(0, X - S) \tag{3}$$

for all $T \geq 0$. Except for numerical methods, which do not produce a formula satisfying partial differential equation (2) above, the solution to this free boundary problem has been considered intractable.

Here we show that there does exist an analytic solution[1] to this partial differential equation subject to the free boundary condition. A key to our solution is the assumption that each exercise decision is a discrete event. Thus, the formula derived is a continuous time solution to partial differential equation (2), subject to the free boundary condition (3) applied at an infinite number of discrete instants. Like the Black-Scholes equation, our formula is easier to use than the numerical methods applied to approximate the solution to the partial differential equation. Our formula would be obtainable by traditional methods for solving partial differential equations, but such procedures would be less tractable. However, since a riskless hedge can be formed, the Cox-Ross [3] technique can be used in conjunction with Geske's [8] compound option valuation, thus circumventing the usual transformation solution to the partial differential equation.

Using the Cox-Ross approach, we can price the American put as the discounted expected value of all future cash flows. The cash flows arise because the put can be exercised at the next instant, dt, or the following instant, $2dt$, if not previously exercised, . . . , ad infinitum. Since the assumption of geometric Brownian motion implies that the stock price at

---

[1]For a definition of "analytic solution," see James and James [13, p. 11]. The use of the word analytical or numerical is tricky in the option context since in the end all methods require numerical procedures.

any future date is a lognormally distributed random variable, the correlation coefficient between the overlapping Brownian increments at times t_1 and t_2 $(t_2 > t_1)$ is given by

$$\varrho_{12} = \frac{\text{Cov}(\Delta z_1, \Delta z_2)}{[\text{Var}(\Delta z_1) \, \text{Var}(\Delta z_2)]^{1/2}} = (t_1/t_2)^{1/2} \tag{4}$$

where $\Delta z_1 = z(t_1) - z(0)$ and $\Delta z_2 = z(t_2) - z(0)$. At each instant, we will exercise the put if (a) the put has not already been exercised and (b) the payoff from exercising the put equals or exceeds the value of the put if it is not exercised. This implies a "critical stock price," $\bar{S}$, at which the exercise occurs. The critical stock price is independent of the current stock price and is determined from the free boundary given in condition (3), whenever the exercise proceeds equal the American put value, or $X - \bar{S} = P(\bar{S}, T)$, for some $S = \bar{S}$ and any T. (This can also be expressed as a derivative boundary condition, $\partial P/\partial S = -1$). At the first instant, there is no probability that the put will already have been exercised, so we just integrate the exercise price less the future stock price over all stock prices less than $\bar{S}_{dt}$, the critical stock price at this date, and then discount to the present. This yields two terms, one being simply the discounted exercise price times the probability that the stock price will be below $\bar{S}_{dt}$. At the next instant, we perform a similar integration up to $\bar{S}_{2dt}$, the new critical stock price, but we must exclude all those cases where the put will be exercised at the first date. Again we obtain two terms, one being the discounted exercise price times the probability that the stock price at the first instant will be above the first critical stock price, $\bar{S}_{dt}$, and that the stock price at the second instant will be below the second critical stock price, $\bar{S}_{2dt}$.

The procedure for the third instant is similar, except now there are trivariate normals instead of bivariates. The correlation coefficient is negative between the argument for the last instant and the arguments for the previous ones, but positive between the arguments for the previous times. The intuition here is that the put will be exercised at this instant if the stock price is below the critical stock price for this instant, given that it was not exercised at all previous instants because the stock price was always above the critical stock price. Proceeding in this way, we obtain the following solution for the value of an American put option:

$$P = Xw_2 - Sw_1 \tag{5}$$

where the weights w_1 and w_2 are [2]

---

[2] This is simply the sum of a series of options on options or compound options. The equation is the solution to an optimal stopping problem. Although the equation contains an infinite series of terms, it is an exact solution of the partial differential equation, subject to an infinite number of discrete exercises, or stopping, boundaries. This is notably different than Fourier, or other infinite series approximations to the partial differential equation.

$$w_1 = \{ N_1(-d_1(\bar{S}_{dt}, dt)$$
$$+ N_2(d_1(\bar{S}_{dt}, dt), -d_1(\bar{S}_{2dt}, 2dt); -\varrho_{12})$$
$$+ N_3(d_1(\bar{S}_{dt}, dt), d_1(\bar{S}_{2dt}, 2dt), -d_1(\bar{S}_{3dt}, 3dt);$$
$$\varrho_{12}, -\varrho_{13}, -\varrho_{23}) + \ldots \}$$

$$w_2 = \{ e^{-rdt} N_1(-d_2(\bar{S}_{dt}, dt))$$
$$+ e^{-r2dt} N_2(d_2(\bar{S}_{dt}, dt), -d_2(\bar{S}_{2dt}, 2dt); -\varrho_{12})$$
$$+ e^{-r3dt} N_3(d_2(\bar{S}_{dt}, dt), d_2(\bar{S}_{2dt}, 2dt), -d_2(\bar{S}_{3dt}, 3dt);$$
$$\varrho_{12}, -\varrho_{13}, -\varrho_{23}) + \ldots \}$$

and where in general

$$d_1(q, \tau) = \frac{\ln(S/q) + (r + \frac{1}{2}\sigma^2)\tau}{\sigma\sqrt{\tau}}$$

$$d_2(q, \tau) = d_1 - \sigma\sqrt{\tau}$$

for any q (i.e., critical stock price or exercise price) and τ (i.e., time interval). The correlation coefficients are, sequentially, as follows:

$$\varrho_{12} = 1/\sqrt{2}$$

$$\varrho_{13} = 1/\sqrt{3}$$

$$\varrho_{23} = \sqrt{2/3}$$

$$\vdots$$

N_1, N_2, and N_3 are the standard cumulative univariate, bivariate, and trivariate normals, respectively. There is an infinite number of terms (each a higher order multivariate normal integral) in the solution, ending when the final instant has been reached.

Although we cannot use Equation (5) to compute actual numbers for the American put values, it does offer intuition about the portfolio which duplicates the American put payoffs. Also, the formula can be differentiated to yield intuition regarding the sensitivity to all specified parameters, and to simplify the computation of the hedge ratio. The American put can be thought of as an infinite series of contingent payoffs. At each date, there is a payoff if and only if the stock price is below the critical stock price for that date and it was not below any critical stock price at any previous date. The American put's contingent payoffs can be duplicated by an infinite series of risk-free, discount bonds, and a short position in the stock. Since we have assumed that the risk-free rate is known and constant, the portfolio of bonds represented by Xw_2 is equivalent to investing the same amount in a risk-free bond of any maturity. However, if one were to introduce uncertainty about future interest rates, then term structure effects could be important. Note that our formula implies the intuitive result that the duplicating portfolio for out-of-the-money puts is skewed toward longer maturity bonds, while for in-the-money puts it is skewed toward shorter maturities.

The European put option is simply a special case of an American put option with only one exercise boundary. Thus, formula (5) above will reduce to the European put formula when boundary condition (3) only holds at $T = 0$. Although the critical stock prices are unknown, they can be determined at any instant for all future dates prior to expiration. The critical stock price is a time-dependent path of stock prices that separates the exercise from the no exercise region in such a way as to maximize the value of the American put. Just at the point where the stock price is equal to the critical stock price, the put value would decrease one dollar for a one dollar increase in the stock price (i.e., $\partial P/\partial S(S = S_c) = -1$). As the stock price approaches the critical stock price, the sensitivity of the American put with respect to time to expiration approaches zero (i.e., $\partial P/\partial T(S \to S_c) \to 0$). Also, at this exercise point, the interest rate effect on the American put exactly offsets the variance effect. Although these points may not be intuitively obvious, they are clarified in the next section, where the derivatives of the American put formula are presented.

B. Comparative Statics

Here the sensitivity of the American put option formula to changes in each of its arguments is presented. Note that because the option value is linearly homogeneous with respect to the stock price and exercise price, either partial derivative implies the other by Euler's Theorem. Also note that because time to maturity only appears in the formula multiplied by the interest rate or the variance rate, any two of the three partial derivatives with respect to r, σ, and T imply the third.

The partial derivative of the valuation formula (5) with respect to the stock price is the hedge ratio, or number of shares of stock to options in a perfectly hedged portfolio:

$$\frac{\partial P}{\partial S} = -w_1 < 0. \tag{6}$$

The negative sign indicates that as the stock price rises the put price falls. The hedge ratio can be thought of as either the negative amount of stock (sold short) to which the put is equivalent, or, under risk neutrality, as the discounted expected cash outflow (divided by the stock price) that the put holder will experience.

As the exercise price rises, the put value rises:

$$\frac{\partial P}{\partial X} = w_2 > 0. \tag{7}$$

This can similarly be considered the expected cash inflow (divided by the exercise price).[3]

As the interest rate rises, the American put value falls:

$$\frac{\partial P}{\partial r} = -X\,dt\,[\,e^{-rdt}N_1(\,') + 2\,e^{-2rdt}N_2(\,') + \ldots\,] \leq 0. \tag{8}$$

This is because the present value of the bonds in the duplicating portfolio decreases as the interest rate increases.

As the variance rate rises, the put value rises:

$$\frac{\partial P}{\partial \sigma^2} = X\,\frac{\sqrt{T}}{2\sigma}\,w_2' \geq 0. \tag{9}$$

An increase in volatility increases the probability of both high and low stock prices, and with the asymmetry of an option's contingent payoffs, increases the option value.

As time to expiration increases, the American put value rises:

$$\frac{\partial P}{\partial T} = -Xr\,\frac{dt}{T}\,[\,e^{-rdt}N_1(\,') + 2\,e^{-2rdt}N_2(\,')\,\ldots\,]$$

$$+ X\,\frac{\sigma}{2\sqrt{T}}\,w_2' \geq 0. \tag{10}$$

The first four partial derivatives are functionally different from their corresponding European counterparts, but they do have the same sign and similar intuition.[4] Although it is not obvious, the partial derivative with respect to time to expiration is strictly positive for the American put (provided $S > \bar{S}$), while its sign is ambiguous for the European put. This ambiguity for the European put is obvious because more time helps if the put is out-of-the-money, but hurts if the holder wants to exercise immediately. The strictly positive sign for the American put is intuitive because extending the life gives the holder more options (i.e., choices). As the stock price approaches the critical stock price and $\partial P/\partial T$ approaches zero, the interest rate effect offsets the variance effect.

---

[3] It may appear that Equations (7)-(10) require taking derivatives of the critical stock prices, but in fact all such terms cancel.

[4] In Equation (8), it may be useful to think of dt as T/n and then take the limit as $n \to \infty$. This relates the derivative to the European put derivative. In Equations (9) and (10), w_2' is the sum of the probability density functions derived from the cumulative distribution functions.

When the American put is alive (i.e., $S > \bar{S}$), the partial derivatives of formula (5), given in Equations (6)-(10), satisfy the original partial differential equation (2). This demonstrates that American put formula (5) is the solution to partial differential equation (2) subject to its boundary conditions.

C. Dividends

The majority of listed put options are traded on stocks paying cash dividends. Geske and Shastri [10] demonstrated for American puts that dividends significantly reduce the probability of early exercise. This diminishes the difference between American and European put option values, and consequently one might conclude that dividends simplify the valuation problem. Although this conclusion is correct in the sense that the errors from using the European formula for American put options would be smaller, dividends complicate the exact valuation of American puts.

Roll [19] developed a formula for valuing American call options on stocks paying a single cash dividend. He avoided the discontinuity in the stock price at the ex-dividend date by escrowing the dividend from the stock price and employing the ''net-of-dividends stock price'' in the valuation problem. In order to incorporate multiple dividends, Geske's [9] adjustment to Roll's dividend procedure is used here for valuing American puts. Although the form of the solution is similar to Equation (5), the next section demonstrates that the evaluation of the formula for American puts on stocks paying dividends is more complex because dividends disrupt the critical stock price path.

II. Formula Evaluation and Applications

In this section, we show how to evaluate the American put formula (5) with a polynomial expression based upon an extrapolation from only a small number of exercise points to the infinite limit. The evaluation is very efficient because we are approximating an exact solution rather than the partial differential equation or the stock price process itself. Arbitrary accuracy can be obtained by adding exercise points. However, we show that only a few (cf. three) critical stock prices need to be computed in order to obtain penny accuracy. We stress that unlike previous authors (Brennan and Schwartz [2] or Parkinson [17]), we do not approximate the partial differential equation or the stock price process (Cox and Rubinstein in [4]). Instead, we evaluate our formula, which is an exact solution to the partial differential equation subject to the (discrete) free exercise boundary.

Let P_1 be the price of a put that can only be exercised at time T (i.e., at expiration); this option is just the European put, and we can write $P_1 = p$, the European put value. Let P_2 be the value of a put that can only be exercised at time $T/2$ (i.e., halfway to expiration) or at time T. Then

$$P_2 = Xe^{-rT/2}N_1[-d_2(\bar{S}_{T/2}, T/2)] - SN_1[-d_1(\bar{S}_{T/2}, T/2)]$$

$$+ Xe^{-rT}N_2[d_2(\bar{S}_{T/2}, T/2), -d_2(X, T); -1/\sqrt{2}]$$

$$- SN_2[d_1(\bar{S}_{T/2}, T/2), -d_1(X, T); -1/\sqrt{2}]. \tag{11}$$

The critical stock price, $\bar{S}_{T/2}$, solves

$$S = X - p(S, X, T/2, r, \sigma) = \bar{S}_{T/2}. \tag{12}$$

Let P_3 be the value of a put that can only be exercised at time $T/3$, time $2T/3$, or time T. Then

$$P_3 = Xe^{-rT/3}N_1[-d_2(\bar{S}_{T/3}, T/3)] - SN_1[-d_1(\bar{S}_{T/3}, T/3)]$$

$$+ Xe^{-2rT/3}N_2[d_2(\bar{S}_{T/3}, T/3), -d_2(\bar{S}_{2T/3}, 2T/3); -1/\sqrt{2}]$$

$$- SN_2[d_1(\bar{S}_{T/3}, T/3), -d_1(\bar{S}_{2T/3}, 2T/3); -1/\sqrt{2}]$$

$$+ Xe^{-rT}N_3[d_1(\bar{S}_{T/3}, T/3), d_1(\bar{S}_{2T/3}, 2T/3), -d_1(X, T);$$

$$1/\sqrt{2}, -1/\sqrt{3}, -\sqrt{2/3}]$$

$$- SN_3[d_2(\bar{S}_{T/3}, T/3), d_2(\bar{S}_{2T/3}, 2T/3), -d_2(X, T);$$

$$1/\sqrt{2}, -1/\sqrt{3}, -\sqrt{2/3}] \tag{13}$$

and the critical stock prices $\bar{S}_{T/3}$ and $\bar{S}_{2T/3}$ solve

$$S = X - P_2(S, X, 2T/3, r, \sigma) = \bar{S}_{T/3} \tag{14}$$

and

$$S = X - p(S, X, T/3, r, \sigma) = \bar{S}_{2T/3}, \tag{15}$$

respectively.

The values $P_1, P_2, P_3, \ldots$ define a sequence, the limit of which is the American put value. Many techniques are available for computing such limits. One method is Richardson extrapolation (see, e.g., Dahlquist and Bjorck [5, p. 269]). This method permits the determination of the limiting value of some quantity as the "step length," h, approaches zero. In our case, the quantity to be determined is the American put price for a particular set of values of S, X, T, r, and σ. The step length is the time between points at which exercise is permitted. The version of Richardson extrapolation we use is developed in the Appendix, and leads to the following equation:

$$P = P_3 + \tfrac{7}{2}(P_3 - P_2) - \tfrac{1}{2}(P_2 - P_1). \tag{16}$$

This polynomial can be used to determine American put values and hedge ratios.

Table I presents our formula values, which are given in the next to last column, while the last column gives values found by numerical integration

Table I. Comparison of American and European Values and Hedge Ratios[a]

r	X	σ	T	$\dfrac{\partial p}{\partial S}$ (European)	$\dfrac{\partial P}{\partial S}$ (Analytic)	p (European)	P (Analytic)	P (Numerical)
0.1250	1.0	0.5	1.0000	-0.309	-0.359	0.1327	0.1476	0.148
0.0800	1.0	0.4	1.0000	-0.345	-0.381	0.1170	0.1258	0.126
0.0450	1.0	0.3	1.0000	-0.382	-0.407	0.0959	0.1005	0.101
0.0200	1.0	0.2	1.0000	-0.421	-0.436	0.0694	0.0712	0.071
0.0050	1.0	0.1	1.0000	-0.460	-0.467	0.0373	0.0377	0.038
0.0900	1.0	0.3	1.0000	-0.326	-0.385	0.0761	0.0859	0.086
0.0400	1.0	0.2	1.0000	-0.382	-0.416	0.0600	0.0640	0.064
0.0100	1.0	0.1	1.0000	-0.440	-0.455	0.0349	0.0357	0.036
0.0800	1.0	0.2	1.0000	-0.309	-0.393	0.0442	0.0525	0.053
0.0200	1.0	0.1	1.0000	-0.401	-0.434	0.0304	0.0322	0.033
0.1200	1.0	0.2	1.0000	-0.242	-0.387	0.0317	0.0439	0.044
0.0300	1.0	0.1	1.0000	-0.363	-0.418	0.0263	0.0292	0.03
0.0488	35.0	0.2	0.0833	-0.008	-0.008	0.0062	0.0062	0.01
0.0488	35.0	0.2	0.3333	-0.088	-0.090	0.1960	0.1999	0.20
0.0488	35.0	0.2	0.5833	-0.128	-0.134	0.4170	0.4321	0.43
0.0488	40.0	0.2	0.0833	-0.460	-0.470	0.8404	0.8528	0.85
0.0488	40.0	0.2	0.3333	-0.421	-0.443	1.5222	1.5807	1.58
0.0488	40.0	0.2	0.5833	-0.396	-0.427	1.8813	1.9905	1.99
0.0488	45.0	0.2	0.0833	-0.974	-1.000	4.8399	4.9985	5.00
0.0488	45.0	0.2	0.3333	-0.794	-0.888	4.7805	5.0951	5.09
0.0488	45.0	0.2	0.5833	-0.694	-0.805	4.8402	5.2719	5.27
0.0488	35.0	0.3	0.0833	-0.051	-0.052	0.0771	0.0774	0.08
0.0488	35.0	0.3	0.3333	-0.171	-0.174	0.6867	0.6969	0.70
0.0488	35.0	0.3	0.5833	-0.206	-0.213	1.1890	1.2194	1.22
0.0488	40.0	0.3	0.0833	-0.464	-0.470	1.2991	1.3100	1.31
0.0488	40.0	0.3	0.3333	-0.428	-0.442	2.4376	2.4817	2.48
0.0488	40.0	0.3	0.5833	-0.406	-0.425	3.0636	3.1733	3.17
0.0488	45.0	0.3	0.0833	-0.898	-0.926	4.9796	5.0599	5.06
0.0488	45.0	0.3	0.3333	-0.691	-0.726	5.5290	5.7012	5.71
0.0488	45.0	0.3	0.5833	-0.608	-0.651	5.9725	6.2365	6.24
0.0488	35.0	0.4	0.0833	-0.106	-0.106	0.2458	0.2466	0.25
0.0488	35.0	0.4	0.3333	-0.222	-0.226	1.3298	1.3450	1.35
0.0488	35.0	0.4	0.5833	-0.247	-0.254	2.1129	2.1568	2.16
0.0488	40.0	0.4	0.0833	-0.463	-0.467	1.7579	1.7679	1.77
0.0488	40.0	0.4	0.3333	-0.426	-0.437	3.3338	3.3632	3.38
0.0488	40.0	0.4	0.5833	-0.403	-0.418	4.2475	4.3556	4.35
0.0488	45.0	0.4	0.0833	-0.823	-0.835	5.2362	5.2855	5.29
0.0488	45.0	0.4	0.3333	-0.627	-0.646	6.3769	6.5093	6.51
0.0488	45.0	0.4	0.5833	-0.556	-0.580	7.1656	7.3831	7.39

[a] Numerical values in far right column are from Parkinson [17] for $X = 1$ and from Cox and Rubinstein [4] for $X \neq 1$. Analytic values in next to last column are from evaluating Equation (5). European values are from the Black-Scholes equation. The stock price equals one dollar for Parkinson and 40 dollars ($S = \$40$) for Cox and Rubinstein.

in Parkinson [17] and by binomial approximation in Cox and Rubinstein [4] (with 150 time steps).[5] The analytic and numerical solutions yield values within a penny of each other. Note that the European values are close to the American values for the parameters presented (these parameters were chosen to match the other established values). Of course the American feature will be most valuable relative to the European when the option is more likely to be exercised early. In Table I the absolute difference is largest, for example, when the exercise price is $45.00. Since this is only $5.00 in-the-money (or about 12.5% when $S = $40.00), more significant differences would be observed for options further in-the-money, or where early exercise is more likely.

Preliminary evidence indicates that the analytic formula evaluation tabulated is faster to compute, by a factor of 10 times, than the numerical methods.[6] This is because the binomial and finite difference methods compute n critical stock prices ($n = $ 150 in Cox and Rubinstein) while our three point extrapolation computes only three, and the tabulated four point method computes six. (The three point extrapolation is about twice as fast as the four point.)

The hedge ratio for the American put is the change in the put value with respect to a change in the stock price. This partial derivative is given analytically in equation (6) as $\partial P/\partial S = -w_1$. In the absence of an analytic formula the hedge ratio is numerically approximated by computing two put values for two different stock prices and then using a different equation to

---

[5]There are many routines available for calculating multivariate normal integrals. Here, the univariate and bivariate normals are calculated using the IMSL routines, MDNORD, and a double precision version of MDBNOR. The trivariate normal integral is evaluated as

$$N_3(h, k, j; \varrho_{12}, \varrho_{13}, \varrho_{23}) = \int_{-\infty}^{j} F'(z) N_2 \left(\frac{k - \varrho_{23}z}{(1-\varrho_{23}^2)^{1/2}}, \frac{h - \varrho_{13}z}{(1-\varrho_{13}^2)^{1/2}}; \right.$$

$$\left. \frac{\varrho_{12} - \varrho_{13}\varrho_{23}}{(1-\varrho_{13}^2)^{1/2}(1-\varrho_{23}^2)^{1/2}} \right) dz$$

where $F'(z)$ is the standard normal density function. The integral can be done using the IMSL routine, DCADRE. The critical stock prices are computed by a Newton-Raphson gradient scheme.

[6]The tabulated values are actually computed from a more accurate four point extrapolation developed similarly to the three point method described above. The resulting four point formula is:

$$P = P_4 + \tfrac{29}{3}(P_4 - P_3) - \tfrac{23}{6}(P_3 - P_2) + \tfrac{1}{6}(P_2 - P_1).$$

The higher order integrals can be evaluated using an integral reduction given in Geske [7]. The comparative times come from the numerical methods presented in Geske and Shastri [11].

approximate the partial derivative at an intermediate stock price. Hedge ratios computed from Equation (6) are given in Column 5 of Table I.

Our technique can also be used for valuing American puts adjusted for cash dividends. However, introducing dividends changes the critical stock price path (or, equivalently, the probability of exercise at different dates) so radically that an extrapolation based on a few exercise points equally spaced through time could result in large errors. Rather than using a large number of exercise points and then extrapolating, we use the following device which finesses the problem in an intuitive way. First, note that any dividend precludes exercise for a period preceding the ex-dividend date (see Johnson [14, p. 42]). Let D' be that dividend which is just big enough to preclude exercise for the entire period between dividends.[7] If the actual dividend, D, is greater than D', then we can put all the exercise points in the period between the last ex-dividend date and the maturity date of the option. If $D < D'$, we find the put value from linear interpolation:

$$P(D) = P(0) + D/D' [P(D') - P(0)]$$

where $P(0)$, $P(D)$, and $P(D')$ are the values of puts when there is no dividend, a dividend D, and a dividend D', respectively. Table II indicates that penny accuracy is obtained with this procedure.

The methods discussed here can also be used to simplify the evaluation of certain contracts, such as coupon bonds, warrants, and currency options. For example, suppose a 30-year bond pays semiannual coupons. Evaluating the analytic formula for this compound option would be very tedious because 60 exercise points involving at least 120 terms of higher order integrals would have to be computed. In fact, it is usually more efficient to evaluate such formulae by finite differences for integral dimensions greater than ten. Richardson extrapolation provides a simple alternative. By extrapolating from three or four payment dates to 60, an efficient computation results. Also, with American currency options and options on futures, since both calls and puts may be exercised early (independent of dividends), this evaluation procedure is applicable. (See Grabbe [12] or Garman and Kolhagen [6] for currency option formulae, Ramaswamy and Sundaresan [18] for options on futures formula, and Shastri and Tandon [20] for an application of this evaluation technique to American currency options.)

III. Conclusion

This paper presents an analytic solution to the American put problem. To our knowledge this is the first formula presented with its comparative statics that satisfies this partial differential equation, subject to the free boundary condition. We attribute the solution of this mathematical problem to simplifications afforded by the economic interpretation. First,

---

[7]Assuming that the stock price drops by the dividend, D, on the ex-dividend date, Johnson [14] shows that there will be no early exercise provided $D \geq X(e^{rT} - 1)$.

Table II. Comparison of American and European Puts Adjusted for Cash Dividends[a]
(S = \$40.00, r = 0.0488 percent annually)

X	σ	T	p (European)	P (Interpolate)	P (Numerical)
35.0	0.2	0.0833	0.01	0.0116	0.01
35.0	0.2	0.3333	0.30	0.3071	0.31
35.0	0.2	0.5833	0.65	0.6580	0.66
40.0	0.2	0.0833	1.09	1.1079	1.11
40.0	0.2	0.3333	1.98	2.0120	2.01
40.0	0.2	0.5833	2.54	2.5717	2.58
45.0	0.2	0.0833	5.33	5.4209	5.41
45.0	0.2	0.3333	5.60	5.69	5.67
45.0	0.2	0.5833	5.93	6.03	6.02
35.0	0.3	0.0833	0.11	0.1073	0.11
35.0	0.3	0.3333	0.88	0.8837	0.88
35.0	0.3	0.5833	1.53	1.5454	1.55
40.0	0.3	0.0833	1.55	1.5590	1.56
40.0	0.3	0.3333	2.88	2.9072	2.91
40.0	0.3	0.5833	3.71	3.7435	3.74
45.0	0.3	0.0833	5.43	5.4996	5.50
45.0	0.3	0.3333	6.24	6.3089	6.29
45.0	0.3	0.5833	6.92	6.9977	6.99
35.0	0.4	0.0833	0.30	0.3049	0.31
35.0	0.4	0.3333	1.57	1.5798	1.58
35.0	0.4	0.5833	2.51	2.5277	2.52
40.0	0.4	0.0833	2.00	2.0120	2.01
40.0	0.4	0.3333	3.78	3.8033	3.81
40.0	0.4	0.5833	4.88	4.9116	4.92
45.0	0.4	0.0833	5.65	5.7015	5.70
45.0	0.4	0.3333	7.02	7.0774	7.07
45.0	0.4	0.5833	8.02	8.0914	8.10

[a] Values in far right column are from Cox and Rubinstein [4]. Values in the next to last column are from a version of Equation (5). The European option values are from the Black-Scholes equation adjusted by reducing the stock price by the scheduled dividend. A 50-cent quarterly dividend is paid in ½, 3½, and 6½ months. Thus one-, four-, and seven-month options (T = 0.0833, 0.3333, 0.5833) have one, two, and three scheduled dividend payments, respectively.

the risk-free hedge allows economists to avoid the complex transformations usually required for solutions to partial differential equations. Second, compound option theory provides a straightforward method for interpreting the infinite series of interrelated probability integrals arising from the free boundary condition. A key to the solution is that each exercise decision is considered as a discrete event. Thus, the formula derived is a continuous time solution to the partial differential equation, subject to the free boundary condition applied at an infinite number of discrete instants. The formula adds to our intuition because it implies an exact duplicating portfolio for the American put, consisting of specific positions in discount bonds and stock sold short. All the comparative statics of the American put formula are presented and discussed. The solution is extended to stock paying cash dividends.

The evaluation of the formula is a separate problem. At first blush the American put formula might be considered intractable due to the infinite series of integrals. However, we demonstrate that because the formula is exact in the limit, arbitrary accuracy can be obtained by extrapolating from a small sequence of terms to the actual solution containing an infinite series.

This formula evaluation procedure leads to a polynomial expression similar to that used to evaluate the integral terms in the Black-Scholes European put option formula.

Before a formula existed that satisfied this boundary value problem, numerical procedures (such as the binomial or finite difference methods) were used for approximating the values of American puts. We demonstrate that our formula allows the use of an evaluation technique resulting in a significant reduction in the number of critical stock price computations necessary for penny accuracy and thus enhances computational efficiency. We also demonstrate that this formula evaluation technique can be used to calculate analytic hedge ratios derived by differentiating the formula. Furthermore, it allows the determination of American put values on stocks that pay cash dividends. A version of this evaluation method can be used to simplify the valuation of American currency options, options on futures, coupon bonds, and many other complex problems.

The technique might also be combined with finite differences and extended in order to evaluate two-dimensional stochastic problems.

Appendix

Let $F(h)$ be the value of the function of interest when a step size of h is used. We wish to find $F(0)$. Suppose that $F(h)$ takes the form

$$F(h) = F(0) + a_1 h^p + a_2 h^r + 0(h^s)$$

where $s > r > p$.

Then we can also write

$$F(kh) = F(0) + a_1 (kh)^p + a_2 (kh)^r + 0(h^s)$$

and

$$F(qh) = F(0) + a_1 (qh)^p + a_2 (qh)^r + 0(h^s)$$

where $q > k > 1$. Substituting for a_1 and a_2 and solving for $F(0)$ yields

$$F(0) = F(h) + \frac{A}{C}[F(h) - F(kh)] - \frac{B}{C}[F(kh) - F(qh)] \quad \text{(A1)}$$

where

$$A = q^r - q^p + k^p - k^r$$

$$B = k^r - k^p$$

$$C = q^r(k^p - 1) - q^p(k^r - 1) + k^r - k^p.$$

Using $P_1 = F(qh)$, $P_2 = F(kh)$, and $P_3 = F(h)$, we have $q = 3$ and $k = \frac{3}{2}$. If we expand $F(h)$ in a Taylor series around $F(0)$ and drop terms of third order or higher, we have $p = 1$ and $r = 2$. Substitution into (16) gives

$$P = P_3 + \frac{7}{2}(P_3 - P_2) - \frac{1}{2}(P_2 - P_1). \quad \text{(A2)}$$

There is some error in (A2) from dropping the higher order terms.

References

1. F. Black and M. Scholes. "The Pricing of Options and Corporate Liabilities." *Journal of Political Economy* 81 (May-June 1973), 637-59.

2. M. Brennan and E. Schwartz. "The Valuation of American Put Options." *Journal of Finance* 32 (May 1977), 449-62.

3. J. Cox and S. Ross. "The Valuation of Options for Alternative Stochastic Processes." *Journal of Financial Economics* 3 (January/March 1976), 145-66.

4. —— and M. Rubinstein. *Options Markets*. Englewood Cliffs, N. J.: Prentice-Hall, forthcoming, 1984.

5. G. Dahlquist and A. Bjorck. *Numerical Methods*. Englewood Cliffs, N. J.: Prentice-Hall, 1974.

6. M. Garman and S. Kohlhagen. "Foreign Currency Option Values." *Journal of International Money and Finance* 2 (December 1983), 231-37.

7. R. Geske. "The Valuation of Corporate Liabilities as Compound Options." *Journal of Financial and Quantitative Analysis* 12 (November 1977), 541-52.

8. ——. "The Valuation of Compound Options." *Journal of Financial Economics* 7 (March 1979), 63-81.

9. ——. "A Note on an Analytical Valuation Formula for Unprotected American Call Options on Stocks with Known Dividends." *Journal of Financial Economics* 7 (December 1979), 375-80.

10. —— and K. Shastri. "The Early Exercise of American Puts." forthcoming, *Journal of Banking and Finance* (1985).

11. —— and ——. "Valuation by Approximation: A Comparison of Alternative Option Valuation Techniques." forthcoming, *Journal of Financial and Quantitative Analysis* (1985).

12. J. Grabbe. "The Pricing of Call and Put Options on Foreign Exchange." *Journal of International Money and Finance* 2 (December 1983), 239-53.

13. R. James and E. James. *Mathematical Dictionary*. 4th Edition, New York: Van Nostrand Reinhold, 1982.

14. H. E. Johnson. "Three Topics in Option Pricing." Ph.D. thesis, UCLA, 1981.

15. ——. "An Analytic Approximation for the American Put Price." *Journal of Financial and Quantitative Analysis* 18 (March 1983), 141-48.

16. R. Merton. "The Theory of Rational Option Pricing." *Bell Journal of Economics and Management Science* 4 (Spring 1973), 141-83.

17. M. Parkinson. "Option Pricing: The American Put." *Journal of Business* 50 (January 1977), 21-36.

18. K. Ramaswamy and S. Sundaresan. "The Valuation of Options on Futures Contracts." Columbia University Working Paper, 1984.

19. R. Roll. "An Analytic Valuation Formula for Unprotected American Call Options on Stocks with Known Dividends." *Journal of Financial Economics* 5 (November 1977), 251-58.

20. K. Shastri and K. Tandon. "The Valuation of American Options on Foreign Currency." University of Pittsburgh Working Paper, 1984.

4

Efficient Analytic Approximation of American Option Values

Giovanni Barone-Adesi and
Robert E. Whaley*

Abstract

This paper provides simple, analytic approximations for pricing exchange-traded American call and put options written on commodities and commodity futures contracts. These approximations are accurate and considerably more computationally efficient than finite-difference, binomial, or compound-option pricing methods.

Options written on a wide variety of commodities and commodity futures contracts[1] now trade in the U.S. and Canada. Nearly all these options are American style[2] and thus have early exercise premiums implicitly embedded in their prices. Unlike the European-style option-pricing problems, however, analytic solutions for the American option-pricing problems have not been

*Associate Professors of Finance, University of Alberta and Duke University, respectively. This research was supported by the Futures and Options Research Center at The Fuqua School of Business, Duke University. Comments and suggestions by Fred D. Arditti, David Emanuel, Hans R. Stoll, Stuart M. Turnbull, Vera Zeidan, Luigi Zezza, and an associate editor of this Journal are gratefully acknowledged.

[1]Options on physical commodities (i.e., commodity options) were traded in the U.S. as early as the late 1800's. (See Mehl [14].) These options convey the right to buy or sell a certain physical commodity at a specified price within a specified period of time. The Commodity Exchange Act of 1936, however, banned trading in such options. Recently the CFTC introduced a pilot program allowing the various exchanges to reintroduce commodity options. Active trading now occurs not only in options on physical commodities such as gold and foreign currencies but also in options on commodity futures contracts (i.e., commodity futures options) such as wheat and livestock.
[2]The Chicago Board Options Exchange now lists European-style options on selected foreign currencies and the S&P 500 Composite Stock Index.

Giovanni Barone-Adesi and Robert E. Whaley, "Efficient Analytic Approximation of American Option Values." Reprinted with permission from *The Journal of Finance,* Vol. XLII, No. 2, June 1987.

found, and the pricing of American options has usually resorted to finite-difference, binomial, or, more recently, compound-option approximation methods. While these approximation methods yield accurate American option values, they are cumbersome and expensive to use.

The purpose of this paper is to provide an accurate, inexpensive method for pricing American call and put options written on commodities and commodity futures contracts. The development of the "quadratic" approximation method is contained in Section I. Commodity option and commodity futures option contracts are defined, the underpinnings of commodity option valuation are discussed, and the solutions to the European call and put option-pricing problems are presented. Unlike the non-dividend-paying stock option case, it is shown that the American call option written on a commodity, as well as the American put option, may optimally be exercised prior to expiration. The approximation methods for the American call and put option values are then derived in the manner in which MacMillan [13] approximated the solution to the American put option on a non-dividend-paying stock pricing problem. In Section II, the programming of the approximations is considered, and the results of comparisons of the finite-difference, compound-option, and quadratic approximation methods are presented and discussed. Comparisons are also made to heuristic option-pricing methods. Section III contains a summary.

I. Valuation Equations for Commodity Options

In this section, the theory of pricing commodity and commodity futures option contracts is reviewed, and the approximations for the American call and put options are presented. At the outset it is useful to clearly define the terms "commodity option" and "commodity futures option." In the context in which the terms will be used here, a commodity option represents the right to buy or sell a specific commodity at a specified price within a specified period of time. The exact nature of the underlying commodity varies and may be anything from a precious metal such as gold or silver to a financial instrument such as a Treasury bond or foreign currency. Usually the commodity option is labeled by the nature of the underlying commodity. For example, if the commodity option is written on a common stock, it is referred to as a "stock option," and, if the commodity option is written on a foreign currency, it is referred to as a "foreign currency option." If the underlying commodity is a futures contract, the options are referred to as "commodity futures options" or simply "futures options."

To begin, the focus will be on a general commodity option-pricing model. The assumptions used in the analysis are consistent with those introduced by Black and Scholes [3] and Merton [15]. First, the short-term interest rate, r, and the cost of carrying the commodity, b, are assumed to be constant, proportional rates. For a non-dividend-paying stock, the cost of carry is equal to the riskless rate of interest (i.e., $b = r$), but, for most other commodities, this is not the case. In Merton's [15] constant, proportional dividend-yield option-pricing models, for example, the cost of carrying the stock is the riskless rate, r, less the dividend yield, d (i.e., $b = r - d$). In

Garman and Kohlhagen's [9] foreign currency option-pricing models, the cost of carrying the foreign currency is the domestic riskless rate, r, less the foreign riskless rate, r^* (i.e., $b = r - r^*$). However, that is not to say that the cost of carry is always below the riskless rate of interest. For the traditional agricultural commodities such as grain and livestock, the cost of carry exceeds the riskless rate by costs of storage, insurance, deterioration, etc.

In the absence of costless arbitrage opportunities, the assumption of a constant, proportional cost of carry suggests that the relationship between the futures and underlying commodity prices is

$$F = Se^{bT}, \tag{1}$$

where F and S are the current futures and spot prices, respectively, and T is the time to expiration of the futures contract. This relationship will prove useful later in this section.

A second common assumption in the option-pricing literature is that the underlying commodity price-change movements follow the stochastic differential equation,

$$dS/S = \alpha \, dt + \sigma \, dz, \tag{2}$$

where α is the expected instantaneous relative price change of the commodity, σ is the instantaneous standard deviation, and z is a Wiener process. It is worthwhile to note that, if the cost-of-carry relationship (1) holds and if equation (2) describes the movements of the commodity price through time, then the movements of the futures price are described by the equation,

$$dF/F = (\alpha - b) \, dt + \sigma \, dz. \tag{3}$$

That is, the expected instantaneous relative price change of the futures contract is $\alpha - b$ and the standard deviation of relative commodity price relatives is equal to the standard deviations of futures price relatives.[3]

Finally, assuming that a riskless hedge between the option and the underlying commodity may be formed, the partial differential equation governing the movements of the commodity option price (V) through time is

$$\tfrac{1}{2} \sigma^2 \, S^2 V_{SS} + bSV_S - rV + V_t = 0. \tag{4}$$

This equation, which first appeared in Merton [15], is the heart of the commodity option-pricing discussion contained herein. Note that, when the cost-of-carry rate b is equal to the riskless rate of interest, the differential

[3] This result is noted in Black [2].

equation (4) reduces to that of Black and Scholes [3], and, when the cost of carrying the underlying commodity is 0, the Black [2] commodity futures option differential equation is obtained. Both the non-dividend-paying stock and the futures option-pricing problems are special cases of this more general commodity option-pricing problem.

A. European Commodity Options

The differential equation (4) applies to calls and puts and to European options and American options. To derive the European call formula, the terminal boundary condition, $\max(0, S_T - X)$, is applied. Merton shows indirectly that, when this terminal boundary condition is applied to equation (4), the value of a European call option on a commodity is

$$c(S, T) = Se^{(b-r)T} N(d_1) - Xe^{-rT} N(d_2),\qquad(5)$$

where $d_1 = [\ln(S/X) + (b + 0.5\sigma^2)T] / \sigma\sqrt{T}$, $d_2 = d_1 - \sigma\sqrt{T}$, and $N(\cdot)$ is the cumulative univariate normal distribution.[4] When the lower boundary condition for the European put, $\max(0, X - S_T)$, is applied to the partial differential equation (4), the pricing equation is

$$p(S, T) = Xe^{-rT} N(-d_2) - Se^{(b-r)T} N(-d_1),\qquad(6)$$

where all notation is defined as above.

B. American Commodity Options

The European call formula (5) provides a convenient way of demonstrating that, under certain conditions, the American call option may be exercised early. Suppose $b < r$, as is the case with most of the non-common-stock commodity options traded. As the commodity price, S, becomes extremely large relative to the exercise price of the option, the values of $N(d_1)$ and $N(d_2)$ approach one and the European call value approaches $Se^{(b-r)T} - Xe^{-rT}$. However, the American option may be exercised immediately for $S - X$, which may be higher than the European option value when $b < r$. Thus, the American call option may command a higher price than the European call option because of the early exercise privilege. If $b \geq r$, as in the case of an option on a non-dividend-paying stock (i.e., $b = r$), the lower price bound of the European option will have a greater value than the exercisable proceeds of the American option for all levels of commodity price, so there is no possibility of early exercise and the European call option model (5) will accurately price American call options. For the American puts, there is always some possibility of early exercise, so the European formula (6) never applies. A more detailed explanation of the conditions for early exercise of the call and put options written on commodities is provided in Stoll and Whaley [19].

The valuation of American commodity options therefore involves addressing the early exercise feature of the options. When the American

---

[4] It is interesting to note that substitution of the cost-of-carry relationship (1) into the European commodity formula (5) yields the Black [2] commodity futures option-pricing equation. This was first pointed out by Black and then later by Asay [1].

option boundary conditions are applied to (4), analytic solutions are not known and approximations must be used. The most common approach uses finite-difference methods. The first applications along these lines were by Schwartz [18], who valued warrants written on dividend-paying stocks, and by Brennan and Schwartz [5], who priced American put options on non-dividend-paying stocks.[5] Recently, Ramaswamy and Sundaresan [16] and Brenner, Courtadon, and Subrahmanyam [6] used finite-difference methods to price American options written on futures contracts.

The most serious limitation of using finite-difference methods to price American options is that they are computationally expensive. To ensure a high degree of accuracy, it is necessary to partition the commodity price and time dimensions into a very fine grid and enumerate every possible path the commodity option price could travel during its remaining time to expiration. This task is cumbersome and can only be efficiently accomplished with the use of a main-frame computer.

An alternative approximation method was recently introduced by Geske and Johnson [10]. Their compound-option approximation method is computationally less expensive than numerical methods and offers the advantages of being intuitively appealing and easily amenable to comparative-statics analysis. However, while being about twenty times more computationally efficient than numerical methods, the compound-option approach is still not inexpensive since it requires the evaluation of cumulative bivariate, trivariate, and sometimes higher order multivariate normal density functions. Needless to say, such integral evaluations require the assistance of fairly sophisticated programs and are not practical on anything below the level of a fast microcomputer.

Johnson [12] and others provide heuristic techniques for valuing American put options on non-dividend-paying stocks. Although these techniques are very fast computationally, they are specific to the stock option-pricing problem and are not directly comparable to the general commodity option-pricing approximations discussed herein. In addition, the accuracy of heuristic techniques is frequently sensitive to the parameter range used in the option-pricing problem, a point that we will return to in the simulation results of the next section.

The American commodity option-pricing approximation method derived here is accurate, is amenable to comparative-statics analysis, and can be programmed on a hand-held calculator. The method is based on MacMillan's [13] quadratic approximation of the American put option on a non-dividend-paying stock valuation problem. To explain the derivation of our approximation, the problem of pricing an American call option on a commodity is addressed.

[5] Geske and Shastri [11] provide a comprehensive analysis of the merits of the explicit, implicit, and binomial finite-difference approximation methods. Cox, Ross, and Rubinstein [7] and Cox and Rubinstein [8] provide detailed discussions of the binomial option-pricing framework.

B.1. Quadratic Approximation of the American Call Value

The key insight into the quadratic approximation approach is that, if the partial differential equation (4) applies to American options as well as European options, it also applies to the early exercise premium of the American option. For an American call option written on a commodity, the early exercise premium $\epsilon_C(S, T)$ is defined as

$$\epsilon_C(S, T) = C(S, T) - c(S, T), \tag{7}$$

where $C(S, T)$ is the American commodity option value and $c(S, T)$ is the European commodity option value as described by equation (5). The partial differential equation for the early exercise premium is therefore

$$\tfrac{1}{2}\,\sigma^2 S^2 \epsilon_{SS} - r\epsilon + bS\epsilon_S + \epsilon_t = 0. \tag{8}$$

For ease of exposition, two simplifications are made. First, in place of time t evolving from the present toward the option's expiration t^*, time T evolving from the option's expiration to the present, that is, $T = t^* - t$, is used. Thus, $\epsilon_T = -\epsilon_t$. Second, equation (8) is multiplied by $2/\sigma^2$, and, third, the notational substitutions $M = 2r/\sigma^2$ and $N = 2b/\sigma^2$ are made. Equation (8) now reads as

$$S^2 \epsilon_{SS} - M\epsilon + NS\epsilon_S - (M/r)\epsilon_T = 0. \tag{9}$$

The early exercise premium is then defined as $\epsilon_C(S, K) = K(T)\,f(S, K)$. It therefore follows that $\epsilon_{SS} = Kf_{SS}$ and $\epsilon_T = K_T f + KK_T f_K$. Substituting the partial derivative expressions into (9), factoring K, and gathering terms on Mf yield

$$S^2 f_{SS} + NSf_S - Mf[1 + (K_T/rK)(1 + Kf_K/f)] = 0. \tag{10}$$

Choosing $K(T) = 1 - e^{-rT}$, substituting into (10), and simplifying give

$$S^2 f_{SS} + NSf_S - (M/K)f - (1-K)Mf_K = 0. \tag{11}$$

Up to this point, the analysis has been exact, and no approximation has been made. The approximation will be made in equation (11); the last term on the left-hand side will be assumed to be equal to 0. For commodity options with very short (long) times to expiration, this assumption is reasonable since, as T approaches $0\,(\infty)$, f_K approaches $0\,(K$ approaches 1), and the term $(1-K)Mf_K$, disappears. As an approximation, therefore, the last term is dropped, and the approximation of the early exercise premium differential equation is

$$S^2 f_{SS} + NSf_S - (M/K)f = 0. \tag{12}$$

Equation (12) is a second-order ordinary differential equation with two linearly independent solutions of the form aS^q. They can be found by substituting $f = aS^q$ into (12):

$$aS^q [q^2 + (N - 1)q - M/K] = 0. \tag{13}$$

The roots of (13) are $q_1 = [-(N - 1) - \sqrt{(N - 1)^2 + 4M/K}]/2$ and $q_2 = [-(N - 1) + \sqrt{(N - 1)^2 + 4M/K}]/2$. Note that, because $M/K > 0, q_1 < 0$ and $q_2 > 0$.

The general solution to (12) is

$$f(S) = a_1 S^{q_1} + a_2 S^{q_2}. \tag{14}$$

With q_1 and q_2 known, a_1 and a_2 are left to be determined. With $q_1 < 0$ and $a_1 \neq 0$, the function f approaches ∞ as the commodity price S approaches 0. This is unacceptable since the early exercise premium of the American call becomes worthless when the commodity price drops to zero. The first constraint to be imposed is, therefore, $a_1 = 0$, and the approximate value of the American call option written on a commodity will be written as

$$C(S, T) = c(S, T) + Ka_2 S^{q_2}. \tag{15}$$

To find an appropriate constraint on a_2, consider equation (15). As $S = 0$, $C(S, T) = 0$ since both $c(S, T)$ and $Ka_2 S^{q_2}$ are equal to 0. As S rises, the value of $C(S, T)$ rises for two reasons: $c(S, T)$ rises and $Ka_2 S^{q_2}$ rises, assuming $a_2 > 0$. In order to represent the value of the American call, however, the function on the right-hand side of (15) should touch, but not intersect, the boundary imposed by the early exercise proceeds of the American call, $S - X$. Below the critical commodity price S^* implied by the point of tangency, the American call value is represented by equation (15). Above S^*, the American call value is equal to its exercisable proceeds, $S - X$, and the fact that $a_2 S^{q_2}$ rises at a faster and faster rate above S^* is not of concern.

To find the critical commodity price S^*, the exercisable value of the American call is set equal to the value of $C(S^*, T)$ as represented by (15), that is,

$$S^* - X = c(S^*, T) + Ka_2 S^{*q_2}, \tag{16}$$

and the slope of the exercisable value of the call, one, is set equal to the slope of $C(S^*, T)$, that is,

$$1 = e^{(b - r)T} N [d_1(S^*)] + Kq_2 a_2 S^{*q_2 - 1}, \tag{17}$$

where $e^{(b-r)T} N [d_1(S^*)]$ is the partial derivative of $c(S^*, T)$ with respect to S^* and where $d_1(S^*) = [\ln(S^*/X) + (b + 0.5\sigma^2)T]/\sigma\sqrt{T}$. Thus, there are two equations, (16) and (17), and two unknowns, a_2 and S^*. Isolating a_2 in (17) yields

$$a_2 = \{1 - e^{(b - r)T} N [d_1(S^*)]\}/Kq_2 S^{*q_2 - 1}. \tag{18}$$

Substituting (18) into (16) and simplifying results in a critical commodity price, S^*, that satisfies

$$S^* - X = c(S^*, T) + \{1 - e^{(b-r)T} N[d_1(S^*)]\} S^*/q_2. \qquad (19)$$

Although S^* is the only unknown value in equation (19), it must be determined iteratively. An efficient algorithm for finding S^* is presented in the next section. With S^* known, equation (16) provides the value of a_2. Substituting (18) into (15) and simplifying yields

$$C(S, T) = c(S, T) + A_2(S/S^*)^{q_2}, \text{ when } S < S^*, \text{ and}$$

$$C(S, T) = S - X, \qquad\qquad \text{when } S \geq S^*, \qquad (20)$$

where $A_2 = (S^*/q_2)\{1 - e^{(b-r)T} N[d_1(S^*)]\}$. Note that $A_2 > 0$ since S^*, q_2, and $1 - e^{(b-r)T} N[d_1(S^*)]$ are positive when $b < r$. Equation (20) is therefore an efficient analytic approximation of the value of an American call option written on a commodity when the cost of carry is less than the riskless rate of interest. When $b \geq r$, the American call will never be exercised early, and valuation equation (5) applies.[6]

In equation (20), it is worthwhile to note that the early exercise premium of the American call option on a commodity approaches 0 as the time to expiration of the option approaches 0. As T gets small, $N[d_1(S^*)]$ approaches 1,[7] $\{1 - e^{(b-r)T} N[d_1(S^*)]\}$ approaches 0, A_2 approaches 0, and, thus, $A_2(S/S^*)^{q_2}$ approaches 0.

B.2. Quadratic Approximation of the American Put Value

Before proceeding with a discussion of how to use this quadratic approximation, it is useful to note how the approximation would change for the American put option on a commodity. Since the partial differential equation (8) applies to the early exercise premium of the American put

$$\epsilon_p(S, T) = P(S, T) - p(S, T), \qquad (21)$$

equations (9) through (14) of the analysis remain the same. In (14), it is now the term $a_1 S^{q_1}$ that is of interest since the early exercise premium of the American put must approach 0 as S approaches positive infinity. The term, $a_2 S^{q_2}$, violates this boundary condition, so a_2 is set equal to zero and the approximate value of the American put option becomes

$$P(S, T) = p(S, T) + Ka_1 S^{q_1}. \qquad (22)$$

[6] In coding the American call option-pricing algorithm, first check whether the cost of carry b is less than the riskless rate of interest r. If not, then price the call using the European pricing formula.
[7] The term $N[d_1(S^*)]$ approaches 1 rather than 0 as T approaches 0 because the critical commodity price S^* is always greater than or equal to the exercise price X.

Again, the values of the coefficient a_1 and the critical commodity price S^{**} must be determined, and the necessary steps pattern those used in determining a_2 and S^*. The value of a_1 is

$$a_1 = -\{1 - e^{(b-r)T}N[-d_1(S^{**})]\}/Kq_1S^{**q_1-1}, \qquad (23)$$

where $-e^{(b-r)T}N[-d_1(S^{**})]$ is the partial derivative of $p(S^{**}, T)$ with respect to S^{**} and where $a_1 > 0$ since $q_1 < 0$ and since all other terms are positive. The critical commodity price S^{**} is determined by solving

$$X - S^{**} = p(S^{**}, T) - \{1 - e^{(b-r)T}N[-d_1(S^{**})]\}S^{**}/q_1. \qquad (24)$$

With S^{**} known, the approximate value of an American put option written on a commodity (22) becomes

$$P(S, T) = p(S, T) + A_1(S/S^{**})^{q_1}, \text{ when } S > S^{**}, \text{ and}$$

$$P(S, T) = X - S, \qquad\qquad\qquad \text{ when } S \leq S^{**}, \qquad (25)$$

where $A_1 = -(S^{**}/q_1)\{1 - e^{(b-r)T}N[-d_1(S^{**})]\}$. Note that $A_1 > 0$ since $q_1 < 0$, $S^{**} > 0$, and $N[-d_1(S^{**})] < e^{-bT}$.

C. American Commodity Futures Options

Up to this point, the focus of the discussion has been on the valuation of commodity options where the cost of carrying the underlying commodity is a constant, proportional rate b. If b is set equal to certain specific values, however, specific commodity option-valuation equations are obtained. For example, the cost of carrying any futures position is equal to 0. Thus, to obtain the commodity futures option-valuation results, simply set b equal to zero in the approximation just described. The approximate value of an American call option on a futures contract is given by equation (20), where the futures price, F, is substituted for the commodity price, S, and where the cost of carry, b, is set equal to zero. The approximate value of an American put option on a futures contract is given by equation (25), where similar substitutions are made. Both of these American futures option-price approximations are used in Whaley [21].

D. American Stock Options

Another special case of the commodity option-valuation framework is the nondividend-paying stock option. The cost of carrying the underlying stock is assumed to be equal to the riskless rate of interest; in other words, b is set equal to r in the above approximation. It is worthwhile to point out that, since $b = r$ for this option-pricing problem, the American call will be valued using the European formula (5). The resulting approximation for the American put is that of MacMillan [13].

E. Summary

The quadratic approximation techniques for pricing the American call and put options on a commodity have now been derived. Before presenting some simulation results intended to show the accuracy of the techniques, it is worthwhile to reiterate that they are useful in a wide range of option-pricing problems. The futures option and the stock option cases are only two examples. American options on foreign currencies, on stock indexes with continuous dividend yields, on precious metal such as gold and silver, and on long-term debt instruments with continuous coupon yields can be accurately priced within this framework.

II. Implementation and Simulation of Approximation Method

In the approximation procedure outlined in the last section, only one step, the determination of the critical commodity price S^*, is not straightforward. In this section, an efficient algorithm for determining S^* is presented, and then simulated results from the quadratic approximation method are compared with results for the finite-difference and compound-option approximation methods.

A. An Algorithm for Determining S^*

To find the critical commodity price S^*, it is necessary to solve equation (19). Since this cannot be done directly, an iterative procedure must be developed.[8] To begin, evaluate both sides of equation (19) at some seed value, S_1, that is,

$$\text{LHS}(S_i) = S_i - X, \quad \text{and} \tag{26a}$$

$$\text{RHS}(S_i) = c(S_i, T) + \{1 - e^{(b-r)T} N[d_1(S_i)]\} S_i/q_2, \tag{26b}$$

where $d_1(S_i) = [\ln(S_i/X) + (b + 0.5\sigma^2)T]/\sigma\sqrt{T}$ and $i = 1$. Naturally, it is unlikely that $\text{LHS}(S_i) = \text{RHS}(S_i)$ on the initial guess of S_1, and a second guess must be made. To develop the next guess S_{i+1}, first find the slope b_i of the RHS at S_i, that is,

$$b_i = e^{(b-r)T} N[d_1(S_i)](1 - 1/q_2) + [1 - e^{(b-r)T} n[d_1(S_i)]/\sigma\sqrt{T}]/q_2, \tag{27}$$

where $n(\cdot)$ is the univariate normal density function. Next, find where the line tangent to the curve RHS at S_i intersects the exercisable proceeds of the American call, $S - X$, that is,

$$\text{RHS}(S_i) + b_i (S - S_i) = S - X,$$

and then isolate S to find S_{i+1},

$$S_{i+1} = [X + \text{RHS}(S_i) - b_i S_i]/(1 - b_i). \tag{28}$$

Equation (28) will provide the second and subsequent guesses of S, with new values of (26a), (26b), (27), and (28) computed with each new iteration. The iterative procedure should continue until the relative absolute error falls within an acceptable tolerance level; for example,

---

[8] Iterative solution to (19) for each of the options on a single underlying commodity is unnecessary. The critical commodity price in (19) is proportional in X; thus, if the critical commodity price S_1^* is computed for an option with exercise price X_1, the critical commodity price for a second option with a different exercise price X_2 is simply $S_2^* = (S_1^*/X_1)X_2$.

$$|\text{LHS}(S_i) - \text{RHS}(S_i)|/X < 0.00001. \tag{29}$$

B. Seed Value

The iterative technique outlined here converges reasonably quickly by setting the seed value S_1 equal to the option's exercise price X and by imposing the tolerance criterion (29). The speed with which the algorithm finds the critical commodity price, however, can be improved by using a starting point closer to the solution.

To arrive at an approximate value of the critical commodity price, consider the information contained in equation (19). If the time to expiration of the call option is equal to 0, the critical commodity price above which the option will be exercised is the exercise price of the option, X. At the other extreme, if the time remaining to expiration is infinite, the critical commodity price may be solved exactly by substituting $T = +\infty$ in (19), that is,

$$S^*(\infty) = X/[1 - 1/q_2(\infty)], \tag{30}$$

where $q_2(\infty) = [-(N-1) + \sqrt{(N-1)^2 + 4M}]/2$. Equation (19) also shows that the critical commodity price is an increasing function of time to expiration of the option.

With this and other information from the call option-pricing problem in hand, it is possible to derive an approximate analytic solution to finding the critical commodity price. Such a derivation is provided in the Appendix. The final form of the approximation is

$$S^* = X + [S^*(\infty) - X][1 - e^{h_2}], \tag{31}$$

where $h_2 = -(bT + 2\sigma\sqrt{T})\{X/[S^*(\infty) - X]\}$. Note that (31) satisfies the critical commodity-price restrictions when $T = 0$ and $T = +\infty$.

For the put option-pricing problem, the critical commodity price must satisfy equation (24). At $T = 0$, the critical price is again the exercise price of the option, and, at $T = +\infty$,

$$S^{**}(\infty) = X/[1 - 1/q_1(\infty)], \tag{32}$$

where $q_1(\infty) = [-(N-1) - \sqrt{(N-1)^2 + 4M}]/2$. It is worthwhile to point out that, when the cost of carry b is equal to the riskless rate of interest r, this result is exactly the same as Merton's [15]. In equation (24), the critical commodity price is a decreasing function of time to expiration, and an approximate analytic expression for the critical commodity price is

$$S^{**} = S^{**}(\infty) + [X - S^{**}(\infty)]e^{h_1}, \tag{33}$$

where $h_1 = (bT - 2\sigma\sqrt{T})\{X/[X - S^{**}(\infty)]\}$.[9]

Equations (31) and (33) provide the seed values for the iterative procedures that determine the critical commodity price in the American call and the American put option algorithms. Both are straightforward computations, and their use usually ensures convergence in three iterations or less.

C. Simulation Results

Tables I through IV contain a sensitivity analysis of the theoretical European and American commodity option values for a variety of cost-of-carry parameters.

In Tables I and II, for example, the cost-of-carry parameter (b) is set equal to -0.04 and 0.04, respectively. Thus, the values in these tables may be thought of as being American foreign currency option prices, where the foreign riskless rate of interest is greater than and less than the domestic interest rate, respectively. In Table III, the cost-of-carry parameter is set equal to 0, so the resulting option values are for American commodity futures options. Finally, in Table IV, the cost of carry is set equal to the riskless rate of interest. Since this is the nondividend-paying stock option case, only American put option values are reported.[10]

In the first three tables, three methods for pricing the American commodity options are used: (a) the implicit finite-difference approximation method with commodity price steps of 0.10 and time steps of 0.20 days or 0.0005479 years, (b) the compound-option approximation method using a three-point extrapolation, and (c) the quadratic approximation method. The European model values are included to provide an indication of the magnitude of the early exercise premium on American options. In the fourth table, the values of Johnson's [12] heuristic technique are also provided.

C.1. Commodity Option Results

Judging by the results reported in Tables I and II, the quadratic approximation is very accurate. The option prices for this method are within pennies of the implicit finite-difference method.[11] The most extreme errors occur for the in-the-money options where the volatility parameter is set equal to 0.40 and where the cost of carry is -0.04 for the calls and 0.04 for the puts (see Tables I and II), but even there the degree of mispricing, when compared with the finite-difference method, is less than three tenths of one percent. Considering that the quadratic approximation costs roughly 2000 times less, this result is impressive.

---

[9] For very large values of b and T, the influence of b must be bounded in the put exponent to ensure critical prices monotonically decreasing in T. A reasonable upper bound on b is $0.6\sigma/\sqrt{T}$, so the critical commodity price declines at least with a velocity $e^{-1.4\sigma\sqrt{T}}$.

[10] Recall that, when the cost of carry is greater than or equal to the riskless rate of interest, the American call option will not be exercised early.

[11] Here, the finite-difference method is assumed to provide the "true" value of the American commodity option.

Table I. Theoretical American commodity option values using finite-difference, compound-option, and quadratic approximation methods (cost of carry (b) = − 0.04 and exercise price (X) = 100)

Option parameters[a]	Commodity price S	Call Options				Put Options			
		European c(S,T)[b]	American C(S,T)			European p(S,T)[b]	American P(S,T)		
			Finite-difference method[c]	Compound-option method[d]	Quadratic approximation method[e]		Finite-difference method[c]	Compound-option method[d]	Quadratic approximation method[e]
r = 0.08, σ = 0.20, T = 0.25	80	0.03	0.03	0.03	0.03	20.41	20.41	20.41	20.42
	90	0.57	0.58	0.58	0.59	11.25	11.25	11.25	11.25
	100	3.42	3.52	3.52	3.52	4.40	4.40	4.40	4.40
	110	9.85	10.35	10.38	10.31	1.12	1.12	1.12	1.12
	120	18.62	20.00	19.97	20.00	0.18	0.19	0.18	0.18
r = 0.12, σ = 0.20, T = 0.25	80	0.03	0.03	0.03	0.03	20.21	20.23	20.23	20.25
	90	0.56	0.58	0.57	0.59	11.14	11.14	11.14	11.15
	100	3.39	3.50	3.49	3.51	4.35	4.35	4.35	4.35
	110	9.75	10.32	10.36	10.29	1.11	1.11	1.11	1.11
	120	18.43	20.00	19.97	20.00	0.18	0.18	0.18	0.18
r = 0.08, σ = 0.40, T = 0.25	80	1.05	1.06	1.05	1.07	21.43	21.44	2.144	21.46
	90	3.23	3.27	3.27	3.28	13.91	13.91	13.92	13.93
	100	7.29	7.40	7.41	7.41	8.27	8.26	8.27	8.27
	110	13.25	13.52	13.51	13.50	4.52	4.52	4.52	4.52
	120	20.73	21.29	21.30	21.23	2.29	2.29	2.29	2.30
r = 0.08, σ = 0.20, T = 0.50	80	0.21	0.21	0.21	0.23	20.95	20.96	20.96	20.98
	90	1.31	1.36	1.36	1.39	12.63	12.63	12.63	12.64
	100	4.46	4.71	4.69	4.72	6.37	6.37	6.37	6.37
	110	10.16	11.00	11.03	10.96	2.65	2.65	2.65	2.65
	120	17.85	20.00	19.98	20.00	0.92	0.92	0.92	0.92

[a] The notation in this column is as follows: r = riskless rate of interest; σ = standard deviation of the commodity price-change relative; and T = time to expiration.

[b] Values are computed using equations (5) and (6).

[c] Values are computed using the implicit finite-difference method with commodity price steps of 0.10 and time steps of 0.20 days or 0.0005479 years.

[d] Values are computed using the three-point extrapolation of the compound-option valuation approach.

[e] Values are computed using the quadratic approximation equations (20) and (25).

The compound-option valuation method appears to do about as well as the quadratic approximation at pricing American options. For options at or out of the money, both techniques provide accurate option values. In-the-money options have minor mispricing errors, but on a proportionate basis the errors are trivial. The overwhelming advantage of using the quadratic approximation, however, lies in the fact that its computational cost is approximately 100 times less than the compound-option approximation.

C.2. Commodity Futures Option Values

In Table III, the simulation results for futures options are reported. With the cost-of-carry parameter set equal to 0, the quadratic approximation shows even more precision across the parameter ranges considered. The largest errors are on the order of one tenth of one percent.

C.3. Stock Option Values

Table IV contains the simulation results for the special case where the cost of carry is equal to the riskless rate of interest, that is, for American options written on non-dividend-paying stocks. Since the call will not rationally be exercised early, only put option values appear in the table. The quadratic approximation method used here is that of MacMillan [13].

With respect to the quadratic approximation and the compound-option approach, the results are qualitatively similar to the previous tables. Slightly larger mispricing errors occur for in-the-money options, but, even in the case where the volatility parameter is set equal to 0.40, the degree of mispricing is less than four tenths of one percent.

Unlike the previous tables, Table IV contains an additional column of values under the heading "Johnson Method." Johnson [12] provides a heuristic technique for valuing American put options on non-dividend-paying stocks.[12] His technique is slightly faster than the quadratic approximation; however, its validity appears to break down for put options that are slightly in the money. Consider the put option values for the first set of parameters. When the stock price is 80, all techniques yield an option value equal to 20.00. This is because the current stock price is below the critical stock price, so that the value of the American put is simply equal to its exercisable proceeds. However, if the stock price is 90, as seen in the second row of the table, the current stock price is in excess of the critical stock price and the approximation methods are invoked. While the quadratic approximation produces an absolute mispricing error of 0.03 (or 0.3 percent) relative to the finite-difference value, the Johnson technique produces a 0.52 (or 5.18 percent) error.

---

[12] When the underlying stock pays known discrete dividends, both the American call and put options written on the stock may be optimally exercised early. Roll [17] and Whaley [20] provide the analytic solution to the American call option-pricing problem where the stock pays known discrete dividends. Analytic solutions to the American put option-pricing problem have not been found; however, Geske and Johnson [10] and Blomeyer [4] provide heuristic techniques for approximating the put option values.

Table II. Theoretical American commodity option values using finite-difference, compound-option, and quadratic approximation methods (cost of carry $(b) = 0.04$ and exercise price $(X) = 100$)

Option parameters[a]	Commodity price S	Call Options				Put Options			
		European $c(S,T)$[b]	American $C(S,T)$			European $p(S,T)$[b]	American $P(S,T)$		
			Finite-difference method[c]	Compound-option method[d]	Quadratic approximation method[e]		Finite-difference method[c]	Compound-option method[d]	Quadratic approximation method[e]
$r = 0.08, \sigma = 0.20, T = 0.25$	80	0.05	0.05	0.05	0.05	18.87	20.00	19.99	20.00
	90	0.85	0.85	0.85	0.85	9.76	10.22	10.25	10.18
	100	4.44	4.44	4.44	4.44	3.46	3.55	3.54	3.54
	110	11.66	11.66	11.66	11.66	0.78	0.79	0.79	0.80
	120	20.90	20.90	20.90	20.90	0.11	0.11	0.11	0.12
$r = 0.12, \sigma = 0.20, T = 0.25$	80	0.05	0.05	0.05	0.05	18.68	20.00	19.99	20.00
	90	0.84	0.84	0.84	0.84	9.67	10.20	10.23	10.16
	100	4.40	4.40	4.40	4.40	3.42	3.52	3.52	3.53
	110	11.55	11.55	11.55	11.55	0.77	0.78	0.78	0.79
	120	20.69	20.69	20.69	20.69	0.11	0.11	0.11	0.12
$r = 0.08, \sigma = 0.40, T = 0.25$	80	1.29	1.29	1.29	1.29	20.11	20.59	20.60	20.53
	90	3.82	3.82	3.82	3.82	12.74	12.95	12.94	12.93
	100	8.35	8.35	8.35	8.35	7.36	7.46	7.46	7.46
	110	14.80	14.79	14.80	14.80	3.91	3.95	3.95	3.96
	120	22.71	22.71	22.71	22.72	1.93	1.94	1.94	1.95
$r = 0.08, \sigma = 0.20, T = 0.50$	80	0.41	0.41	0.41	0.41	18.08	20.00	19.96	20.00
	90	2.18	2.18	2.18	2.18	10.04	10.75	10.79	10.71
	100	6.50	6.50	6.50	6.50	4.55	4.77	4.75	4.77
	110	13.42	13.42	13.42	13.42	1.68	1.74	1.74	1.76
	120	22.06	22.06	22.06	22.06	0.51	0.53	0.53	0.55

[a] The notation in this column is as follows: r = riskless rate of interest, σ = standard deviation of the commodity price-change relative; and T = time to expiration.

[b] Values are computed using equations (5) and (6).

[c] Values are computed using the implicit finite-difference method with commodity price steps of 0.10 and time steps of 0.20 days or 0.0005479 years.

[d] Values are computed using the three-point extrapolation of the compound-option valuation approach.

[e] Values are computed using the quadratic approximation equations (20) and (25).

Table III. Theoretical American futures option values using finite-difference, compound-option, and quadratic approximation methods (cost of carry (b) = 0.00 and exercise price (X) = 100)

Option parameters[a]	Futures price F	Call Options				Put Options				
				American $C(F,T)$				American $P(F,T)$		
		European $c(F,T)$[b]	Finite-difference method[c]	Compound-option method[d]	Quadratic approximation method[d]	European $p(F,T)$[b]	Finite-difference method[c]	Compound-option method[d]	Quadratic approximation method[e]
$r = 0.08, \sigma = 0.20, T = 0.25$	80	0.04	0.04	0.04	0.04	19.64	20.00	20.00	20.00
	90	0.70	0.70	0.70	0.70	10.50	10.59	10.58	10.58
	100	3.91	3.92	3.93	3.93	3.91	3.92	3.93	3.93
	110	10.74	10.82	10.81	10.81	0.94	0.94	0.94	0.94
	120	19.75	20.03	20.04	20.02	0.14	0.14	0.14	0.15
$r = 0.12, \sigma = 0.20, T = 0.25$	80	0.04	0.04	0.04	0.04	19.45	20.00	19.99	20.00
	90	0.69	0.69	0.69	0.70	10.40	10.53	10.53	10.53
	100	3.87	3.89	3.90	3.90	3.87	3.89	3.90	3.90
	110	10.63	10.76	10.76	10.75	0.94	0.93	0.93	0.93
	120	19.55	20.01	20.02	20.00	0.14	0.14	0.14	0.15
$r = 0.08, \sigma = 0.40, T = 0.25$	80	1.16	1.16	1.16	1.17	20.77	20.94	20.94	20.93
	90	3.52	3.53	3.53	3.53	13.32	13.39	13.39	13.39
	100	7.81	7.83	7.84	7.84	7.81	7.83	7.84	7.84
	110	14.01	14.08	14.08	14.08	4.21	4.22	4.22	4.23
	120	21.71	21.87	21.86	21.86	2.10	2.11	2.11	2.12
$r = 0.08, \sigma = 0.20, T = 0.50$	80	0.30	0.30	0.30	0.30	19.51	20.06	20.09	20.04
	90	1.70	1.71	1.71	1.72	11.31	11.48	11.47	11.48
	100	5.42	5.46	5.47	5.48	5.42	5.46	5.57	5.48
	110	11.73	11.90	11.89	11.90	2.12	2.14	2.14	2.15
	120	19.91	20.36	20.37	20.34	0.69	0.69	0.69	0.70

[a] The notation in this column is as follows: r = riskless rate of interest; σ = standard deviation of the commodity futures price-change relative; and T = time to expiration.

[b] Values are computed using equations (5) and (6).

[c] Values are computed using the implicit finite-difference method with commodity futures price steps of 0.10 and time steps of 0.20 days or 0.0005479 years.

[d] Values are computed using the three-point extrapolation of the compound-option valuation approach.

[e] Values are computed using the quadratic approximation equations (20) and (25).

Table IV. Theoretical American put option on stock values using finite-difference, compound option, quadratic, and Johnson approximation methods (exercise price (X) = 100)

			American P(S, T)			
Option parameters[a]	Stock price S	European c(S, T)[b]	Finite-difference method[c]	Compound option method[d]	Quadratic approximation method[e]	Johnson method[f]
b = r = 0.08, σ = 0.20, T = 0.25	80	18.09	20.00	20.00	20.00	20.00
	90	9.05	10.04	10.07	10.01	10.56
	100	3.04	3.22	3.21	3.22	3.21
	110	0.64	0.66	0.66	0.68	0.65
	120	0.09	0.09	0.09	0.10	0.09
b = r = 0.12, σ = 0.20, T = 0.25	80	17.13	20.00	20.01	20.00	20.00
	90	8.26	10.00	9.96	10.00	10.00
	100	2.63	2.92	2.91	2.93	2.90
	110	0.52	0.55	0.55	0.58	0.53
	120	0.07	0.07	0.07	0.08	0.07
b = r = 0.08, σ = 0.40, T = 0.25	80	19.45	20.32	20.37	20.25	20.08
	90	12.17	12.56	12.55	12.51	12.52
	100	6.94	7.11	7.10	7.10	7.12
	110	3.63	3.70	3.70	3.71	3.72
	120	1.76	1.79	1.79	1.81	1.80
b = r = 0.08, σ = 0.20, T = 0.50	80	16.65	20.00	19.94	20.00	20.00
	90	8.83	10.29	10.37	10.23	10.73
	100	3.79	4.19	4.17	4.19	4.17
	110	1.31	1.41	1.41	1.45	1.38
	120	0.38	0.40	0.40	0.42	0.39

[a] The notation in this column is as follows: b = cost of carrying underlying stock; r = riskless rate of interest; σ = standard deviation of the stock price-change relative; and T = time to expiration.

[b] Values are computed using equations (5) and (6).

[c] Values are computed using the implicit finite-difference method with stock price steps of 0.10 and time steps of 0.20 days or 0.0005479 years.

[d] Values are computed using the three-point extrapolation of the compound-option valuation approach.

[e] Values are computed using the quadratic approximation equations (20) and (25).

[f] Values are computed using the Johnson [12] method.

For the second and third set of option-pricing parameters, the Johnson technique produces reasonable values, but, for the fourth set of parameters, the first in-the-money put option again has a large mispricing error. This is indicative of the problems one faces when using heuristic procedures. While the option prices may be well behaved in general, they may lead to serious mispricing errors for arbitrary combinations of parameters.

C.4. Long-Term Option Values

The parameters of the options in Tables I through IV were chosen so as to represent typical exchange-traded options with times to expiration of less than six months. The most actively traded options, in fact, have maturities of less than three months. In the interest of completeness, however, it is worthwhile to point out that over-the-counter markets for long-term options are slowly developing, particularly in the area of U.S. Treasury obligations, and the impact of the time-to-expiration parameter on the accuracy of the approximation methods is of particular importance. For this reason, simulations are performed using times to expiration of up to three years. Table V contains the three-year time-to-expiration results.

The results in Table V show that all the approximation method results are weakened considerably. In some cases, the three-point extrapolation compound-option method does better than the quadratic approximation, and in other cases vice versa. The Johnson technique produces the largest mispricing errors for the American put option on a non-dividend-paying stock.

Based on the results of Table V and the other simulation results (not reported here) using time-to-expiration parameters of between 0.5 and 3 years, it is reasonable to use either the three-point compound-option extrapolation method or the quadratic approximation method for pricing commodity options with less than one year to expiration, with the obvious preference being for the quadratic approximation method because of its computational expediency. For times to expiration beyond one year, finite-difference or binomial option-pricing methods should be used to ensure pricing accuracy.

III. Summary

More than thirty commodity option and commodity futures option contracts now trade in a variety of markets in the U.S. and Canada. These options are, in general, American style and, as such, are exercisable at any time up to and including the expiration date of the option. Previous attempts at pricing these options have been accurate but computationally expensive. This paper provides simple, inexpensive approximations for valuing exchange-traded American call and put options written on commodities as well as commodity futures contracts.

Table V. Theoretical American commodity option values using finite-difference, compound-option, quadratic, and Johnson approximation methods (exercise price $(X) = 100$)

Option parameters[a]	Call Options				Put Options				
			American $C(S,T)$				American $P(S,T)$		
Commodity price S	European $c(S,T)$[b]	Finite-difference method[c]	Compound-option method[d]	Quadratic approximation method[e]	European $p(S,T)$[b]	Finite-difference method[c]	Compound-option method[d]	Quadratic approximation method[e]	Johnson method[f]
$b = -0.04, r = 0.08, \sigma = 0.20, T = 3.00$									
80	1.93	2.34	2.31	2.52	24.78	25.66	25.59	26.25	
90	3.75	4.76	4.71	4.97	19.62	20.08	20.05	20.64	
100	6.36	8.49	8.54	8.67	15.25	15.50	15.51	15.99	
110	9.75	13.79	14.08	13.88	11.67	11.80	11.83	12.22	
120	13.87	20.89	21.29	20.88	8.81	8.88	8.91	9.23	
$b = 0.00, r = 0.08, \sigma = 0.20, T = 3.00$									
80	3.79	3.98	3.99	4.20	19.52	22.20	22.35	22.40	
90	6.81	7.25	7.23	7.54	14.68	16.21	16.18	16.50	
100	10.82	11.70	11.65	12.03	10.82	11.70	11.65	12.03	
110	15.71	17.31	17.28	17.64	7.85	8.37	8.34	8.69	
120	21.35	24.02	24.11	24.30	5.62	5.93	5.93	6.22	
$b = 0.04, r = 0.08, \sigma = 0.20, T = 3.00$									
80	6.88	6.88	6.88	6.97	14.59	20.35	20.60	20.33	
90	11.49	11.48	11.49	11.62	10.33	13.50	13.69	13.56	
100	17.20	17.19	17.22	17.40	7.17	8.94	8.95	9.11	
110	23.80	23.80	23.85	24.09	4.90	5.91	5.85	6.12	
120	31.08	31.08	31.18	31.49	3.32	3.90	3.85	4.12	
$b = 0.08, r = 0.08, \sigma = 0.20, T = 3.00$									
80					10.25	20.00	19.44	20.00	20.00
90					6.78	11.69	11.96	11.63	12.89
100					4.41	6.93	7.06	6.96	6.69
110					2.83	4.15	4.13	4.26	3.71
120					1.80	2.51	2.45	2.64	2.16

[a] The notation in this column is as follows: b = cost of carrying underlying stock; r = riskless rate of interest; σ = standard deviation of the commodity price-change relative; and T = time to expiration.

[b] Values are computed using equations (5) and (6).

[c] Values are computed using the implicit finite-difference method with commodity price steps of 0.10 and time steps of 0.20 days or 0.0005479 years.

[d] Values are computed using the three-point extrapolation of the compound-option valuation approach.

[e] Values are computed using the quadratic approximation equations (20) and (25).

[f] Values are computed using the Johnson [12] method.

Appendix *Derivation of Analytic Approximation of Critical Commodity Price S^*:*
Equation (19) shows that the critical commodity price is an increasing
function of time to expiration of the option bounded by the exercise price
when $T = 0$ and by

$$S^*(\infty) = X / [1 - 1/q_2(\infty)], \tag{A1}$$

where $q_2(\infty) = [-(N - 1) + \sqrt{(N - 1)^2 + 4M}] / 2$ when $T = +\infty$.
To derive an approximate analytic equation for the critical commodity price
as a function of time, consider the call option holder's dilemma when the
time to expiration of the option is some arbitrarily small time increment, $\triangle$.
If the call is exercised at time $\triangle$, the exercisable proceeds are $S(\triangle) - X$,
which will earn interest to become $[S(\triangle) - X](1 + r\triangle)$ at $T = 0$. On the
other hand, if the option holder chooses to leave the call position open, the
worth of the call is equal to the expected terminal value of the option,
$E[S(0) - X | S(0) > X]$. Thus, the critical commodity price above which
the call option holder will choose to exercise early is determined by

$$[S^*(\triangle) - X](1 + r\triangle) = E[S^*(0) - X | S^*(0) > X]. \tag{A2}$$

To evaluate the right-hand side of (A2), represent the commodity price at
the expiration of the option using the Cox-Ross-Rubinstein [7] risk-neutral
binomial approach, that is,

$$S^*(0) = S^*(\triangle)(1 + b\triangle \pm \sigma\sqrt{\triangle}). \tag{A3}$$

Equation (A3) says that, in a risk-neutral world, the expected rate of return
on commodity S is equal to its cost of carry, $b\triangle$, plus or minus the
stochastic component, $\sigma\sqrt{\triangle}$, with equal probabilities. Thus, the expected
value of holding the call to expiration is

$$E[S^*(0) - X | S^*(0) > X] = 0.5[S^*(1 + b\triangle + \sigma\sqrt{\triangle}) - X], \tag{A4}$$

and, if (A4) is substituted into (A2), the critical commodity price is
determined by

$$(S^*(\triangle) - X)(1 + r\triangle) = 0.5[S^*(1 + b\triangle + \sigma\sqrt{\triangle}) - X]. \tag{A5}$$

Rearranging equation (A5) to isolate $S^*(\triangle)$ provides

$$S^*(\triangle) = [X(1 + 2\triangle r)] / [1 + (2r - b)\triangle - \sigma\sqrt{\triangle}], \tag{A6}$$

which, in turn, provides the approximations

$$S^*(\triangle) \approx X(1 + 2\triangle r)[1 - (2r - b)\triangle + \sigma\sqrt{\triangle}]$$

$$\approx X(1 + b\triangle + \sigma\sqrt{\triangle}). \tag{A7}$$

Equation (A7) ignores terms of order higher than $\triangle$. Moreover, $\triangle$ is assumed to be small enough to make opportunities of exercising the call at intermediate times before expiration negligible. Therefore, equation (A7) holds exactly only in the case where $\triangle$ approaches 0.

To approximate S^* for arbitrary times to expiration, expand $S^*(0)$ around $S^*(\triangle)$, that is,

$$S^*(0) = S^*(\triangle) + (\delta S^*/\delta T)_{T = \triangle}\triangle. \tag{A8}$$

(The reason for choosing $T = \triangle$ in lieu of $T = 0$ as the origin of the expression (A8) is that at $T = 0$ the slope is discontinuous.) Substituting (A7) for $S^*(\triangle)$ and recalling that $S^*(0) = X$, it follows that the critical commodity price satisfies the differential equation

$$\delta S^*/\delta T = S^*(0)(b + \sigma/\sqrt{\triangle}) \tag{A9}$$

in a neighborhood of $T = 0$, with boundary condition $S^*(0) = X$. The general solution of (A9) is of the exponential form, with exponent $(bT + 2\sigma\sqrt{T})$.

Now, drawing the results together, the critical commodity price function is bounded at $T = 0$ and at $T = +\infty$ and has a slope described by the differential equation (A9). An appropriate final form for the critical commodity price of an American call option is therefore

$$S^* = X + [S^*(\infty) - X][1 - e^{h_2}], \tag{A10}$$

where $h_2 = -(bT + 2\sigma\sqrt{T})\{X/[S^*(\infty) - X]\}$. A parallel analysis can be made in deriving an approximate analytical critical commodity price equation for the American put option.

References

1. M.R. Asay. "A Note on the Design of Commodity Contracts." *Journal of Futures Markets* 2 (Spring 1982), 1-7.

2. F. Black. "The Pricing of Commodity Contracts." *Journal of Financial Economics* 3 (January-March 1976), 167-79.

3. —— and M.S. Scholes. "The Pricing of Options and Corporate Liabilities." *Journal of Political Economy* 81 (May-June 1973), 637-54.

4. E.C. Blomeyer. "An Analytic Approximation for the American Put Price for Options on Stocks with Dividends." *Journal of Financial and Quantitative Analysis* 21 (June 1986), 229-33.

5. M.J. Brennan and E.S. Schwartz. "The Valuation of American Put Options." *Journal of Finance* 32 (May 1977), 449-62.

6. M. Brenner, G.R. Courtadon, and M. Subrahmanyam. "Option on the Spot and Options on Futures." *Journal of Finance* 40 (December 1985), 1303-17.

7. J.C. Cox, S.A. Ross, and M. Rubinstein. "Option Pricing: A Simplified Approach." *Journal of Financial Economics* 3 (September 1979), 229-63.

8. J.C. Cox and M. Rubinstein. *Options Markets.* Englewood Cliffs, NJ: Prentice-Hall, 1985.

9. M. Garman and S. Kohlhagen. "Foreign Currency Option Values." *Journal of International Money and Finance* 2 (December 1983), 231-37.

10. R. Geske and H.E. Johnson. "The American Put Valued Analytically." *Journal of Finance* 39 (December 1984), 1511-24.

11. R. Geske and K. Shastri. "Valuation by Approximation: A Comparison of Alternative Valuation Techniques." *Journal of Financial and Quantitative Analysis* 20 (March 1985), 45-71.

12. H.E. Johnson. "An Analytic Approximation for the American Put Price." *Journal of Financial and Quantitative Analysis* 18 (March 1983), 141-48.

13. L.W. MacMillan. "Analytic Approximation for the American Put Option." *Advances in Futures and Options Research* 1 (1986), 119-39.

14. P. Mehl. *Trading in Privileges on the Chicago Board of Trade.* U. S. Department of Agriculture, Circular No. 323, December 1934.

15. R.C. Merton. "The Theory of Rational Option Pricing." *Bell Journal of Economics and Management Science* 4 (Spring 1973), 141-83.

16. K. Ramaswamy and S.M. Sundaresan. "The Valuation of Options on Futures Contracts." *Journal of Finance* 40 (December 1985), 1319-40.

17. R. Roll. "An Analytical Valuation Formula for Unprotected American Call Options on Stocks with Known Dividends." *Journal of Financial Economics* 5 (November 1977), 251-58.

18. E.S. Schwartz. "The Valuation of Warrants: Implementing a New Approach." *Journal of Financial Economics* 4 (January 1977), 79-93.

19. H.R. Stoll and R.E. Whaley. "The New Option Instruments: Arbitrageable Linkages and Valuation." *Advances in Futures and Options Research* 1 (1986), 25-62.

20. R.E. Whaley. "On the Valuation of American Call Options on Stocks with Known Dividends." *Journal of Financial Economics* 9 (June 1981), 207-11.

21. ——. "Valuation of American Futures Options: Theory and Empirical Tests." *Journal of Finance* 41 (March 1986), 127-50.

Section 6
Dynamic Replication

Underlying the development of the Black-Scholes model is the premise that an option position can be dynamically replicated using an investment in the underlying commodity and some riskless bonds. A long call position, for example, can be synthetically created using a dynamically rebalanced portfolio of a long commodity position and a short riskless bond position. A long put is equivalent to a dynamically rebalanced short commodity/long riskless bond position.

Dynamic replication of any number of possible security positions in any number of commodities is possible where two or more of the markets for commodities, futures, options, and/or futures options are reasonably liquid. In the finance literature, the lion's share of the research work has focused on one form of dynamic replication in one particular market—stock portfolio insurance. Perhaps, the two best-known works—Rubinstein and Leland [1981] and Rubinstein [1985]—are reprinted here. Many other articles have also been written. Some of them are listed in the bibliography. Since dynamic replication involves frequent portfolio revision, an important

consideration is transaction costs. Leland [1985] analyzes the role transaction costs may have on option pricing.

References and Bibliography

Asay, M., and C. Edelberg, 1986, "Can a Dynamic Strategy Replicate the Returns on an Option?" *Journal of Futures Markets* 6, 63-70.

Black, F., and R. Jones, 1987, "Simplifying Portfolio Insurance," *Journal of Portfolio Management* 14, 48-51.

Bookstaber, R., and J.A. Langsam, 1988, "Portfolio Insurance Trading Rules," *Journal of Futures Markets* 8, 15-31.

Etzioni, E.S., 1986, "Rebalance Disciplines for Portfolio Insurance," *Journal of Portfolio Insurance* 13, 59-62.

Gatto, M.A., R. Geske, R. Litzenberger, and H. Sosin, 1980, "Mutual Fund Insurance," *Journal of Financial Economics* 61, 283-317.

Leland, H.E., 1985, "Option Pricing and Replication with Transactions Costs," *Journal of Finance* 40, 1283-1301.

Merrick, J.J., 1988, "Portfolio Insurance with Stock Index Futures," *Journal of Futures Markets* 8, 441-55.

Rubinstein, M. 1985, "Alternative Paths for Portfolio Insurance," *Financial Analysts Journal* 41, 42-52.

——, and H.E. Leland, 1981, "Replicating Options with Positions in Stock and Cash," *Financial Analysts Journal* 37, 63-72.

Tilley, J.A., and G.O. Latainer, 1985, "A Synthetic Option Framework for Asset Allocation," *Financial Analysts Journal* 41, 32-43.

1

Replicating Options with Positions in Stock and Cash

Mark Rubinstein and Hayne E. Leland

A call option can be replicated by a "portfolio" that combines borrowing and holding shares in the underlying stock, provided the number of shares is continually revised so that it always equals the slope of the option curve at the current stock price. Using replicating portfolios, many institutions can create protective puts and covered calls on stock for which there is no options market.

In most situations of practical relevance, the price behavior of a call option is very similar to a combined position involving the underlying stock and borrowing. The call price and the stock price will change in the same direction. The effect on the call price of a one dollar change in the stock price, however, will depend on the current price of the stock; the number of shares of stock in the replicating portfolio must equal the slope of the call price curve at that price.

When the call is deep out of the money—i.e., when the stock price is much lower than the striking price—a one dollar change in the stock price has

Hayne Leland and Mark Rubinstein are Professors of Finance at the Graduate School of Business, University of California at Berkeley, and cofounders, along with John O'Brien, of Leland O'Brien Rubinstein, Associates, an investment counselling firm specializing in risk management through dynamic investment strategies.

John Cox has not been listed as an author of this article, although the authors feel his contribution merited more than equal coauthorship. The authors also thank John O'Brien for his many useful comments.

little effect on the call price. When the stock price is equal to the striking price, a one dollar change in the stock price produces roughly a half-dollar change in the call price. If the stock price rises until the call is deep in the money, a one dollar move in the stock price results in nearly a one dollar move in the call price.

Because the call price behaves this way, we must revise the replicating portfolio as the stock price changes—selling stock as the share price falls and buying stocks as the share price rises. Since we are never fully invested when the stock price rises, nor fully disinvested when the stock price falls, this process will deplete our initial investment. By the call's expiration date, the accumulated depletion will, in principle, exactly equal the initial value of the call.

This concept permits one to replicate, not only calls, but many other option positions. Using replicating portfolios, institutions can create for themselves protective puts and covered calls on stocks for which there is no options market.

The volume of trading in exchange-traded puts and calls (in terms of share equivalents) now rivals share volume on the New York Stock Exchange.[1] Yet, for most investors, options remain an arcane or complex subject. One thing is obvious, however: An option provides a comparable alternative to a direct investment in its underlying stock. To decide between the two alternatives, we would like to know

— how to value an option,

— how to measure the expected return and risk of an option position,

— how the margin requirements and transaction costs of option positions compare with common stock,

— who should be buying and who should be selling options, and

— how to create an option position if options on a stock or on a portfolio do not exist.

It is quixotic to hope that there is a single, simple principle that can provide satisfactory answers to all these questions? We think not. The key insight to modern option pricing theory is that, *in most situations of practical relevance, the price behavior of an option is very similar to a portfolio of the*

---

[1] A *call* option is a contract giving its owner the right to buy a fixed number of shares of a specified common stock at a fixed price at any time on or before a fixed date. The act of making this transaction is referred to as *exercising* the option. The fixed price is termed the *striking price* and the given date, the *expiration date.* The individual who issues a call is termed the *writer* and the individual who purchases the call is termed the *buyer.* A *put* option is identical except it conveys the right to sell the stock.

underlying stock and cash that is revised in a particular way over time.[2] That is, there exists a *replicating portfolio strategy,* involving stock and cash only, that creates returns identical to those of an option.

Why the Principle Makes Sense

Suppose we want to replicate a *purchased call option* using only stock and cash. To succeed, our replicating strategy must satisfy three conditions:

(1) for small changes in the stock price, the initial out-of-pocket investment must give the same absolute, *dollar return* as a call;

(2) to equalize the *rate of return* as well, the initial out-of-pocket investment must equal the value of the call; and

(3) thereafter, since a call requires no further investment, the replicating strategy must be self-financing.

If it satisfies these three conditions, we have reason to believe our strategy will resemble a purchased call at any time prior to expiration as well as at expiration.

A brief study of exchange-traded options and their underlying stocks shows that their respective daily price movements tend to parallel each other. In particular, (a) *call prices and stock prices change in the same direction,* but (b) *a one dollar change in the stock price causes a change of less than one dollar in the call price.* To satisfy Condition 1, the value of our stock-cash portfolio must, at a minimum, share these properties. This will be easy to achieve if we have a long position in less than one share of stock.

Further observation of call prices shows that they have additional important properties our replicating portfolio will have to match. More precisely, how a call option responds to a one dollar change in the stock depends largely on the relationship of its striking price to the stock price. (c) *When the stock price is much lower than the striking price (deep out of the money), a one dollar change in the stock price has little effect on the call price. If the stock price rises and becomes equal to the striking price (at the money), a one dollar change in the stock price produces about a half-dollar change in the call price. If the stock price rises further so the call becomes deep in the money, then a one dollar move in the stock price results in almost a one dollar change in the call price.*

Because the call price behaves this way, we will have to revise our replicating portfolio as the stock's price changes. We will hold almost no shares when

---

[2] The seminal articles developing the theory are Fischer Black and Myron Scholes, "The Pricing of Options and Corporate Liabilities," *Journal of Political Economy,* May-June 1973 and Robert C. Merton, "Theory of Rational Option Pricing," *Bell Journal of Economics and Management Science,* Spring 1973. A considerably simplified development of this theory appears in John C. Cox, Stephen A. Ross and Mark Rubinstein, "Option Pricing: A Simplified Approach," *Journal of Financial Economics,* September 1979.

the stock price is low, and we will buy more shares as the stock price rises. In particular, when the call is at the money, we will hold about half a share. As the stock price rises further and the call becomes deep in the money, we will gradually buy in until we hold almost one share. Conversely, whenever the stock price falls, we will reduce the number of shares held.

Exhibit A compares the value of a call with various positions in stock and cash. Both the striking price and current stock price are $30, so the call is currently at the money. The straight line from the origin with a slope of one shows how the value of an unlevered position in one share of stock depends on the stock price; in this very simple case, these values are identical. In contrast, the value of a fixed, fully levered position in the stock is represented by the straight line with a slope of one cutting the horizontal axis at 30.

The curve describing the call price as the stock price changes is positively sloped throughout (corresponding to property a). Although the slope of this curve is always lower than the unlevered stock line (property b), it increases continually as the stock price rises (property c).[3] Indeed, *the slope of the call price curve at the current stock price is equal to the number of shares in the replicating stock-cash portfolio.* At very low stock prices, the slope is almost zero; at a stock price of 30 the slope is one-half; and at very high stock prices the slope is almost one.

Equalizing dollar return is not enough. We must also equalize the rate of return (Condition 2). Observation of call prices shows that (d) *a one per cent change in the stock price causes a more than one per cent change in the call price.* Our stock-cash portfolio will share this property if the stock position is financed partly through borrowing.

For example, suppose the initial at-the-money call value equals three dollars and the stock price is $30. In this case, we will buy one-half share by investing three dollars and borrowing $12. The current value of our portfolio is thus three dollars—$15 worth of stock minus the $12 owed on borrowing. If the stock price then goes up by one dollar, the value of the portfolio will increase by only 50 cents. However, this represents a $16\frac{2}{3}$ per cent increase for our portfolio, compared with a $3\frac{1}{3}$ per cent increase for the stock.

Exhibit A shows that the amount of borrowing in the replicating portfolio ($12) can be read off the vertical axis by extending the dashed line tangent to the call price line at the current stock price ($30). The distance between the corresponding call price ($3) and the amount borrowed ($12) equals the dollar value of the stock in the replicating portfolio ($15).

---

[3] To simplify the figure, the interest rate on borrowing is assumed to be zero. If this were not the case, the call price curve would have the same zero vertical intercept, but be shifted somewhat to the left. The exact position and shape of the curve is also influenced by the time remaining to expiration and the stock volatility.

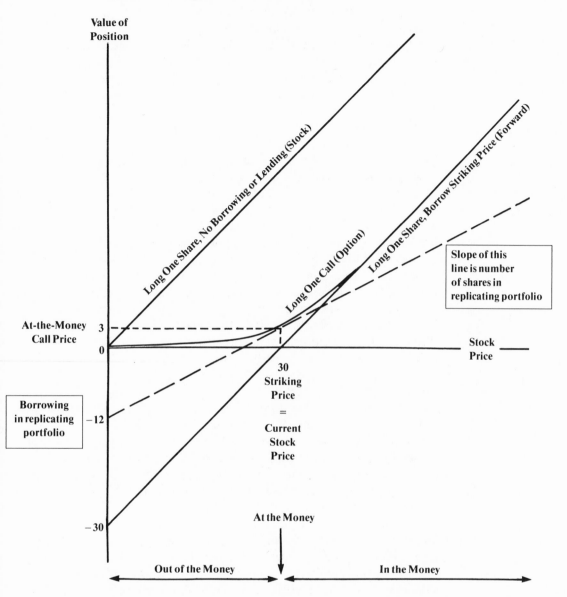

Finally, to satisfy Condition 3, our strategy must be self-financing from this point on. To accomplish this, we borrow more to buy more shares as the stock price rises and, as the stock price falls, we sell some of our shares and use the proceeds to retire a portion of our loan. Exhibit A shows what is happening. As the stock price rises, the dashed tangent line pivots counterclockwise, taking on increasing slope and an intercept farther from zero along the vertical axis. As the stock price falls, the tangent line pivots clockwise, with decreasing slope and an intercept closer to zero.

By the expiration date, if the call ends up in the money, we will find ourselves owning one share of stock and owing from our borrowing an amount exactly equal to the striking price. If the call finishes out of the money, we will find ourselves fully disinvested with our borrowing fully repaid. This is, of course, equivalent to the position of the call buyer at expiration. In either case, since, prior to expiration, we were never fully invested when the stock price rose nor fully disinvested when the stock price fell, we will have depleted our initial out-of-pocket investment. It is a fact of modern option pricing theory that, subject to certain conditions, in either case this "shortfall" will always be the same and exactly equal to the initial value of the call.

Some Additional Factors

In conclusion, we can replicate a purchased call position by a strategy of *buying shares plus borrowing, where we buy (sell) shares and increase (decrease) our borrowing as the stock price rises (falls).* Of course, the current level of the stock price and its relation to the striking price will affect how much stock we should be holding and how much we should be borrowing. In addition, the exact composition of our replicating portfolio will also depend on other factors. For example, if the call is sufficiently in the money, we should be holding more shares, the closer the option is to *expiration* or the lower the *stock volatility,* because profitable exercise is then more likely. Since we are borrowing against purchased shares, it should be obvious that we will also need to take account of *interest rates* and *cash dividends.* The appendix shows how a call option can be replicated exactly by a properly adjusted stock-cash portfolio.

The accuracy of the replicating strategy depends on four considerations. First, since the strategy may involve frequent trading, it is necessary that transaction costs be relatively insignificant. Second, it must be possible to borrow whatever is required to form the replicating stock-cash portfolio (or, in the case of other option positions, it must be possible to short the stock). Third, the possibility of gap openings or jump movements in the stock price means that a call can provide something that a levered stock position cannot. To take an extreme case, suppose a catastrophic event suddenly causes the stock price to collapse to zero. This may happen too fast for us to adjust our stock-cash position. A call, on the other hand, will pay off our borrowing even in such a catastrophe. Fourth, there may be significant uncertainty surrounding future rates of interest, the stock's volatility or cash dividends on the stock. For example, while an unanticipated increase in volatility will increase the value of a call, it is certainly conceivable that such a change could occur without affecting the price of the underlying stock. Consequently, the value of the call would change but the value of our stock-cash portfolio would not, no matter how we revised it.

Although it may be impossible to find a strategy that will allow a portfolio of stock and cash to duplicate exactly the returns of a call under all possible conditions, we nonetheless strongly believe that the concept of an option being equivalent to a carefully adjusted position in the underlying stock and cash is close enough to being true in most situations of practical interest to make it an invaluable tool for understanding options.

Translating Option Positions into Stock-Cash Equivalents

If we can replicate a call, we can replicate any other type of option position as well. Exhibit B, which translates the language of options into the more familiar language of stock and cash, shows what we would need to do. For each option position in the center of the table, the corresponding stock-cash portfolio is given at the top of its column and the appropriate adjustment strategy is given at the ends of its row. For example, the exhibit shows that buying a put is equivalent to a short position in the stock combined with lending, which will be revised by lending more and shorting more stock when the stock price falls and by lending less and buying back stock to reduce the short position when the stock price rises.

Some option positions are likened to "insurance." For example, an at-the-money put purchased against a long share of stock protects the investor against loss if the stock price falls. Our analysis implies that this insurance effect arises because the *protective put* is equivalent to a long stock-lending portfolio that is systematically shifted (1) away from stock and into cash as the stock price falls, providing a floor on losses, and (2) into stock and away from cash as the stock price rises, permitting future gains or losses to be realized.

To generalize, any hedged option position whose replicating portfolio involves shifting away from a long or short stock position toward no stock as the stock price falls implicitly involves the purchase of insurance. Conversely, any hedged option position whose replicating portfolio involves shifting further into a long or short stock position as the stock price falls implicitly involves the sale of insurance. Therefore, the far left and far right upper (lower) option positions in Exhibit B amount to buying (selling) insurance. For example, buying protective puts is similar to the purchase of insurance, while writing *covered calls* (buy one share and write one call) is similar to the sale of insurance.

Option positions have also been compared to forward contracts, which promise delivery of an underlying asset on a given date (delivery date) in the future at a currently agreed price (forward price). Like a call, a forward contract is equivalent to a levered position in the underlying asset. In contrast to a call, however, a forward contract requires unconditional delivery, rather than exercise at the option of the buyer. A forward contract could be replicated by borrowing to finance the *entire* holdings of the underlying asset and leaving this stock-cash position *unrevised* through the delivery date.[4] This is represented in Exhibit A by the straight line cutting the horizontal axis at 30.

Is there an option position that also has these two properties? If so, we can replicate forward contracts with options. Exhibit B shows that the

---

[4] This conclusion presumes there are no carrying costs or cash payouts involved in holding the underlying asset. However, the conclusion of the next paragraph holds even with possibly uncertain carrying costs or cash payouts, as long as the replicating options are not protected against these costs or payoffs and cannot be exercised prior to expiration.

replicating portfolios for both long calls and short puts involve long stock and borrowing. Moreover, the revision strategies for these two positions move in opposite directions. Therefore, we might suspect that the proper combination of the two positions would neutralize the required revisions. As the stock price changes we would find ourselves simply transferring stock between the two replicating positions with no net purchases or sales required. Indeed, as it turns out, we can replicate a purchased forward contract exactly by buying one call and shorting one put with a common expiration date equal to the delivery date and a common striking price equal to the forward price.[5]

We are now prepared to answer the questions posed at the beginning of the article. In each case, we simply need to examine the composition of the stock-cash portfolios that replicate option positions.

How to Value an Option

If we can exactly duplicate an option with a stock-cash position, we can also accomplish the reverse. If it turns out that the current market price of an option differs from that of the replicating portfolio, then we will have found an arbitrage opportunity, since both the option and its replicating portfolio (which is self-financing) are sure to have identical payoffs at expiration.[6] Thus the value of an option is equal to the value of its replicating stock-cash portfolio.

From this perspective, the problem of valuing an option is the same as the problem of determining the composition of its current replicating portfolio. The appendix provides an example where the current replicating portfolio consists of $5/7$ shares of stock at $50 per share financed partially with $22.50 of borrowing. This implies that the current value of the call must be $13.20 ([$50 × $5/7$] − $22.50).

The Black-Scholes option pricing model provides another way of determining the composition of the replicating portfolio. The Black-Scholes formula for a call takes the following form:

[5] Readers may want to refer to Eugene Moriarty, Susan Phillips and Paula Tosini, ''A Comparison of Options and Futures in the Management of Portfolio Risk,'' *Financial Analysts Journal,* January/February 1981. —Ed.

[6] Indeed, many floor traders of options exchanges acting on their own account follow trading strategies based on this observation. They will almost simultaneously buy or sell an option and take an opposing position in the stock (or a related deep-in-the-money option that behaves like the stock). Over time, they will adjust the composition of this portfolio to keep its value insensitive to stock price movements, hoping to profit from mispricing of the option.

$$\text{call value} = (\text{stock price} \times \text{delta}) - \text{borrowing.}[7]$$

The "delta" is the standard terminology used in the options market for the number of shares in the replicating portfolio. If the market price of the call exceeds this value, the call is overpriced; if it is less, the call is underpriced.

How to Measure the Expected Return and Risk of an Option Position

If we know how to measure the risk and return of stock-cash portfolios, we can easily measure these variables for option positions as well. The leverage of any stock-cash portfolio will be:

$$a \equiv \frac{\text{stock price} \times \text{number of shares}}{(\text{stock price} \times \text{number of shares})}, \; - \text{borrowing}$$

where the leverage a will exceed one if we are borrowing and be less than one if we are lending. From this formula we can derive the expected return, volatility and beta of any stock-cash portfolio:

$$\text{expected return} = a \times \text{stock expected return} + (1 - a) \times \text{interest rate,}$$

$$\text{volatility} = a \times \text{stock volatility,}$$

$$\text{beta} = a \times \text{stock beta.}$$

Measuring the return and risk of an option position (on a given underlying stock) entails three steps. First, we translate each option into its current replicating stock-cash portfolio; second, we aggregate across all the options to find their replicating net position as a group in stock and cash; third, we

---

[7] According to the original Black-Scholes formula, the current value of a call C depends only on its underlying stock price S, striking price K, time to expiration t, the interest rate $r - 1$, and the stock volatility σ. The composition of the replicating portfolio consists of $N(x)$ shares of stock, where $N(x)$ is the area under a standard normal distribution function to the left of x and

$$x \equiv \frac{\log(S/Kr^{-t})}{\sigma\sqrt{t}} + \tfrac{1}{2}\sigma\sqrt{t}.$$

The amount borrowed is $Kr^{-t}N(x - \sigma\sqrt{t})$ where $N(x - \sigma\sqrt{t})$ is the area to the left of $x - \sigma\sqrt{t}$. The value of a call is then

$$C = SN(x) - Kr^{-t}N(x - \sigma\sqrt{t}).$$

Although this formula applies only to stocks that do not pay dividends prior to the expiration date, it can be modified to include the effects of dividends.

calculate the leverage parameter a for this netted position and apply the formulas for return and risk.[8]

For example, since a properly priced purchased call is replicated by a margined long position in the stock, a will exceed one and the call will be both more risky and have greater expected return (provided the stock's expected return is greater than the interest rate) than the stock itself. Similarly, a covered call will have both lower risk and lower expected return than the stock, since a will be less than one.[9]

Moreover, observe that the leverage measure a of the option position's replicating portfolio will typically change continually through the future. Therefore, even if the expected return and risk of the underlying stock remain unchanged, the expected return and risk of the option position will typically change over time.

How the Margin Requirements and Transaction Costs of Option Positions Compare with Common Stock

Margin requirements on common stock involve (1) limits on borrowing against long positions, (2) limits on the use of proceeds of short sales and (3) collateral to guarantee performance of short positions. An examination of their equivalent stock-cash positions shows how options can be used to relax each of these requirements.

For example, buying a call will often prove a way to relax the first requirement. Currently an investor can borrow only up to 50 per cent to initiate purchase of stock. In contrast, one of our previous examples showed that one at-the-money call selling at three dollars was equivalent to the purchase of one-half share for $15, $12 of which was borrowed. In other words, the call implicitly allows borrowing 80 per cent ($^{12}/_{15}$) of the price of the stock.[10] Moreover, the call may implicitly permit borrowing at more favorable rates than otherwise obtainable. Indeed, this is likely to be the case for retail investors if it is the interest rates available to professionals that determine option prices. In this event, the lower borrowing rates available to professionals will be passed along to the public through lower call prices.

---

[8] This technique will only work exactly over the very short run, since the composition of the replicating portfolio changes as the expiration date approaches. However, as shown in John C. Cox and Mark Rubinstein, *Options Markets* (Prentice-Hall, 1981), these short-run measures of return and risk will usually be adequate approximations of the longer run exact measures. This makes sense intuitively, since if the chances are roughly equal that the stock price may rise or fall, then the chances are roughly equal that the short-run return and risk measures will increase or decrease in the future.

[9] Note that the conclusions of this paragraph will hold exactly in the long run as well. For example, since a covered call *always* involves a replicating portfolio consisting of long no more than one share of stock and lending, it must always have less *expected* return and risk than the stock by itself, although for some stock price outcomes its *realized* return may be greater.

[10] A full analysis of margin requirements should consider maintenance margins on stock and that the implicit leverage obtained through a call will change as the stock price changes.

Buying puts may relax the second and third margin requirements. Remember that the replicating portfolio of a put consists of selling stock short and lending. Unlike many professionals, most retail investors cannot earn interest on the proceeds of short sales. Again, however, if these professionals determine option prices, then the interest they can earn on short sale proceeds will be passed along to the public in the form of lower put prices.[11] In addition, the lending contained in the replicating portfolios for many puts will be less than the collateral required to guarantee performance of short stock positions.

With respect to transaction costs, options and stock can be compared, (1) dollar for dollar of investment, (2) option contract vs. round lot of stock or (3) option vs. replicating stock-cash portfolio. Under the first approach, options come out unfavorably; under the second, options look very good for holding periods not exceeding the life of the option. However, if we want to compare positions of similar expected returns and risks, then neither of these approaches is correct. The third approach, which will generally have implications intermediate between the first two, is what we want. An analysis of the commissions usually charged for exchange-traded options shows that options tend to dominate stock for short holding periods, but that the advantage shifts to stocks for longer term positions that exceed the life of the option.[12]

Who Should Be Buying and Who Should Be Selling Options

The most frequently given reason for trading options is that they offer *new desired patterns of returns.* Yet, as we have seen, much of what options offer can be replicated by properly adjusting a stock-cash position over time. There must be other considerations that incline investors toward options.

As we have just seen, options may offer investors *more favorable implicit borrowing or lending opportunities, margin requirements, transaction costs or tax exposure.* Also, as we mentioned earlier, changes in stock volatility or dividends may very well leave the current stock price unchanged while affecting the option price.[13] Thus options can offer *opportunities either to take advantage of information about stock volatility or dividends or to hedge against their impact.*

The question remains, however, whether the investor who decides to hold an option position should be buying or selling. The correspondence between

---

[11] Since the buyer of a put is implicitly lending, then the higher the interest rate he receives, the less he will need to lend to come up with the striking price on the expiration date if the put finishes in the money. Therefore, the lower the current value of the put. Since calls involve implicit borrowing, similar reasoning shows their values will be higher, the higher the interest rate, other things equal.

[12] A complete analysis would also consider any differences in the bid-ask spread typically sacrificed or gained by various classes of investors in options and stock.

[13] This will also be true of interest rates. But, in this case, interest rate futures would typically be superior to currently listed options for hedging or taking advantage of special information.

Exhibit B: Stock-Cash Portfolios to Replicate Option Positions

		Long Stock (no more than one share)		Short Stock (no more than one share)			
		+ Lending	+ Borrowing	+ Lending	+ Borrowing		
As Stock Price Rises	Buy stock financed by borrowing	long stock (one share) + long one put*	long one call	long one put	short stock (one share) + long one call	Sell stock and lend proceeds	As Stock Price Falls
	Sell stock and lend proceeds	long stock (one share) + short one call†	short one put	short one call	short stock (one share) + short one put	Buy stock financed by borrowing	

Note: In all cases, any dividends received will be used to increase lending or reduce borrowing. Restitution for dividends paid while stock is held short will be financed by reduced lending or more borrowing.
*Protective put.   †Covered call.

options and replicating stock-cash portfolios can help answer this question. For example, an average investor might want simply to buy and hold stock, with no borrowing or lending. But if he were more risk-averse than average, he might not want to assume the risk inherent in holding a typical stock. He can reduce his risk by investing only part of his money in the stock and lending the remainder. If the stock price subsequently rose, his risk would tend to increase as the relative dollar value of the stock-cash position shifted toward the stock. At the same time, as his position became more valuable, he might become willing to accept more risk. Indeed, if he were average in this respect, he would find that the increase in the stock price automatically injected just the desired amount of risk into the portfolio. He would then be content to buy and hold, and would have no need for options.

However, suppose that, as the stock price rose and he became wealthier, the investor's willingness to accept more risk was less than the average investor's. Then he would want to shift from stock to cash gradually as his position became more valuable, and into stock from cash as his position became less valuable. He could, of course, do this by continually revising his stock-cash position. On the other hand, he could let a fixed covered call position achieve the same result automatically. Which strategy he prefers will typically depend on the comparative transaction costs.

In brief, covered call writers should typically be investors whose risk aversion *does not decrease as rapidly* as the average investor's as the value of their portfolios increases. Conversely, protective put buyers should typically be investors whose risk aversion *decreases more rapidly* than the average investor's as the value of their portfolios increases.[14] Similar reasoning applies to the other option positions in Exhibit B.

[14] This correspondence was first discussed by Hayne Leland, "Who Should Buy Portfolio Insurance?" *Journal of Finance,* May 1980.

A completely separate reason for a preference between buying or selling options rests on certain technical theories of stock price behavior. If investors believe in trends, they may want to buy protective puts or buy uncovered calls. If they believe in reversals, they should prefer writing covered calls or writing puts.

What to Do When the Corresponding Option Doesn't Exist

If options on a particular stock or on a portfolio do not exist, we can create them by using the appropriate strategy for the underlying asset and cash. For example, we can effectively create an at-the-money protective put option on our equity portfolio. We would begin by placing part of our capital in the equity portfolio and part in cash and then, without changing the composition of the equity portfolio, shift between the portfolio and cash as the equity portfolio value changes and as the "expiration date" approaches. Such an investment strategy would be tantamount to insuring the equity portfolio against losses by paying a fixed premium to an insurance company.[15]

Even in the unlikely event that exchange-traded put options of synchronous maturity existed on all the stocks in a portfolio, a combination of put options could not match the above strategy in terms of cost. If we purchase put options against each stock in the portfolio, we would be insuring each individual stock, rather than the portfolio as a whole, against loss; even if our portfolio rose in value, as long as the price of at least one stock fell the insurance would pay off. The insurance provided by a stock-cash strategy would pay off if and only if the portfolio fell in value. As such, the implicit premium of the latter strategy will be less because only the portfolio as a whole, not every individual stock, is insured.

Total portfolio option replicating strategies, since they involve shifts between equities and cash, are similar to rebalancing strategies that seek to maintain the risk level by keeping the same relative amounts invested in equities and cash. In contrast, the total portfolio protective put option strategy systematically increases the risk of the overall position as the portfolio becomes more valuable and decreases exposure to risk as the portfolio falls in value.

For many financial institutions, the replicating strategies for protective puts and covered calls will be feasible because they do not require borrowing or short selling. However, replication of many other option positions will not be possible because they do require borrowing or short selling.

---

[15] Remember that the analogy to insurance breaks down under a sudden catastrophic loss that does not leave sufficient time to adjust the replicating portfolio.

Appendix

A Simple Example of Replication of Option Returns with a Portfolio of Stock and Cash

Suppose the current price of an underlying stock is $50 and that, over the next period, it will either move up to $70 or down to $35. If it moves up to $70 during the first period, then it will move to $100 or $50 during the second period. If it moves down to $35 during the first period, then it will move to $50 or $25 during the second period. The tree diagram in Exhibit AA illustrates this behavior.

Exhibit AA

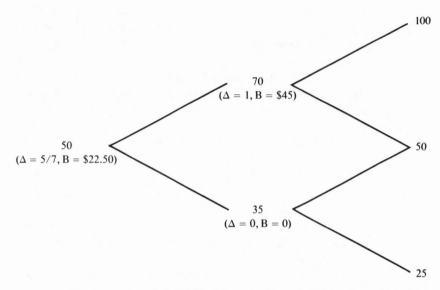

Suppose that we can borrow money at an 11 per cent rate of interest in each period. How can we replicate the returns of an at-the-money purchased call that expires at the end of the second period? First, let us see what we would do with just one period remaining when the stock price is at $70. At expiration, the call will be worth $50 ($100 − $50) if the stock price goes up or zero if the stock price goes down (since we would then be indifferent to exercising it).

What mixture of stock and cash would produce these same returns? Suppose we let Δ stand for the number of shares we would need to buy and B for the number of dollars we would need to borrow. Then our problem is to find values of Δ and B such that:

$$(100 \times \Delta) - (1.11 \times B) = 100 - 50 = 50,$$

$$(50 \times \Delta) - (1.11 \times B) = 0.$$

The first equation insures that our stock-cash portfolio has the same return as the option if the stock goes up and the second assures us the returns will also be equal if the stock goes down. It is easy to see that setting Δ equal to one and B approximately equal to $45 will solve both these equations and therefore give us a stock-cash position with the same returns as a call.

On the other hand, suppose we have one period remaining and the stock price is at $35, then our problem is to find values of Δ and B such that:

$$(50 \times \Delta) - (1.11 \times B) = 0,$$

$$(35 \times \Delta) - (1.11 \times B) = 0.$$

In this case the call has no chance of finishing in the money, so it makes sense that our solutions are Δ equals zero and B equals zero.

Finally, let us go back to the first period when the stock price was $50. Now we must find a portfolio of stock and cash that will (1) provide us with just enough money to buy one share of stock, financed by $45 of borrowing, if the stock price goes up over the first period to $70, or (2) provide us with just enough money to buy zero shares of stock, financed with zero borrowing, if the stock price goes down over the first period to $35. That is, in the first period we must choose Δ and B so that:

$$(70 \times \Delta) - (1.11 \times B) = (70 \times 1) - 45 = 25,$$

$$(35 \times \Delta) - (1.11 \times B) = 0.$$

In this case, Δ equals $\frac{5}{7}$ and B equals approximately $22.50.

To summarize, to replicate the call we will need to start by buying $\frac{5}{7}$ shares financed partially by borrowing $22.50. This implies we will have to put up $13.20 ([50 \times \frac{5}{7}] - 22\frac{1}{2})$ of our own money. If we do this, we will have just enough money to take the appropriate position during the second period, whether the stock price goes up or down. If the stock price goes up, we will find ourselves subsequently buying in, financing the additional $\frac{2}{7}(1 - \frac{5}{7})$ shares by additional borrowing. If the stock price goes down, we will find ourselves subsequently completely selling out and thereby raising just enough money to repay our borrowing. In either case, on the expiration date we will find that the value of our replicating portfolio is exactly equal to the value of the call.

2

Alternative Paths to Portfolio Insurance

Mark Rubinstein*

Portfolio insurance is equivalent to a securities position comprised of an underlying portfolio plus an insurance policy that guarantees the portfolio against loss through a specified policy expiration date. Under true portfolio insurance, the probability of experiencing a loss is zero; the position's return is dependent solely on the ending value of the underlying portfolio, regardless of interim movements in portfolio value; and the expected rate of return is greater than that on any other strategy possessing the first two properties.

European payout-protected puts could be used to provide perfect portfolio insurance. The investor would select a put option on the underlying portfolio such that exercising the put would yield just enough to make up for any decline in portfolio value plus the initial cost of the option. Unfortunately, European options are not available on listed exchanges in the U.S.

In their absence, portfolio insurance may be approximated by using listed options or by a systematic dynamic asset allocation strategy employing either cash and the underlying portfolio or a replicating futures position. Because the longest effective maturities of listed options are two or three months, a portfolio insurance strategy of any reasonable length will be susceptible to interim movements in the underlying portfolio, hence will generally have lower expected returns than true portfolio insurance. Dynamic asset allocation strategies designed to replicate a long-term European protect put come closest to perfect portfolio insurance.

This article was awarded first prize in the 1984 Institute for Quantitative Research in Finance competition.

*Mark Rubinstein is Professor of Finance at the Graduate School of Business of the University of California at Berkeley and a principal of Leland O'Brien Rubinstein, Associates.

The author thanks Hayne Leland for his helpful comments.

Mark Rubinstein, "Alternative Paths to Portfolio Insurance." Reprinted with permission from *Financial Analysts Journal,* Vol. 41, July/August 1985.

Portfolio insurance, in its purest and simplest form, is equivalent to a securities position comprised of an underlying portfolio plus an insurance policy that guarantees the insured portfolio against loss through a specified policy expiration date. Should the underlying portfolio (including any income earned and reinvested in the portfolio but deducting the cost of buying the insurance) experience a loss by the policy expiration date, the insurance policy can be used to refund the amount of the loss. On the other hand, should the underlying portfolio show a profit, all profit net of the cost of the insurance is retained.

Consider a portfolio with the same composition as the Standard & Poor's 500 and suppose it is covered by an insurance policy that has one year until expiration. The S&P 500 is at 100 at the start of the policy, and the one-year insurance policy costs $3.33. After buying the insurance, an investor with $100 has $96.67, which can buy 0.9667 "shares" of the S&P 500.

Table I shows the pattern of returns this investor will realize at the end of the year. The *minimum* value of the insured portfolio is $100; there will be no loss, even after the cost of the insurance is deducted. On the upside, the value of the insured portfolio depends on the behavior of the full $100 investment in the S&P 500. Because the insured portfolio owns 0.9667 shares of the S&P 500, its value on the upside will always be 0.9667 times the value of the S&P 500 with dividends reinvested (e.g., $125 \times 0.9667 = 120.84$). This number is sometimes referred to as the "upside capture."

Table I. Pattern of returns from portfolio insurance after one year

Value of S&P 500 with dividends reinvested	Value of insured S&P 500 portfolio
$ 75	$100
80	100
85	100
90	100
95	100
100	100
105	101.50
110	106.34
115	111.17
120	116
125	120.84
130	125.67

Properties of Insured Portfolios

The return pattern of the insured portfolio has several important properties:

(A) The probability of experiencing any losses is zero.

(B) The return on any profitable position will be a predictable percentage of the rate of return that would have been earned by investing all funds in the S&P 500.

(C) If the portfolio is restricted to investments in the S&P 500 and cash loans, if the expected rate of return on the S&P 500 exceeds the return on cash, and if the insurance is fairly priced, then among all investment strategies possessing properties (A) and (B), the insured portfolio strategy has the highest expected rate of return.

Stop-loss orders are perhaps the simplest examples of investment strategies that have property A (ignoring jumps through the stop-limit price) but lack property B. To implement a stop-loss order strategy, one invests the entire $100 in the S&P 500 and instructs the broker to sell out completely and convert to cash if the S&P 500 (with dividends reinvested) falls so low that a conversion to cash, given then current interest rates, would result in a value of exactly $100 at the end of the year.

Clearly, this strategy possesses property A. However, the value of the portfolio is not completely determined by the level of the S&P 500. If, midway through the year, the S&P 500 fell low enough to trigger the conversion into cash, then the return on the portfolio from then on would be entirely unrelated to the S&P 500.

It is easy to devise other strategies that have both properties A and B but lack C. Suppose an investor is restricted to "buy and hold" positions using only the S&P 500 and cash and wants to maximize expected rate of return while insuring against a loss. If the interest rate is 10 per cent, he can invest $90.91 in cash and $9.09 in the S&P 500. Now, even if the S&P 500 falls to zero, he would just break even (since $90.91 × 1.1 = $100). If the expected rate of return on the S&P 500 is 16 per cent, the overall expected rate of return from following this strategy would be 10.5 per cent (= (90.91 × 10%) + (9.09 × 16%)).

The proof that portfolio insurance satisfies property C, hence must have a higher expected rate of return than the buy and hold strategy, will not be reproduced here.[1] However, it will be demonstrated by example in the course of the discussion.

Why Purchase Portfolio Insurance?	Clearly, anyone who wants to insure against any losses while maximizing expected return is a candidate for the purchase of portfolio insurance.[2] Equally clearly, for every investor who purchases portfolio insurance there needs to be an investor who sells it.[3] We are thus led to conclude that intelligent buyers of portfolio insurance are typically more sensitive to downside risk than the average investor.

[1] The proof of this proposition is contained in an unpublished note by Hayne Leland.
[2] For a more complete treatment, see Hayne Leland, "Who Should Buy Portfolio Insurance?" *Journal of Finance*, May 1980.
[3] It is hypothesized that an investor who sells portfolio insurance wants to maximize the probability of obtaining a specified level of profit (the insurance premium in the case of a no-loss policy). In compensation for this, the investor must absorb all losses in the index.

For either the buyer or seller of portfolio insurance, property B still holds: The return from the insured portfolio (S&P 500 plus insurance policy) will be fully determined by the return from the underlying portfolio (S&P 500) at the insurance expiration date. The path taken to reach this level of return will have no effect on the outcome.

Outcomes of "path-dependent" strategies are usually much more difficult to describe and evaluate than those of "path-independent" strategies.[4] That is, predicting returns from path-dependent strategies requires knowledge of many more factors. It is also difficult to see why an investor would want his return to be influenced by intermediate levels of the index, apart from their cumulative effect on the ending level of the index.

The remainder of this article focuses on the purchase of portfolio insurance—specifically, how is it done?

Alternative Paths

We assume that the investor wants to insure against losses in the S&P 500 with dividends reinvested. We further assume the economic environment that gives rise to the Black-Scholes option valuation formula.[5] In particular, the interest rate is known and constant, the dividend yield of the S&P 500 is known and constant, the volatility of the S&P 500 is known and constant, the value of the S&P 500 moves smoothly over time without jumps or gap openings, there are no opportunities for riskless arbitrage profits, and transaction costs are zero.

In the interest of comparability, we will assume that the interest rate is 10 per cent per year, the expected rate of return on the S&P 500 is 16 per cent, the dividend yield on the S&P 500 is 5 per cent, and the (arithmetic) volatility of the S&P 500 is 18 per cent.[6]

---

[4]For a proof that rational, risk-averse investors in a complete-markets, random-walk, time-additive utility environment should prefer path-independent to path-dependent strategies, see John C. Cox and Hayne Leland, "A Characterization of Path-Independent Policies." For the special case of investors who maximize the terminal value of their wealth at the end of a specified horizon, the intuition behind their proof is easily grasped. Suppose the only thing an investor cares about is the amount of wealth he will have at his horizon date and he has no reason to be concerned about the implications of past outcomes for future returns (the random walk assumption). Then, if he can achieve path-independent outcomes for the pattern of returns that he desires at his horizon date, he will prefer these to path-dependent outcomes. The additional uncertainty from path-dependence is uncompensated risk. It is as though, in addition to his desired outcome of $120.84, the investor had to flip a coin to determine whether he receives $5 more or $5 less. No risk averter would willingly accept this gamble.

[5]See Fischer Black and Myron Scholes, "The Pricing of Options and Corporate Liabilities," *Journal of Political Economy*, May-June 1973.

[6]The Black-Scholes option pricing formula uses the logarithmic or continuous volatility (the standard deviation of the *natural logarithm* of one plus the rate of return) as an input, rather than the arithmetic or discrete volatility (the standard deviation of the rate of return). In our case, the S&P 500 is assumed to have an arithmetic mean and volatility of 16 and 18 per cent, respectively. Assuming lognormality of its rate of return, this translates into a logarithmic volatility of 15.5 per cent.

Each technique for creating portfolio insurance is designed to be 100 per cent reliable in preventing losses. Our comparison will focus on differences in path-independence and expected rate of return.

Stop-Loss Orders

The analysis of stop-loss orders as a method for approximating portfolio insurance is complicated by path-dependence. Suppose, for instance, that the investor executes a stop-loss order at the end of each quarter. To keep things as simple as possible without sacrificing the main elements of the problem, suppose that the S&P 500 (with dividends reinvested) moves either up or down by a fixed percentage over each quarter.

Figure A gives the S&P 500's pattern of movement over the year, given its assumed expected rate of return and volatility.[7] Both the S&P 500 and the value of the stop-loss portfolio (in parentheses) begin at $100. In each quarter, the probability of the index moving up by 8.02 per cent is 0.721, and the probability of the index moving down by 7.42 per cent is 0.279.

As the stop-loss portfolio starts out fully invested in the S&P 500, both the index and the portfolio are at either 108.02 or 92.58 after the first quarter. During the second quarter, however, path-dependence appears. If the index moved up in the first quarter, the portfolio remains fully invested in the S&P 500 during the second quarter; whether the index moves up or down, the portfolio tracks it to either 116.68 or 100.

If, on the other hand, the index moved down during the first quarter, the stop-loss order would be triggered. It is easy to see why. The interest rate must be 2.41 per cent during any quarter if it is to compound out to 10 per cent over the year while remaining at a constant level. If the portfolio is down to 92.58 at the end of the first quarter, it can only reach 99.45 ($= 92.58 \times 1.0241^3$) by the end of the year, even if it is invested in cash over the remainder of the year. Because this ending level is less than 100, the stop-loss order is executed and the portfolio reverts for the remainder of the year to 100 per cent cash. At the end of the second quarter, the portfolio is thus at 94.81 ($= 92.58 \times 1.0241$). The dashed lines in Figure A indicate that the portfolio has been stopped out.

When the index is at 100, there is a 0.201 probability (0.721 × 0.279) that the portfolio will be at 100 and a 0.201 probability (0.279 × 0.721) that it will be at 94.81. That is, although the index may reach the same level either by moving up and then down or by moving down and then up, the same is not true of the portfolio. The *path* by which the index reaches 100 leads to different values for the stop-loss portfolio.

[7]Formulas for transforming the mean and volatility of a lognormal security price process into the sizes and probabilities of the up and down moves of a discrete binomial process are given in John C. Cox, Stephen A. Ross and Mark Rubinstein, "Option Pricing: A Simplified Approach," *Journal of Financial Economics,* September 1979.

To evaluate a stop-loss order as a method for creating portfolio insurance, it is necessary to measure its expected rate of return, given its degree of path-dependence. Path-dependence can be measured by the expected absolute deviation of the rate of return conditional on the level of the index; the appendix illustrates the calculation. Perfect portfolio insurance requires that path-dependence be zero; the stop-loss order has a path-dependence of 3.14 per cent. Table II lists the nine distinct possible outcomes from the stop-loss strategy considered above.

European Payout-Protected Puts

The stop-loss strategy is path-dependent, but it *is* a step in the right direction. It suggests that there may be a way to transfer systematically between the S&P 500 and cash to generate portfolio insurance. By moving *gradually* into stock from cash as the stock price goes up, and *gradually* out of stock into cash as the stock price falls, it is possible to generate the equivalent of an insured position in stock.[8]

Alternatively, if one-year European payout-protected puts on the S&P 500 were available, these instruments could provide perfect portfolio insurance. An investor would select a put option on the index with striking price K such that K satisfies the following equality:

$$P(K) = K - S$$

Here, P is the price of the put (shown above as a function of its striking price) and S is the concurrent level of the S&P 500 index.[9] If the index, with

Table II. Possible outcomes of stop-loss strategy

Value of S&P 500 with dividends reinvested	Stop-loss portfolio return	Probability
$136.14	36.14%	0.270
116.68	16.68%	0.314
116.68	−0.56%	0.105
100.00	0.00%	0.081
100.00	−0.56%	0.121
100.00	−5.19%	0.040
85.71	−0.56%	0.047
85.71	−5.19%	0.016
73.46	−0.56%	0.006

[8] See M. Rubinstein and H. Leland, "Replicating Options with Positions in Stock and Cash," *Financial Analysts Journal,* July/August 1981.

[9] Readers familiar with options may wonder if a striking price K can be chosen satisfying this equation. If the put were American (permitting early exercise), then the striking price would be so high that the put should be immediately exercised. But the put under consideration here is European (it cannot be exercised early), so its price must only satisfy $P > Kr^{-t} - S$, which permits its price to fall such that $P < K - S$ prior to expiration. Here, r is one plus the annual rate of interest and t is the time to expiration. Since a protective European put is always worth $S + P$, it follows that at no time in its life can the value of this position fall below Kr^{-t}. This implies that if, at any time during its life, the put were converted into cash, the investor could realize a minimum $Kr^{-t} \times r^{t} = K$ by the expiration date.

dividends reinvested, were to fall below its initial level by the end of the year, it could be sold by exercising the put at price K; this would be just enough to make up for the index decline and the initial cost P of the put.

This strategy is 100 per cent reliable in preventing losses. In addition, because the payoff of such a put would be solely dependent on the year-end level of the S&P 500 (with dividends reinvested), the protective put position would be completely path-independent. Assuming, as before, that the S&P 500 has an arithmetic expected rate of return and a volatility of 16 and 18 per cent, respectively, the striking price of the put would need to be 103.45 to provide insurance against losses. The expected rate of return on the insured portfolio (S&P 500 plus put) is 14.30 per cent.[10] The payoff pattern given in Table I is from just this strategy.

Of course, the investor must pay for the index put out of his initial $100. The ratio of the initial S&P 500 level to the striking price of the put is 0.9667 (100/103.45). The investor thus ends up with 0.9667 shares of the S&P 500 and 0.9667 puts, each at a striking price of 103.45. He must invest $3.33 ($3.45 × 0.9667) in puts and $96.67 in the S&P 500.

Several other types of instruments can be used to effect the same pattern of returns. From the European put-call parity relation, we know that a protective put is equivalent to a *fiduciary call* (purchased call plus cash), where the call has the same time to expiration and striking price as the put.[11] Moreover, with known rates of interest, a European put (or call) on the S&P 500 is equivalent to a European put (or call) on S&P 500 futures contracts, provided the expiration date of the option coincides with the delivery date of the underlying futures contracts.[12] Perfect portfolio insurance could be provided by either a *protective index futures put* or a *fiduciary index futures call*.

---

[10]This technique for calculating the expected rates of return of European options is developed in Mark Rubinstein, "A Simple Formula for the Expected Rate of Return of an Option over a Finite Holding Period" (Working paper #119, Research Program in Finance, Institute of Business and Economic Research, University of California at Berkeley, March 1984).

[11]If S is the stock price, C the call price, P the price of an otherwise similar put, r one plus the annual rate of interest, t the time to expiration of the options, and K their common striking price, according to the put-call parity relationship, at all times during the lives of the options:

$$P + S = C + Kr^{-t}.$$

The left-hand side of this equation is a protective put and the right-hand side is a fiduciary call.

[12]Because neither the European spot call nor the European futures call can be exercised early, and because the spot and futures prices must be equal on the expiration date of the options, the cash flows received from either option must be identical.

If a one-year European payout-protected option were available on each stock in the S&P 500, these instruments could be used to insure the S&P 500 by insuring each stock in the portfolio against loss for the year. However, use of conventional options on individual stocks leads to path-dependent outcomes with lower expected rates of return than index option strategies.[13]

Unfortunately, currently listed index options do not have the terms we have assumed. First, all listed options are *American*. American options can be exercised at any time before expiration, whereas European options can be exercised only at expiration. Because American options have every advantage of European options (they can be turned into European options by holding them to expiration) as well as the increased flexibility of early exercise, American options should be more expensive than otherwise identical European options. Second, listed options are not protected against dividends. As a result, they can be used to insure the capital appreciation component of stock returns, but not the dividend component. Third, all listed options have maturities of less than nine months. Because almost all trading volume is concentrated in the nearest maturities, the longest effective maturities are about three months for index futures options and two months for index spot options.[14] Finally, listed options have highly standardized striking prices that do not typically match the striking prices needed for portfolio insurance. This, combined with the advisability of early exercise of some American options, means that no American options of particular striking prices may survive in the market, even though European options of the same striking price would.

Sequential Short-Term Index Options

Although the listed markets do not offer options with the proper terms, there may still be some way of using these options to approximate portfolio insurance. In order to focus on the most significant feature of listed index options, we will assume that payout-protected European options are available in maturities of less than a year.

If six-month payout-protected European options were available, an investor could approximate portfolio insurance by rolling over a position in index puts every six months. He might start with a protective put that would insure the portfolio against loss over the first six months. If, at mid-year, the S&P 500 has declined so that it pays to exercise the put, the investor will buy another protective put to insure the portfolio over the next six months. At worst, by the end of the year, he should break even.

But suppose the S&P 500 rises over the first six months, so that the put is not exercised. In this case, the investor would buy a put that will insure the

[13]See Mark Rubinstein, ''Alternative Paths to Portfolio Insurance: A Detailed Analysis'' (Expanded version of this article, May 1984).
[14]The most active listed index options, the CBOE S&P 100 options, are not even listed with maturities beyond three months. A casual glance at the *Wall Street Journal* reveals that about 90 per cent of the volume in listed index puts is concentrated in puts with less than 40 days to expiration, with negligible volume in puts with more than 60 days to go.

portfolio's mid-year value with a deductible equal to the profit earned over the first six months.

Figure B illustrates this strategy when the year is divided into four (binomial) intervals. Using the Black-Scholes formula, the striking price of the purchased six-month put at the beginning of the year is $103.86 (in brackets). After two quarters, the S&P 500 index is at 85.71, 100 or 116.68. In each case, the striking price of the six-month put purchased next is different.

When the index is at 85.71 or 100, the portfolio has just broken even over the first six months; the investor can't afford to lose money over the next six months. He must purchase a put with the same striking price relative to the stock price as the put he purchased at the beginning of the year.[15] When the index is at 116.68, however, such conservatism is not needed. Now, the investor can afford to lose $12.34 during the next six months and still break even at the end of the year. He can purchase a put with a striking price considerably below the current value of the portfolio.

This strategy is 100 per cent reliable in preventing losses, but it does suffer from path-dependence. Its expected rate of return, moreover, will usually fall short of the expected rate of return that could be achieved with a one-year protective European put, if one were available or could be created from a dynamic asset allocation strategy. Table III (which assumes the year is divided into 144 binomial intervals) provides estimates of the magnitudes of path-dependence and rate of return for different roll-over periods. As the roll-over becomes more frequent, the path-dependence increases and the expected rate of return decreases.

The limited availability and liquidity of listed striking prices that are distant from the money, and the five-point intervals at which they are listed, force the investor to be more conservative in practice than he might want to be.[16]

Table III. Path-dependence and expected rates of return for roll-over of short-term protective European puts*

Roll-over period	Path-dependence	Expected rate of return
one year	0.00%	14.30%
six months	1.50 (1.67%)	14.04 (13.74%)
four months	2.12 (2.39)	13.96 (13.63)
three months	2.56 (2.90)	13.90 (13.53)
two months	2.97 (3.45)	13.86 (13.44)
stop-loss orders	3.73	14.70

*These results are particularly sensitive to the assumptions that volatility is known in advance and that there are no jump movements in the S&P 500 index.

[15]Observe that when the index is at 85.71, the striking price of the next six-month put, relative to the index level is 103.86. (= 89.02/85.71).
[16]To preserve reliability at three-point intervals, the investor must buy puts at slightly higher striking prices than optimal. Moreover, when the S&P 500 rises, the eight-point limitation will also force one to buy options at higher than optimal striking prices.

Suppose that striking prices are only available in three-point intervals and the deepest out-of-the-money put available is at most eight points out-of-the-money (relative to an S&P 500 level of 100). The numbers in parentheses in Table III show the degree to which this constraint increases path-dependence and reduces expected rate of return.

Real-World Considerations

The discussion so far has ignored complications created by American options, uncertain interest rates, uncertain volatility, jumps in security price movements, apparently mispriced securities, and transaction costs.

American Options

As building blocks for portfolio insurance, even long-term American index puts pose an unfortunate dilemma: It is either impossible to provide path-independence and 100 per cent reliability in preventing losses, or the insurance must be purchased at an excessive price!

As noted, if it is to insure a portfolio against loss, the index put must have a striking price K such that $P(K) = K - S$. Because of the possibility of early exercise, however, this is the lowest price an American option can have. Furthermore, if the option is priced properly, it would pay to exercise it immediately.

If the put were worth less than $K - S$, an investor could earn a riskless arbitrage profit by buying the put and the underlying stock and then immediately exercising the put to receive $K > P + S$. If the put were worth exactly $K - S$, the investor who exercised the option immediately would get the full benefit of the put and also be able to start earning interest on the net receipt of $K - S$. By pricing the put at its exercisable value, the market implies that the interest that can be received through early exercise of the put outweighs its time value.

Using American puts to generate portfolio insurance thus presents an awkward choice. On the one hand, buying a put priced higher than $K - S$ can lead to a portfolio loss equal to the premium over parity $(P - (K - S))$ if the index falls. On the other hand, a put priced such that $P = K - S$ will be overpriced, inasmuch as the insurance purchaser doesn't plan to exercise it immediately. The investor must steer between Scylla and Charybdis; as he avoids one difficulty, he approaches the other. In brief, the American put purchaser pays for something he doesn't want—the right to exercise the option early.

Uncertain Interest Rates

In all the strategies we have considered, except the use of long-term European payout-protected index options, uncertain interest rates increase the difficulty of predicting upside returns. The strategies' ability to protect against loss is unaffected, however, if care is taken to measure changes in interest rates and to factor these changes into the ongoing strategy.

In the case of the stop-loss strategies, for example, declining interest rates during the year translate into a shorter time to the stopout point. For the sequential option strategies (since option prices are partly determined by interest rates) uncertainty regarding interest rates increases the uncertainty regarding the prices that must be paid for options at future dates; nevertheless, changes in the option prices offset interest rate changes, preserving full loss protection.

Within the context of Black-Scholes assumptions, there is no reason to distinguish between options and their replicating dynamic asset allocation strategies; both produce identical results. With uncertain interest rates, however, dynamic strategies no longer have the power to replicate long-term European options exactly. Nonetheless, dynamic strategies that transfer holdings between stock and cash can hedge changes in interest rates over the year. Proper implementation using one-year Treasury bills as the hedging instrument (cash) should make conventional dynamic strategies less susceptible to shifts in shorter-term rates than either the stop-loss or sequential option strategies.

Dynamic option replication strategies can be implemented by using index futures. A purchased index futures contract, if held to the delivery date, implicitly embodies a long position in the index coupled with an equal amount of borrowing at a risk-free rate over the life of the contract. Instead of selling stock and lending the proceeds (as in conventional dynamic asset allocation), the investor can sell futures to accomplish similar ends by much simpler means. If the futures delivery date is less than a year, however, it will be necessary to roll over the futures hedge during the year. The strategy is thus more susceptible to uncertainty surrounding upside returns than conventional dynamic asset allocation utilizing one-year Treasury bills.

Uncertain Volatility

In practice, the source of the greatest difference between options and dynamic strategies is uncertain volatility. Not only does predicted volatility have an important effect on option prices but, of all their determinants, it is the most difficult to measure. Purchasing an index option amounts to insuring against fluctuations in the volatility of the index through the expiration date of the option. Proper implementation of the replicating dynamic asset allocation strategy retains full loss protection, but the upside capture now depends on the realized volatility over the year. The greater the volatility, the less the upside capture. This introduces a form of path-dependence into the outcome.

Sequential option strategies are exposed to a similar form of path-dependence. The prices of options to be purchased at future dates are dependent on the market's future predictions of volatility.

Security Price Jumps

As noted, stop-loss strategies may be threatened by jumps in security prices. For this reason, as contingent immunization (a form of stop-loss order applied to bond portfolio management) is practiced, the position remains 100 per cent invested in the actively managed bond portfolio as long as the stopout point is sufficiently distant. However, when the stopout point comes into view, the active portfolio is gradually transferred into the immunized portfolio.

In the case of dynamic asset allocation, this gradual transition to cash is an automatic and continuous feature. Because the portfolio will tend to be invested mostly in cash just before a jump that could create a loss, jumps will be less of a problem. The additional conservatism required of stop-loss orders to prevent losses from jumps will tend to equalize the expected rates of return from the stop-loss and dynamic asset allocation strategies.

Mispriced Securities

The investor who believes he can identify mispriced index futures, index options or even conventional options on common stocks may want to consider different approaches to portfolio insurance at different times. For example, when index calls are underpriced relative to index puts, he should give preference to fiduciary calls in place of protective puts as a means of creating portfolio insurance. If he thinks he can identify relatively underpriced calls on individual stocks, he may want to use a portfolio of fiduciary calls on individual stocks, despite the disadvantages of this strategy. If index futures appear to be underpriced, the preferred method may be to buy futures against a position in cash, rather than selling futures against a long position in the index.

Transaction Costs

By far the most liquid spot index option contracts are the S&P 100 options traded on the CBOE, which now comprise in total about 33 per cent of all CBOE options volume—typically representing trades to more than 20 million shares of the index per day (about $3 billion). The S&P 500 index futures traded on the CME are also highly liquid, representing trades to over 25 million shares per day (about $3.750 billion).

Currently, almost all trading volume for both index futures and options is concentrated in the nearest maturing contracts. As a result, it is necessary in the case of large trades to turn over options hedges about once every two months and futures hedges about once every four months to obtain sufficient liquidity. For options, we assume a 2 per cent one-way commission and a 1 per cent one-way spread give-up for a total one-way transaction cost of 3 per cent—about 12 cents on a $4 option, or about 0.08 per cent of the spot index. Additional costs from terminating index options at their expiration are ignored, because of their cash resettlement feature. For futures, we estimate a round-trip commission of $30 per contract and a $25 spread give-up for a total round-trip transaction cost of 0.07 per cent of the spot index price.

With a turnover of six times per year for a sequential options strategy, the total annual options transaction cost is 0.48 per cent of the spot index price. For dynamic asset allocation using index futures, turnover comes from two sources—from rolling the futures over three times per year (each time on an average of half the index portfolio) and from the requirements of dynamic asset allocation (which, based on the simulation, is roughly 50 per cent per year). In total, futures would need to be bought or sold on 2.5 times the value of the index portfolio, which in turn implies a total annual futures transaction cost of 0.18 per cent of the spot index price.

Conventional dynamic asset allocation, which requires transferring assets between S&P 500 stocks and Treasury bills, is estimated from experience to cost 0.56 per cent of the spot index price.

In summary, conventional dynamic asset allocation is only slightly more expensive than a sequential index options strategy (0.56 per cent versus 0.48 per cent per annum). Dynamic asset allocation implemented with index futures is the cheapest, at about one-third this cost.

Conclusion   Long-term European payout-protected index options provide perfect portfolio insurance, but they do not currently exist in exchange-traded markets. Until they do, it will be necessary to use other instruments to approximate portfolio insurance on broad-based stock market indexes.

Stop-loss order strategies suffer from extreme path-dependence. Sequential index option strategies are also path-dependent and have a lower expected rate of return than perfect portfolio insurance. Of all the methods examined above, dynamic asset allocation, which attempts to replicate a long-term European protective put, seems to come closest to perfect portfolio insurance.

Figure A. Portfolio insurance with stop-loss orders

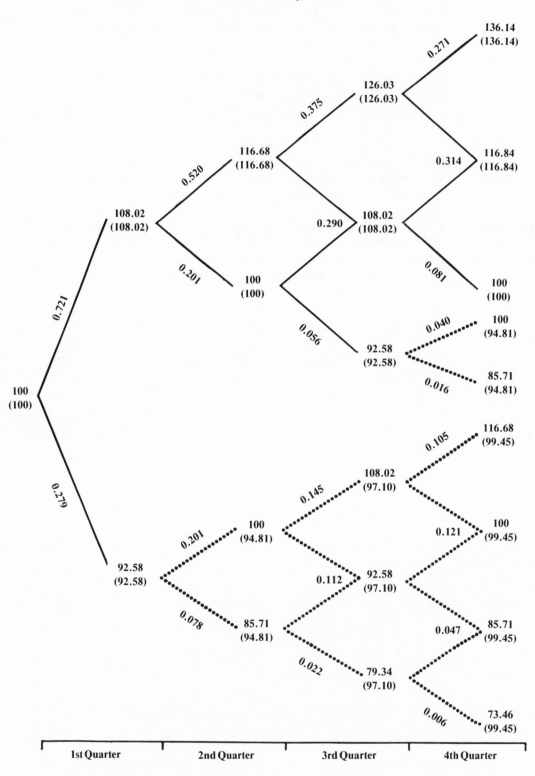

| 1st Quarter | 2nd Quarter | 3rd Quarter | 4th Quarter |

Figure B.   Sequential short-term European index options

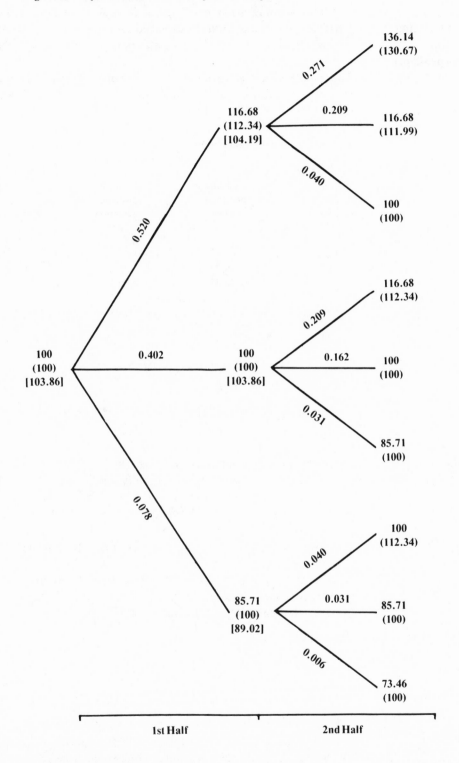

Appendix

Calculating Path-Dependence

For each ending level of the index, make the best possible estimate of the portfolio rate of return. On average, as Table AI shows, the realized portfolio rate of return may be expected to err by 3.14 per cent. At worst—if the index ends at 116.68—the error may be expected to be 6.47 per cent.

The overall expected rate of return on the stop-loss strategy is calculated by summing the products of the second and third columns of Table II in the text. This results in 14.57 per cent.

Table AI.   Calculation of path-dependence

Value of S&P 500 with dividends reinvested	Conditional portfolio expected value	Expected absolute deviation	Probability
$136.14	$136.14	0.00	0.271
116.68	112.37	6.47	0.418
100.00	98.85	1.35	0.243
85.71	98.28	1.74	0.062
73.46	99.45	0.00	0.006

Path Dependence = $(0.418 \times 6.47) + (0.243 \times 1.35) + (0.062 \times 1.74) = 3.14\%$

Example: When S&P 500 = 116.68:

$$112.37 = \frac{(0.314 \times 116.68) + (0.105 \times 99.45)}{0.314 + 0.105}$$

$$6.47 = \frac{[0.314 \times |116.68 - 112.37|] + [0.105 \times |99.45 - 112.37|]}{0.314 + 0.105}$$

For a very close approximation of the results from continuous S&P 500 movements, divide the year into 50 equally spaced intervals with binomial moves over each interval.[17] In this case, the path-dependence and expected rate of return are 3.73 and 14.70 per cent, respectively. With a continuous process, the stop-loss order could be executed at exactly 100; in that case, the stop-loss strategy would be 100 per cent reliable in preventing losses.

Also of interest for the stop loss strategy are the stopout probability, which is 40 per cent, and the expected time to stopout, which is 0.76 of a year (roughly, the beginning of the fourth quarter).

[17] With 50 intervals, the minimum number of separate nodes at the end of the tree is 51 and the maximum number is 2^{50} or 123 trillion. In the stop-loss strategy, the number of different ending nodes turns out to be 638.